The Inside Story of OMB

How the President's Swiss Army Knife Wields Power

Rob Fairweather

The Inside Story of OMB

How the President's Swiss Army Knife Wields Power

First Edition: 2024

Library of Congress Control Number: 2024905551

1. POL040010   2. POL017000   3. POL028000

Paperback ISBN: 979-8-9902943-0-1
Ebook ISBN: 979-8-9902943-1-8

Printed by RSF Publications LLC, Arlington, VA.

Table of Contents

INTRODUCTION

I first thought about writing this book during the month-long Federal Government shutdown in January 2019. As I will explain later, I was in the office for the entire shutdown as an "excepted" worker, but there are only limited tasks that I was legally allowed to perform during this period. Because one of those tasks was to organize my files for archiving in preparation for the totally fictitious end of the Federal Government, I had time to reflect on my forty years of service at the Office of Management and Budget (OMB) as I went through various files during my down time.

It dawned on me that I had seen and participated in a wide range of budget and policy making and that the lessons that I had learned should be valuable to others. That is not to say that I didn't always try to impart some of my wisdom to my staff during my thirty-plus years as a supervisor. In fact, I am sure that some of my longer-tenured staff got tired of hearing me repeat stories or guidance to new junior staff. Nevertheless, I concluded that it would be useful to communicate some of my knowledge not only to policy nerds like me, but to a wider range of interested citizens as well.

Writing a book is probably the last thing my classmates at Princeton expected of me. In fact, my close friends used to joke that my mediocre writing skills could be explained by the fact that English was not my native language. It was always unclear what my native language was alleged to be, particularly since I had taken French from third through twelfth grade and still couldn't pass out of Princeton's language requirement, but the best guess was that it was a computer programming language called Fortran.

The perception about my writing skills perhaps stems from the first paper I wrote in the required literature course that emphasized paper writing. The course was set up as one large lecture each week by a full professor, followed by two "precepts," which were small classes of roughly fifteen students gathered to discuss the assigned book for the week. In many top colleges, such small classes might be taught by graduate students, but that was rare at Princeton, where most precepts were taught by assistant professors. I was fortunate, however, in not only having a full professor teach my precept, but a famous one at that. While I was oblivious to who Carlos Baker was, my classmate who lived down the hall at my dorm clued me in after our first precept that Professor Baker was Ernest Hemingway's official biographer and had written a best-selling book about Hemingway.

Our first paper had to be on the works of one of the authors we had studied during the first few weeks. I chose to write about Edgar Alan Poe. After the papers were graded, Professor Baker took a portion of one class to discuss what he liked about several of the papers without identifying their authors. To my astonishment, he was effusive in praise about my paper, calling it humorous and well thought out. My classmate from down the hall, who was the only one in the class who knew it was my paper, came up to me afterward and congratulated me on getting an "A". I sheepishly had to tell him that actually I got a "B-" and showed him that, while Professor Baker liked the substance of my paper, he had ripped my grammar and spelling to shreds in a sea of red ink.

Substance had always been of paramount importance to me in drafting papers, with spending energy on good grammar having been viewed as an annoying waste of time. However, Professor Baker's comments were a wake-up call that being able to communicate those ideas effectively was important as well. That marked the beginning of a decade-plus-long effort to improve my writing skills, a process made more difficult by my undergraduate engineering curriculum, during which time my vocabulary skills worsened rather than improved. It really wasn't until business school at Stanford and my first few years as an OMB budget examiner that my writing skills improved. This was due to the intense pressure and critical importance of being able to communicate complicated policy issues to political officials in a concise manner, particularly in short but information-rich issue papers.

The fact that it is painful to go back and review some of my college papers is perhaps evidence of the vast improvement in my writing skills during my OMB career. Nevertheless, my desire to write a book ebbed and flowed several times since my initial musing about it during the 2019 shutdown.

A major boost came in June 2019 at an early forty-fifth reunion event for my Princeton classmates living in Washington, D.C. While talking to Jay Powell about economic issues we were involved in as part of our respective roles at OMB and the Federal Reserve Board, he made an unsolicited suggestion that I write a book about my career at OMB. While I didn't tell him that I had already had that thought, having the Chairman of the Federal Reserve Board make such a suggestion gave some credibility to the thought that somebody, other than myself, might actually be interested in reading such a book.

As it was impossible to work on a book while still working full time at OMB, I knew that any writing would have to wait until I retired. Unfortunately, my retirement got delayed a year when one of my branch chiefs left OMB and I felt obligated to stay and hire a replacement. My retirement was then delayed another four months when I was asked to serve as the Acting Director of OMB if Joe Biden was elected President.

Even after retiring, there were family medical issues that needed to be addressed first followed by a long list of delayed projects and home maintenance that needed attention. Many of these projects were not critical but provided an easy excuse to not start the book. In fact, it seemed like I was scared to even attempt to start writing, because I prioritized any task that came along over starting the book, even tasks that I found distasteful. Consequently, I didn't actually start writing until almost five months after my retirement. However, once I started, I didn't want to stop, except for my weekly golf outing.

The hardest part of writing the book was figuring out what message or information I wanted to convey and for whom the message was intended. Part of my interest in writing the book is that OMB is a powerful yet little-known agency about which relatively few books have been published. My plan to fill that information gap was almost torpedoed when the Brookings Institution issued a book — *Executive Policymaking: The Role of the OMB in the Presidency* — in the fall of 2020.[1] However, when I finally got around to looking at the book, I realized that it was basically a compilation of papers from an academic conference and not the kind of book that I wanted to write anyway.

During the writing of this book, I became aware of two earlier books about OMB. The first was a Princeton University PhD dissertation on the history of OMB from 1921-1979,[2] a period which conveniently ended when I started at OMB. The second, *The Evolution of OMB*,[3] was written by a couple of my former Senior Executive Service (SES) colleagues at OMB and covered the agency's history from 1921 through 2009. Both of these books were very academic in nature, although the latter includes some interesting anecdotes.

Instead, I wanted to write a book for budding policy analysts and members of the public who were interested in how the Federal government works in practice, not in theory. In this book, I tried to explain all the various functions of OMB and how they can work together to achieve policy goals.

In addition, I wanted to highlight for the public how to interpret what they read in the press about policy issues, especially budget issues. Finally, I wanted to imbue readers with a sense of skepticism for interpreting claims made by advocates on various issues, including for issues on which they may share the same goals as the advocates.

Interestingly, *The Evolution of OMB* starts with a quote from Paul O'Neill, former Deputy Director of OMB, who said:

> *"One of the interesting things about OMB is that it is unexplainable to everyone who lives outside of the Beltway and misunderstood by nearly everyone who lives inside the Beltway.*[4]*"*

The second part of the quote is definitely correct, while this book is my attempt to prove that the first part of the quote is incorrect.

As a long-time "nameless, faceless bureaucrat," I have no illusion that anybody, other than my wife, daughters and possibly my friends, cares about the specifics of my life or career at OMB. Nevertheless, I have included in this book many references to my personal experiences to illustrate how OMB works to get things done in practice, not just in theory. To do this, however, I must spend some time educating the reader about the programs involved in the examples. Following the arc of my career from junior examiner to Acting Director also has the advantage of showing what roles staff play at various levels in the organization, as well as how they think and react to the issues being addressed. Hopefully you will find this book illuminating and will view public policy issues, and press coverage of them, in a new, informed, and possibly more skeptical light.

GLOSSARY OF KEY TERMS AND ACRONYMS

ACRE – Average Crop Revenue Election

BA – Budget Authority

BC – Branch Chief

BRD – Budget Review Division

CAA – Clean Air Act

CAAA – Clean Air Act Amendments of 1990

CARES – Coronavirus Aid, Relief & Economic Security Act

CBO – Congressional Budget Office

CCC – Commodity Credit Corporation

CDC – Centers for Disease Control

CEQ – Council on Environmental Quality

CERCLA – Comprehensive Response, Compensation and Liability Act

CFC – Chlorofluorocarbon

CHIMP – Change in Mandatory Program

CN – Congressional Notification

CO – Carbon Monoxide

CO_2 – Carbon Dioxide

CR – Continuing Resolution

CSP – Conservation Security Program

DAD – Deputy Associate Director

DDM – Deputy Director for Management

DFC – Development Finance Corporation

DOD – Department of Defense

DOE – Department of Energy

DOI – Department of the Interior

DPC – Domestic Policy Council

EEOB – Eisenhower Executive Office Building (aka OEOB)

E-Gov – Office of E-Government and Information Technology

EO – Executive Order

EPA – Environmental Protection Agency

EXOP – Executive Office of the President

FCRA – Federal Credit Reform Act

FMF – Foreign Military Financing

FRM – Final Rulemaking

FSRIA – Farm Security and Rural Investment Act

FTE – Full-time equivalent

FY – Fiscal Year

GAO – General Accounting Office

GHSA – Global Health Security Agenda

GNP – Gross National Product

HHS – Department of Health and Human Services

IAD – International Affairs Division

ICA – Impoundment Control Act of 1974

IIM – Individual Indian Money trust system

IT – Information Technology

MBA – Master of Business Administration

NAAQS – National Ambient Air Quality Standards

NAPAP - National Acidic Precipitation Assessment Program

NCP – National Contingency Plan

NSC – National Security Council

NEOB – New Executive Office Building

NGO – Non-Governmental Organization

NOx – Nitrogen Oxide

NPL – National Priority List

NPRM – Notice of Proposed Rulemaking

NRD – Natural Resources Division

NSD - National Security Council

OCO – Overseas Contingency Operations

OEOB – Old Executive Office Building

OFFM – Office of Federal Financial Management

OFPP – Office of Federal Procurement Policy

OGAC – Office of the Global AIDS Coordinator

OGC – Office of General Counsel

OIRA – Office of Information and Regulatory Affairs

OMB – Office of Management and Budget

PAD – Program Associate Director

PAYGO – Pay-As-You-Go

PEPFAR – President's Emergency Plan for AIDS Relief

PM – Particulate Matter

PMA – President's Management Agenda

PRA – Paperwork Review Act

RIA – Regulatory Impact Analysis

RMO – Resource Management Office

SES – Senior Executive Service

SO2 – Sulfur Dioxide

SRF – State Revolving Fund

TB – Tuberculosis

USAID – United States Agency for International Development

USDA – United States Department of Agriculture

VOC – Volatile Organic Compound

VSL – Value of a Statistical Life

VSLY – Value of Statistical Life-Years

WH – White House

CHAPTER ONE: Shining Light on the Black Box -- *OMB 101*

In order to fully understand and get the most out of this book, the reader will need a basic understanding of both the structure of the Office of Management and Budget (OMB) and the terminology used in budgeting. While I realize that some readers may view this chapter and the following chapter on budget process as good cures for insomnia, I urge you to prop your eyelids open and pay attention as it will make it easier to understand the remainder of the book. Unfortunately, non-fiction writers don't have the luxury available to novelists of adding a sex scene to spice up a slow portion of the book, so bear with me.

OMB's Relationship to the White House

By federal government standards, OMB is a small agency of around 480 full-time equivalents (FTE).[5] An agency's FTE level is the calculated number of full-time work years used by the agency in a particular fiscal year. For example, an employee who worked four months and an employee who worked eight months would together be one FTE, the same as a single employee who worked the entire year.

This FTE level is down from about 630 when I started at OMB 42 years earlier,[6] despite OMB having accumulated significant new statutory responsibilities over the years. A significant portion of the reduction is due to a dramatic downsizing of the amount of administrative (i.e. secretarial) staff due to productivity gains from using modern computer systems.

However, the reduction is also due to various directors wanting to show leadership in fiscal restraint by holding down OMB budget requests as well as congressional Appropriations Committee retaliation against OMB related to various policy disputes. Regardless of the reason, OMB has become a leaner agency at a time when domestic agencies in the aggregate have gone in the opposite direction and the Congressional Budget Office (CBO) has remained roughly constant in size.[7]

Though a small agency, OMB is the largest component of the Executive Office of the President (EXOP), which had about 1,700 FTE in 2020.[8] However, the 1,700 figure is a gross underestimate of the number of people who actually work in the White House complex. For instance, it doesn't include General Services Administration staff who maintain the buildings, National Park Service staff who maintain the grounds, Navy personnel who man the White House mess, and Army personnel who staff the motor pool. It also doesn't include hundreds of non-reimbursable agency staff detailed (i.e. short-term assignments) to the White House, such as Defense and State Department personnel who provide the bulk of the staff to run the National Security Council (NSC).

The White House complex has three primary buildings — the White House (WH), the Eisenhower Executive Office Building (EEOB, aka the Old Executive Office Building, or OEOB), and the New Executive Office Building (NEOB). Within the complex, these are often referred to as the White Building, the Gray Building, and the Red Building, based on the color of the stone or brick facade of each building.

The White House has offices for the President's most-senior political aides while the EEOB offices are mostly for less-senior political staff, detailees, as well as a few career staff, and the NEOB contains career and contractor staff offices. Ironically, in general, the closer an employee's office is to the President, the smaller the office. Nevertheless, for political staff, proximity to the Oval Office trumps office size in the competition for office space.

OMB political staff work in the EEOB while the career OMB staff occupy half of the NEOB, which is across Pennsylvania Avenue from the White House and EEOB (and despite what many people in Washington believe, there is no tunnel under Pennsylvania Avenue to get from the NEOB to the EEOB). OMB leadership sometimes refer to issues as "White Building problems," "Gray Building problems," or "Red Building problems" depending on which level of staff has the action on the issue.

When I started at OMB in 1979, it had three presidential-ly-appointed and Senate-confirmed positions — referred to as PAS positions — whereas now there are six. The Director and Deputy Director positions have been PAS slots since 1970, when the Bureau of the Budget (BOB) was reorganized into OMB. Four additional PAS slots were subsequently added to the Management side of OMB: the Administrator of the Office of Federal Procurement Policy in 1974; the Deputy Director for Management, and the Controller of the Office of Federal Financial Management in 1990; and the Administrator of the Office of Information and Regulatory Affairs in 1995.

Given that OMB has always had a policy that only Senate-confirmed appointees testify before Congress, the additional confirmed positions gave Congress more OMB staff they could hold accountable in open congressional hearings. Although the total number of OMB political positions (both confirmed and non-confirmed) has fluctuated over time, the number of positions in recent years has been at an all-time high, even as the total OMB staff has shrunk.[9]

As OMB is an agency rather than a department, the Director is not automatically a member of the president's cabinet but is generally designated by the President to be a cabinet member. Consequently, the Director is typically invited to all principal level (i.e. cabinet secretaries without the President) meetings of the policy councils (i.e. National Security Council, Domestic Policy Council, and National Economic Council). Unlike department secretaries, however, the Director of OMB is also a White House senior staff member and attends the WH's regular (usually daily) senior staff meetings.

While OMB is sometimes referred to in the press as the "White House Office of Management and Budget," that is not technically correct. OMB is part of the broader Executive Office of the President but is not part of the White House. The White House has its own internal budget account that pays for less than 400 of the president's political staff.

Nevertheless, the distinction between OMB and the White House can be confusing depending on the situation being considered. For instance, the Director is an OMB staff member, but has a White House security badge and is considered part of the president's senior staff. However, there are some legal distinctions, particularly relating to records retention and disclosure policies, that differentiate OMB from the White House. Furthermore, OMB internal communications are not covered by the president's constitutional executive privilege in the same manner as internal White House communications are.

Organization of OMB

When one of my examiners introduced herself to former OMB Director Jack Lew on a transatlantic flight, he told her what a great organization it was and how OMB "punches above its weight." What he meant is that OMB wields a significantly disproportionate amount of clout for an agency of its size. There are multiple reasons for this, including OMB's proximity to the White House and ability to attract extremely capable staff. However, the same can be said for other EXOP offices that don't wield the same level of clout.

From my standpoint, what sets OMB apart are the processes it runs and the tasks it has been assigned by both the President and Congress. The multiple tools that OMB has at its disposal make it like a Swiss army knife. In other words, it is a versatile organization that can use multiple tools in different situations with the singular goal of accomplishing the objectives in the President's policy agenda.

When I was a branch chief and used to recruit new staff, I would emphasize the five roles that OMB plays and that the budget staff played a key part in each of those roles.

These roles, which will be discussed in more detail throughout the book, are:

1. *Budget* — OMB runs the process for developing the President's Budget for the executive branch in accordance with OMB Circular A-11, a role which necessarily involves giving agencies fiscal guidance, evaluating agency requests, making budget decisions, resolving agencies appeals, and preparing the final budget documents.

2. *Legislation* — Under OMB Circular A-19, OMB runs the inter-agency clearance process and resolves disputes between agencies for proposed Administration legislation, testimony on Congressional legislation, and testimony for controversial oversight hearings, to ensure that the Administration "speaks with one voice."

3. *Regulations* — Under Executive Order 12866 and the Paperwork Reduction Act, OMB reviews all major agency regulations to help ensure that rules achieve their objective in the most efficient and effective manner possible and approves information collection requests to minimize paperwork burden on the public.

4. *Management* — Under a range of statutes and executive orders, OMB is charged with improving the efficiency and effectiveness of federal government programs and ensuring that they are implemented in a consistent and transparent manner.

5. *Executive Orders* — Pursuant to Executive Order 11030[10], OMB is responsible for running the inter-agency clearance process and resolving disputes between agencies prior to Executive Orders and Presidential Memorandums being submitted to the President for signature.

While somewhat of a simplification, OMB is generally viewed as having a "management side" (i.e. the "M" in OMB) and a "budget side" (i.e. the "B" in OMB). When I first became interested in working at OMB during graduate school, my inclination was to work for the M side. This was in part because budgeting sounded boring. Furthermore, I was pursuing a master's in business administration (MBA) degree at Stanford and helping manage the federal government seemed more consistent with that degree. After a little digging, however, I realized that budgeting in the federal government is very different than in the private sector and that budgets are the government's biggest sources of leverage and power to achieve public policy objectives.

The "B" Side

Thus, my first job at OMB was as a Budget Examiner in the Environment Branch, which was responsible for the Environmental Protection Agency (EPA). I always hated the title of Budget Examiner, because it didn't convey the real nature of the job. In fact, vacancy announcements for Budget Examiners tended to elicit a lot of applications from individuals in agency budget execution offices, who were good at rote tasks, such as tracking money, but couldn't understand the big picture policy significance of various proposals. Consequently, I switched my vacancy announcements to advertise for policy analysts, because that was a more fitting description of the staff's duties. Unfortunately, after a reorganization 1994, known as OMB 2000, all the budget staff positions were recategorized as program examiners and I was forced to use the new job categorization.

After OMB 2000, the offices within the budget side became known as Resource Management Offices (RMO), of which there are 4 or 5 depending on the organizational set-up in each administration. Each RMO is headed by a non-confirmed political appointee under the title Program Associate Director or PAD. There are eight budget divisions that report to the PADs, each headed by a Deputy Associate Director or DAD. The DAD positions are career Senior Executive Service (SES) slots that are generally held by long-serving OMB career staff. I served as the DAD for Natural Resources for nine years and as DAD for International Affairs for eleven years.

The budget divisions have between two and four branches, each headed by a career SES Branch Chief (BC). The branches themselves generally have between five and ten program examiners. The examiners are paid according to the General Services (GS) pay scale and OMB examiners are on a career ladder from a GS-9 (which requires one year of experience at a GS-7 entry level position or a master's degree) through a GS-15 (which is the level just below the SES). A career ladder means that the individual can be promoted up to the top of the career ladder without recompeting for the job. While career ladders are common for positions in Washington, career ladders to a GS-15 are extremely rare and provide a major advantage for working at OMB.

The branches themselves line up with the Federal Government's organization structure. Most branches are responsible for a department or large independent agency (e.g. EPA), although large departments, such as the Department of Defense (DOD) or Health and Human Services (HHS), will have multiple branches working on their programs. Given the small number of examiners assigned to each Department, the span of control of each examiner is huge. A typical examiner would be responsible for all the programs under a Presidentially appointed, Senate confirmed Assistant Secretary for a Department. Assistant Secretaries with line, as opposed to staff, functions would typically run a large Bureau within the Department.

What makes an examiner's job so challenging, particularly for new staff straight out of graduate school, is that they need to become expert on all the programs within their assigned Bureau. In addition, they need to have a "big picture" mentality to understand how that Bureau's programs fit within the Department and how those programs need to be coordinated with other Federal agencies, as well as their partners in state and local governments. Furthermore, the examiner will be involved in virtually all the same issues as the relevant Assistant Secretary for their bureau, because examiners in the RMO's are very involved in all five of OMB's principal roles (i.e. budget, legislation, regulation, management, and EOs), not just on budget as many people assume.

As a case in point of how an examiner can leverage these multiple roles, I will cite my work as an examiner and branch chief in implementing the Montreal Protocol, which required a ramp down in the production of chemicals, mainly chlorofluorocarbons (CFCs), that deplete the ozone layer protecting the Earth from excessive ultraviolet radiation. The Environment Branch view was that the fairest and most efficient method of implementing the Protocol was to auction off the fixed amount of production allowances -- a radical idea at the time -- and devote the revenue to deficit reduction.

We first tried to get the allowance auction into the Administration's proposal for needed implementing legislation but lost that fight to EPA. After Justice provided public comments on EPA's proposed rule that allowances could be auctioned under existing law, we tried to get the auction into EPA's final regulation carrying out the implementing legislation. We lost that fight as well. Finally, we got the auction proposal into the annual Budget passback as a deficit reduction measure that was projected to save almost $4 billion over 5 years. As EPA didn't have a multi-billion mandatory offset to offer as a replacement for our deficit reduction proposal, and had other priorities on appeal, we succeeded in getting the auction proposal in the Budget.

Unfortunately, the business community wasn't yet comfortable with the auction concept, so Congress enacted an excise tax as part of the 1989 reconciliation bill to get the same amount of revenue. While only a partial victory, the debate on tradeable allowances and auctions for the Protocol paved the way for enactment of both to address acid rain in subsequent Clean Air legislation. Furthermore, as CFC substitutes became available faster than expected, the excise tax likely resulted in more revenue than the CFC allowance auction would have raised, savings me from an embarrassing shortfall in my estimate.

The "M" Side

The "M" side of OMB is headed by the Senate confirmed Deputy Director for Management. It consists of four offices, which are generally referred to as the statutory offices because each is established in statute and has its own set of statutory responsibilities. The primary task of three of the offices is to set government-wide policies consistent with their statutory role. These offices and their roles are:

Office of Federal Procurement Policy (OFPP) — provides policy direction and guidance on procurement issues for all Federal agencies in order to promote efficiency and effectiveness in Federal acquisitions and is responsible for Federal cost accounting standards.

Office of Federal Financial Management (OFFM) — performs a similar function to OFPP for financial management issues under the Chief Financial Officers Act of 1990. OFFM issued guidance is aimed at providing transparency of Federal finances and safeguarding against "fraud, waste, and abuse" of taxpayer dollars.

Office of E-Government and Technology (E-GOV) — created by the E-Government Act of 2002 and headed by the Federal Chief Information Officer, a non-Senate confirmed political appointee. E-GOV provides guidance and oversight in order to maximize the return on Federal Information Technology (IT) investments. E-GOV also conducts cybersecurity oversight for non-classified Federal computer systems. (Note, this office is also sometimes known as the Office of the Federal Chief Information Officer.)

These offices are staffed by experts on procurement, financial management, and IT issues respectively. However, these subject experts do not have broad knowledge of individual departments and agencies, and they lack much in the way of leverage over the agencies. For these reasons, these offices are most effective in getting their policies implemented when they are working with the examiners in the RMOs who have the expertise about, and budget leverage over, the individual agencies. In fact, many management directives are issued as part of the annual budget passback to increase the likelihood that agencies will give priority to implementing various management initiatives.

The Office of Information and Regulatory Affairs (OIRA) also issues some government-wide guidance, but they have more of an operational role. This role includes reviewing, under Executive Order 12866, major agency rulemakings prior to publication, at both the proposed and final stage, and in approving information collection requests under the Paperwork Reduction Act. Unlike the other statutory office, OIRA has "desk officers" who are agency experts, but only on the agencies with major regulatory programs.

Major regulations are supposed to be reviewed by both the OIRA desk officer and the relevant RMO examiner. However, RMO involvement varies depending on the importance of regulations in the overall scheme of agency programs, whereas OIRA must review all of the regulations. Consequently, in my two decades in the Environment Branch, I spent a huge portion of my time on regulatory review, because EPA had the most complicated statutes and most expensive rules in the Government. In contrast, the State Department had few rulemakings and the only ones of sufficient interest to merit my time related to fee setting regulations for consular programs (e.g. passports and visas).

Support Offices

OMB also has several agency-wide support offices, most of which don't fit neatly under the "M" or "B" sides. The key support offices are discussed below due to their role in running key OMB-led processes.

Budget Review Division (BRD) — issues guidance and runs the budget process both within OMB and government-wide. BRD is also the budget scorekeeper for the Executive branch, develops Statements of Administration Policy on appropriations bills, and is responsible for budget concepts, a wonky but important, if underappreciated, role. While BRD is generally viewed as part of the "B" side, the Assistant Director for Budget reports directly to OMB's front office and has an office in the EEOB, rather than the NEOB. This close proximity to the front office is needed in order to facilitate quick internal collection of information requested by the Director.

Legislative Review Division (LRD) — runs the inter-agency clearance process for testimony and Administration legislative proposals. LRD staff are organized by agency and are expert at resolving inter-agency conflicts on a short time frame. RMO staff review all testimony and bills to ensure consistency with established policy and are responsible for getting decisions on open policy issues. LRD also drafts the Statements of Administration Policy for non-appropriation bills prior to floor action, indicating whether the Administration supports or opposes the bill. In addition, LRD prepares an enrolled bill memo on every bill passed by the Congress, which are sent by the Director to the President to give him a summary of the bill as well as agency positions on whether to veto or sign it.

Office of General Counsel (OGC) — among OGC's tasks is running the inter-agency clearance process on draft EOs and preparing a memo for the President summarizing the EO and agency positions on whether to sign. OGC is also the Executive branch's foremost authority on legal issues relating to budgets and funds control. However, OGC also provides an extremely valuable function in providing OMB budget and management staff with legal reads on virtually any statute. It is not uncommon for an agency to brief OMB staff on a new policy proposal and argue that the proposed policy is the only possible interpretation of the underlying statute. OMB staff with a commonsense knowledge of the statute will generally know that is not true, but need the legal firepower in OGC to get the agency to admit that other policy options are available besides the agency's preferred position.

Budget Terminology

If I were a member of the general public, I suspect that I would be very confused by press reporting on budget issues. Even with forty years of budget expertise, it sometimes takes me awhile to understand either what is being reported or the limitations of what is being reported. As press articles don't always provide sufficient information to fully understand the situation, I can't provide a complete guide to deciphering the articles. The best that I can do is provide a guide that, hopefully, will allow the reader to know what questions are being left unanswered.

To compound matters, the terminology and concepts of budgeting are tricky as there are three basic measures of spending and two basic types of spending. The three spending measures are as follows:

Budget Authority (BA) — provides the legal authority to incur obligations. The most common type of BA is provided as appropriations through the appropriations bill process. However, BA can also be provided through authorization bills.

Obligation (OB) — refers to a binding agreement that commits the use of BA. The signing of a contract or grant incurs an obligation, as does the purchase of expenses and any labor provided by staff.

Outlay (OL) -- means a payment for work performed under an obligation. Thus, an electronic funds transfer (or a check) for progress in constructing a road under a contract, or an employee paycheck would both be outlays.

The press can sometimes refer to any of these three measures as spending without specifying which measure. Understanding which measure can be important because of the time lag between the three. Appropriations bills specify how long BA is available for obligation. Salary accounts are typically one-year accounts, meaning that they must be obligated in the fiscal year they are appropriated. However, BA may also have two-year availability or, as is often the case with construction funding, the BA can be classified as no-year funding, meaning that the BA is available for obligation indefinitely. Similarly, there is a lag between obligation and outlay. For salaries, the lag between work and paycheck is about two weeks, but outlays for complicated infrastructure projects stretch out over years. This means that the total lag between the availability of the BA and the final outlay can be over a decade.

If a press report doesn't specify a measure of spending, it can sometimes be inferred from the context of the article. Thus, if the article is about an appropriation's spending bill, the measure is likely BA. If the article refers to "year-end spending", the measure is obligations because that term refers to agencies obligating all their funds before the availability of the BA expires. Finally, if an article refers to spending in the context of the deficit, the measure is outlays, because the deficit in a particular year is calculated as the amount of outlays (i.e. value of checks issued) in excess of the amount of revenue (i.e. taxes and fees) received. The two types of spending are as follows:

Discretionary — as a general rule, discretionary spending is provided as BA through the appropriations process and becomes available in the fiscal year (FY) for which the appropriations are funded. However, appropriations bills can also provide advance appropriations for future years. Obligation limitations on permanent budget authority are also classified as discretionary. There is a statutory exception, however, for limitations on transportation trust funds where the BA remains mandatory.

Mandatory — as a general rule, mandatory spending (sometimes referred to as direct spending) is provided by laws other than appropriations acts and the bills are developed by the authorizing, rather than appropriations committees. The bulk of mandatory spending are entitlements, which are programs for which the Federal Government is legally required to make payments if certain criteria are met (e.g. an individual retires and meets the age and work requirements to receive social security payments). Some entitlements (e.g. Medicaid) are referred to as "appropriated entitlements", because the funding is provided in appropriations acts, even though the Federal Government is legally required to make the payments.

Conceptually, the model of discretionary funding through the annual appropriations process and ongoing mandatory entitlements legislated through the authorizing committees make a lot of sense. However, there is little logic to the many exceptions to the model. Basically, the exceptions reflect the ongoing parochial power struggle between the appropriations committee and the various authorizing committees in each House. In most cases, the exceptions probably resulted from deals cut as part of the "sausage making" needed to enact legislation.

For instance, appropriated entitlements are designed to give the Appropriations Committees a role in an ongoing entitlement program, whose permanent authority should preclude the need for annual appropriations action. In fact, Medicare is very similar to Medicaid, except that it provides health care for the elderly instead of the indigent, but it is not an appropriated entitlement and the Appropriations Committee has no role in the program. Nevertheless, as a practical matter, the clout of the appropriators on the Medicaid program is limited.

Non-entitlement mandatory programs can be seen as a power grab by the authorizing committees. For instance, conceptually there is little difference between some of the mandatory programs in the Farm Bill and many similar types of programs that get discretionary funding. It is simply a reflection of the Agriculture Committees having sufficient clout to provide multiple years of mandatory funding in the Farm Bill and prevent those programs from being automatically subject to the annual appropriations process.

However, this does not prevent the Appropriations Committee from seizing a role in discretionary-like mandatory programs through a "change in a mandatory program" or "CHIMP" as it is known. A typical CHIMP would effectively rescind (i.e. take away) a portion of the mandatory program funding scheduled to become available in a year. As such a CHIMP would be scored as a negative in the discretionary appropriations process, it allows an appropriations subcommittee to provide an equivalent amount of additional appropriations for other programs in its portfolio. Of course, the authorizing committees hate CHIMPs, which they view as stealing their money, but they are usually powerless to stop it and, in many cases, are supportive of the programs which receive the additional appropriations.

Just as the authorizers use non-entitlement mandatory funding to mimic discretionary programs, except with multiple years of funding provided up-front, the appropriators sometimes use appropriations to mimic mandatory spending. The best example of this is the Infrastructure Investment and Jobs Act (IIJA) of 2021 (aka the Bipartisan Infrastructure Deal), which provided almost a half-trillion dollars in multi-year discretionary funding. The appropriators did this by classifying the four years of funding after the budget year as advance appropriations to get the same advantage as if the funding had been enacted as mandatory.

All of this funding was also classified under budget scorekeeping rules as an "emergency" requirement. This classification was established to allow funding for severe hurricanes, earthquakes and other disasters that couldn't easily be funded quickly within the constraints of annual appropriations. It is primarily important when budget caps are in place on discretionary spending, because emergency spending is in addition to the statutory cap. As a technical matter, the cap is adjusted for emergency appropriations rather than having such spending exempt from the cap.

Unfortunately, use of the emergency classification is often misused by both parties to fund longer-term items and activities that aren't really emergencies. In fact, often the way to get sufficient votes to enact a disaster supplemental is to add funding for minor emergencies, often from prior years, until enough Senators and Representatives benefit from the bill. The IIJA is certainly the largest abuse of the classification. However, as the current discretionary caps expired at the end of FY 2021, the emergency classification is less important in this case, unless new caps are established in the five-year window when most of this funding becomes available.

CHAPTER TWO: Budgeting is Like a Rubik's Cube --
Congress Rarely Fully Solves the Puzzle

In this chapter I will explain how the budget process works and the timeline for formulating and enacting the budget. The first section discusses the process for developing the President's Budget request while the second section attempts to explain the congressional budget process.

Budget Process — Administration

The budget formulation process for the President's Budget lasts nearly a year as shown in Figure 2-1. The first several months of this process are internal to the agencies. While agency budget submissions must be submitted to OMB in accordance with OMB Circular A-11, internal budget processes may be very different from one agency to the next. OMB's role during this period is limited to providing Spring planning guidance, which gives the agencies target levels for the discretionary budget and issuing the annual update to Circular A-11. Agencies may also get guidance on reducing mandatory programs. OMB typically refers to these as budget ceilings, but agencies tend to view the level as a floor and usually submit requests well above the ceiling.

The fact that agencies ignore the guidance is not terribly surprising. In most years, the guidance requires a cut of a few percentage points from the previous year's level. The rationale for such a cut is that it gives the President fiscal room to shift funding between agencies to address new priorities. This is particularly important in years when there is a statutory cap on discretionary spending.

The guidance also usually gives the agencies the option of identifying an increase over the ceiling level — 5 percent is typical — for consideration as part of any re-prioritization between agencies. Most agencies jump at the chance to

Figure 2-1

President's Budget Development Timeline

(The budget process is always delayed in Presidential transition years to allow the new President time for input)

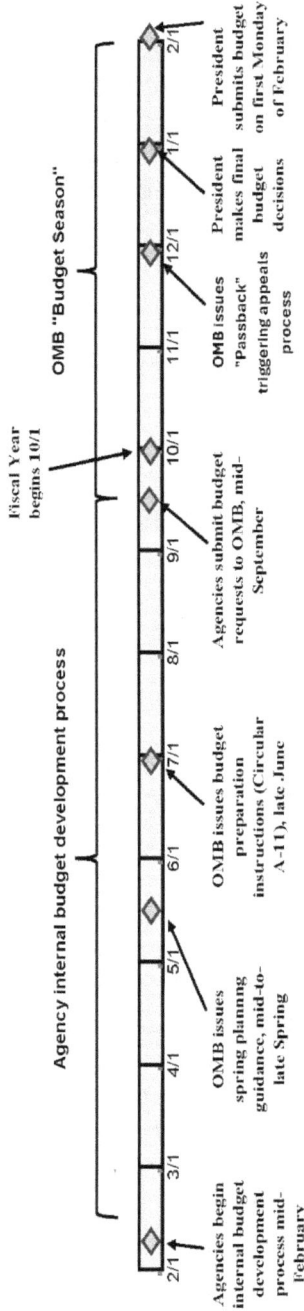

While the budget process always starts on time, in recent years the statutory budget transmittal date (as well as Passback) have often been missed, in large part due to the Congressional delay in enacting current year appropriations.

request funding at the higher level but are loath to identify which programs would need to be cut if the President's request restrained them to the ceiling level.

OMB's involvement in the budget process consumes the final four and a half months — from mid-September through the beginning of February — and is referred to internally as "budget season". One of the interesting things about the budget process at OMB is how little it has changed during my 42 years in the organization. In non-transition years, the cadence of the budget process is virtually the same every year as summarized below:

1. OMB issues budget ceilings to agencies in mid-to-late spring;
2. Agencies submit their requests to OMB in mid-September;
3. OMB examiners hold agency hearings on the submission in late September;
4. Budget recommendations are developed in October;
5. OMB's Director makes decisions in late October through mid-November;
6. OMB passes back decisions to agencies in late November;
7. Agencies appeal the passback in early December;
8. Final budget levels are negotiated no later than early January:
9. The Budget is released in early February.

In the interest of full disclosure, the Budget release in recent years has sometimes slipped later than the statutory early February due date, usually due to delay in Congressional action of the prior year budget or a late deal changing the discretionary budget caps. Nevertheless, this process has been remarkably consistent over my four decades at the institution because it works well for OMB staff, for the Federal Government, and, most importantly, for the President.

Budget season is simultaneously challenging and exciting for RMO staff. Part of what makes it challenging is that staff are working on three budgets concurrently. Execution of the prior year budget (i.e. enacted appropriations) is a year-round task but can be particularly busy at the end of a fiscal year in September. As will be discussed in the next section on the Congressional budget process, appropriations for the fiscal year beginning October 1st are supposed to be enacted by September. However, as that rarely happens, RMO staff spend a substantial amount of time each fall monitoring and reacting to Congressional action on appropriations (or continuing resolutions) to ensure enactment of bills that the President can sign. Finally, the point of budget season is to formulate the President's Budget proposal for the next fiscal year, which begins the following October.

The exciting part for examiners is being part of the policy development process at a lower GS grade level than anywhere else in government — budget is policy as well as power. Two steps in this process are particularly important for the examiners: 1) the budget hearings and 2) Director's Review. The budget hearings are a chance for the examiners to grill high level agency officials on their submissions. The hearings have two purposes: 1) get a firm understanding of what is being proposed and how it differs from prior budgets; and 2) for new initiatives, probe to see how well they are thought out.

My experience has been that most agency budget initiatives have good intentions but are rarely better than half-baked. The impetus for many initiatives is pressure from non-governmental organizations (NGOs), but agency officials are often reluctant to spend much time fleshing initiatives out until they have evidence that the program is likely to get funded. Of course, this sets up a chicken and the egg problem, because OMB, and often the appropriators, are reluctant to fund programs that haven't been well developed.

Even more important for examiners is Director's Review. After the budget hearings, the examiners develop funding and policy recommendations, which the Branch Chief, DAD and PAD must assure will fit within OMB's internal guidance level for a particular agency, while also funding previously decided Presidential priorities. This internal budget ceiling is often lower than the Spring Guidance ceiling given to the agencies but, unlike the agencies, OMB staff must produce and recommend a level at guidance.

However, the guidance level is not necessarily the level that the Director will choose. In addition to a guidance solution, the Director will receive a briefing book (aka Director's Review book) that will contain 5 to 10 decision papers on major budget and policy issues. These issue papers will usually have options that would allow the Director to choose a budget level either above or below the recommendation.

The Director's Review itself is typically a meeting with the Director for the branch, the DAD, and the PAD to explain and defend the recommended level for a particular Department or large agency. Typically, the examiners present and answer most of the questions that the Director or other senior staff have about any issue papers related to their programs. This annual opportunity to get "face time" with a cabinet rank official is one of the biggest motivations for OMB staff and also one of our best recruiting tools.

The focus of most Director's Review papers is on discretionary programs, although papers on issues with mandatory programs may be included as well. An agency such as HHS, which has huge mandatory programs, will usually have a separate Director's Review just on mandatory programs.

Prior to giving the decisions back to the agencies, the Director briefs and/or sends a memo to the President to get his sign-off on the overall budget outlook and the major issues that require presidential attention. A cabinet meeting is also often scheduled to lower the expectations of department secretaries on the size of their budgets. It is especially important for the President to send a message that he has signed off on the Budget when agency marks are particularly austere. Cabinet officers tend to nod their heads in support of the President's austerity message but assume that the message is directed to other members of the cabinet, since they have all heard individually from the President about how important their department's or agency's mission is to the Administration.

The document transmitting decisions on the agency's budget request is referred to as the "passback" and is typically sent to the agencies the week after Thanksgiving. Agencies typically have three days to send any appeals of those decisions back to OMB. The period up through Christmas is when most appeals are resolved. The PADs resolve most appeals, after clearing appeals resolution with the Director, with more difficult appeals going to the Director.

In general, significant efforts are made to keep appeals away from the President. Both the Director and Cabinet Secretary are reluctant to take up the President's time to resolve remaining differences after resolution of some issues at lower levels unless there is a really fundamental policy disagreement. Often a "Budget Review Board (BRB)" is used to resolve appeals rather than taking them to the President. The makeup of the Board can vary, but typically might include the Vice-President, the Chief of Staff, and the OMB Director. Appeals of BRB decisions by secretaries are rare.

RMO staff consider the month of January to be the most boring part of budget season because the period is almost entirely devoted to process after the final decisions have been made. Among the most important tasks is finalizing a huge database that contains the detailed data to publish the 1,000 plus page Budget Appendix as well as summary data that goes into the actual President's Budget document. RMO staff also work on various budget rollout tasks including finalizing Budget chapter text; preparing questions and answers (Q&As) to prep the Director for press briefings and congressional hearings; and clearing agency congressional budget submissions to ensure consistency with both final budget decisions and White House messaging themes.

When the President's Budget request is released on the first Monday in February, at least some critics will declare it "dead on arrival". While it is certainly true that the President's Budget will not be enacted in total, it nevertheless sets the overall fiscal framework for the Budget and, thereby, puts some constraints on congressional action. In fact, in many years, the President's Budget is the only complete budget proposal developed that covers appropriations, mandatory spending and taxes. Furthermore, even congressional committee chairs lobby to get proposals included in the President's Budget, because it increases the chances of a proposal getting enacted.

Preparation of a budget request is a constitutional responsibility of the President. However, it is important to remember that is only a proposal. Occasionally a critic will argue that a proposal in the Budget is "illegal". Certainly, implementing a proposal without any statutory authority would be illegal, but the criticism misses the point. The Budget is replete with proposals for changes to mandatory programs and taxes that knowingly require statutory change.

Budget Process — Congress

Legislative staff like to remind OMB that "the President proposes, and Congress disposes". That is certainly correct when it comes to the 30 percent[11] of the budget devoted to appropriations, although with the caveat that the President can veto what the "Congress disposes". When it comes to mandatory spending and tax changes, however, the saying might more appropriately read "the President proposes and Congress dithers" as the congressional process seems more broken as time goes by, as will be discussed below.

The congressional process begins almost immediately after the President's Budget is transmitted, starting with "big picture" hearings for the OMB Director to testify before the budget and finance committees. These are followed by a couple of months of agency hearings before the appropriations committees. The OMB Director also testifies on the proposal for OMB's budget. However, that is always an odd hearing, with virtually no questions about the OMB request. Instead, it is used as an opportunity for appropriation committee members to ask the Director about parochial issues of importance to their districts or any other issue that appears in the Budget.

As can be seen on Figure 2-2 on the congressional budget process, there are two statutory deadlines for Congress — April 15th to complete the budget resolution and October 1st to enact appropriations — which Congress virtually never makes. This is particularly galling for many executive branch staff who may have to comply with multiple congressionally imposed deadlines. In many cases, failure to meet those deadlines will result in citizen suits to compel action or trigger other penalties. When Congress misses its own

Figure 2-2

Congressional Budget Development Timeline

(This timeline shows how the process is supposed to work, not how it works in practice)

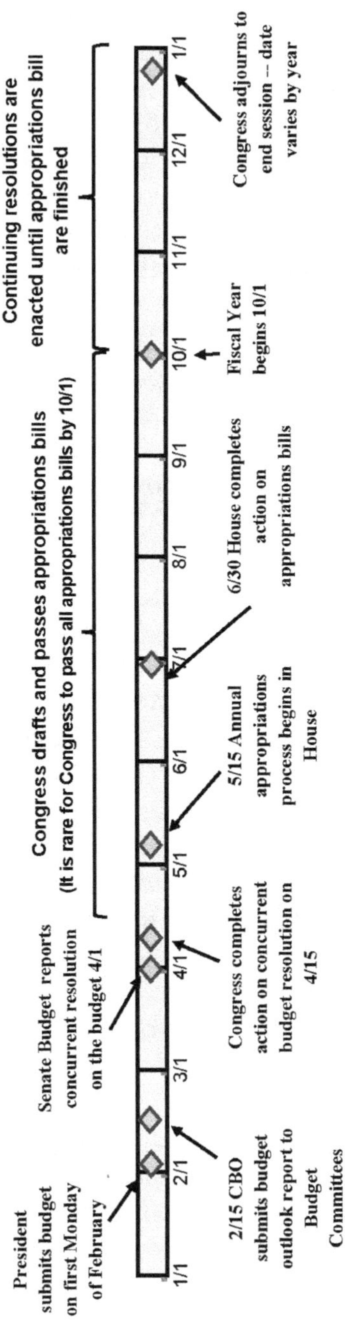

President submits budget on first Monday of February

2/15 CBO submits budget outlook report to Budget Committees

Senate Budget reports concurrent resolution on the budget 4/1

Congress completes action on concurrent budget resolution on 4/15

Congress drafts and passes appropriations bills
(It is rare for Congress to pass all appropriations bills by 10/1)

5/15 Annual appropriations process begins in House

6/30 House completes action on appropriations bills

Fiscal Year begins 10/1

Continuing resolutions are enacted until appropriations bill are finished

Congress adjourns to end session — date varies by year

1/1 2/1 3/1 4/1 5/1 6/1 7/1 8/1 9/1 10/1 11/1 12/1 1/1

deadlines, however, there are no consequences other than potential political pressure. Unfortunately, such pressure is rarely sufficient to force Congress to get its work done on time and, in many cases, political pressure actually works against taking any action.

There are three key budget actions that Congress can, and arguably should, take during a year: 1) passage of a budget resolution; 2) enactment of a reconciliation bill; and 3) enactment of appropriations bills. Unfortunately, Congress performs poorly on all three, even the must-have appropriations bills. Confusingly, the press often refers to any of these three actions as the "budget". Thus, when the press reports that Congress has passed the budget, as shorthand for the budget resolution, most people would assume that Congress has done its work for the year. **WRONG**, because at a minimum Congress still must enact appropriations in some form.

Budget Committee Process

The requirement for adoption of an annual congressional budget resolution was enacted as part of the Congressional Budget Act of 1974. It is a "concurrent" resolution, which means that it does not go to the President for signature, even after passage by both the House and Senate. Consequently, it is not a law, but provides a framework for further congressional action on the budget, with spending allocations that can be enforced by points of order during floor action, although the 60 vote Senate points of order are the only ones with any teeth.

Like the President's Budget, the congressional budget resolution provides an overall picture of the budget (i.e. aggregates for BA, outlays, revenue, and the budget surplus or deficit), but does not provide anywhere close to the level of detail. While the House and Senate Budget Committees prepare the budget resolution, the details of the actual budget are to be filled in during the appropriations process, reconciliation, or other authorizing legislation.

Furthermore, the BA and outlay aggregates in the budget resolution are compiled by budget function rather than agency. Unfortunately, these are numbers that nobody recognizes, other than possibly the wonks on the Budget Committees. While the President's Budget also provides numbers by budget function, they are derived from agency account levels. In contrast, there is no real backup to the function numbers in the resolution and none of the function numbers are binding on the congressional committees. The budget resolution numbers that can be enforced by a point of order are the discretionary total for the appropriations committees and the reconciliation instructions, which are included in the resolution, for mandatory spending and tax changes issued to specific authorization committees.

Congress enacted a budget resolution every year from FY 1976 through FY 1998. However, a resolution was enacted in only 8 of the 12 years between FY 1999 and 2010.[12] Unfortunately, the process has fallen further since FY 2010, with a resolution enacted only 5 times in the succeeding 12 years through FY 2022.[13] However, two of those resolutions were passed after the beginning of the fiscal year and had nothing to do with providing a framework for congressional action in that fiscal year. Their sole purpose was to provide an opportunity for a second reconciliation bill at the beginning of a new administration (i.e. Trump and Biden).

Reconciliation is a special process that Congress can use to bring direct (i.e. mandatory) spending, revenue, and debt limits into compliance with the budget resolution. The carrot for Congress to use reconciliation is that it can be enacted under special rules in the Senate with a majority vote. Thus, it is not subject to the normal Senate rules allowing filibusters of pending bills, which require 60 of the 100 Senators to vote to end debate.

The reconciliation process was originally set up to allow a majority vote to enact bills that reduced the deficit. As a second safeguard to limit reconciliation to budget matters, the Congressional Budget Act included what is known as the "Byrd rule", which prevents consideration of extraneous items in the Senate. Thus, a bill on voting rights, which has no budget impact, would be stricken from a reconciliation bill on a point of order by the Senate Parliamentarian during floor action. While the point of order can be overridden, it requires 60 votes (i.e. 3/5th of the Senate) to do so, rather than a simple majority. The original reconciliation rules were subsequently relaxed to allow enactment of bills that raise the deficit, through either tax cuts or more spending, but the Byrd rule remains intact.

Reconciliation has been attempted in slightly less than half of the years (22 of 47) since the Congressional budget process was established. In most cases, it has resulted in enacted reconciliations bills, with four years having produced two reconciliation bills, as direct spending, revenue, and debt legislation can be considered separately under the same budget resolution. Four reconciliation bills have been vetoed and three reconciliation attempts have failed to be adopted by Congress.[14] The most recent of these was in 2017 at the beginning of the Trump Administration when the sole purpose of both the budget resolution and reconciliations was to try to repeal the Affordable Care Act (aka Obamacare).

It is important to note that reconciliation is possible only in years when a budget resolution is enacted. As indicated earlier, budget resolutions have been enacted in only 5 of the last twelve years and only when there is going to be a serious attempt to enact reconciliation. Two of these attempts (both related to Obamacare repeal) failed and two were enacted at the beginning of the Trump and Biden Administration on party line votes. The two bills enacted through reconciliation fulfilled major campaign commitments to cut taxes (Trump - 2017) and provide pandemic stimulus (Biden -2021).

The reason that a budget resolution is not enacted on an annual basis as the Congressional Budget Act intended, is that the resolution is usually considered a political liability, unless the stars are aligned to make a serious attempt to enact reconciliation. For this to occur, it usually requires that the same party control both houses of congress as well as the presidency.

Senators and Representatives, often of both parties, love to bash the President's Budget as "dead on arrival" because it lays out a complete budget. Unfortunately, the budget can never accomplish all the objectives that the public and Congress want to achieve (i.e. simultaneously increase spending, cut taxes, and balance the budget). Consequently, both parties often view it as not politically worthwhile, particularly in the Senate, to present their own budget solution. The view of the majority party is that producing and voting on a budget resolution will leave their members open to attack during the next campaign for what many members view as meaningless votes on controversial issues. Given Congressional reluctance to implement the congressional budget process on an annual basis, it raises the questions of whether the Budget Committees still have any value.

Appropriations Committee Process

As mentioned earlier, the appropriations process begins almost immediately after the transmission of the President's Budget, with the first three months consisting of numerous budget hearings. The committee in each house is composed of twelve subcommittees which are each supposed to produce a separate bill. Under regular order in both the House and the Senate, each of the twelve bills would be marked up and subject to amendment in the bill's subcommittee and full appropriations committee before being sent for floor action.

The total that the appropriations committees must work with is supposed to be established in the congressional budget resolution, which is supposed to be completed by April 15th. As the budget resolution in recent years is rarely produced on time, if at all, each house may have to "deem" an appropriations total to allow the committee to begin its markups in the absence of timely action on the resolution. The appropriations committee then sub-divides this total among its subcommittees in a process known as the 302(b) allocations.

Subcommittee markups typically begin in early June with the House marking up each bill first. The House is generally pretty good at marking up all its bills in committee and completing floor action on most bills. Historically, appropriations bills were considered under an open rule that allowed unlimited amendments, but all the amendments had to be germane to the bill. Furthermore, attempts to authorize programs in the appropriations bill could be struck on a point of order. In recent years, the House has often used structured or closed amendments rules to limit the number of amendments, which speeds the process and protects majority members from controversial votes. However, even the House doesn't always bring bills to the floor separately, often resorting to enacting multiple bill "minibuses".

The Senate is a whole different level of dysfunction. For one thing the Senate doesn't have a rules process like in the House that can be used to limit amendments. Second, appropriations bills are subject to potential filibusters, like most other non-reconciliation legislation. Third, amendments do not need to be germane to the bill being considered, which means that all sorts of controversial amendments can be proposed for inclusion in the bill.

The combination of these factors means that Senate floor action on appropriations bills can be very lengthy and can result in votes on wedge issues that the Senate Majority Leader would like to avoid.   Furthermore, the increasing polarization of the parties means that authorizing legislation as well as both judicial and executive branch nominations also takes up an increasing amount of Senate floor time. Whichever party is in the minority has found that it can frustrate the majority party's agenda by using the filibuster and other maneuvers to draw out debate on various issues. The fallout of this tactic is that the Senate Majority Leader — of whichever party is in power — has shown increased reluctance to waste limited floor time on appropriation bills.

The FY 2022 appropriations process is illustrative of the broken process. The House marked up all twelve of its bills prior to the August recess. Nine of the twelve were passed in House floor action, although seven of those nine bills were passed as a minibus and the votes on all the bills were largely passed on party line votes.[15] In the Senate, three bills were reported out of committee prior to the August recess on a bipartisan basis. However, the remaining nine bills weren't even introduced until October and were developed without input from Senate Republicans.[16] None of these bills were marked up in committee and none of the Senate bills was subject to floor action.

In the absence of enacted appropriations by October 1st, either a continuing resolution (CR) must be enacted, or portions of the Federal Government shut down. A CR generally extends prior year funding levels for a short period, with a limited number of anomalies to address situations where the prior year level doesn't work for technical reasons (e.g. a new program that got only start-up funding in the prior year). See Chapter 12 for a more detailed discussion of CRs and shutdowns.

In most years, at least a few bills are enacted separately, with the remaining bills rolled into what is referred to as an omnibus appropriations bill. The bills rolled into an omnibus are generally ones that either the House or Senate (or both) couldn't pass through floor action. The legislative vehicle used to enact the omnibus has to be an appropriations bill already passed by the House.

Essentially, the Congress bypasses floor, and often committee, action and goes directly to conference. While the House may be able to pass bills without minority votes, conference is another matter because the conference bill is subject to Senate filibuster rules requiring 60 votes for final passage. This means that the two parties must reach a compromise acceptable to the Senate minority, as well as the President who must sign the bill. One consequence of the need to reach a compromise is that "poison pill" legislative riders added by the majority party usually get stricken.

The good news is that appropriations, even if included in a full year CR, must be enacted annually. Furthermore, the appropriations committees are composed of better deal cutters than most, if not all, other committees. Unfortunately, the leadership blessed compromises needed to enact an omnibus appropriations bill are rarely made until just before Christmas. In some years, the process can extend into March. If an omnibus hasn't come together by the end of March, the Appropriations Committees will usually default to a full year CR, although with a substantial number of non-controversial anomalies both technical and policy.

CHAPTER THREE: Becoming a Skeptic -- *The Education of an OMB Examiner*

This is the first of two chapters that focus on the role of the budget examiner, arguably the most important position in the organization. This chapter focuses on how a newly minted junior examiner learns to conduct the budget examining responsibilities of the job as well as adapt to OMB's unique culture.

By the end of the first year of my MBA program, I had decided that I was more interested in applying my learning to the public sector than the private sector. My final choice of jobs came down to public sector consulting or a job with a federal agency. Consulting had the advantage of paying on the order of 50 percent more than a federal position and would provide a better opportunity to use the analytic tools that I had learned in business school. However, the chance to work directly on public policy, rather than indirectly as a consultant, was an overriding attraction in my job choice.

Consequently, when an offer came through for an examiner position in the Environment Branch at OMB, I jumped at the chance, even though I had been hoping for a job in another branch. While environment as a subject matter appealed to me, the branch chief — Jim Tozzi — evoked strong opinions when I asked around about him, not all of which was positive. As examiners in the Environment Branch rarely stayed more than five years, I figured that I could handle three budget seasons before moving on to a line agency.

I started in mid-July 1979 and had two months to get up to speed on my assigned programs — the $4 billion per year wastewater treatment grant program and the noise regulatory program among others. The demands on OMB staff at the time were not as numerous as they are now, particularly in the seven months outside of budget season. Nevertheless, I felt overwhelmed by the demands of the job and, for a time, I was unsure I could handle the responsibilities of being an OMB examiner. Consequently, I am always impressed at how our new examiners straight out of graduate school handle themselves in today's environment, because I am not sure that I would have survived.

Jim Tozzi turned out to be quite the character. Hailing from Waynesburg, Ohio,[17] he liked to portray himself as a poor southern boy, at least when it suited his purposes. While Waynesburg is not exactly the south, Jim did get a degree from the University of Florida and spent some time in New Orleans,[18] where his trumpet playing skills somehow resulted in a long-term connection to the Preservation Hall Jazz Band. Despite his identification as a southerner, complete with southern drawl, his choice of dress reflected his Italian heritage, as he tended to wear dark suits that would be fitting of a mafia don.

Avoiding Failure on My First Assignment

My first major assignment at OMB was to find a more accurate method for estimating outlays for the wastewater treatment grant program. The program had undergone a major expansion after passage of the Clean Water Act of 1972 to help municipalities achieve secondary treatment standards. Secondary treatment uses bacteria to biodegrade organic material in sewage to achieve a pollutant removal level of 85-90 percent, up from a 50 percent level for primary treatment. Despite sophisticated, contractor developed estimating models, outlays were consistently overestimated by 25 percent or $1 billion a year.

Tozzi told me in no uncertain terms that I was to come up with a method to substantially cut the outlay estimation error for the program. As a first task, he told me to call Henry Longest, the head of the program, and demand he come to my office to explain why the agency's estimates were so full of.... sewage. When I looked Longest up in the EPA phone directory, I saw that he had the imposing title of Deputy Assistant Administrator for Water Program Operations. My first thought was that I was in danger of failing my assignment because I didn't think he would call me back.

Although Longest was in a meeting when I called, I was surprised that he called me back promptly after his meeting. The reason that I didn't think he would call me back was that I was a relatively low graded staffer just out of graduate school, and he was at the top level of the career Senior Executive Service (SES). What I hadn't considered was the concept of position power. In other words, Longest called me back not because of who I was, but because of the position I held — as his budget examiner with significant influence over his program's budget.

This was the first important lesson that I learned as an examiner and over time I would learn how to use that position power to my advantage to carry out my job. Eventually I also would learn a corollary to that lesson — don't let the power go to your head. Unfortunately, too many examiners, including me at times, forget that power comes from the position, not the individual, and that it needs to be used judiciously and respectfully.

While I asked, rather than demanded as Tozzi appeared to want, that Longest come to OMB for the discussion, he proposed that I come to EPA to meet his staff and have them brief me on their efforts. I accepted this offer as reasonable, but unsure whether Tozzi was going to yell at me for not sticking to the letter of his instructions. To my surprise, Tozzi was fine with the arrangement. This was my second lesson that, while Tozzi often gave instructions in very demanding and rigid terms without raising his voice, he did so to convey the importance of the assignment even though he was flexible on the details if you got results. In other words, his bark was worse than his bite.

My discussion with EPA staff was very useful in that they were sufficiently embarrassed about the poor estimates that they gave me access to a lot of raw program data. I then embarked on what would now be called "data mining", except that I did it by hand as this was the era before personal computers. It turned out that the problem with EPA's estimates is that they were assuming a straightforward relationship between BA and outlays, in a program that was ramping up sharply in an out-of-control manner. In reality, there was a consistent relationship, but it was between obligations and outlays, not BA and outlays, and the pace of obligations for a particular year's BA varied radically by year. Program outlays were incurred over a 7-to-10 years after obligation.

Based on these data relationships, I constructed a much simpler model than EPA had been using, which I incorporated into spreadsheet software when the branch got its first personal computer a few years later. This simpler methodology successfully resulted in a much more accurate outlay forecast than was off by only a couple of percent that first year and never much more in the future. In fact, 40 years later one of my former examiners, who had moved to another branch, told me that she had given the basic model to one of her agencies to straighten out estimation problems that they were having.

The Agony and Ecstasy of Budget Season

Shortly after receiving EPA's budget submission in mid-September, we held our budget hearings with the agency. Tozzi ran the hearings as a bigger more formal event than was the case with most branches. EPA was organized by what was referred to as "media" program offices -- air, water, land (i.e. waste sites), and products (i.e. pesticides and chemicals), with several crosscutting offices — research, enforcement, and management. Each of these offices was headed by a Senate confirmed Assistant Administrator and each would have his own budget hearing where the Assistant Administrator was given an opportunity to make a pitch for the office's request followed by OMB questions.

The hearings were 3 hours long and all Environment Branch staff were required to come to every hearing, including ones for which an examiner may not have any specific responsibility. The rationale for having every examiner attend was to gain an understanding of all parts of the agency, both for purposes of backing up the other examiners and for common issues, such as the regulation of the same pollutants by several offices.

Tozzi liked his examiners to ask direct, no-holds barred questions at these hearings. His own questioning style, however, was much different and reminded me of Peter Falk's character in the television series Columbo, except without the trench coat. Tozzi would use his "poor southern boy" schtick to ask basic questions and elicit unguarded an-

swers. His "one more question", a la Columbo, would inevitably point out the fallacies or contradictions in the Assistant Administrator's rationale for why a big new initiative
was needed to address the trendy problem highlighted in
that year's request.

After the hearings the hard part began to winnow down
EPA's request, which was always way above ceiling, and
put forth a recommendation that maximized environmental
protection and met our guidance level. One of the management reforms of the Carter Administration was to require
agencies to use "zero based budgeting" or ZBB. The concept
of ZBB was to achieve better outcomes by having agencies
compete for resources by justifying all resources starting at
zero every year.

Most agencies only gave lip service to ZBB, but EPA
took it very seriously. Each program's budget was broken
into packages for the purpose of ranking the packages in
an agency-wide process. As a practical matter, the process
didn't really start at zero, as the first packages contained 75
percent of the program's prior year budget and ranked highly without much thought given. However, the competition
above that level was fierce with senior executives devoting
huge amounts of time arguing over the relative rankings of
their programs versus those of other offices.

The advantage of this process for OMB was that we were
given a ranking of all the budget packages requested by the
agency and could theoretically draw a line anywhere within
that ranking and know the agency's priorities for whatev-
er amount of funding was available. However, it is not in
OMB's DNA to accept an agency's priorities without question. Furthermore, an agency's priorities might not be consistent with overall Administration priorities. For instance,
EPA may have weighed environmental protection over energy security during an energy crisis or might have given
short shrift to a government-wide financial management
improvement initiative. Consequently, the branch had to
develop its own recommendation using the agency ranking
as important input.

Unfortunately, I was floundering when it came time to
make decisions on which packages to fund and which to re-

ject. The agency budget staff had done their job in making justifications for each package that made them sound critical because babies would die or workers would get cancer if a funding package was not funded. I would go to bed at night thinking that I was being given a sort of "Sophie's choice" between doing my job to avoid being fired and making decisions that would doom people to death.

The more I dug into the justifications, however, the more I began to doubt their apocalyptic tone. Assuming that EPA's ranking was accurate, the highest ranked packages should have had the biggest bang for the buck. In other words, the marginal number of diarrhea or cancer cases avoided per million dollars spent should be the highest for the highest rated packages within a program. Comparing across programs is more complicated because the regulatory cost of controlling a pollutant like benzene may be much higher in water than air and the regulatory costs always dwarf the budget costs.

What I found, however, was that lower ranked packages often had higher marginal benefits than higher ranked packages, which is contrary to any rational ranking of the packages. As an illustration, the next to lowest rated package for a program might be $20 million and avoid 20 cases of cancer annually (i.e. 1 cancer case avoided per $1 million spent), while the lowest rated package might be $10 million and avoid 15 cases of cancer (i.e. 1.5 cancer cases avoided per $1 million spent). Once I realized this, I understood that games were being played to beef up the justification for the lowest rated packages.

The more questions I asked the more skeptical I became. While having quantified outputs was great, the supporting evidence for those outputs was usually shaky and often a WAG (i.e. wild ass guess). Furthermore, lower ranked packages were often ranked lower because the ability of EPA and the states to implement the proposal might be questionable and, even if implementable, it might not be until some point in the future.

Finally, there were issues of whether a particular program was a proper Federal role or should be left to the discretion of the states. After considering these kinds of factors, the decisions on which programs to cut no longer seemed like a Sophie's choice.

Preparing for Director's Review

After marking up our programs (i.e. deciding which parts of EPA's request to fund) with Tozzi and developing an overall branch recommendation, we began to prepare our Director's Review book for the FY 1981 Budget. Despite being the junior staffer, I had two of the five issue papers to prepare — one on the funding level for the wastewater treatment Construction Grants program and second on a policy issue that EPA had raised. EPA's proposal would expand eligibilities to allow funding of multiple purpose projects (i.e. non-wastewater projects where there were some economies to be had by constructing at the same time as a wastewater project).

As I was not a fast writer, I spent long hours preparing the papers and rewriting them to incorporate Tozzi's edits before taking the book to the DAD for Natural Resources, Don Crabill. At our markup with Crabill, he accepted almost all of our recommendations and complemented us on our work. I was very pleased with the outcome until Crabill said that he wanted us to cut the length of the papers in half with no loss of content. As I had struggled to make my papers as short as they were, I was furious and vented to the other examiners once we were back in the branch.

The more experienced examiners took the task in stride and said that papers can always be shortened. In fact, one of them suggested that I cross out every other word in my paper and see how it read. I thought it was a stupid exercise, but I did it anyway. To my horror, although the grammar was terrible, I could still understand the issue. Embarrassed by the exercise, I went back to work to dramatically shorten the paper.

Drafting good Director's Review papers is an art because the papers have to be short, sweet, to the point, and even handed or as Tozzi's successor, Dave Gibbons, used to say, "they need to sing". Consequently, we spent enormous amounts of time writing and rewriting our papers to make sure that the Director could quickly comprehend the issue.

It was not a matter that Directors couldn't comprehend complex issues, it was a matter of the volume of issues that the Director needed to comprehend in a short period.

The task confronting Directors is that they need to make decisions on up to 20 review books averaging perhaps 75 pages of text and tables (1,500 pages total) in a span of three weeks. This workload is on top of the Director's myriad normal responsibilities, which may include Hill negotiations to resolve appropriations for the current year because Congress didn't complete them on time.

Consequently, it was constantly drilled into me that I needed to go to great lengths to make the papers concise because the Director's time is much more valuable than mine. Among other shortcuts, this would include replacing three and four syllable words with one or two syllable words (e.g. cut instead of reduction). This is contrary to the experience of many examiners at top colleges where getting a good grade on papers often meant replacing one and two syllable words with three and four syllable words to impress the professor with the student's erudition...er...smarts.

Even though short papers are emphasized in master's in public administration (MPA) programs, brevity is still a tough sell for eager beaver examiners just out of graduate school who are anxious to impress the Director whenever given a chance. When the Director's office sends down a question, a junior examiner's preferred response is to put in long hours over a couple of days to give a comprehensive ten-page response to the question which demonstrates the examiners thorough knowledge of the issue. In reality, however, the Director is usually looking for a short two-paragraph response by the next morning because that is all that is needed, and a timely response is often critical.

Decisions and Appeals

When I was a junior examiner, the hours leading up to Director's Review were always ones of heart-pounding anxiety. Once the review started, however, I tended to relax. Until relatively recent times, most Director's Reviews were held in the Director's conference room — Room 248 in the Old Executive Office Building (OEOB), before it was renamed for President Eisenhower and became the EEOB in 2002. Now, many Director's Reviews are held in larger conference rooms in the NEOB. Generally, the Director and Deputy Director sit in the middle with other political staff on one side of the table and the PAD, DAD, branch chief and examiners with issue papers sit on the other side. All the staff have name plates in front of them to help the Director get to know the staff better.

In general, the examiners present the issues and answer most of the questions from the Director and his/her team. However, if the examiner hesitates, the PAD, DAD or branch chief will jump in. The Reviews have two purposes: 1) get decisions from the Director on open issues or any PAD-decided issues on which the Director may disagree; and 2) prepare the Director for potential appeals and budget rollout. The purpose of preparing the Director for appeals is often underappreciated because most agency appeals are resolved without the personal involvement of the Director.

As mentioned earlier, one of the objectives of the Director's Review papers is to make them evenhanded. The agency request is always an option discussed in the Director's Review paper. As the agency doesn't get to attend the Reviews, it is important that the agency's position is accurately reflected in the paper for two reasons. First, good staff work requires ensuring that the Director has the best unbiased analysis possible to make the best decision that reflects the priorities of the President, even if that view is contrary to the staff position. The second reason is that you never want the Director taken by surprise in an appeal meeting with the Secretary.

The Director's advantage in those meetings is that he/she knows the trade-offs between agencies better than the Secretary and knows how much money is available to give back without violating the President's overarching fiscal goals. The disadvantage is that the Secretary virtually always knows more about the Department's specific programs than does the Director. Thus, the easiest way to lose an appeal is for the Secretary to make a clear and convincing argument that the Director hasn't heard before and has no basis to rebut. Consequently, the Review paper needs to be transparent about the Department's best arguments on an issue, while also pointing out the weaknesses of those arguments.

While our appeals my first year didn't go to the Director, they did highlight the disadvantage OMB sometimes faces on appeal, particularly when the budget is the last one submitted before the President is up for reelection and there is no statutory budget cap. Our PAD at the time was a former Rhodes Scholar, but he had no budget background and had only been in OMB a couple of months. He had the task of resolving appeals with Doug Costle, who had been the EPA Administrator for three years at that time.

The appeals session, which didn't go well from the standpoint of Environment Branch staff, lasted three hours one evening. The examiners weren't allowed to attend, but we were standing by in our office in case we were needed to answer questions. Periodically the senior examiner would go to the conference room where the discussion was taking place to get Tozzi's notes. Invariably, he would come back and announce that the PAD had made "another cave" that added back money to EPA.

Cleaning Up the Budget Mess

The last President's Budget released before a President stands for reelection always has outsized political significance. It is the last opportunity to show the constituents who elected the President that he is dedicated to their causes. Presumably that was part of the reason for so many "caves" during the EPA appeals. Unfortunately, the Administration's generosity to various causes resulted in a projected $16 billion deficit for FY 1981.[19] By today's standards, this seems tiny but, given that Carter had campaigned on balancing the budget by the end of his first term, his failure to even propose a balanced budget caused a major political problem for him.

The political problem became worse when inflation spiked up, rather than declining from the already high existing rate, and the bond markets tanked. Consequently, within a couple weeks of submitting the FY 1981 Budget, President Carter decided to revise the Budget to project a surplus. The revised FY 1981 Budget, developed after consulting with the Democratic leadership in Congress, was formally transmitted to Congress on March 31, 1980, and projected a surplus of $16 billion rather than a deficit of $16 billion.[20]

Revisions to the Budget were made across the government. In the case of EPA, the branch was given an outlay reduction target and developed a proposal to meet the target. The Director subsequently accepted our proposal to defer $3.65 billion in wastewater treatment Construction Grant funding during FY 1980. This deferral was formally transmitted to Congress as a Presidential special message.[21] Under the Congressional Budget Act, a deferral prevents the obligation of funding for some period of time but does not eliminate the funding as would be the case with a rescission. In that sense, it was not a real cut, but instead just shifted the timing of some outlays out of FY 1981 and into a future year.

Construction Grant appropriations were no-year funds and the funding for the program was allotted to states based on a statutory formula. Despite being no-year funds, a state only had two years to obligate its allotted funding, with any unobligated funding being reallotted to other states. As it would have been politically, if not legally, untenable to force reallotment, the amount proposed for deferral was made up almost entirely of funding that was appropriated in FY 1980. This is funding that would have a second year of availability for the allotment, even if the funding was deferred through the end of the fiscal year.

In fact, besides being just a timing shift, the outlay savings were not huge because Construction Grant funding paid out very slowly, reflecting in part that much of the funding does not get obligated until the second year of availability. As outlay savings only occurred for projects whose obligation is delayed, projects funded by FY 1980 appropriations, which were not going to be obligated until FY 1981 anyway, were largely unaffected by the deferral.

The outlay savings target that the branch had been given for the Budget revision required deferring all remaining

FY 1980 appropriations. However, according to my newly developed outlay estimation methodology, our target could still be met if we released $400 million at the beginning of September, a month ahead of the release of the remaining funds at the beginning of FY 1981.

We were aware that the early release of these deferred funds would allow some projects, particularly in northern states, to get funded before winter delayed many projects. However, at the time the deferral was proposed, we did not have a plan for determining which funds to release. This might not have been a problem without the unintended political jockeying that ensued. Unfortunately, about ten Governors weighed in with letters to the Director or President arguing that priority be given to their states in the early release of the funding.

I eventually hosted a meeting in my DAD's conference room with the relevant EPA Assistant Administrator and a representative from the White House Intergovernmental Affairs (IGA) Office to make decisions on allotting the early release funding. During the meeting, the IGA representative was called out of the meeting to take a call from Air Force One. His boss was apparently with President Carter at the time doing a flyover of Mount St. Helens, which had erupted earlier that summer, and called to report on the awesome scene.

Shortly after the IGA staffer returned to the meeting and reported on the call, I got called out of the meeting by my DAD, Don Crabill. He wanted to know who the...heck...I was meeting with that was getting a call from Air Force One. I explained the situation and got a lecture about how he should have been informed about the meeting and given the opportunity to attend. This was even though my branch chief was aware of the meeting and chose not to attend.

Unfortunately, I had an uneasy relationship with Crabill. Although my branch chief told me that Crabill considered me to be a great examiner, it never seemed that way to me. This incident taught me the importance of keeping some separation between work and my personal life — in other words compartmentalization, although that word did not come into vogue until the Clinton Administration. Fortunately, in this case, I was too preoccupied outside of work with figuring out how to get a phone number for a girl I had recently met at a Georgetown bar to let being chewed out at work bother me.

CHAPTER FOUR: It's a Bird, It's a Plane, No It's Superfund -- *The Birth of an Environmental Program*

This chapter focuses on the full range of responsibilities
of a budget examiner and how the tools available to OMB
staff can be used to help shape a new Federal program, in
this case Superfund. In particular, it demonstrates how a
seasoned examiner can leverage OMB's role not only in the
budget, but the legislative, regulatory review and executive
order processes as well, to help a program more cost-effec-
tively carry out its mission.

The impetus for the creation of Superfund was the chemical contamination of the Love Canal neighborhood in Niagara Falls, NY. Love Canal was a never completed project to
bypass Niagara Falls and allow barge traffic on the Niagara River. In the 1940's, Hooker Chemical began to use the
site for hazardous waste disposal, in part because the clay
soil at the canal provided a natural liner for the dump that
prevented seepage. Eventually Hooker Chemical put a clay
cap over the dump and sold the site to the Niagara Board of
Education for $1[22].

If the site had been just used as a park, the chemicals in
the dump might not have posed a problem for a long time.
Unfortunately, construction at the site to build a school and
houses, while not directly exposing the chemical waste,
broke the clay cap covering the site. Consequently, heavy
rains at the site produced what is known as the "bathtub
effect" where water couldn't seep out of the clay sides and
bottom of the site but could overflow the top and now laced
with dangerous chemicals. This led to emergency declara-
tions by both the state and Federal government in August of
1978, the closing of the school, and eventual evacuation of
all the residents.

The Love Canal disaster, as well as a related crisis at the
"Valley of the Drums" in Kentucky, led to calls for national legislation to address chemical waste cleanup resulting
in the drafting of expansive legislation known as the Com-

prehensive Environmental Response, Compensation, and Liability Act (CERCLA). The draft legislation had stalled in Congress in 1980 until an unlikely turn of events spurred its passage. That event, the election of Ronald Reagan as President in November 1980 and the shift in control of the Senate to Republicans, shocked the environmental community.

Realizing that significant cleanup legislation was unlikely to be enacted during a Reagan Administration, environmentalists and their allies in Congress worked feverishly to meld very different House and Senate cleanup bills. This led to the enactment of CERCLA during the lame duck Congressional session before Reagan took office and the Senate flipped parties. The environmental groups had a key ally in Senator Robert Stafford, a moderate Republication and environmental champion, who was poised to become Chair of the Senate Environment and Public Works Committee in the new Congress. Although a Committee Chairmanship is a much more powerful position than that of Ranking Minority Member, Senator Stafford understood that, if he waited until he became Committee Chair, the legislation may never pass.

Consequently, Stafford was the key Senator in quickly revising the bill to produce a draft that could be enacted. The need to move rapidly resulted in Congress punting on the assignment of various tasks by agency, as is normally the case with legislation. Instead, the vast majority of the authorities in the bill enacted on December 11, 1980, were assigned to the President, rather than the Administrator of EPA or other cabinet officials.

Superfund Executive Order

The implication of most authorities being assigned to the President is that, since the President wasn't in the position of actually implementing the bill, his authorities needed to be delegated by Executive Order (EO) to the heads of various Federal agencies to implement the statute. The Council on Environmental Quality (CEQ) quickly drafted an EO that President Carter signed before he left office. However, the Carter Administration's assignment of those authorities was never going to be acceptable to the Reagan Administration, necessitating the need for a new EO.

The responsibility for drafting this new EO was assigned to the Environment Branch in OMB. I became the examiner for the new program in the spring of 1981 shortly after a rough draft of the EO was completed, largely by my branch chief, Dave Gibbons, who had succeeded Jim Tozzi in mid-1980. My job was to work with OMB's Office of General Counsel to produce a final draft, including resolving two rounds of interagency comments, before the EO went to the Office of Legal Counsel (OLC) at Justice for final review and forwarding to the President.

The Reagan version of the EO (No. 12316 signed on August 14, 1981),[23] included two major changes to the Carter EO, in addition to a slew of more minor changes. First, it assigned response authority to DOD and DOE for waste sites on their facilities. One thing that few people understood at the time was the enormous impact that CERCLA would have on Federal facilities and that cleanup costs for those facilities needed to come from agency budgets, not the Superfund. In fact, the Department of Defense (DOD) and Department of Energy (DOE) cleanup budgets were actually much larger than EPA's Superfund budget.

Assigning response authority to DOD and DOE meant that those agencies were in charge of the cleanup process at their facilities, although all cleanups had to be consistent with the cleanup rules in the National Contingency Plan (NCP) promulgated by EPA. This delegation of authority was strongly opposed by the environmental community. OMB's concern prompting this delegation was that putting EPA in charge would result in excessive costs for cleanups that in some cases were already going to cost hundreds of million dollars.

In particular, the fear was that giving zealous EPA staff access to the "deep pockets" of DOD and DOE would result in "cleanup for cleanup sake". Instead, the Reagan Administration wanted cleanup decisions based on actual risk to the public, where risk is determined by both the exposure of a chemical to the public as well as the danger posed by the chemical. Thus, at Rocky Mountain Arsenal in Colorado, when DOD was faced with hundreds of millions in clean-up costs to reduce the health risk sufficiently to allow residential use of the property, the Department instead chose to achieve both lower health risk and cost by limiting the amount of remediation and turning the site into a National Wildlife Refuge.

The second major change was to subject the NCP and all revisions to review <u>and approval</u> by the Office of Management and Budget. Many people interpreted this provision of the EO as redundant with OMB's general regulatory review authority under the Reagan EO 12291 (subsequently revised by President Clinton as EO 12866). However, the regulatory review order was issued under the President's general authority to efficiently manage the government, but EOs do not have the legal authority to override enacted statutory authorities given to an agency head. In the case of CERCLA, the statutory authority for issuing the NCP was given to the President. Thus, in the Superfund EO 12316, President Reagan had statutory authority to give OMB <u>approval</u>, not just review, authority for the NCP, which presidents do not have in most other statutes.

The rationale for providing approval authority to OMB was to serve as a potential check on EPA developed NCP provisions for which the benefits might not be commensurate with the costs. This was particularly important for DOE cleanups. Whereas DOD cleanups were for substances like those found at private sites, the radioactive cleanups at DOE facilities were often unique to those facilities. Given the huge cost involved in radioactive cleanup, the Reagan Administration wanted protective standards, but not "cleanup for cleanup sake". Due to the cost implications of the NCP on Federal budgets, I drafted the internal OMB delegation giving NCP approval authority to the PAD for Natural Resources, Energy and Science, not to OIRA.

Superfund Authorities

Superfund was the first of its kind hazardous waste cleanup program. It was hoped to be a model for other countries, but I don't believe that it has been emulated elsewhere.

The program employed two strategies to achieve waste site cleanup. The first strategy was to get responsible parties to clean up the site to tiny residual contamination levels that EPA determined were protective of human health and the environment. Potential responsible parties included not only the owner and operator of the site, but anybody who generated or transported waste to the site. EPA had several enforcement tools to compel such cleanup, the most powerful being joint and several liability.

Joint and several liability was common for tort claims, but it was new in environmental legislation. The basic concept is that when multiple parties share liability for a waste site, any of the parties can be held liable for the cleanup of the entire site. This contrasts with proportionate liability where each party is responsible for their share of the contamination. The implication of joint and several liability is that if household cleaners, which contain hazardous substances, that an individual disposed of ended up in Love Canal, that individual could theoretically be held responsible for the entire cleanup of the site.

While that would be very unfair, as a practical matter that is not how the program is implemented, as it would be prohibitively expensive for EPA to pursue such de minimis contributors to the site. Joint and several liability is used by EPA to get a large responsible party with deep pockets (e.g. Dow Chemical) to foot the bill so they don't have to chase down potentially thousands of minor responsible parties.

In practice, EPA uses the sledgehammer of joint and several liability to bring responsible parties to the negotiating table. However, many of the settlements mirror proportionate liability, where each of the identifiable responsible parties pay their share of the cleanup. The remaining "orphan shares" of parties that are bankrupt or couldn't be identified can be divided up among the viable responsible parties, assigned to a deep pocket, or paid out of the Superfund. The enforcement negotiations also determine whether the cleanup is managed and paid for directly by the responsible parties or, if the responsible party group is too unwieldy, have the Superfund pay for the cleanup and be reimbursed by the responsible parties.

The second strategy involves using funds appropriated to EPA's Hazardous Substance Superfund account, generally just referred to as Superfund, to pay directly for a Federally managed cleanup. This is never EPA's choice but is often necessary at the many "orphan sites" that were abandoned long ago and have no viable responsible party who can be compelled to conduct the cleanup. In addition to cleanup costs, the Superfund account pays for EPA's research and enforcement expenses as well as expenses for other agencies that implement pieces of CERCLA, such as the Department of Justice and a new Agency for Toxic Substances and Disease Registry (ATSDR). The funding for the account is a discretionary appropriation out of a trust fund. When first enacted the trust fund was financed by excise taxes on petroleum and chemical feedstocks as well as fines, recovery of cleanup costs from responsible parties, and a payment from the general fund.

The rationale for the excise taxes on petroleum and chemical feedstocks was that the polluter should pay. However, major responsible parties (e.g. chemical companies such as Monsanto) already were required to pay for their share of waste site cleanups and possibly orphan shares as well under CERCLA's joint and several liability standards. The excise tax was essentially a third bite at the apple to make companies like Monsanto pay for cleanup of long closed orphan sites. The environmental community viewed this as rough justice, although the most expensive of these orphan sites tended to be mining sites for which the petrochemical industry had no role in creating.

Early Implementation of CERCLA

When a new Federal program starts, particularly after a high-profile event such as Love Canal, the Congress, the press, and the public always want it implemented immediately. Unfortunately, those expectations are usually unrealistic. While the Carter EO delegating CERCLA responsibilities was done quickly, and stayed in place until the Reagan EO was completed, the statute was enacted too late in the "lame duck" session of Congress to receive any FY 1981 appropriations. Although EPA reprogrammed some funds to begin preliminary assessment work at sites, any significant funding had to wait until after the Reagan Administration requested a March 15, 1981, supplemental and Congress had time to enact the supplemental.

Aside from the funding lag, EPA had a large amount of technical work to perform in order to develop procedures and standards for responding to releases of hazardous substances. In particular, they had to revise the NCP, which had originally been developed for response to oil spills. While not minimizing the difficulty in responding to oil spills, the existing plan was no match for dealing with the wide variety of pollutants and types of sites that needed to be addressed under CERCLA's response authority.

CERCLA gave EPA only six months to revise the NCP, a ridiculously short period given that virtually any major EPA rulemaking requires at least a year to develop and go through the notice and comment requirements of the Administrative Procedures Act. Such short deadlines are not uncommon in environmental statutes and, most likely, the committees understand that the deadlines will not be met. However, a short unachievable deadline sets up the dynamic that an environmental group can go to court once the deadline is missed and get EPA on a court ordered schedule. This gives the environmental organization significant leverage over the agency if any deadline extensions are needed, which is often the case.

OMB approved the proposed NCP in March 1982 to meet a court-ordered deadline. There were two main issues discussed with EPA during OMB review. The first concerned the vagueness of the NCP, particularly concerning the issue of "how clean is clean". EPA's view was that the NCP should contain only very general criteria to preserve flexibility in determining the appropriate extent of cleanup on a site-by-site basis. The rationale for this policy was that conditions at each site are so different that it is virtually impossible to develop site specific methods and criteria that would be appropriate at all sites. Instead, they wanted to develop further guidance later. We weren't happy about the "vagueness" of the rule but didn't have any solution to the problem.

The second issue concerned the inadequate role EPA was assigning to cost in the decision process. In response to our concerns, EPA changed its decision process to take costs into account in determining the needed level of cleanup. Given the importance OMB always places on cost, I often wondered in situations like this whether EPA's deemphasis of cost as a consideration was simply a negotiating tactic that allowed the agency to make a concession to OMB on cost language they always intended to include anyway.

The NCP included two key appendices — the Hazard Ranking System (HRS) and the National Priorities List (NPL) — which also had to be developed to get the program off the ground. The HRS was a crude risk scoring system, issued in 1982, which took data from site investigations and ran it through an algorithm to produce a ranking of the sites for long-term cleanup based on the actual or potential release of hazardous substances from the site. This ranking produced the NPL which statutorily was required to have an initial list of at least 400 sites, although each state was entitled to have its most important site included on the list regardless of how well it scored under the HRS. The HRS scored sites on a 0 to 100 scale with sites qualifying if they scored higher than 28.5. The determination of the cut-off score wasn't based on a rigorous analysis of an appropriate risk level, rather it was the cut-off score needed to meet the statutory requirement to include at least 400 sites on the initial list published in 1983.

Cleanup Actions

There are actually two types of cleanups under CERCLA, the first being short term responses called removal actions. While sometimes these are emergency actions, removals can also be undertaken in non-time critical situations that don't require extensive planning and generally can be completed within one year for less than $2 million. The second type of response is a remedial action which is undertaken after extensive planning and design work for sites on the NPL.

The focus of media and public attention has always been on remedial actions with the most important metric of program success being the number of sites delisted from the NPL. In certain respects, this is understandable as communities view having a Superfund NPL site in their midst as a black eye for the community and are often a real detriment to local property values.

From a risk standpoint, however, removal actions are far more important, and cost-effective, in protecting public health and the environment than remedial actions. Removal actions are often undertaken to removal barrels or other containers of hazardous waste from the site as well as removing heavily contaminated surface soils. Barrel removal prevents further leaching of contaminants into the soil, and eventually groundwater, as well as reducing the risk of fire and explosions that can quickly spread the contaminants widely from the site. Removing contaminated surface soils prevents runoff of contaminants to surface water, which can pose risks to fishing, swimming, and drinking water.

Remedial actions address the remaining contamination at NPL _after_ any removal actions have been taken, even though the sites are ranked based on the wastes at the site _before_ the removal action. Remedial actions are often extremely complex and require extensive planning, going through a standard, but time consuming, three step process of remedial investigation/feasibility study (RI/FS), design and construction. The type of remedial action can vary widely depending on the type of site. It can involve incineration of debris and, in some cases, soil; pumping and treating of groundwater to keep it from reaching surface water; and dredging of contaminated river bed segments.

Groundwater contamination is the most typical type of problem addressed by remedial action. Contaminants in soil around a site eventually leach into the groundwater below the site and slowly get transported to surface water. These contaminants pose a health risk if either groundwater is being pumped out of the aquifer underlying the site for public use or if the contaminants reach surface water, particularly if the surface water is used for drinking water.

The most common remedial actions for this type of contamination is to first stop pumping groundwater from the affected underground aquifer for public use and find an alternative source of water for those uses. Second, pump the groundwater out of the aquifer to prevent the plume of contaminants from moving toward surface water, and run the groundwater through a treatment system before discharging it back into the aquifer. This process is referred to as pump and treat and can take up to 20 years to complete in order to comply with the relevant pollution control, usually drinking water, standard.

The fact that so many sites require pump and treat provided a dilemma for EPA given the public's demand for quick action. It became impossible to be successful in meeting the most important program metric of delisting sites from the NPL once EPA realized how many sites required multiple years of pump and treat, after already lengthy planning, design and construction periods. To address this problem, EPA came up with a new metric, called construction complete, to get credit for taking all the needed steps to protect public health and the environment while the pump and treat process took place.

Unfortunately, EPA was never able to develop a metric for actual risk reduction that would highlight the risk reduction achieved through removal actions. Consequently, EPA never got the credit from the public that it deserved for those actions. However, developing such a metric would have had the downside of highlighting the much smaller risk reduction of remedial actions and potentially imperiled EPA's ability to get needed funding.

The Reagan Administration was heavily criticized for the slow implementation of Superfund, some of which was warranted and some not. From my standpoint, there were three general reasons for the slow implementation. The first was the normal growing pains of any new program in setting up the infrastructure and rules (e.g. NCP, HRS, and NPL) needed to ramp up implementation of the program, as discussed above. Second, the program was more complex than anybody realized. Unfortunately, the wide variety of contaminants and sites meant that there were few "cookie cutter" solutions that could be applied to multiple sites. Further, as mentioned above, EPA struggled with the "how clean is clean" question.

The "how clean is clean" issue wasn't just an academic thought exercise but involved economics, practical considerations, and risk-risk tradeoffs. As an illustration, consider contamination of a riverbed. In most such cases new contamination has stopped, some of the contamination has been covered by silt, but some is also being carried further down the river. It would be nice to totally eliminate the contamination by dredging it out of the river bottom. Obviously, the more dredging the higher the cost. However, the act of dredging itself stirs up deeply buried contaminants causing some portion to be carried further down river. Consequently, a portion is usually left undisturbed or possibly capped with sand.

Finally, there is the question of what to do with the dredged material, which is mostly dirt — the Fox River contamination for instance contained 40 tons of PCBs in 11,000,000 tons of sediment.[24] While the dirt can be partially treated, ultimately it requires a huge landfill for final disposal. Finding a community willing to take Superfund sediment was a problem that continually bedeviled EPA. Communities were reluctant to want such a landfill because of the notoriety attached to Superfund waste as well as the risk of some level of local contamination in transporting and disposing of the waste.

Scandal Plagued Leadership

Finally, there was the self-inflicted wound known as Rita Lavelle. Lavelle was designated as the nominee for Assistant Administrator for Solid Waste and Emergency Response at EPA in February 1982. Prior to coming to EPA, she was a communications official to Aerojet-General Corporation in California.[25] Unfortunately, the program suffered from Lavelle's scandal plagued year in office due to her lack of management skills as well as her disdain for the ethical rules that govern Executive Branch political employees. Lavelle was fired by EPA Administrator Anne Gorsuch — mother of Supreme Court Justice Neil Gorsuch -- in February 1983[26] and Lavelle was convicted and sent to prison in 1984.[27] As is often the case with Washington scandals, she wasn't fired for her actual performance in the job — incompetence is not a crime — but for lying to Congress.

At a Christmas party before Lavelle was fired, I complained to an acquaintance from the Carter White House about the poor quality of many of the Reagan appointees, such as Lavelle, who appeared to have been selected more for loyalty than competence. I was stunned when he said that Reagan had the right approach, and he wished the Carter Administration had followed a similar policy. His view was that Carter had too many capable but out of control officials. He specifically mentioned Health, Education and Welfare Secretary Joe Califano, whose personal anti-smoking crusade prior to the 1980 election was alleged to have killed Carter's election chances in several tobacco growing states. Over time I came to understand the importance of loyalty in political appointments but believe it doesn't work well when there is a very narrow ideological pool to draw from such as in Reagan's first term and the Trump Administration.

Anne Gorsuch followed Lavelle out the door a month later, tripped up by some of the same irregularities concerning the politicization of funding at the Stringfellow Acid Pits Superfund site.[28] Unlike Lavelle, Gorsuch was not incompetent nor was she ever convicted of any crime. However, she was a lightning rod for a range of Reagan Administration environmental policies that drew the ire of environmentalists.

I had my own reasons to dislike Gorsuch. The career OMB staff view the budget as an adversarial but rules-based process. I never minded that agencies disputed our budget passbacks or called me names in their appeals. That was all part of the process. However, leaks to the press or Congress infuriated me because that was outside the process.

In her book, "Are You Tough Enough?", written under her remarried name of Burford, Gorsuch discusses a leak of EPA's budget appeal letter to the New York Times, just in advance of a 1981 appeal meeting with the President. The book indicates that the leak by her Chief of Staff was without her knowledge, and she told him afterwards that she wanted to deal with such matters head on and to never do it again.[29]

Certainly from my standpoint that was the correct position to take. Unfortunately, a year later while watching Nightline with my girlfriend, the cover of our budget passback flashed up on the TV screen. I always assumed, but had no proof, that Gorsuch had a hand in the leak, given how few people had the entire passback document. In addition to ruining what should have been a blissful night, to an institutionalist like me, leaking the entire passback was the equivalent of budget treason.

Developing the Superfund Reauthorization Proposal — Policy Provisions

The word "Superfund" actually never appears anywhere in CERCLA, the program's original authorizing statute. At the time, both the trust fund and the appropriations account went by the name "Hazardous Substance Response Trust Fund". However, Superfund quickly became the popular term for the program and the name became formally attached to the program in the 1986 reauthorization.

What I didn't realize initially was how appropriate the name was given the extensive cleanup authority CERCLA provided. Particularly in the early years of the program, an often-panicked public would report rumors of buried waste, particularly if anybody in the neighborhood had recently come down with cancer. Not knowing what they would find, EPA contractors would show up in protective gear, popularly referred to as moon suits, to check out the report. For EPA, use of moon suits was a best practice when not knowing the potential risk a spill or site posed. Unfortunately, to residents of the neighborhood, it was often interpreted as a sign of major problems prompting questions about whether to evacuate.

While the Superfund legislation was originally sold as a response to chemical waste dumps, every new revision to the NPL that EPA sent for OMB approval seemed to include a new category of site for cleanup. These included mining sites, contaminated riverbeds, naturally occurring substances and, my favorite, pineapple farms in Hawaii with soil residue from the legal application of pesticides. The variety of sites was due to very broad definitions of releases, facilities, and hazardous substances, with few statutory constraints on EPA response authority.

From the standpoint of the environmental community, the broad scope of Superfund was an advantage and what they intended. Thus, it was useful in responding to anthrax laced letters received on Capitol Hill shortly after 9-11. However, the broad scope is an impediment to a new program trying to get up to speed. Most Federal programs start out more focused and expand over time as their original goals are met.

Particularly for a program that was struggling with how to address defined waste dumps and answer questions about "how clean is clean", the broad scope of potential cleanup was an unneeded complication. The program would probably have been better served if the removal authority had been broad, to deal with the emergency but unforeseen situations such as the anthrax letters, while having a more defined remedial action authority that Congress could have potentially expanded over time with more appropriately defined funding sources.

In the lead up to the reauthorization of the program when its initial authorization expired at the end of 1985, I started to develop proposals for reauthorization. My objectives were to reign in the program to a more manageable scope by limiting cleanups of minor environmental problems and better focusing limited cleanup dollars to ensure maximum environmental protection.

To help explain the issue, I created a graphic of a cube. One axis of the cube was the type of sites, the second axis was the uses of the fund, and the third axis was the risk of sites. The size of the cube represented the current program. There were proposals floating around that would have enlarged the cube (e.g. new types of sites, pay more types of claims, reduce the NPL cutoff score) which would have enlarged the scope of the program. I provided my bosses with options for reducing the size of the cube and, consistent with OMB procedures, provided pros and cons for each of the options. The reforms to reduce the size of the cube were designed to limit the program to problems that: 1) could not be addressed under other statutes; 2) were not more appropriately addressed by state and local governments; and 3) were focused on protection of human health.

OMB Director David Stockman loved the graphic of the cube. After choosing which options he wanted to pursue, he wanted it included in a decision memo to the President on Superfund reauthorization proposals. Unfortunately, not everybody can visualize a three-dimensional graphic drawn on a two-dimensional piece of paper. Consequently, when the memo got to Don Regan, the Chief of Staff for Reagan, his reaction was that if he didn't understand the graphic neither would the President. Due to Regan's opposition, the graphic was dropped from the final memo.

Developing the Superfund Reauthorization Proposal — Budget & Tax Provisions

In addition to the policy aspects relating to program scope, I was responsible for estimating the needed size of the program over the next five years and providing options for financing the expanded program. Everybody understood that the original authorization of $1.6 billion was start-up funding and would need to be increased significantly when it was reauthorized. While Superfund financed a range of activities, many of which did not need to expand further, the high-cost remedial action portion followed the same type of ramp-up as most construction programs.

EPA liked to explain this with a "pig in the python" graphic. The "python" was essentially the timeline as a project moved from the study phase, to design, and finally construction. The "pig" was the number of sites going through the cleanup process. In the early 1980's, numerous sites were put into the initial Remedial Investigation/Feasibility Study phase leading to a bulge at the start of the python because there were no sites in the construction phase. Over time, the bulge (i.e. the pig) would move through the python towards the construction stage. By 1986 much of the bulge was centered in construction.

As a numbers guy, I loved to build spreadsheet models once OMB moved into the age of office personal computers. I had developed one on Superfund for use in the annual budget process, but it became even more valuable as we worked on estimating the needed size of the program over the five years reauthorization period and, consequently, how much tax revenue would be needed to support it.

The model estimated budget needs, based on program outputs as projects moved through the construction cycle, including BA, obligations, and outlays, as well as keeping track of funding balances in the trust fund. Like any model, it is only good as the assumptions used for the projections. This model had over 60 input assumptions on the number and types of projects, project pricing, and revenue. The advantage of such a large number of assumptions is that it provides flexibility to test the sensitivity of the model to various input assumptions. The downside is that more assumptions provide the potential for greater error due to faulty assumptions.

Ultimately, the President decided to propose a $5.3 billion five-year authorization that more than tripled the size of the program. While the existing oil and chemical feedstock taxes were maintained, the proposal included a new "end waste" tax on waste disposal companies. EPA had designed the tax to promote improved waste management practices by imposing a lower tax rate for companies that use the best technology and a higher rate for companies that didn't.[30]

Interestingly the proposal did not include any general fund payment as in the original authorization. As a Congressman, Stockman had viewed the oil and chemical taxes being used to fund orphan shares and sites as not consistent with "user pays" and, consequently, supported significant general fund financing. As Director, however, he was faced with large deficits caused by Reagan's 1981 tax cut bill and wanted the program fully financed by industry.

While the size of the Superfund increase was worked out during the budget process, the substantive policy proposals were developed by an ad-hoc cabinet council working group in which I participated. The group was chaired by the White House Office of Policy Development and included representatives from EPA and Justice. My guidance was to make sure that the legislative package focused on the most significant environmental problems while ensuring that cleanups were cost-effective. Of course, this meant including the reforms we had discussed with the Director to limit the scope of Superfund's unnecessarily broad authority.

The proposal included new enforcement tools developed by EPA and an OMB proposal to double the State cost share for remedial cleanups to be more consistent with the cost sharing levels in other EPA programs. The proposal also included key changes to limit Superfund to hazardous waste problems and emergency spills, such as by preventing its use for mining sites which could already be addressed under another statute, and cleanup of residues from the normal application of pesticides. In addition, it included elimination of funding eligibility for restoring natural resources.

As Administrator Lee Thomas stated at the roll-out press conference: "We're saying Superfund's purpose in life is not to clean up everything that's contaminated"[31]. While Administrator Thomas might not have really supported all our reforms, he can't have been too upset, since he sent me a nice letter of appreciation for my work in helping prepare the Administration's proposal.

Administrations have the discretion to decide how much detail to provide Congress on its legislative proposals. The proposal that the Reagan Administration sent to Congress on Superfund was actual bill language. In other cases, an Administration may send a set of principles, or as in the case of the Biden Administration's Build Back Better bill, Congress got a fact sheet with a paragraph on each multi-billion spending proposal.

The choice of the level of detail often depends on who controls the Congress. When the President's party is in control, such as in the early Biden Administration, there is a tendency to provide less detail and let the Administration's friends on the Hill flesh out the bill. This is particularly true when the majority party in Congress has a very narrow majority. When Congress is controlled by the opposition party, Presidents are more likely to send a detailed bill. Much to the consternation of OMB's Legislative Reference Division, over time there has been less tendency to send actual bill language, as it often is introduced in Congress only by courtesy before the relevant committee drafts its own bill.

The President agreed to the proposed legislative package at a February 1985 Cabinet Council meeting, and it was transmitted to Congress as a major Administration Initiative. The day that the Reagan Administration released the bill that February was chaos. I was called to attend a morning West Wing meeting with the communications folks as a subject expert. They immediately raised issues with labeling the new "waste end" revenue as a tax. As part of Reagan's mantra was to oppose new taxes, it was decided that it was acceptable to call the existing excise taxes as taxes, but the new "waste end" excise tax had to be labeled a fee.[32]

Of course, this silliness meant that changes needed to be made to both the bill and roll-out materials. Unfortunately, there was a version control problem that wasn't caught until just before the Director sent the package to the White House. Consequently, I caught flak from the Director's office when having to explain how the wrong version got sent forward to them.

Congressional Action on Reauthorization

Predictably Congressional Democrats and environmental groups, who wanted up to $10 billion for the program blasted the bill as inadequate, with a Sierra Club spokesman labeling the proposal as "Superfarce".[33] Surprisingly, the Washington Post's editorial on the bill noted the environmental groups criticism of the bill and said that "perhaps some of that denunciation is deserved".[34] In general, however, they seemed to believe that the proposal was worthwhile and noted the difficulty in ramping up a program quickly.

The Superfund Amendments and Reauthorization Act (SARA) wasn't enacted until October 1986 after a nearly year and a half legislative process. Whereas CERCLA was 45 pages long, SARA included 170 pages in amendments to CERCLA as well as new stand-alone legislation. Included in the bill were new titles on community right to know, radon gas research and a new cleanup trust fund for leaking underground storage tanks which EPA staff quickly dubbed the LUST program.

Only minor parts of our effort to roll back the scope of Superfund cleanups were included, such as prohibiting cleanup of naturally occurring substances and products used in building construction. However, there was a major tug of war between the environment committees and the finance committees over whether to include the Administration's proposal to prevent use of Superfund to pay for natural resource damage restoration.

Although SARA still includes language allowing such funding, the finance committees were footing the bill and had the final say in the matter. Consequently, the very last provision of SARA includes a "notwithstanding" provision in the tax title's use of funds section, which trumps the use of funds section drafted by the environment committees and prohibits use of Superfund money for natural resource damage restoration.

The final bill authorized $8.5 billion over 5 years and did not include the Administration's proposed "waste end" tax. Instead, it included a controversial tax on corporate income, based on an already required calculation of alternative minimum taxable income. The concept was that hazardous waste was generated by a wide array of businesses and, therefore, a tax with broad reach was needed. However, this broad-based tax infuriated groups, such as grocery manufacturers, who felt they were being forced to finance a problem that they had no role in creating.

When we told EPA that OMB was seriously considering recommending veto of the bill over the new tax, they were apoplectic and quickly wanted to meet to discuss the benefits of the bill. Ultimately, President Reagan signed the bill but expressed his displeasure with such broad-based taxes in his signing statement.[35] The taxes in the 1986 bill would be extended once as part of a deficit reduction effort in the Omnibus Budget Reconciliation Act of 1990, before expiring in 1995.

Revising the Superfund Executive Order

Despite environmental group criticism of many of the delegations in the original Reagan Superfund EO 12316, there was no serious attempt to override those delegations during reauthorization. Apparently, it is hard to put the genie back in the bottle. In fact, not only did Congress not take away DOD's response authority, although they did provide some additional oversight, but SARA included a codification of DOD's environmental restoration program. Unfortunately for the environmental community, the Armed Services Committees and the Defense Appropriations subcommittees supported DOD's response authority and the environment committees needed their support to get SARA enacted.

Surprisingly, Congress also neglected to prohibit OMB's approval authority of the NCP. As I feared that EPA might change the delegation if they drafted the new EO, I volunteered to draft the new revised EO, even though SARA was passed in the middle of budget season. It was a daunting task to track down every one of the roughly 250 references to the President in CERCLA, as amended by SARA, and figure out how to word the EO when a section was being delegated to multiple agencies. EPA's Office of General Counsel could have done that job quicker by dividing the task among multiple lawyers, but any EPA effort would have been greatly slowed down by the cumbersome approval process inherent in a large bureaucracy.

In addition to drafting the EO, I had to organize a small ad-hoc group of agency representatives (i.e. EPA, Justice, Defense, Energy, Interior, and Agriculture) to resolve an array of technical issues, and mediate turf battles between agencies. Fortunately, only a few controversial issues required resolution at the political level.

Despite the need to get through interagency review, final Office of Legal Counsel review, and a process slowed by the Christmas holidays, the revised Executive Order 12580 was signed in January 1987[36] a little over three months after enactment. While EPA was chomping at the bit to get the new EO finished, I thought it had been done relatively quickly. I was particularly pleased given the complexity of the EO and the fact that the sheer number of needed delegations had ballooned the EO to 13 pages from the 7 in the previous EO.

Superfund Post-SARA

In 1994 when I was Chief of the Environment Branch, the Clinton Administration embarked on a major internal effort to revise SARA and further expand Superfund, including a doubling of the tax on corporate alternative minimum taxable income. As the Administration was simultaneously working on Clean Water reauthorization, and I had been through a Superfund reauthorization before, I opted to lead the Clean Water effort and delegated two of my senior examiners to work on Superfund.

Ultimately, both efforts crashed and burned. The Clean Water effort died shortly after the Administration released its bill because EPA, at the last minute, slipped in uncleared language on control of chlorine that led to attacks that the Clinton Administration was trying to eliminate chlorine from the periodic table of elements. The Superfund effort was weighed down by the unpopularity of the taxes supporting the program, but the nail in the coffin was that the Democrats loss of control of Congress in the 1994 mid-term elections.

The reauthorization effort wasn't helped by the fact that the unappropriated balance in the trust fund was $3.7 billion at a time when the appropriation was around $1.4 billion.[37] Some in the environmental community were panicked about getting funds appropriated for Superfund once the trust fund was exhausted. However, this fear reflected a misunderstanding of the budget process.

The key piece of information that many people misunderstood was that the Superfund account was funded by annual discretionary appropriations and was not mandatory funding. In other words, despite the existence of the trust fund, the funding was not automatically available. The purpose of the taxes was to minimize the deficit impact of the program and the purpose of the trust fund was to assure the companies paying the tax that those funds would only be used for purposes authorized by the Superfund legislation.

However, the amount appropriated annually had nothing to do with the trust fund balance. Instead, it reflected the competition for funding against other appropriated programs within an overall budget restraint, which ultimately was the appropriations committees' 302(b) allocations. Superfund appropriations were always below trust fund collections when the taxes were in effect and were largely financed by general revenue once the taxes expired.

Superfund annual appropriations grew rapidly in the early years but reached a plateau of around $1.5 billion in the early 1990's. At that point, the bloom was off Superfund as a major problem. Comparative risk studies began to emerge in the late 1980's showing that, while the public still viewed hazardous waste sites as a top risk, EPA experts viewed them as a medium-to-low risk.[38]

The situation at Times Beach, Missouri, a community 17 miles southwest of St. Louis, was symptomatic of the problem. The town had become contaminated when waste oil was sprayed on dirt roads to keep down dust. Unfortunately, the waste oil included tiny quantities of dioxin, which was a byproduct of the production of certain chemicals. At the time even minute quantities of dioxin were considered deadly. In December 1982, the town was evacuated, and the Centers for Disease Control (CDC) recommended that the community be permanently relocated, prompting a $33 million EPA buyout[39].

By 1991, however, the scientific understanding of dioxin had changed. Data had accumulated over the past decade showing no adverse health risk due to dioxin at the levels of contamination at Times Beach. Consequently, Dr. Vernon Houk, the CDC official who recommended the relocation in 1982, admitted in May 1991 that the recommendation had been wrong. In addition to the cost of relocation, EPA was spending on the order of $200 million on cleanup of the dioxin at the site.[40]

While environmentalists blamed slow cleanup completions on inadequate appropriations, other experts questioned the stringent level of cleanups being required (i.e. how clean is clean) for driving excessively expensive cleanups. Tom Grumbly of Clean Sites, a nonprofit that advised communities on cleanups, maintained that "the last couple turns of the screw could not be justified on economic criteria". This is particularly true because, as Bill Ralston of consulting firm SRI International pointed out, "when you look for deaths from hazardous wastes, you just don't find them".[41]

Superfund continued to make incremental progress on remedial cleanups for 26 years after the trust fund's dedicated taxes expired in 1995. At the end of 2019, roughly 1,750 sites had been listed on the NPL. Of those, 424 had been removed from the list and construction had been completed at another 1,212, but the treatment measures at those sites needed to be operated well into the future.[42]

In an unexpected turn of events, in 2021 Superfund, and virtually every other Federal infrastructure program, got a huge slug of funding as part of the Infrastructure Investment and Jobs Act of 2021. Even more surprising, after a 26 year hiatus, the bill reimposed through 2031 a tax on chemical feedstocks, but not oil or corporate alternative income, in order to raise $14.5 billion.[43] Unlike earlier authorizations, the revenue from this tax will be made available as a mandatory appropriation with a year lag after receipt.[44] In addition, Superfund got an upfront discretionary appropriation of $3.5 billion to address its existing site backlog.

CHAPTER FIVE: Anatomy of a Bill -- *President Bush's Clean Air Act Revisions*

This chapter provides an example of the extensive role OMB can play in shaping an Administration legislative proposal and helping get it enacted. It also shows the clout and access an OMB branch chief sometimes can have in working with West Wing political staff. Admittedly this is a somewhat unusual example in terms of the depth of OMB's involvement in a legislative issue, particularly in working with the Congress.

Working on the Clean Air Act Amendments of 1990 stands out as probably the most exciting period of my career. While the original Clean Air Act was enacted in 1963, the Clean Air Act Amendments of 1970 was the first major environmental statute enacted after the initial Earth Day and the establishment of the Environmental Protection Agency earlier in 1970. Further major amendments were enacted in the Clean Air Act Amendments of 1977, but the Act still had major shortcomings that Congress had tried and failed to rectify during the 1980's.

Primer on the Clean Air Act

Implementation of the Clean Air Act (CAA) starts with the establishment of outdoor National Ambient Air Quality Standards (NAAQS). There are NAAQS primary standards for six pollutants (usually secondary standards as well)— ozone (O_3), carbon <u>monoxide</u> (CO), nitrogen oxides (NOx), sulfur dioxide (SO_2), particulate matter (PM), and lead (PB). At the time of the 1990 amendments EPA only had a standard for PM 10 but has since established a standard for PM 2.5. The numbers 10 and 2.5 refer to the diameter of the particles in micrometers, which are far smaller than even the 70-micrometer diameter of a human hair.

To avoid confusion with climate related issues, there is no NAAQS for carbon <u>dioxide</u> (CO_2), only CO, because ambient levels of CO_2 are far below the level that would cause direct health effects. However, CO_2 is a greenhouse gas that contributes to warming the atmosphere and the creation of ambient ozone, which does have health impacts. Furthermore, while ozone is a pollutant requiring control in the lower atmosphere, the same chemical needs to be protected from depletion in the upper atmosphere where it is needed to shield the Earth from harmful ultraviolet radiation.

Primary NAAQS standards are set by EPA to protect public health "with an adequate margin of safety". The CAA does not allow cost to be considered in the setting of primary standards. Secondary standards are welfare-based standards that are promulgated to protect against environmental effects such as impacts to crops, forests, and wildlife. Cost can be considered in establishing secondary standards.

Once NAAQS are established, EPA can establish national emissions standards on new, and sometimes existing, stationary sources (e.g. factories) and mobile sources (e.g. cars and trucks) to help achieve the NAAQS. These emissions standards are usually based on a demonstrated technology but are generally set as a performance standard that gives a factory or car maker flexibility to use a different technology as long as the performance standard is met. Cost can be considered in setting these emissions standards.

As the achievement of NAAQS is determined at a local level, many metropolitan areas need to impose additional controls beyond the emissions standards that apply nationwide. These additional controls are determined as part of a State Implementation Plan (SIP), which sets forth additional controls to meet the NAAQS and must be approved by EPA. EPA has various enforcement tools to penalize municipalities that don't reach attainment and, in rare circumstances, can develop a Federal Implementation Plan (FIP) when a state does not prepare an adequate SIP.

The CAA is the most important, most complex, and most costly of EPA's several mega regulatory statutes. It is largely a regulatory and enforcement statute. While the statute authorizes funding for research and implementation of the Act, including grants to states for their implementation costs, it does not provide grants to comply with the statute as the Clean Water Act does for municipal wastewater treatment. Instead, pollution emitters are expected to foot the bill for compliance with the Act and, to the extent they can, pass the costs along to their customers. In the case of electric and gas utilities, those rate increases are regulated by state public utility commissions.

Success and Limitations of the Clean Air Amendments of 1970 and 1977

The CAA amendments of 1970 and 1977 were hugely successful in reducing emissions and bringing many metropolitan areas into attainment with the relevant NAAQS. Under the CAA prior to the 1990 amendments, many large point sources had already been required to reduce emissions by roughly 80 percent from uncontrolled levels and tailpipe emissions from new vehicles had been reduced by 90 percent.

These reductions in emission requirements, however, were mitigated to some extent by emissions from increased industrial output due to economic growth and increased vehicle miles traveled (VMT) of an increasingly mobile population. In addition, for motor vehicles the reductions weren't fully achieved until the entire fleet of existing cars was replaced by new cars. At the time, EPA was estimating that the nation was spending $33 billion per year on air pollution control,[45] a figure that translates into roughly $68 billion in today's dollars.

In 1989, there were two NAAQS for which a significant number of metropolitan areas were still out of attainment — ozone (O_3) and carbon monoxide (CO). Of these, CO was the easier to address. CO ambient levels had decreased 32 percent from 1978 to 1987 and the number of eight-hour exceedances deceased by 91 percent during that same period. Furthermore, many of the 52 areas still out of attainment with the CO standard were expected to achieve attainment as older cars built to less stringent emissions standards were phased out of the fleet and replaced by newer cars built to stringent standards. Ozone, on the other hand, had 81 cities out of attainment and, for various reasons that will be discussed further below, attainment was going to be extremely difficult to achieve for many of these cities, particularly Los Angeles.

A second unresolved problem was toxic air pollutants. While some toxic air pollutant emissions would be controlled by the NAAQS, the CAA also included a separate Section 112 that governed health based-emission standards for these hazardous air pollutants. However, the statutory requirement for EPA to protect public health and welfare "with an ample margin of safety" was almost impossible to administer as it was unwieldy, fraught with contradictions, and provided little regulatory discretion. In particular, for carcinogens there simply is no identifiable threshold at which they pose no health risk. Yet a zero-emission requirement is tantamount to shutting down many of the largest and most vital U.S. industries. As a result, EPA had only promulgated seven regulations controlling air toxics since enactment of the section.

The marquee problem driving the push for CAA amendments, however, was acid rain. The term acid rain is something of a misnomer as unpolluted rain is naturally acidic[46]. While the NAAQS SO_2 standards were successful in reducing SO_2 by 40 percent from uncontrolled levels by 1990,[47] emissions were still around 20 million tons annually. Further, there was not sufficient scientific evidence to tighten the national SO_2 standards. As the environmental community has always hated coal as a particularly dirty fuel, they were looking for reasons to reduce SO_2 emissions further and the threat of acid rain provided that opportunity. It was only after enactment of the acid rain controls in the CAA Amendments of 1990, that the environmental community began demonizing coal for its CO_2 emissions as well.

Acid rain started to become an issue after research coming out of the Northeast in the 1970s had begun to indicate that unusually acidic rain could have adverse regional effects on ecological species due to long range transport of pollutants. In response, Congress adopted the Acid Deposition Act of 1980 which established a $500 million, eighteen-year research program — the National Acid Precipitation Assessment Program (NAPAP) --to assess the problem.[48]

However, eighteen years was too long for the environmental community to wait, and they began ratcheting up pressure for earlier action, in part by usefully exploiting the imagery of rain as an acid destroying substance.

Reagan Administration Consideration of Acid Rain Control

Part of the pressure for addressing acid rain was coming from the Canadians, who felt their lakes in the eastern provinces were threatened by acid rain from the long-range transport of pollutants from the mid-western United States. When Bill Ruckelshaus became Administrator of EPA for the second time in May 1983, after the resignation of Anne Gorsuch, he wanted to change the narrative of the Reagan Administration's position on environmental issues as well as address the concerns of the Canadians.

Consequently, Ruckelshaus developed an acid rain control proposal with a 3.5-million-ton SO2 reduction -- not enough to please the environmental community, but it was as far as he thought he could push the Reagan Administration. This set up an epic battle on the proposal between Ruckelshaus and OMB Director David Stockman, the boy wonder of the Reagan Administration, before the Domestic Policy Council (DPC) in October 1983.

Ruckelshaus didn't prepare a visual presentation, but rather made a verbal pitch about the political benefits of taking a pro-environment position as well as the diplomatic benefits of eliminating a sore point in our relationship with Canada, a key ally on a whole range of foreign policy issues. Stockman, on the other hand, spent weeks preparing a detailed presentation. While the concept for the presentation was pure David Stockman, most of the leg work fell to my fellow examiner, Barbara Chow, who would later become a high-level Obama political appointee. The presentation covered acid rain science, economics, and politics. It was brilliant!!

The presentation summarized the small amount of demonstrated adverse environmental effects based on the limited research available at the time. It also summarized the legislative dynamics of trying to limit an acid rain reduction program to the level proposed by Ruckelshaus. Finally, it included cost figures for various potential legislative outcomes and translated those figures into costs per pound of fish population protected, which ranged from $6,000 to $66,000 per pound[49].

In Stockman's Book, "The Triumph of Politics — Why the Reagan Revolution Failed", he talks about a presentation by Defense Secretary Casper Weinberger to the President in September 1981. Weinberger, who had been nicknamed "Cap the Knife" during his work as OMB Director, was defending the enormous and unsustainable multi-year defense increase included in the prior budget. The presentation included a cartoon style graphic showing soldiers, which represented different budget options, ranging from a small wimpy soldier with no gun to a buff GI-Joe fully decked out in advance armament.[50]

Stockman badly lost that battle with Weinberger, but he must have learned the importance of simple and clear visualizations in these types of policy presentations. Consequently, in his presentation on acid rain, Stockman had a graphic showing cartoon dead fish in a tiny portion of highly acidic lake surface area and happy swimming fish in the huge portion of lake surface area unaffected by acid deposition.[51] By the time his presentation to the DPC was done, it had been a knockout victory for Stockman.

The acid rain issue did not go away, however, even in the Reagan Administration. In March 1987, President Reagan announced several steps the U.S. was taking in working closely with the Canadian Government to determine and address the environmental effects of acid rain. The first two steps were to fully fund $2.5 billion in demonstration projects of innovative control technologies over five years and establish an advisory panel, with participation by state governments and Canada, in selecting the projects.

The third step was to have Vice President Bush's Task Force on Regulatory Relief review Federal and State economic and regulatory programs to identify opportunities for addressing environmental concerns under existing laws.[52] In essence this step was an attempt to find administrative ways to reduce acid rain precursor pollutants (i.e. SO2 and NOx). This was to be accomplished by reviewing Federal and state regulations to see if there were disincentives to deployment of new emissions control technologies that could be removed, or incentives for such technologies that could be provided by amending the rules.

At this point, Dave Gibbons had moved up to become the DAD for Natural Resources and I had become the Acting Chief of the Environment Branch. In this role, I was chosen to lead the Task Force working group, under the direction of C. Boyden Gray, the Vice President's right hand man for regulatory relief, and draft the final report within 6 months. My role also included scheduling working group activities, organizing meetings, coordinating agency assignments, and frequently chairing meetings. Given the divergent policy positions of the participating agencies, the task required looking for compromises and negotiating recommendations acceptable to all agencies.

The final Innovative Emissions Control Technology Report, released in October 1987, contained some useful, but not earth-shattering recommendations, all of which were accepted by the President. The recommendations were subsequently incorporated as one of two key elements in the Administration's position for negotiations with the Canadian Government on acid rain issues. For my effort, I got to help brief the Vice President on the final report in his West Wing office and received a nice commendation letter from the VP.

President George H. W. Bush Clean Air Act Amendment Proposals

On the campaign trail in August 31, 1988, despite running for President partly on Ronald Reagan's record, Vice President Bush strove to distinguish himself from Reagan on several key issues including acid rain[53], by committing:

"On the question of acid rain, the time for study alone has passed. We know enough now to begin taking steps to limit future damage... As President, I will ask for a program to cut millions of tons of sulfur dioxide emissions by the year 2000, and to reduce significantly nitrogen oxide emissions as well."

As President, he reiterated this stance in his February 9, 1989, statement to the Joint Session of Congress, promising that he would shortly send legislation for a new more effective Clean Air Act.

Roger Porter, Bush's Domestic Policy adviser, was chosen to lead the effort, with long time Bush aide Boyden Gray, now the White House Counsel, also having a significant role. Within OMB, Bob Grady, the PAD for Natural Resources Energy and Science, was given the lead. After graduating from Stanford Business School in June 1988, Bob joined the Bush campaign as a speech writer working particularly on environmental issues. As the Chief of the Environment Branch, I would become his right-hand man on clean air authorization.

Although the Clean Air Act was a regulatory statute, the budget side had always taken the lead on legislative issues, even though the $100 billion in annual regulatory costs imposed by EPA dwarfed EPA's $5 billion annual budget. However, controlling EPA's operating budget, which financed the regulatory programs, arguably was the best tool OMB had for preventing over-regulation by EPA. Consequently, to do their job, the Environment Branch staff had to develop a deep understanding of EPA's statutes and regulatory programs and spent a significant portion of their time working on regulatory reviews with OIRA, although we could pick and choose which rules to review.

Unfortunately, the Clean Air Act was one of the two EPA statutes for which I did not have a deep understanding at the time. Consequently, I engaged in a crash effort to understand the key titles that would be involved in reauthorization. Fortunately for me, it is easier to learn an additional EPA statute when you already have a good understanding of five others. This allowed me to quickly get to the point where I could give Grady a crash course on the Clean Air Act.

In April 1989, the Environment Branch had been tasked with taking the technical analysis that EPA staff had prepared and distill that analysis into lengthy options papers for use in cabinet level DPC meetings. Options papers were drafted for each of the three key reauthorization issues — acid rain, air toxic, and ozone non-attainment. Unfortunately, I had the audacity to get married and take my honeymoon at the end of April leaving Dave Gibbons and my air examiner, Ed Watts, to draft the air toxics paper without me.

Acid Rain Issues and Approach

Even though research developed by NAPAP still hadn't demonstrated a dire environmental problem in either lakes or forests, the President had already made his commitment to significantly reduce SO2 and NOx, with reductions in the range of 7 to 10 million tons being considered. In developing the Administration's proposal, there were two contentious issues that needed to be navigated which had stalemated acid rain legislation for years. The first was the impact of required emissions reductions on high sulfur coal producers and coal mining employment. The second was electricity rate increases in states with utilities affected by acid rain control.

Required installation of "scrubber" technology to coal utility smokestacks would have mitigated job loss among high sulfur coal producers but maximized utility rate increases. However, President Bush wanted to take a least-cost, market-based approach towards achieving the reductions. This could be accomplished by allocating the required reduction to states according to excess emissions, allowing fuel switching, and allowing emissions through trading marketable permits. To mitigate the loss of high sulfur coal jobs, there was a decision to provide incentives for the deployment of clean coal technology.

Air Toxics Issues and Approach

Air toxics were viewed as a problem because the 2.7 billion pounds of toxic chemicals emitted annually included 280 toxic compounds identified as being emitted in quantities posing some risk. In particular, 45 were carcinogens that were estimated to cause between 1,500 and 3,000 additional cancer cases per year, of which 25 percent were caused by the large stationary sources that Section 112 was intended to regulate.[54]

While a considerable portion of the air toxics problem was going to be addressed by the other components of the reauthorization proposal, as well as controls through the hazardous waste statute, the rigidity of the zero-risk test under the existing Section 112 air toxics program still needed to be fixed. In designing its proposal, the DPC's clean air working group, identified four legislative principles to guide finding a way to make Section 112 workable:

1) Achieve toxic pollutant reductions as soon as possible;
2) Provide flexibility to allow risk reduction to be balanced against economic and technical feasibility;
3) Set in place a long-term strategy leading to additional reductions; and
4) Encourage industries to make reductions on their own.

Non-Attainment Issues and Approach

Ozone (often referred to as smog) non-attainment was easily the most intractable of the issues the working group faced. At the time, the NAAQS ozone standard was 0.12 parts per million (ppm) measured over a one-hour period (the standard has been subsequently lowered to 0.07 ppm measured over an eight-hour period). A city was considered in non-attainment if the standard was exceeded four times over a three-year period. The press would often portray citizens in non-attainment cities as breathing "dirty air", while never explaining that the air in a city just above the standard was dirty less than 0.1 percent of the time.

Los Angeles, however, had dirty air a significant portion of the time, with 140 exceedances in a year and levels that could reach 200 percent above the standard. In fact, Los Angeles had exceedances four times higher than Houston, the second most polluted city in the US.[55] Other California cities also ranked among the worst, due to the car-oriented culture, the warm weather, and the mountains to the west of the cities that would keep the polluted air from being dispersed by eastward blowing prevailing winds.

The fact that California's ozone problem was different and more severe than other areas meant that national standards did not make sense to address California's problem fully, because it would impose unneeded cost burdens on the rest of the nation. For that reason, the Clean Air Act already included a provision allowing California to set its own mobile source (i.e. car and truck) emission standards.

California has since wanted to use that authority to restrict mobile source CO_2 emissions to reduce (very marginally) global warming. As climate change is a global issue, conceptually it makes little sense for California to have such authority. The Obama Administration was going to allow it, before being blocked by the Trump Administration. The Biden Administration has now reversed the Trump policy. However, the courts have yet to weigh in on whether the statute is written in a way for California to use this authority for climate change when it doesn't face a problem different than the rest of the nation.

The other complication in addressing ozone is that, unlike the other NAAQS pollutants, ozone is not directly emitted. Instead, it is formed when volatile organic compounds (VOCs), which can be toxic chemicals, are mixed with nitrogen oxides (NOx) in the presence of sunlight. As heat speeds up the reaction, it is a particular problem in the summer months and is why global warming can exacerbate the problem. The Bush Administration's ozone control strategy focused on VOCs. NOx controls generally reduce ozone but can increase its formation in certain situations as well.

The 0.12 ppm ozone health-based standard at the time was designed to protect healthy exercising individuals from acute respiratory symptoms (coughing, chest pain, shortness of breath) that are usually temporary and reversible. Ozone was also suspected of playing a role in chronic lung diseases, but EPA's Clean Air Science Advisory Committee didn't have enough evidence to tighten the standard based on chronic effects. The ozone secondary standard was based on adverse effects on vegetation and forest damage.

The bulk of the options considered affected mobile sources, with some control options on the cars and some on the fuels. The options also differed by whether they were imposed nationally or were measures that non-attainment areas could choose to impose. EPA had done an enormous amount of excellent technical work estimating the VOC reductions for various control options, the level of VOC reductions needed to get various cities into attainment, and the cost-effectiveness of various options. For the DPC options paper we drafted, my staff and I were able to take that information and summarize it in a one-page graphic showing the number of cities remaining out of attainment as additional control options were added, roughly in the order of cost-effectiveness (See Figure 5-1[56])

Decisions on the Proposal

Eventually our papers, which were drafted for discussion by the Cabinet principals, were condensed by DPC staff into shorter memos (ozone non-attainment went from 40 pages to 10) from the DPC to the President. After separate meetings on each of the three issues for the Cabinet to debate the issues in front of the President, Chief of Staff John Sununu huddled with the President to get final decisions. Time Magazine had an article in August of 1989 on how President Bush made decisions. It included an eight-frame cartoon which, despite its simplicity, captured the essence of the Clean Air Act decision process remarkably well.[57]

I attended a Rose Garden ceremony on June 12, 1989, at which President Bush announced the outlines of his proposal:

- *Acid Rain* — A two phased approach was proposed to cut SO2 emissions by 10 million tons annually, or 50 percent, and cut NOx emissions by 2 million tons annually. The first phase, to get half of the reductions by 1995, would target 107 power plants in 18 states, with the remaining reductions by 2000. To reduce costs, trading of acid rain allowances would be allowed and, to help high sulfur coal, use of clean

Figure 5-1 Clean Air Ozone Attainment Options

Clean Air Act Options Paper: Ozone NonAttainment   May 22, 1989   Page 9

Graph 1

EFFECT OF VOC CONTROL MEASURES ON # OF CITIES
BROUGHT INTO ATTAINMENT IN 2005

This chart shows how many cities will be brought into attainment by achieving incremental reductions of VOCs; the reductions could be achieved by the kinds of measures listed.

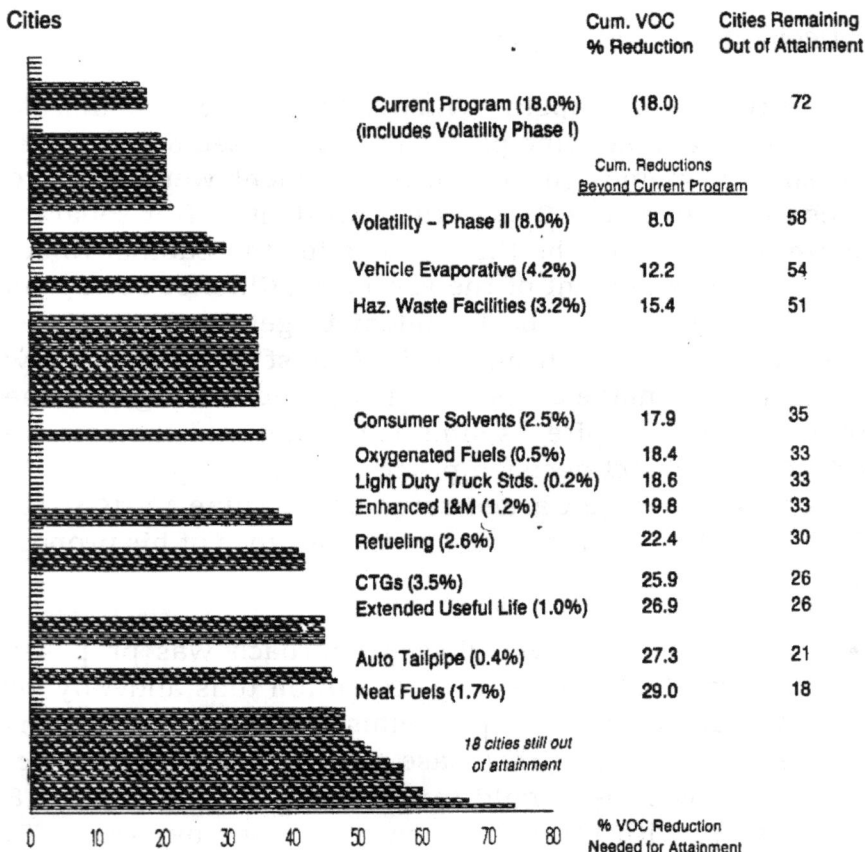

Cities

Measure	Cum. VOC % Reduction	Cities Remaining Out of Attainment
Current Program (18.0%) (includes Volatility Phase I)	(18.0)	72

Cum. Reductions Beyond Current Program

Measure		
Volatility – Phase II (8.0%)	8.0	58
Vehicle Evaporative (4.2%)	12.2	54
Haz. Waste Facilities (3.2%)	15.4	51
Consumer Solvents (2.5%)	17.9	35
Oxygenated Fuels (0.5%)	18.4	33
Light Duty Truck Stds. (0.2%)	18.6	33
Enhanced I&M (1.2%)	19.8	33
Refueling (2.6%)	22.4	30
CTGs (3.5%)	25.9	26
Extended Useful Life (1.0%)	26.9	26
Auto Tailpipe (0.4%)	27.3	21
Neat Fuels (1.7%)	29.0	18

18 cities still out of attainment

0 10 20 30 40 50 60 70 80

% VOC Reduction Needed for Attainment

coal technology would get an additional three years to meet the deadline[58]. The acid rain trading system eventually put in place was estimated to reduce costs by $1 billion per year.

- *Air Toxics* — A schedule would be established for regulating major industrial sources which would require achievement of a 75 to 90 percent reduction in toxic emissions through Maximum Available Control Technology (MACT). If EPA determined residual risks remained after MACT, EPA could set additional standards to prevent "unreasonable risk". The proposal was estimated to eliminate three-fourths of the annual cancer deaths attributed to air toxics.[59]

- *Non-Attainment* — The plan was designed to meet the ozone standard in two thirds of the cities by 1995, and all but New York, Houston, and Los Angeles by 2000, with those cities to meet the standard by 2010. While the plan included VOC controls on emissions from hazardous waste operations and consumer products (e.g. paint), it focused heavily on motor vehicles. Tailpipe emissions in 1993 models were to be reduced 40 percent for hydrocarbon VOCs and 30 percent for NOx.[60] There was also a big emphasis on alternative fuels, particularly in the more polluted cities where bus fleets would be required to use compressed natural gas or methanol. Cities out of attainment with the carbon monoxide standard would be required to add oxygenated fuels (e.g. ethanol) in winter. To cut costs, automakers could engage in emissions trading and oil companies could adopt fuel pooling.

EPA Administrator Bill Reilly told the press that the cost of complying with the proposal could reach $14 to $18 billion annually when fully implemented[61]. The cost would have been much higher without the proposal's market-oriented approach. The inclusion of such an approach was a triumph for EPA economists, particularly in the policy office, who had been working on pollution trading and other market-based policies for a decade with little success.

As discussed in Chapter 1, OMB had included a proposal in the last Reagan Budget for auctioning the limited number of allowances allowed under the Montreal Protocol to use ozone depleting CFCs. The proposal had originally been suggested by EPA before they recanted. Unfortunately, industry wasn't quite ready for such a proposal at that time. However, less than a year later, and with different legislative dynamics, industry embraced the concept of pollution trading for the Clean Air Act. It was also a huge success for the Environmental Defense Fund, which also had been working on allowance trading, even at the risk of alienating other environmental groups.

The reaction to the President's proposal was generally favorable with most parties applauding the President's objectives while wanting to make changes favorable to their interests. Of course, that meant that the environmental organizations wanted to make the bill more stringent and limit the market-based approaches, whereas industry favored the market-based approaches but viewed the plan as more stringent and costly than needed.

The key dissenting voice was Democratic Senator Robert Byrd of West Virginia who said the proposal would "decimate" the companies that mine high sulfur coal.[62] While the President's proposal energized the reauthorization effort, the reaction of the various stakeholders made it clear that the solution to the reauthorization stalemate had not yet been found. Senator Byrd's opposition also highlighted that the key fault line that needed to be bridged in order enact a bill was along regional rather partisan lines.

The President's proposal outlined the key policies that the President wanted in the bill. However, as discussed in the previous chapter, it is often advantageous to submit bill language when the President's party does not control Congress. Unlike in the case of Superfund, where the President's party at least controlled the Senate, President Bush always had to cope with a Congress where the Democrats controlled both houses. Consequently, after the President announced his proposals, the Administration undertook a difficult two-month period of bill drafting.

Many people assume that once the President has made policy decisions on the key issues, that drafting the needed legislation is straightforward. Unfortunately, that has never been my experience and that is certainly not the case for a bill with the mind-numbing complexity of the Clean Air Act. In fact, changes of a few words in a regulatory statute, such as the CAA, can have a huge impact on the stringency, and therefore cost, of a particular provision.

EPA prepared the initial draft of the bill and OMB's Legislative Reference Division was responsible for running the inter-agency review process. My branch's role was to provide comments on the draft consistent with OMB's policy position. In addition, I was also responsible for trying to mediate inter-agency disputes, often between EPA and DOE. Typical of the issues that might be raised in the acid rain context was how stringent to make the reporting and enforcement requirements for allowance trading. EPA wanted airtight rules to prevent any loss of tonnage reductions. On the other hand, DOE didn't want the trading requirements to be so burdensome that nobody would even attempt to trade, which would undermine the innovative policy.

To the extent that issues could not be resolved at my level, they bumped up to my political boss, Bob Grady. To the extent that Bob couldn't resolve the issues they would go back to the DPC. As you could never be sure whether Cabinet officials would understand, or how they would react to, the technical nuances in language issues, there was a powerful incentive for all agencies to strike deals before issues got elevated that far.

Breaking the Stalemate

Once the Administration released its bill language, it was introduced in the House with 148 sponsors, including Michigan Democrat John Dingell, Chairman of the House Energy and Commerce (E&C) Committee, the committee that had jurisdiction of the bill. However, the bill first had to go through the E&C's subcommittee on Health and the Environment, chaired by California Democrat Henry Waxman. Chairman Waxman wanted more stringent controls than proposed by the Administration, which the Washington Post characterized as strengthening the bill.[63]

The environment community would always characterize adding more stringent controls as "strengthening" the bill and deleting some controls as "weakening" the bill. As advocacy groups, this is a perfectly logical strategy since the word "strengthening" conveys positive connotations. This is even though there are trade-offs between stringency and cost that need to be balanced in making policy.

Consequently, what strengthens a bill is in the eye of the beholder. For instance, the environmental groups might view eliminating a bill's trading provisions as strengthening the bill, whereas industry might view adding trading to a bill that doesn't have it as strengthening the bill. I would always view a particular journalist as biased if they picked up the environmental community's use of the word "strengthen" rather than the more accurate and unbiased characterization of a bill provision as tightening emissions controls or making them more stringent.

Although Waxman began his markup of the Presidents' bill in September 1989, the crazy dynamics in the House eventually bogged it down. While Dingell and Waxman agreed on most issues under the Committee's jurisdiction, Dingell was a Detroit Congressman who had to protect his constituency in the auto industry. This put him in direct conflict with Waxman on motor vehicle standards. While Dingell had the votes to control his committee, including Waxman's subcommittee in which a majority of the subcommittee had sponsored the Bush bill,[64] his control when the bill hit the House floor was more tenuous.

In the Senate, Max Baucus, Chair of the Environment and Public Works Committee, introduced his own bill, drafted with considerable environmental group input, in September 1981. Although he had several Republican co-sponsors, his bill did not have enough support to overcome a filibuster and get to the Senate floor. Senate Majority leader George Mitchell understood that the Baucus bill was dead without significant changes and that he needed Bush Administration support for any bill to pass on the Senate floor.

To jump start the process, Senator Mitchell took the unusual step of inviting the Bush Administration to participate in negotiating the bill to be taken to the floor. As a general rule, both parties in Congress jealously guard the legislative branch's prerogatives (i.e. the President proposes, and Congress disposes). Thus, Congress would introduce Administration drafted bills by courtesy, have Administration appointees testify on bills, meet with Administration representatives, and consider Administration views expressed in letters and Statements of Administration Policy. However, Congress had to be desperate to let the Administration into the room for actual negotiations.

The Administration's negotiating team consisted of five individuals led by Roger Porter. The others were Bob Grady from OMB, Assistant Administrator for Air and Radiation Bill Rosenberg from EPA, Linda Stuntz from the Department of Energy (DOE), and Dick Schmalensee from the Council of Economic Advisers (CEA). Most of the principals also had a plus one who attended the negotiations as well as most of the internal Administration strategy sessions. I was fortunate to be Bob Grady's plus one and got to see history unfold from a cramped seat in the back bench.

One of my roles, in conjunction with my colleague Howard Gruenspecht from CEA, was to serve as scorekeeper for the regulatory costs of the bill. The basis for the estimates were various EPA, and sometimes DOE, contractor analyses on different provisions in the bills. Even these estimates were only ballpark projections compared to those EPA would prepare as part of a detailed Regulatory Impact Analysis (RIA), which is required to accompany every major rule sent to OMB for review. Furthermore, Howard, my air examiner and I often had to massage the contractor estimates to reflect fast moving changes.

Our initial estimate of the Baucus bill was about $40 billion annually, or over twice the cost of the President's bill. Therefore, part of the Administration's negotiating strategy was to drastically reduce the cost of the bill, while maintaining key aspects of the President's proposal. In particular, any bill had to include innovative market-based approaches, such as allowance trading, that were in the President's bill.

The negotiations took place in Majority Leader Mitchell's conference room and consumed most of February 1990. The Majority Leader was not a participant but would appear periodically to keep the pressure on the negotiators to reach a deal while Senate floor time was easier to schedule because it was still early in the Congressional session. As the negotiations had to be fit around other Senate business, the negotiations often went late into the night. There were times when we came back from the Hill after midnight and held a strategy session in Porter's office before we were allowed to go home to get a few hours of sleep. It was simultaneously exhilarating and exhausting.

One of the issues that must be dealt with in this type of negotiation is the lack of trust between parties with conflicting views. This was particularly important because neither side was able to commit the rest of their caucus to the changes worked out by the Environment and Public Works Committee members in the negotiations. While everybody understood that some floor changes were inevitable, changes to key compromises could kill the bill. Thus, one strategy for bill opponents was to try to amend a key compromise in the hope that it would make the bill implode. To prevent this, the negotiators, as well as the Majority and Minority leaders, all had to pledge to vote against "deal breaker" amendments even if they would normally support them.

Part of the Administration's negotiating strategy was to emphasize getting a good deal on stationary source (e.g. factories) non-attainment and air toxic issues. The Administration's assumption was that House Committee Chairman Dingell would make sure that the motor vehicle standards weren't overly stringent and, therefore, the Administration didn't need to use much negotiating capital on those issues.

Senate Democrats were fearful of the same thing. Consequently, like the deal on Senate floor action, they proposed that all the parties to the Senate negotiations would commit to supporting the Senate compromise "through conference". This meant that after the bill passed both houses and went to conference committee for resolution, the parties to the Senate compromise were bound to oppose any changes to the agreement unless all parties agreed to the change. The

Administration rejected the proposal hoping for a better outcome in the final bill.

After weeks of negotiation, a final deal was reached. The Administration had largely achieved its objectives of maintaining the innovative market-oriented approaches in the bill and my recollection was that the annual cost of the bill was cut to around $22 billion. The deal set off a furious effort to quickly draft a bill, which had to be done by Senate legislative counsel, and get it to the Senate floor. Since the Administration wasn't involved in the drafting, we were heavily reliant on Republican committee staff, some of whom the Administration didn't trust, to make sure the bill adhered to the deal.

Senate floor action was also a lengthy process, but the compromise held and all "deal breaker" amendments failed. Towards the end of floor action EPA came forward with a huge number of "technical" amendments needed to make the bill more implementable, which were to be submitted as a large manager's amendment. Minority Leader Dole was not thrilled, as he did not really trust EPA staff. However, he announced that he would support the manager's amendment because, at some point, you must trust your partners.

Nevertheless, the White House wanted to be sure that the amendments were truly technical, and that EPA staff weren't slipping in any language that would be contrary to the Administration's policy. I drew the short straw to wade through the stack of technical amendments to make sure they were legitimate. While I had a good lay understanding of the CAA, as a non-lawyer I felt somewhat under-qualified to comprehend the legal nuances of some of these changes.

At the time we were working out of the Vice President's large, ornate office in the Senate, which served as a base of operations for White House legislative staff given that the Vice President was only rarely present. The amendments were being funneled to me by John Beale a graduate of Princeton's Woodrow Wilson school and a senior staff member in the policy shop of EPA's Office of Air and Radiation. I worked well with John as he was bright, hardworking, and struck me as a straight shooter I could trust, unlike some of the other EPA staff who seemed to have their own agenda.

Consequently, I was astonished when, two decades later, Beale was convicted and sentenced to 32 months in prison for defrauding the Federal Government out of almost $1 million. Almost as bad, he was ridiculed mercilessly by Jon Stewart and John Oliver in a Daily Show segment entitled Charlatan's Web.[65] Apparently, starting in the year 2000, he kept collecting his EPA salary when not working by telling EPA management the he was secretly working for the CIA.[66] As I thought I was a good judge of character, and in the vast majority of cases correctly, I was stunned when the news of John's arrest broke because I never saw it coming. Fortunately, he is the only felon I have ever worked with, or ever personally known for that matter.

While my review of the technical amendments resulted in a few minor changes, I didn't find any major problems. Much to my relief, since my credibility was on the line, no problems showed up later after the interest groups got eyes on the changes. The manager's amendment with the technical fixes was added to the bill and the Senate passed the bill on April 3, 1990. At that point, action moved to the House.

End Game and Bill Passage

The Administration's participation in the Senate bill had been so successful, and so much fun, the Administration had some hopes of playing a similar role in the House. Realistically, however, that was never going to happen. Once the Administration had served its purpose of helping surmount the filibuster in the Senate, it was time for Congress to go back to regular order. In the House it really came down to whether Dingell and Waxman could cut a deal. If they could, the rest of the House Democrats would line up behind the bill and it would pass the House.

Unfortunately, despite Dingell being the most powerful House Committee Chairman, the Administration had miscalculated his ability to control the outcome when the bill came to the floor. While many House members feared Dingell, he knew that his caucus was much more sympathetic to the environmental cause than the auto industry. Consequently, Dingell cut a deal with Waxman.

Dingell got the best deal he could to protect the auto industry from too many new requirements. In the process, however, he gave up many of the Bush Administration's hard-won gains in the stationary source non-attainment title. Furthermore, it was reported that Dingell and Waxman cut their deal "through conference", making it more difficult for the Administration to get improvements to the House bill in conference. Consequently, the strategy of not agreeing to the Senate negotiated deal "through conference", as proposed by Senate Democrats, ended up backfiring on the Administration.

The House bill passed at the end of May triggering a multi-month conference process to hammer out a final bill. The Administration again was not a participant in the negotiations, although the Administration was allowed a representative to attend and answer questions in the public sessions. Unfortunately, much of the work took place in private sessions. In the end the Hill knew that the final bill had to be acceptable to the President, because they wouldn't have the votes to override a veto. However, they also knew that the President badly wanted a bill as part of his legacy.

The conference reached agreement on October 22, 1990. The New York Times referenced annual compliance cost estimates of various economists as being between $25 and $35 billion.[67] The Administration's estimate of the final cost was around $25 billion annually. Certainly, this was higher than the $18 billion high end estimate for the Administration's bill, but still far lower than the original Senate bill. Furthermore, the Administration had always assumed that Congressional action would increase the bill's cost.

While the bill was more stringent than hoped, it nonetheless accomplished the Administration's core objectives and included the innovative and cost saving flexibilities and market-oriented approaches that the Administration had proposed. Both industry associations and environmental groups supported the bill. Consequently, it passed the House and Senate with overwhelming bipartisan support in late October and was sent to the President for signature.

President Bush signed the bill at a ceremony in the East Room of the White House on November 15, 1990. The ceremony was attended by a bipartisan group of bill sponsors, industry organizations, environmental groups, and key executive branch staffers including my examiner and I. Bob Grady obtained one of the limited red border copies of the bill with the President's signature and had the front and back pages framed along with a letter from Grady thanking the staff for our work on the bill. As the last one who worked on the bill who was still at OMB, I took the framed bill pages with me when I stepped out the door for my retirement.

CHAPTER SIX: Playing Whack-a-Mole — *Adventures in Farm Policy*

Previous chapters looked at OMB's role in shaping programs whose costs largely were either financed through discretionary budget authority (e.g. wastewater treatment grants and Superfund) or imposed on the public through the regulatory process (e.g. Clean Air Act). This chapter focuses on mandatory funding provided in legislation enacted through the authorizing committees. It also begins to look at the role of the career Deputy Associate Directors, a discussion which is continued in the following three chapters.

In May 2001, I made the jump from Chief of the Environment Branch to Deputy Associate Director (DAD) of Natural Resources. I had turned down the opportunity to become a DAD nine years earlier because I had a one-year-old and another child on the way. Since my daughters were older, this seemed like a good time to make the move.

One thing that I hadn't realized was how bored I had become with environmental policy after 22 years. It wasn't until I got energized learning about the other parts of my new portfolio, the Departments of the Interior (DOI) and Agriculture (USDA), that it even dawned on me that I had been bored. In fact, once exposed to these new issues, I tried to minimize the amount of time I spent on EPA, even though it was still part of my portfolio.

Surprisingly, it was agricultural issues that fascinated me most. For one thing, it was my first significant experience working on mandatory and credit programs. Even more curious, however, were the farm support programs. Working on farm issues was like entering an alternate universe -- a Disneyland on the Potomac -- where the normal concepts of good public policy do not apply.

It was also stunning to discover that farmers were not only among our nation's best capitalists, who responded quickly to incentives to maximize their income, but also our most prominent socialists, who were politically strong enough to enact a vast array of farm social safety net programs.

The amazing thing about farmers' political strength is how few farmers there actually are. In 2012, there were only 2.1 million principal farmers (i.e. the person primarily responsible for the day-to-day operation of the farm) or less than 1 percent of the U.S. population. Even among principal farmers, it was the primary occupation for less than half of those individuals.[68]

Nevertheless, the farm community remains politically strong for two reasons. First, every state has a vocal farm constituency, which their Senators cannot ignore. However, that is not true in the House, where only a minority of districts have a significant number of farmers. Second, the jurisdiction of the House and Senate Agriculture Committees provides the support needed in urban and suburban areas to enact farm bills.

In particular, the Agriculture Committees have jurisdiction over: 1) the food stamp program --now called the Supplemental Nutrition Assistance Program (SNAP) — which is of importance to inner city House members; and 2) farm conservation programs, which are important to many suburban House members with environmental constituencies. Getting support for farm support programs requires the Agriculture Committees buying off these constituencies in the farm bill process, which occurs every five years. Consequently, lasting reform of farm programs may require moving jurisdiction for SNAP and other nutrition programs out of the Agriculture Committees.

The Agriculture Committees also have another ace up their sleeves referred to as permanent law. This permanent law, which consists of two Acts from 1938 and 1949, takes effect if a Farm Bill is not enacted, thereby putting parity pricing back into effect. As parity pricing is indexed to prices in the early 1900's, without taking productivity into account, it would produce much higher subsidies than recent farm bills, particularly for large farms that can take advantage of significant economies of scale.[69] The Agriculture Committees use the threat of higher cost permanent law to spur enactment of farm bills costing more than would otherwise be the case. However, as the Agriculture Committees haven't wanted permanent law to take effect either, it may be that permanent law is a double-edged sword which could unleash a backlash against farm legislation if ever triggered.

Early Action on the 2002 Farm Bill

By the time I became DAD, four months into the Administration of George W. Bush, the Congress was already working on a new farm bill. Given the normal lag in getting USDA political appointees in place, the Administration was not well positioned to have a major impact in shaping the bill. Furthermore, I had my own staffing issues, with my new Agriculture Branch Chief, Adrienne Lucas, going on maternity leave a few months after she was selected and my commodities examiner, who had lost out on competition for the branch chief job, having one foot out the door.

In September 2001, shortly before the House was to mark up its very traditional farm bill, with generous increased commodity subsidies, USDA threw a hand grenade into the debate. They released a lengthy policy document which, while not containing specific proposals, laid out the general direction the Administration wanted the bill to take. In particular, the document expressed a desire to reorient the focus of the bill away from commodity subsidies for large producers, as almost half the subsidies were paid to eight percent of farmers. Instead, the Administration wanted more funding for conservation programs, greater access to foreign markets, and expanded research into pest and disease control[70].

The non-profit Environmental Working Group (EWG) announced that they were pleasantly surprised by the policy and hoped it could mark a watershed change in agriculture policy. EWG has done yeoman's work over the past two decades using Freedom of Information Act (FOIA) requests to compile a database on farm subsidies and particularly in publicizing how much of the funding has gone to wealthy farmers, including absentee farm owners living in Manhattan. In line with the USDA policy document, and with the Administration's strong support, Congressman Kind tried to amend the farm bill on the House floor to shift $19 billion from commodity subsidies to conservation. Sadly, the amendment narrowly failed[71].

Shortly before that vote, USDA Secretary Ann Veneman announced that there might not be enough money to finance the $76 billion in new spending over 10 years ($171 billion total) in the House bill. Her caution was due to the need for the Federal Government to shift funding to homeland security in response to the 9/11 attack earlier in the month. She indicated that OMB would have to determine how much was available.[72]

When the FY 2003 Budget was announced in February 2002, it provided $73.5 billion in new funding over a 10-year period. Initially OMB Director Daniels just wanted to set a spending cap without targeting the funds. However, wearing my oversight hat for environmental programs, I knew that the overall environment budget was going to be heavily criticized as inadequate. Consequently, I proposed a win-win solution to target $10 billion of the additional farm spending to conservation programs. In addition to achieving the President's conservation objectives, it limited the amount of funding available for trade distorting subsidies. Additional funds were also set aside for improvements in the food stamp program, and establishment of new risk management Farm Savings Accounts for farmers.[73]

A Word About Scoring Estimates

While the amount of new farm bill funding in the FY 2003 Budget was generous, it was not as close to the House bill total as it seems ($73.5B versus $76B). First, it is necessary to understand that the baseline used to score bills changes each year with the new budget. The baseline essentially is the estimated cost of extending existing law with no policy changes but considering changes in commodity prices or other economic assumptions since the previous year. In this case, the baseline for FY 2003 was several billion higher than FY 2002.

It should be noted that all farm bill costs refer to mandatory spending, as opposed to a statute like the Clean Air Act which only authorized discretionary spending. While farm bills also include authorizations for discretionary spending, such funding is not scored until included in an appropriations bill. This convention not only prevents the double counting of such spending, but also avoids the scoring of numerous authorizing provisions littered throughout enacted laws which never receive any funding.

The second complication in making scoring comparisons is that bills undergoing floor action are scored by the Congressional Budget Office (CBO), while the President's Budget and enacted bills are scored by OMB and the agencies. As CBO and OMB economic assumptions and technical methodologies always have some differences, it means that Congressional and Administration bill scores never provide "apples to apples" comparisons. This can be very confusing to the public, not to mention OMB DADs, because CBO and OMB analysts are really the only ones capable of cross walking the two estimates.

Another caution in comparing bill estimates is that readers need to understand the numbers of years the estimate covers. Unfortunately, that information is not always identified in press reports. Farm bills generally last five years and costs are sometimes given for the five-year period. However, pay-as-you-go (PAYGO) rules always use ten years of funding, with most of the policies in the farm bill being assumed to extend for a total of ten years.

Finally, when articles or press releases refer to "new funding", that means funding over the baseline. On the other hand, total funding is the sum of baseline and new funding. In issuing press releases, choosing between five- and ten-year estimates, or between new and total funding, is often determined by which estimate provides the best political spin for whoever is issuing the press release.

Farm Security and Rural Investment Act of 2002 (FS-RIA)

When the Senate took up the bill in January, Senator Grassley made effective use of EWG's data base on absentee landowners of huge farms to pass an amendment, with heavy Administration support, that significantly lowered the cap on total subsidy payments for any farmer. While the Administration also supported the Senate's increase for conservation programs, the overall cost of the Senate bill ballooned during markup and floor action. The conference agreed version of the bill increased conservation spending and cut the cap on farm subsidies, but not as much as in the Senate bill. The final bill had a CBO scored cost of $190 billion over ten years, an increase of $90 billion.[74]

The Farm Security and Rural Investment Act of 2002 became law on May 13, 2002, at a White House signing ceremony. While the bill was significantly more expensive than proposed in the President's Budget, the political spin in the White House fact sheet claimed that the Administration had made the bill more fiscally responsible because it cost 29 percent less than the Senate bill.

President Bush touted the bill as being generous in increasing conservation spending and providing a safety net for farmers, without encouraging overproduction and depressing prices. Despite lamenting that the bill did not include his proposed Farm Savings Accounts, he nonetheless predicted — incorrectly as it turned out --that the bill would eliminate the need for ad-hoc disaster supplementals.[75]

The White House fact sheet also claimed that the bill preserved the main market-oriented features of the Freedom to Farm Act of 1996, including planting flexibility, price responsive payment programs, and no government stockpiling of crops or forced-idling of cropland. While Freedom to Farm had been a landmark bill in allowing farmers to better respond to the market, FSRIA backtracked on some of that progress.

One of the key changes in the Freedom to Farm Act, officially known as the Federal Agriculture Improvement and Reform (FAIR) Act, was the elimination of countercyclical payments, also referred to as deficiency payments. These were replaced by fixed Federal payments that were independent of current farm prices and production for farmers who signed production flexibility contracts.[76] I will refer to these as direct payments, although they have also been called decoupled payments, production flexibility contract payments, and AMTA payments after the name of the commodity title in the 1996 bill.

Direct payments were paid whether prices were at record highs or record lows and whether there was a bumper crop or a poor crop. Only a farm bill could get away with touting the elimination of the link between income support payments and farm prices, which addressed a genuine risk to farmers, and replacing it with what were effectively welfare payments to often rich farmers. Furthermore, the claim that the linkage between payments and farm prices had been severed wasn't even correct. While countercyclical payments had been eliminated, marketing loan gain payments, which were also linked to price, remained in effect.

The direct payments were supposed to be temporary adjustments that would decline over the seven-year reauthorization period before ending. Unfortunately, they were boosted at times in ad-hoc supplemental bill and didn't end for almost two decades. In fact, FSRIA not only maintained the direct payments, it re-instituted the countercyclical payments. So much for that highly touted Freedom to Farm reform.

Understanding Farm Subsidy Payments

By the end of my first year as NRD DAD, I had learned a lot by going through the farm bill process. While I had a good understanding of the big picture for farm policy, I will admit that I was super confused when it came to the specifics of farm subsidy programs. Part of my confusion stemmed from my incredulity that farms, which are essentially small businesses, could be treated so much more generously than small businesses in other economic sectors. Whereas farmers have programs to protect them from both adverse price changes and reductions in output to keep them operating, most small businesses get no Federal aid, except after major disasters.

Consequently, small businesses in other sectors are subject to a continual churn of bankruptcies and new entrants. Farm organizations justify their special treatment by arguing that commodity pricing and crop yield are more volatile than business risks faced by other sectors. While there is some truth to that argument, it doesn't explain the need for the range of farm programs supported or why some crops can compete with little Federal support.

Farm advocates also point to the generous subsidies provided by other nations. There is also truth to this statement, as many countries want to maintain a viable farm sector either for security reasons or to protect products of cultural importance (e.g. French wines, Dutch cheese, and Japanese rice). While the focus of much trade policy is to prevent inefficient producers from subsidizing exports, the U.S. also has some inefficient farm sectors that we want to protect. Unfortunately, it is an impediment to our trade negotiators in achieving their free trade objectives if we are imitating other nation's bad behavior.

When my new commodities examiner, Susan Leetmaa, tried to verbally explain the various subsidy programs my eyes would glaze over. In particular, I was having a tough time understanding why the same row crops (e.g. wheat, corn, soybeans, and cotton) were eligible for so many subsidies. Unfortunately, this is a situation where you need to suspend disbelief to wrap your mind around farm programs.

Note that most of this chapter will focus on these bulk commodity row crops. I won't even attempt to explain the dairy and sugar programs which are focused on maintaining high prices by managing supply. Those programs are sufficiently bizarre that they would make an old-time Soviet central planning apparatchik smile.

As noted earlier, in business school I was categorized as a quant jock, or numbers guy if you prefer. Even though DADs are not supposed to do this kind of work, I sat down with my copy of the recently passed FSRIA and developed a spreadsheet to show me graphically what was happening with these subsidy programs. Although FSRIA is a long statute — 300+ pages — comprehending statutory funding language is far easier than trying to decipher the type of regulatory provisions found in environmental statutes.

The spreadsheet was designed to allow different crops, prices and yields as inputs to test the model's sensitivity. The spreadsheet generated two graphs, with the first showing the effect of price on revenue, taking the subsidy programs into account, and the second showing the effect of yield on revenue. The two graphs (Figure 6-1 and Figure 6-2) for wheat are re-creations of the graphics I produced and, while they may be too complicated for some people to understand, for me they were highly enlightening.

To understand the graphs, it is first needed to understand the four subsidy programs that applied to the full range of row crops under FSRIA. As explained further below, these are all payments that provide farmers with revenue in addition to what they would obtain by selling their crops. Sales revenue is the shaded triangle at the bottom of both figures that goes up linearly as market price increases in Figure 6-1 and as crop yield per acre increases in Figure 6-2.

The market price and yield assumptions in the graphs are in the ballpark of actual levels for wheat at that time, although rounded for illustrative purposes. All prices are shown as dollars per bushel and all yields are shown as bushels per acre. The horizontal lines are operating and total cost levels which can be compared to revenue. These lines indicate that 90 percent of the wheat crop can be produced at this level or lower cost. Finally, these graphs do not show ad-hoc disaster payments, which are often appropriated to provide additional assistance on top of these programs in counties designated as disaster areas.

Direct Payments - As discussed above, these are what I referred to as "welfare payments" because eligible farmers (i.e. those having grown row crops in prior years) received them regardless of market prices or yield in a year, although they are subject to payment limits. In these graphs, the direct payments are the band just above the sales revenue triangle that adds the same amount of revenue on top of sales revenue at every price and every yield level. To simplify the analysis, they have also been reduced by the farmer's cost to purchase crop insurance.

Figure 6-1 Subsidy Protection Against Price Change

Wheat Revenue & Cost -- FSRIA of 2002 (2004-2007)
(Effect of Changes in Market Price)

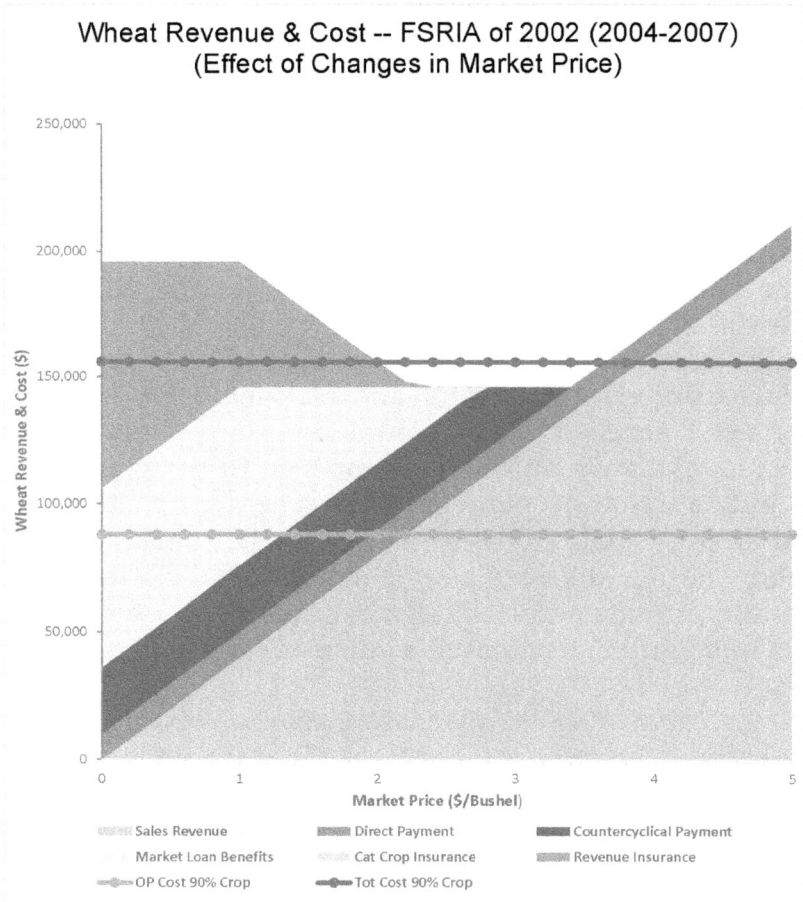

Sales Revenue		Direct Payment		Countercyclical Payment	
Market Loan Benefits		Cat Crop Insurance		Revenue Insurance	
OP Cost 90% Crop		Tot Cost 90% Crop			

Statutory Levels			
Target Price	$3.92	Loan Rate	$2.75
Direct Payment Rate	$0.52	Note: Direct Payment is Net of Crop Insurance Cost	
Example Assumptions			
Farm Acreage	1,000	Actual Yield per Acre (Bushels)	40
Crop Revenue Coverage %	75	Expected Harvest Price (Future Contract $/Bushel)	$3.00

Figure 6-2 Subsidy Protection Against Yield Change

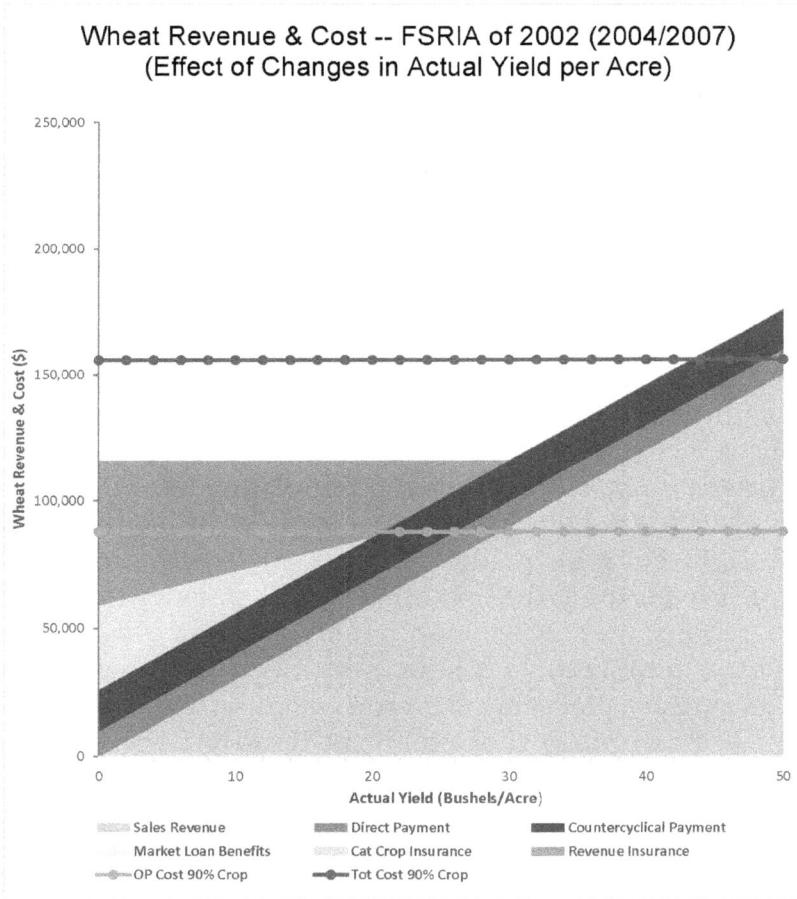

Wheat Revenue & Cost -- FSRIA of 2002 (2004/2007)
(Effect of Changes in Actual Yield per Acre)

Legend:
- Sales Revenue
- Direct Payment
- Countercyclical Payment
- Market Loan Benefits
- Cat Crop Insurance
- Revenue Insurance
- OP Cost 90% Crop
- Tot Cost 90% Crop

Statutory Levels

Target Price	$3.92	Loan Rate	$2.75
Direct Payment Rate	$0.52	Note: Direct Payment is Net of Crop Insurance Cost	

Example Assumptions

Farm Acreage	1,000	Market Price	$3.00
Crop Revenue Coverage %	75	Expected Harvest Price	$3.00
Expected Yield per Acre (Bushel)	40	(Future Contract $/Bushel)	

Countercyclical Payments - These payments are referred to as countercyclical because they provide extra revenue to farmers to offset lower sales revenue when prices are low. Countercyclical payments, which are shown as the darkest band in the graphs on top of the direct payments band, start when market price drops below the difference between the crop's target price and direct payment rate (i.e. $3.40 per bushel), both of which are specified in FSRIA ($3.92 and $.52 per bushel respectively). The payments reach their maximum of 65 cents per bushel when the price drops to the statutorily set loan rate of $2.75 per bushel.

In Figure 6-2 this dark band appears at all yield levels because the market price assumption in this graph is below the price that triggers the payments. If market price were to exceed $3.40 per bushel, the band would disappear, although higher sales revenue would offset the loss of countercyclical payments except at low yield levels.

Marketing Loan Benefits - While not labeled as countercyclical, these benefits provide extra revenue, shown as the light-colored quadrilateral in Figure 6-1, at prices even lower than the countercyclical payments. Farmers can get marketing loan benefits in two ways. First, farmers may receive a loan from USDA at the statutory loan rate by pledging the crop as collateral. However, farmers can repay these loans at less than the loan rate when market prices drop below the loan rate, giving rise to the subsidy, or they can forfeit the pledged crop. The repayment rate at low market prices is set by USDA to minimize forfeitures.

The second way to receive marketing loan benefits is through what is known as a loan deficiency payment (LDP). Essentially an LDP gives the farmers the same level of subsidy as they would get with a marketing loan, but they don't have to bother getting the loan!! As a long-time bureaucrat, with an occasional Machiavellian streak, I appreciate the diabolical elegance of this scheme to funnel subsidies to farmers. As a taxpayer, however, I find it outrageous.

Note that in Figure 6-1, marketing loan benefits start when market prices drop below the loan rate, which is the point at which countercyclical payments no longer increase. In Figure 6-2, there are no marketing loan benefits showing because the market price is assumed to be $3 per bushel but would appear if the market price assumption had been below the $2.75 per bushel loan rate.

Crop Insurance - Two types of crop insurance are available to farmers. Both are paid on top of any other USDA subsidies that a farmer might receive (i.e. direct, countercyclical, and marketing loan payments are not considered in determining crop insurance payment amounts).

The first type of insurance, catastrophic (CAT) coverage, provides a payment equal to 55 percent of the expected price at harvest on crop losses more than 50 percent of expected yield. Eligible producers received this coverage for a nominal $100 fee. Revenue from CAT coverage is not shown in Figure 6-1 because yield is assumed to be normal. It shows up as a light-colored triangle on top of the countercyclical payments band in Figure 6-2, with payments starting at 20 bushels per acre, which is 50 percent of the expected yield.

The second type of coverage is "buy-up" coverage which can protect against either yield losses or revenue losses. This darker colored band is for 75 percent revenue coverage and appears on top of the marketing loan band in Figure 6-1 and on top of the CAT coverage band in Figure 6-2. This coverage level prevents revenue from dropping if 1) prices are 25 percent or more below expected levels in Figure 6-1: or 2) yield is 25 percent or more below expected yield in Figure 6-2, although net of the CAT payment. As the name implies, "buy-up" coverage means that farmers pay a premium that increases with the level of coverage purchased. However, even "buy-up" coverage is heavily subsidized with the premium subsidy averaging 63 percent in 2018[77] and costing taxpayers over $6 billion that year.[78]

I had four takeaways from these graphs which greatly influenced my thoughts on farm subsidy programs in the following years. First, at least 90 percent of wheat farmers in the 2004 to 2007 period who bought crop insurance revenue coverage had sufficient revenue to fully cover operating costs even in years with very low yields or prices. Farmers don't need to cover total costs every year, but they will go out of business quickly if they can't cover operating costs.

Second, somewhat less than 90 percent of farmers could fully cover total costs for a range of prices (Figure 6-1) that included the expected harvest price, which at the time was low by the standards of the prior 30 years. Third, coverage for low yield levels (Figure 6-2) was not nearly as good for many farmers as coverage for low prices. Finally, and most stunningly, wheat farm revenue for a farmer would actually increase if prices dropped more than 25 percent below the expected price!!

Post Farm Bill Actions

From the standpoint of the Agriculture Committees, once the Farm bill is enacted there should be no changes to its provisions for the next five years. Of course, they lobby heavily for farm disaster assistance — there is always a drought or flood disaster somewhere in the country every year --whenever a supplemental bill is being considered.

OMB does not share the Committee's view that farm programs are untouchable once the Farm bill passes. In fact, the Farm bill is such a target rich environment of excessive spending, that it is viewed as a good source of potential offsets no matter who is President. Between Farm bills, there are three types of actions that OMB takes to attempt to limit the cost of mandatory farm spending.

CHIMPs

First, OMB almost always includes what are known as changes in mandatory programs (CHIMPs) — also referred to as mandatory savers — in the annual budget. While food stamps and crop subsidy payments are legitimately mandatory spending, a significant amount of Farm bill funding is spent on programs that should be discretionary.

If it were up to the authorizing committees, all spending would be mandatory under their control, except possibly salary costs. In part due to appropriations committee opposition, however, it is difficult in most cases to shift programs from discretionary to mandatory. Unfortunately, the Agriculture Committees often are allocated enough funding for reauthorization that they can sprinkle it around to create new mandatory programs, which effectively become grandfathered as mandatory once the program is created. Most of these mandatory programs, which would be discretionary in virtually any other department, fall within the conservation and rural development bureaus. In making trade-offs during development of the annual discretionary budget, we took these mandatory programs into account.

Consequently, we would propose CHIMPs in the budget as offsets to discretionary spending in order to fund other discretionary programs within USDA. For instance, in FSRIA of 2002, mandatory funding for the Environmental Quality Incentives Program (EQIP) was scheduled to grow from $400 million in 2002 to $1,300 million in 2007. While the Bush Administration supports the EQIP program, we thought the size of the increase was excessive. Starting in the 2005 Budget, a CHIMP was included to block the program from increasing above the $1,000 million level, with the $200 or $300 million in savings being used to fund other priorities.

During the six budgets between the 2002 and 2008 farm bills, the Administration proposed an average of over $800 million in farm bill CHIMPs annually. While the appropriators didn't necessarily include all our proposed CHIMPs, they shared our interest in using CHIMPs as offsets to essentially expand their 302(b) allocation (i.e. the subcommittees share of overall appropriations). In the case of EQIP, they included the proposed CHIMP every year.

Legislative Proposals

The second action OMB would take between farm bills,

was to propose actual changes in the farm bill as part of the annual budget process to get mandatory savings, which could be used for either deficit reduction or PAYGO offsets to fund other mandatory spending proposals or tax cuts. The size of these proposed savings varied dramatically by year, depending on the overall fiscal outlook and whether the Administration wanted to pursue a reconciliation bill. The amount of these proposals during this period ranged from zero in the FY 2005 Budget to $8.9 billion over ten years in the FY 2007 Budget.

Unlike CHIMPs, which block funding by preventing use of salaries to carry out a program above a certain level, these proposals require legislative action that would need to be initiated by the Agriculture Committees. Unfortunately, in the absence of a broad government-wide reconciliation bill for deficit reduction, the Agriculture Committees have zero incentive to open up the Farm bill for any reductions. Consequently, most of these proposals went nowhere. However, the FY 2006 and 2007 proposals in some ways foreshadowed reductions that the Administration would include in its proposal for the 2008 Farm bill.

Administrative Actions

The third type of actions that OMB staff would undertake between Farm bill were administrative actions, although sometimes coupled with CHIMPs or legislative proposals. Two examples show the multiple ways that OMB staff sometimes take on a policy issue. The first relates to the Conservation Security Program (CSP), a new program created by FSRIA in the Natural Resources Conservation Service (NRCS). CSP was designed as a voluntary program that would provide payments to farmers for adopting management, vegetative, or structural practices to conserve or improve resources such as soil, water, or wildlife habitat.

CSP was originally estimated to cost $2 billion over 10 years. However, as my staff and I looked deeper into the legislation, we became convinced that it would produce only marginal environmental benefits at a likely cost of $8 billion over ten years. My examiner at the time was Jason Weller, who ironically would become the Chief of NRCS roughly a decade later.

Our initial option was to include in the FY 2004 Budget, the first budget after enactment of FSRIA, a proposal to amend the CSP provisions in FSRIA and save $5.2 billion. As the chances of that proposal being enacted were slim, we then began to work with USDA on the regulation to implement the program. The thrust of our efforts was to target the program on problematic areas (mainly watersheds), tighten the environmental standards for eligibility, and require real environmental improvements.

Due to special farm bill provisions, the rule was issued before the first year's sign-up, which targeted 18 priority watersheds, as interim final rather than taking comment on a proposed rule. Under an interim final rule (IFR), comments are taken after the IFR is issued. We used those comments to fix problems discovered in the first sign-up. However, we also had NRCS issue another IFR before the second year's sign-up to give us flexibility to make further fixes based on the results of the larger second sign-up, which opened up enrollment to about 200 watersheds.

Ultimately, the targeting of the rule had the dual benefit of maximizing the impact of the program and limiting the cost, by saving an estimated $3 billion over 10 years. As the resulting cost was still higher than originally intended, we then began proposing to cap annual CSP costs using a CHIMP. The Appropriations Committees not only agreed with this approach, but they also sometimes set the cap lower than proposed by the Administration.

The second example of use of administrative actions to control farm programs relates to crop insurance which, unlike the commodity programs, is permanently authorized. Crop insurance was designed to be the primary risk management tool to help farmers cope with natural disasters, such as flood and drought. Beginning in the late 1990's with the advent of revenue insurance, it also protected against prices drops below the levels expected at the time planting decisions were made. One of the purposes of crop insurance was to eliminate the need for large disaster payments on top of crop insurance and other subsidy payments. Unfortunately, at least through 2010, it failed miserably in achieving that goal (see Figure 6-3).[79]

While USDA subsidizes, regulates, and reinsures crop insurance policies, the policies themselves are sold to producers by Approved Insurance Providers (AIP). The AIPs make their money through Administrative and Operating payments which are calculated as a percentage of annual premiums, with the percentage established in the Standard Reinsurance Agreement (SRA). As this percentage was established when the program was much smaller, it was providing huge profits for the AIPs by the early 2000s because it did not reflect the economies of scale that had developed in the program over the years.

My Agriculture Branch Chief, Adrienne Lucas, and her examiner, Jennifer Bell, realized that the need to renegotiate the SRA in 2004 provided an opportunity to save the taxpayers money without harming the program. Consequently, they worked with USDA to develop a proposal to significantly reduce the excessive amount of reimbursement that the companies were receiving. Unfortunately, USDA was not willing to fight hard for the proposal and it was only through OMB's tenacity that the negotiation resulted in $35 million in annual savings.

Fortunately, Adrienne and Jennifer got another swing at the bat when we were asked to include significant mandatory savings in the FY 2006 Budget. My staff produced a crop insurance savings proposal of $1.3 billion over ten years that reduced the subsidies for both the insurers and the farmers. While it seemed at one point that the proposal would be enacted, unfortunately Congress left the proposal out of the final 2006 Budget reconciliation bill. Despite strike two, those same proposals were included in the Administration's 2008 Farm bill reforms. This time the staff's perseverance paid off as Congress, needing offsets and recognizing the merit of the reforms, included much of the proposal in the final bill.

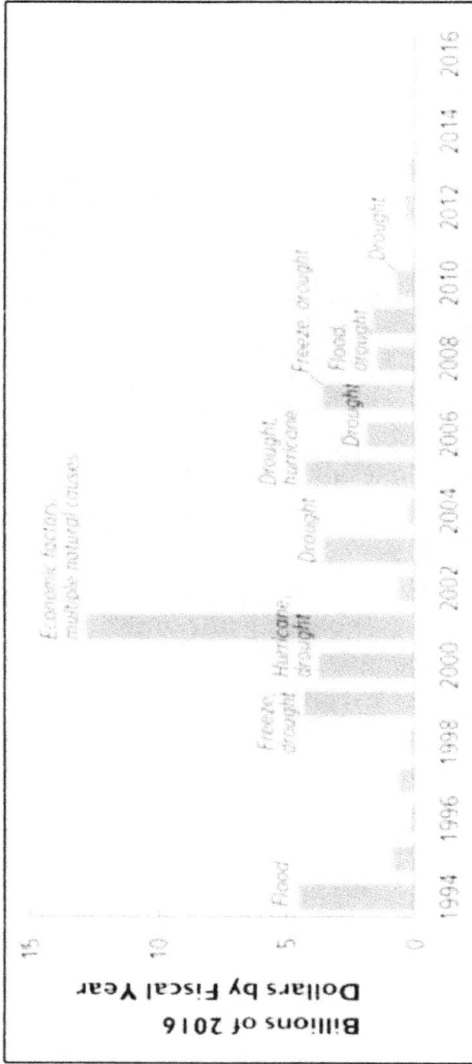

(FY1994 to FY2016)

Billions of 2016 Dollars by Fiscal Year

Source: CBO, using data and information from RMA, CRS, and a review of enacted legislation.

Notes: The bar labels identify reasons for supplemental assistance in all years that it totaled more than $1 billion. That assistance, which is provided separately from scheduled appropriations, consists of payments to crop producers for major losses attributable to natural disasters and other unscheduled support that addresses the types of perils covered by crop insurance. It does not include support provided through market-loss payments to producers to compensate for low commodity prices, standing disaster programs created by the Food, Conservation, and Energy Act of 2008, or nonfarm programs.

Bush Administration 2008 Farm Bill Proposals

When the Farm bill came up for reauthorization in 2007, my division was far better prepared to help shape it than in 2002, and virtually the entire Agriculture Branch was involved. USDA was better prepared as well, having begun preparations in 2005 by conducting 52 Farm Bill Forums across the country and collecting over 4,000 sets of comments.[80] The Secretary of Agriculture at the time was Mike Johanns, a smart, thoughtful, and capable executive. Despite being a former Governor of a farm state, Nebraska, he was genuinely interested in program reform and understood that he needed to support the broader Bush Administration agenda and not just farm interests.

In developing the FY 2007 Budget, we had received internal guidance to develop farm bill proposals that included significant policy reforms, produce $20 billion in savings, and be consistent with U.S. trade obligations under our most recent proposal at the Doha round of trade negotiations. Ultimately, the savings requirement was relaxed and the 2007 Budget included a $5 billion increase in funding over 10 years. Nevertheless, this required our helping scale back USDA's proposed funding levels while working to improve upon the reforms in their initial proposals.

On many issues we were in general agreement with USDA, such as the need for tighter payment limitations, while on other issues we disagreed, such as my desire to eliminate or phase out direct payments. However, any chance of that happening blew up when OMB leadership backed away from requiring large savings.

As mentioned earlier, we were successful in getting our crop insurance reforms in the Administration proposal. Given the problems we encountered in implementing CSP, my staff had developed a new targeted regional conservation program that was designed to improve water quality and water conservation on working agricultural lands. A version of this concept was included in the enacted bill.

In addition, working with an examiner in the International Affairs Division, Nancy Schwartz, the two of us began an effort, which spanned the remainder of our careers, to reform the Federal government's international food assistance programs to allow faster response at lower costs. Our proposal, which would have allowed more flexibility in managing a portion of food aid under the P.L. 480 Title II Food for Peace program, was included in the Administration's reform package, but rejected by the Congress.

The Administration's Farm bill proposals were announced by Secretary Johanns on January 31, 2007, just ahead of the release of the FY 2008 Budget. The package included 65 proposals addressing a wide range of agricultural and rural development issues. It was intended to represent a comprehensive, reform-minded, and fiscally responsible approach to supporting America's farm community. Major increases included: $7.8 billion in conservation funding; $5 billion to support fruit, vegetable, and other specialty growers, who had received little Federal assistance in the past, by increasing nutrition in food assistance programs; $1.6 billion for renewable energy research; and even $1.6 billion in loans to rehabilitate Rural Critical Access Hospitals.

The proposals also reduced payments to farmers through the traditional commodity programs by $10 billion, which were intended to make commodity programs less market-distorting and reduce friction with America's trading partners. This total included $3.7 billion over 10 years from revising countercyclical payments to be more responsive to actual market conditions. The proposals also tightened payment limits, including preventing any payments to farmers earning more than $200,000 per year.

Some of the reactions to the proposals were predictable. For instance, the American Farm Bureau had "serious concerns" about the commodity payment cutoff, which they estimated would affect 75,000 farmers, or more than 10 percent of those receiving payments under FSRIA. Conversely, critics of current farm policies, such as the Environmental Working Group, described the proposals as the most reform-minded in decades.[81]

Food, Conservation, and Energy Act of 2008

Unfortunately, the Agriculture Committees were not re-form-minded, or at least not in the same way as the Administration. Consequently, it was like we were playing a real-life version of the arcade game Whack-a-Mole. The Committees would grant some of our reforms, such as on payment limits, but often replace them with a new provision or program, which in many cases was worse than what it replaced.

For over a year, my staff and I expended enormous amounts of time and energy in a valiant but ultimately unsuccessful effort to get a signable bill for the President. Activities included analyzing numerous bills, costing out key provisions, developing charts for meetings with the President, drafting Statements of Administration Policy, developing Administration counterproposals, identifying acceptable offsets, and preparing a book for White House use on flaws in the enrolled bill.

Congress was supposed to enact a new farm bill by the end of FY 2007 in September. As the Agriculture Committees had too many priorities to fill, it took them until spring of 2008 before they found enough gimmicks to pay for the bill. In the meantime, they had to temporarily extend the 2002 Farm Bill a few times.

The official CBO score upon enactment showed a five-year cost of $5 billion and a ten-year cost of only $600 million. However, that score masked the fact that the bill included almost $10 billion in tax changes, mostly gimmicks, that were outside the jurisdiction of the Agriculture Committees.[82] In particular, the bill exploited a quirk in the baseline for customs fees which, unlike other revenue provisions, are not assumed to continue beyond ten years. As the ten-year PAYGO scoring window shifts a year later for each new fiscal year, this means that the baseline only includes nine years of customs fees. Consequently, by extending the fees for a year, Congress gets credited with several billion in new revenue, even though there was no real change in the law.

The scoring of the bill also took other phony savings using timing changes in payments. In fact, the biggest revenue raising provision involved requiring corporations to prepay their estimated tax payments but did not change their overall tax liability. In addition, the bill was given credit for $2.8 billion in savings through changes in the timing of crop insurance receipts and payments, which had no effect on overall subsidies. This was far more than the $1.1 billion in actual crop insurance savings included in the bill from cutting insurer reimbursements and charging farmers higher premiums as the Administration had proposed.[83]

The final gimmick was using the baseline for FY 2007 instead of FY 2008, which would have raised the Farm Bill score by an additional $4 billion.[84] This was justified on the basis that the House and Senate bill were marked up using the FY 2007 baseline, before the eight-month delay in finishing the bill. While that is true, Congress routinely uses an updated baseline whenever it results in lower costs and, thereby, allows more goodies to be stuffed into a bill.

The scoring gimmicks weren't the only problems with the bill. My biggest concern was a new program for row crops known as Average Crop Revenue Election (ACRE), which provided a new option for farmers. Farmers who signed up for ACRE had to give up 20 percent of their direct payments and their loan rates for marketing loans were cut by 30 percent. In exchange, they received a 90 percent revenue guarantee based on the previous two years' experience.

The Magazine Pro Farmer described the new program as "lucrative beyond expectations" and a "no brainer" for farmers to sign up. USDA estimated that subsidy payments to corn farmers alone could be $10 billion in a year under a realistic price scenario.[85] An Iowa State University analysis that summer could only find one set of circumstances — a continuation of the high commodity prices at the time — where the normal subsidy programs would provide higher payments than ACRE[86].

My performance appraisal for the year stated that I played Paul Revere in trying to alert the public about the enormous potential costs of the ACRE program. While I didn't go to the public myself, I badgered the OMB press office until they got the attention of a Washington Post reporter, who was similarly appalled once we had the chance to explain the issue to him. Unfortunately, his article didn't appear until May 21, 2008, the day President Bush vetoed the bill, with the House overriding the veto the same day before the ink on the Post article was barely dry.

Getting a Republican President to veto a Farm bill that is important to a key Republican constituency is difficult, but President Bush stood tall. The veto message (Figure 6-4) hit all the key problems that my staff and I had been raising. The summary line in the message was:

> "At a time of high food prices and record farm income, this bill lacks program reform and fiscal discipline. It continues subsidies for the wealthy and increases farm bill spending by more than $20 billion, while using budget gimmicks to hide much of the increase."

After Congress overrode the President's veto, it was discovered that the bill that passed the Senate was different from the bill that passed the House. This made the enrolled bill sent to the White House invalid. Consequently, Congress had to pass the bill again and President Bush vetoed it for a second time. In their offices, the Agriculture Branch still proudly displays a framed copy of the two veto messages with a handwritten note from the President thanking them for a good job. Congress overrode the second veto the same day, June 18, 2008, and the Food, Conservation, and Energy Act (FECA) of 2008 became law.

Despite the sting of the veto override, FECA included a requirement for renegotiation of the Standard Reinsurance Agreement (SRA). Although called a renegotiation, USDA can essentially impose the terms if necessary, leaving the insurers with the choice of whether to remain in the business. Having learned from our mistakes in the last renegotiation, this time we were able to get USDA to drive a harder bargain resulting in $6 billion in savings. Most importantly, we got the savings incorporated in the budget baseline. Although CBO's estimate was well below ours, it was enough to prevent the Agriculture Committees from being able to

Figure 6-4 Farm Bill Veto Message

For Immediate Release
Office of the Press Secretary
May 21, 2008

Farm Bill Veto Message

TO THE HOUSE OF REPRESENTATIVES:

I am returning herewith without my approval H.R. 2419, the "Food, Conservation, and Energy Act of 2008."

White House News

For a year and a half, I have consistently asked that the Congress pass a good farm bill that I can sign. Regrettably, the Congress has failed to do so. At a time of high food prices and record farm income, this bill lacks program reform and fiscal discipline. It continues subsidies for the wealthy and increases farm bill spending by more than $20 billion, while using budget gimmicks to hide much of the increase. It is inconsistent with our objectives in international trade negotiations, which include securing greater market access for American farmers and ranchers. It would needlessly expand the size and scope of government. Americans sent us to Washington to achieve results and be good stewards of their hard-earned taxpayer dollars. This bill violates that fundamental commitment.

In January 2007, my Administration put forward a fiscally responsible farm bill proposal that would improve the safety net for farmers and move current programs toward more market-oriented policies. The bill before me today fails to achieve these important goals.

At a time when net farm income is projected to increase by more than $28 billion in 1 year, the American taxpayer should not be forced to subsidize that group of farmers who have adjusted gross incomes of up to $1.5 million. When commodity prices are at record highs, it is irresponsible to increase government subsidy rates for 15 crops, subsidize additional crops, and provide payments that further distort markets. Instead of better targeting farm programs, this bill eliminates the existing payment limit on marketing loan subsidies.

Now is also not the time to create a new uncapped revenue guarantee that could cost billions of dollars more than advertised. This is on top of a farm bill that is anticipated to cost more than $600 billion over 10 years. In addition, this bill would force many businesses to prepay their taxes in order to finance the additional spending.

This legislation is also filled with earmarks and other ill-considered provisions. Most notably, H.R. 2419 provides: $175 million to address water issues for desert lakes; $250 million for a 400,000-acre land purchase from a private owner; funding and authority for the noncompetitive sale of National Forest land to a ski resort; and $382 million earmarked for a specific watershed. These earmarks, and the expansion of Davis-Bacon Act prevailing wage requirements, have no place in the farm bill. Rural and urban Americans alike are frustrated with excessive government spending and the funneling of taxpayer funds for pet projects. This bill will only add to that frustration.

The bill also contains a wide range of other objectionable provisions, including one that restricts our ability to redirect food aid dollars for emergency use at a time of great need globally. The bill does not include the requested authority to buy food in the developing world to save lives. Additionally, provisions in the bill raise serious constitutional concerns. For all the reasons outlined above, I must veto H.R. 2419, and I urge the Congress to extend current law for a year or more.

I veto this bill fully aware that it is rare for a stand-alone farm bill not to receive the President's signature, but my action today is not without precedent. In 1956, President Eisenhower stood firmly on principle, citing high crop subsidies and too much government control of farm programs among the reasons for his veto. President Eisenhower wrote in his veto message, "Bad as some provisions of this bill are, I would have signed it if in total it could be interpreted as sound and good for farmers and the nation." For similar reasons, I am vetoing the bill before me today.

GEORGE W. BUSH

THE WHITE HOUSE,

May 21, 2008.

block the needed $4 billion in PAYGO offsets. Score one for the taxpayer.

Subsequent Farm Bills

FCEA was my last farm bill before I moved to the International Affairs Division, consequently I am not as familiar with the two subsequent farm bills in 2014 and 2018. While the 2018 bill appears to be largely a continuation of the 2014 bill, the Agricultural Act of 2014 was a major departure from previous farm bills in that it repealed direct payments, countercyclical payments, and the ACRE programs. In the end, the taxpayers dodged a bullet with the ACRE program because commodity prices stayed high throughout the life of FECA before it got repealed.

I would be tempted to cheer the demise of those programs except that Congress replaced them with two new programs — Price Loss Coverage (PLC) and Agriculture Risk Coverage (ARC) — and gave producers the option to choose between the two. Under PLC, row crop farmers essentially receive a payment amounting to 85 percent of the difference between a newly established reference price and the market price for the year. Under ARC, when revenue drops below 86 percent of recent levels the payment is essentially 85 percent of the revenue drop below that level.

While I haven't researched this new scheme in detail, my previous experience is that the Agriculture Committees only make changes when it benefits the farmers based on the market conditions at the time of Farm bill enactment. The only time that the Agriculture Committees even gives lip service to the general taxpayer is when they are forced to provide reductions as part of a government-wide reconciliation bill to reduce the deficit.

In this case, the fact that the reference prices used for PLC appear to be at least 30 percent higher than the target prices used for countercyclical payments is a giant red flag. I suspect that the program would have been hugely expensive for the taxpayer if commodity prices had dropped during the reauthorization period. Fortunately, I think they generally stayed high.

Whether these programs are needed at all is questionable given the widespread use and availability of heavily subsidized revenue crop insurance. With buy-up coverage, farmers can manage their own risk without these extra programs. Ideally, even the subsidies ought to be phased out over time as the cost of buy-up coverage gets internalized in farm operating costs the same way that unsubsidized insurance is a cost of doing business in other sectors of the economy.

The farm community and its political representatives, however, will always have small, inefficient farmers working marginally productive land to point to for why farm subsidies are needed. Leaving aside the issue of whether inefficient farms ought to be saved, they certainly can be maintained at a much lower cost through better targeted assistance than under current programs. Unfortunately, during Farm bill consideration, these small farms serve as the poster child for enacting excessively costly subsidy programs that funnel most of the largess to the big, wealthy farmers who don't need the assistance.

CHAPTER SEVEN: Defending the Treasury — *Cobell Indian Trust Lawsuit & Other Raids*

I was once told that my first OMB DAD, Don Crabill, viewed himself as akin to a marine on a 19th century sailing vessel whose job was to repel pirates attempting to board, although in his case, the threat was from various constituencies trying to fleece the Treasury. At the time, I had trouble relating to that role as the mega dollar issues for EPA mostly related to expensive regulations imposing high costs on the private sector. However, within a short time of taking Don's old job as DAD for Natural Resources in 2001, I fully understood where he was coming from.

Consequently, this chapter is about how OMB protects against raids on the Treasury beyond our role in the annual budget process. First, I will discuss a lawsuit that plaintiffs hoped would result in a settlement in excess of $100 billion. Second, I will discuss how USDA can use the Commodity Credit Corporation (CCC) as a piggybank to provide aid to the farm community. Finally, I will discuss how OMB helped develop and implement a creative way to eliminate costly distortions in the use of Federal credit programs.

Cobell Indian Trust Lawsuit

The Cobell lawsuit was set in motion over 100 years earlier with the passage of the General Allotment Act of 1887 (more generally known as the Dawes Act). The Dawes Act was a well-meaning, if misguided and ultimately unsuccessful attempt to assimilate American Indians into 19th century non-Indian society. It divided and assigned to Indian heads of households individually owned parcels, normally either 80 or 160 acres in size, which were previously communally held by Tribes. Under the Act, the Secretary of the Interior held the lands in trust for 25 years (i.e. roughly until 1912), after which individual Indians were free to sell or use their lands as they saw fit.

After the initial allotment, individual Indians owned 138 million acres compared to only 10 million acres today, with Tribes currently owning an additional 45 million acres.[87] The number of acres owned by individual Indians had already dropped to 17 million acres by 1934[88] when Congress passed the Indian Reorganization Act which permanently reimposed DOI's trust responsibilities for individual Indian allotments.

In its role as trustee, DOI can lease allotted lands to oil, timber, mineral and other companies on behalf of the allotment holders. Revenues received from these leases are distributed to allotment holders through Individual Indian Money (IIM) accounts. Unfortunately, the number of allotment holders and IIM accounts has exploded over the years.

The reason for this explosion in accounts is that when an allotment holder dies, probate proceedings generally divide the property equally among eligible heirs. Although a will can specify otherwise, wills are not typically used by Indians. This process, known as fractionation, can easily result in a 160-acre parcel, allotted in 1887, having more than 100 owners today. Such unwieldy ownership makes it extremely difficult to effectively use those lands. Furthermore, fractionation gets exponentially worse the longer the problem is not addressed.

As the number of accounts and criticism of the process ballooned, Congress enacted the American Indian Trust Fund Management Reform Act (Reform Act) of 1994 which required the Secretary to account for:

> "the daily and annual balance of all funds held in trust by the United States for the benefit of an Indian tribe or an individual Indian which are deposited or invested pursuant to the Act of June 24, 1938 (25 U.S.C. 162a)."

The Act also created the Office of Special Trustee for American Indians as a Senate confirmed position within DOI, which was initially filled by a banker named Paul Homan.

Unfortunately, land fractionation probably played a role in creating the impression in Indian country that tens of billions of dollars had gone missing. With $500 million a year being collected from use of Indian lands, Indians with small shares of an allotment that doesn't produce much income wondered what happened to their share.

Unfortunately for them, a disproportionate amount goes to a small number of original owner descendants who receive six or seven figure sums yearly. This is because their land is valuable to lease for oil wells in Oklahoma, resorts in Palm Springs, or rights of way for roads in Scottsdale.[89] Compounding matters, many checks for small allotments have never been paid because the Government can no longer find the heirs, furthering the impression of mismanagement.

Frustration with DOI culminated in June 1996 with the filing of the lawsuit Cobell v. Babbitt by Elouise Cobell and four other named plaintiffs on behalf of more than 300,000 individual Indians, although it wasn't formally a class action suit. The defendants were the Secretaries of the Interior and Treasury as well as the Assistant Secretary of Indian Affairs. The plaintiffs charged that the defendants:

> "...individually and in combination and conspiracy with employees of the Department of the Interior, have willfully and purposely obstructed and harassed efforts of the Special Trustee to carry out the mandate under the 1994 Act."

The plaintiffs went on to ask the court:

> "For a decree ordering an accounting and directing the defendants to make whole the IIM accounts of the class members.[90]".

Technically, the case was about requiring a complete accounting, not about money damages, which would have had to have been brought in the U.S. Court of Federal Claims. Nevertheless, the bottom-line objective was to produce a huge money settlement for the plaintiffs, with the battle being fought in the press and Congress in addition to the courts.

Plaintiff Winning Streak

Plaintiffs caught a break when Judge Royce Lamberth was assigned to the case, as he was very sympathetic to the Indians cause. In fact, my impression was that he seemed like he was on a mission from God to right centuries of wrongs to Indians by pressuring the Government to give the Indians a massive financial settlement to resolve this case.

Initially, the plaintiffs were on a winning streak. In February 1999, Judge Lamberth issued a judicial order castigating the Government's for its handling of the case. More specifically, it found Interior Secretary Bruce Babbitt, Treasury Secretary Robert Rubin, and Assistant Interior Secretary for Indian Affairs Kevin Gover in civil contempt for failure to produce and protect records.[91]

This was followed by a December 1999 ruling on Phase One of the trial on reform of the system where Judge Lamberth found for the plaintiffs on five specific breaches of the Government's trust obligations to the Indians. Lamberth ordered Interior to provide an historical accounting of all trust funds and appointed both a special master, to oversee preservation and production of documents, and a court monitor, to provide periodic reports on Interior's execution of trust reform. When DOJ appealed this ruling, the D.C. Court of Appeals unanimously upheld Judge Lamberth's ruling in a February 2001 opinion.[92]

Following on these victories, plaintiff's attorneys pursued what I would call a "scorched earth strategy" in the courts as a way of putting heavy pressure on Interior, Treasury and Justice to agree to a huge settlement. For instance, at the request of plaintiffs, in December 2001 Judge Lamberth shut down significant portions of DOI's website, including the Bureau of Indian Affairs, and prohibited DOI employees from using the internet.

Ostensibly this step was taken to prevent trust data from being manipulated by people outside the Department. Given that most of the required accounting involved accessing 100 years of paper records before DOI started automating IIM data, this action seemed to have little real purpose. It wasn't until July 2006 that the Appeals Court restored the internet connection for most of DOI[93] and until May 2008 when the key DOI offices working on Indian trust issues were reconnected.

The plaintiffs scored another victory in September 2002 when Judge Lamberth found Interior Secretary Gale Norton and Assistant Secretary for Indian Affairs Neal McCaleb in contempt, for failing to carry out his 1999 ruling, based on reports from Joseph Kieffer, the court monitor that Judge Lamberth had appointed.

Plaintiff's attorneys also attempted to intimidate career Department of Justice (DOJ) and DOI lawyers, as well as other DOI officials, through filings with Judge Lamberth requesting "personal sanctions" for alleged serious misconduct.[94] While no such sanctions were ever imposed, several lawyers requested to be removed from the case due to the harassment. Given the positions that OMB was taking in relation to the suit, I thought there was sufficient risk that plaintiff's attorneys might propose similar sanctions on OMB employees. Consequently, for the first time in my career, I decided to get professional liability insurance in case I needed an attorney to represent me in a court case.

The plaintiffs final victory came in a September 2003 ruling, following Judge Lamberth's Phase Two trial that began in May 2003. The structural injunction issued by Judge Lamberth required a three-year accounting effort to provide a complete history of all financial and ownership transactions in the trust since 1887. This included accounting for deceased IIM account holders, closed IIM accounts, and even direct pay rents sent directly to Indians and never held in trust.

While Judge Lamberth had no authority to award money damages to the plaintiffs, he did the next best thing. He required an impossible accounting, unlike any accounting previously undertaken anywhere in the world, in an unreasonable time frame. While never stated, the clear intent of his ruling seemed to be to force the Government to settle with plaintiffs or be subject to more expansive contempt and personal sanction rulings. DOI estimated that the accounting would cost between $6 and $13 billion.[95] Unfortunately for the plaintiffs, by the time of this ruling their strategy was already beginning to unravel.

Historical Accounting and OMB's Strategy

Despite the contempt citations, DOI had been slowly working on the monumental task of finding and organizing the over 100 years of Indian Trust records within the resource levels made available by Congress. Even as records were being pulled together and digitized, the question remained as to how to perform the accounting. Late in the Clinton Administration, Secretary Babbitt decided to use a statistical sampling technique.

While Secretary Norton initially endorsed that approach when she took office, she quickly changed her mind and established the Office of Historical Trust Accounting (OHTA) in the spring of 2001. Over the next year, that Office developed a plan for an accounting without statistical sampling. Unfortunately, that plan would cost at least $2.4 billion, take 10 years and might not produce a usable result.[96]

At this point, I had been DAD for Natural Resources for a year and my Interior branch staff and I were beginning to seriously engage on this issue due to the large accounting costs, even before any potential settlement. From our perspective, $2.4 billion for accounting was a poor use of resources that would provide little additional information beyond what a statistical sampling plan could provide.

Faced with the budget realities of trying to finance that proposal, however, Interior was forced to go back to using statistical sampling in the Historical Accounting Plan they submitted to Judge Lamberth in January 2003. Under that plan, DOI would verify all transactions over $5,000 through a document review and verify a sample of transactions under $5,000. Unlike the structural injunction that Lamberth would issue later in the year, the plan would not cover deceased Individual Indian Money (IIM) trust system account holders, closed IIM accounts, or direct payments to Indians never held in trust. The plan was estimated to cost $335 million over 5 years and we included $130 million in the FY 2004 Budget to implement the plan.[97]

Earlier in January 2003, the plaintiffs gave Judge Lamberth a detailed filing claiming that they had been cheated out of $137 billion over the past 115 years. The filing was based on private historical records.[98] This contrasts with the testimony of Jim Cason, DOI Associate Deputy Secretary, later in the year that only $13 billion in IIM funds had flowed through the trust since 1887, the majority of which moved through a small number of accounts. Of the $13 billion total, $3.3 billion had occurred in the electronic record era between 1985 and 2000. By the time of Cason's testimony in October, the plaintiffs had upped the amount they believed they were owed to $176 billion.[99]

Although the D.C. Court of Appeals had backed up Lamberth in his initial 1999 ruling, July 2003 marked the beginning of a long losing streak for the Judge. First, the Appeals Court threw out the contempt charges against Norton and McCaleb. This was followed by a stay of Judge Lamberth structural injunction in November.

The stay was somewhat superfluous due to an appropriations rider enacted earlier in the month that prevented funding from being used to implement the structural injunction until December 31, 2004. The stated reason for the rider was to give Congress time to clarify the accounting obligations under the Reform Act and avoid diverting, in order to pay for the accounting, other Bureau of Indian Affairs (BIA) funds that would be "devastating to Indian county".[100] OMB had strongly supported the rider as a way to head off proposals within the Administration for mandatory spending to implement the structural injunction.

With the structural injunction on hold and the prospects for legislation appearing dim, the plaintiffs and the Government agreed to the selection of two mediators in April 2004 to try to negotiate a resolution. However, OMB and DOI were far apart on an Administration negotiating strategy. Consequently, a high-level meeting was held between DOI, OMB and others in the White House. OMB was represented by our Deputy Director Joel Kaplan.

The fact that the publicly stated high end cost estimate of carrying out the structural injunction was $13 billion, aside from making plaintiffs whole for any errors uncovered, provided one option for settling the case. I don't blame Interior for taking that view, since they were being vilified unmercifully in the press as well as being harassed by plaintiff's frivolous motions for contempt and sanctions. Unfortunately, a $13 billion settlement would have been a terrible deal for the taxpayer.

Along with my Interior Branch Chief, Janet Irwin, and her BIA examiners, we had been getting periodic briefings on the OHTA's progress on the accounting. While OHTA wasn't at the point of providing good data, in court filings they were reporting a high percentage of needed documents and weren't discovering major errors. In fact, in response to an earlier appropriations provision requiring a report to Congress, the previous spring OHTA had finished an accounting for the named Cobell plaintiffs. While it cost $20 million to conduct, they had only found a single error of $61.[101] Needless to say, this result cast significant doubt on the claims being made by the plaintiffs and their lawyers.

There were two arguments for not settling quickly. First, as more data became available over time, the magnitude of the real problem decreased. Consequently, a strategy of letting the accounting continue would likely lower the ultimate settlement cost. Second, there were good reasons to hope that the D.C. Appeals Court would continue ruling against Judge Lamberth and eventually clarify the accounting requirements resulting in a lower cost to finish the job.

Of course, the OMB strategy was the exact opposite of the plaintiff's strategy. Although technically the plaintiffs filed the suit to get a complete accounting, they didn't really want an accounting. They wanted to make the process so costly and onerous that the Government would quickly agree to a huge settlement without doing an accounting.

It seemed unlikely that the plaintiffs wouldn't accept $13 billion anyway, because Louise Cobell had whipped up such high expectations in Indian country that accepting a mere $13 billion would have appeared to be a sell-out. Unfortunately, even mentioning such a high figure would in practice set an undesirably high floor for any future negotiations. In any event, in October 2004 the mediators declared settlement efforts to be hopeless and resigned.

The plaintiffs used the $176 billion claim figure to shock the public about the magnitude of Federal Government mismanagement and the press uncritically accepted the figure. However, the disconnect between that figure and the accounting data showing that only $13 billion ever flowed through the trust should have been a red flag for the press about the absurdity of the plaintiff's loss claim.

Plaintiff's estimate seemed to be relying on some, perhaps far-fetched, principle of private trust law that if the trustee couldn't verify payment of the full trust, it had to be assumed that none of the trust had ever been paid. The total then got inflated under the assumption that all the funds simply sat in the trust and collected interest. Such an interpretation would be consistent with the plaintiff's desire for Judge Lamberth to require an unreasonably extensive accounting that all sides would agree was impossible to implement, thereby triggering an absurdly large payout. Of course, this case was not being governed by private trust law, with a major difference being that the general taxpayer was paying for the trust services, not the Indian beneficiaries.

On December 8, 2004, the Interior FY 2005 appropriations bill was enacted. While it did not extend the rider blocking Lamberth's structural injunction, it did cap funding for historical accounting at $58 million in FY 2005, an amount that we increased to $95 million in the FY 2006 President's Budget issued two months later. Even more devastating for the plaintiffs, on December 10, 2004, the D.C. Court of Appeals struck down most of the structural injunction and ruled that DOI could use statistical sampling. Undaunted, in February 2005 Judge Lamberth noted that the appropriations rider had expired and issued a new structural injunction which again required an accounting back to 1887 and prohibited statistical sampling[102].

In March 2005, Senator John McCain, Chairman of the Senate Committee on Indian Affairs, pledged to address trust reform but indicated that he would give it "only one good shot". In response, a national tribal task force, which included the Cobell plaintiffs, developed a set of principles to guide trust reform and proposed a settlement amount of $27.5 billion. Senators McCain and Byron Dorgan used these principals to draft a proposed bill[103], although without specifying a settlement amount in the bill.

On behalf of the Administration, Jim Cason testified on the issue before McCain's Committee in July 2005 and lambasted the tribal proposal. In particular, he pointed out that the $27.5 billion payment only relieved the Government of conducting an historical accounting but would still allow individuals to pursue mismanagement claims with no accounting basis to determine the amount of mismanagement.

Cason also reported on the accounting to date. Of 22,000 IIM accounts fully reconciled, there were only 21 instances of underpayments totaling $52. An accounting for the large IIM transactions in the electronic era (1985-2000), discovered underpayments of only $47 thousand.[104] Based on the available accounting at the time and insights from a spreadsheet I developed, the estimated cost of DOI mismanagement appeared to be no more than $100 million, not billions.

Judge Lamberth's frustration over the case showed in a July 2005 opinion in which he ordered DOI to admit to the trustees that its accounting may be inaccurate and labeled the department a "dinosaur". He went on to call DOI "the morally and culturally oblivious hand-me-down of a disgracefully racist and imperialist government that should have been buried a century ago".[105] A month later, the Justice Department seized the opportunity to request an appeals court hearing to remove Judge Lamberth from the case.

Before addressing that issue, the D.C. Appeals Court in November 2005 put the final nail in the coffin of Judge Lamberth's structural injunction by vacating Lamberth's February 2005 ruling[106]. Finally, in July 2006, the D.C. Appeals Court ordered the removal of Judge Lamberth from the case, due to his lack of objectivity, and ordered that the case be reassigned to provide an opportunity for a fresh start[107].

<u>Working Towards Resolution</u>

In July 2006, Senator McCain also revised his settlement bill, S.1439, and this time included a proposed settlement amount of $8 billion. In response, OMB worked with DOJ,

DOI, and the White House on a legislative proposal to settle not only the Cobell case, but a panoply of other potential litigation on individual Indian and tribal claims, including the fractionation problem.

OMB considered fractionation to be an important issue that needed to be addressed. In fact, the FY 2005 President's Budget released in February 2004 included an unprecedented $75 million request to finance land consolidation of highly fractionated Indian land allotments.

Probate legislation was pending when including land consolidation as part of any settlement was first proposed. Ultimately the American Indian Probate Reform Act (AIPRA) would be enacted in October 2004. While that Act was not intended to either stop all fractionation or pay for land consolidation to address past fractionation, we knew it would have a significant impact on the rate of growth in fractionation. By 2006, the expected slowing of fractionation due to the AIPRA made including funding for land consolidation in any future settlement more appropriate than when it was first considered.

The staff of the Senate Indian Affairs Committee (SIAC) convened several meetings with the Administration that summer to discuss the contours of settlement legislation. While I attended those meetings, OMB's delegation was led by our new General Counsel Jeff Rosen. Jeff was a super sharp, very conservative, and straight-shooting individual. Those qualities were quite evident in January 2021 when, as Acting Attorney General, he faced down President Trump's effort to overturn the 2020 Presidential election results.

While I don't believe the Administration ever put a settlement figure on the table, the meetings were cordial and productive. The SIAC staff were clearly trying to mediate a resolution but were constrained by the demands of their constituents in Indian country. By October 2006, the effort had fallen apart when the plaintiffs rejected SIAC's proposals.[108]

In December 2006, Judge James Robertson was assigned to the case to replace Lamberth. In January 2008, Judge Robertson rejected DOI's historical accounting plan, ruling that it was impossible to "achieve an accounting that passes muster as a trust accounting" because Congress wasn't providing sufficient funding. Consequently, he ordered a bench trial to determine an appropriate remedy.[109]

For the bench trial, both the plaintiffs and the Government were allowed to propose a methodology for determining restitution. My staff and I worked with DOI to help refine their methodology and improve the DOJ filing in the case. The plaintiffs claimed a shortfall of $4 billion, which they alleged resulted in a $43 billion benefit to the government, for a total claim of almost $48 billion.

Judge Robertson rejected the plaintiff's model as defective and was critical of plaintiff's failure to try to discredit the Government's model. Instead, he selected the "maximally conservative"[110] estimate from the government model and awarded the plaintiffs $456 million in restitution. Needless to say, the ruling was devastating to the plaintiffs.

In July 2009, the D.C. Court of Appeals overturned the restitution award, but the damage had already been done to the plaintiffs. Furthermore, the Court didn't directly overturn the award but vacated Judge Robertson's "impossibility" finding that led to the bench trial and remanded the case to the District Court. Basically, they concluded that Judge Robertson should have given deference to DOI's accounting methodology to do the best accounting possible with the resources Congress made available.[111]

Given that ruling and the change in Administrations, settlement negotiations started anew. My staff and I were not heavily involved other than to try to make sure the settlement was as airtight as possible and covered as many potential claims as possible. The $3.4 billion settlement was announced in December 2009, fulfilling an Obama campaign pledge to resolve the issue.

Of that total, however, only $1.4 billion went to the Cobell plaintiffs for compensation of errors in the historical accounting. Ironically, they might have gotten a bigger settlement if Senator McCain had been elected, since his earlier legislation included $8 billion in restitution. The remaining $2 billion in the settlement was earmarked for land consolidation to address the fractionation problem.[112]

In December 2010, after I had moved to the International Affairs Division, the Claims Resolution Act of 2010 was signed into law essentially codifying the settlement. While Native Americans have been egregiously wronged multiple times by the U.S. and prior western European governments over the centuries, the work of OHTA would seem to indicate that accounting of the IIM trust accounts was not one of those wrongs. Although the $1.4 billion settlement for accounting — three times the Robertson award — was probably significantly higher than the actual losses, I viewed this as a good settlement and a win for the taxpayer.

USDA Discretionary Piggybanks

One of my biggest surprises when I became DAD for Natural Resources is that there was effectively a third type of spending in addition to discretionary and mandatory spending, which I termed "discretionary, mandatory spending". Technically, it was mandatory spending under various USDA statutes, but was available at the discretion of the Secretary of Agriculture subject to certain limitations.

The only check on this spending was that USDA needed OMB (i.e. the DAD for Natural Resources) to sign the apportionment which, if approved, in essence could create new spending, almost out of thin air. While the DAD had to sign the apportionment, these were essentially policy and/or political decisions made by OMB leadership, or in some cases the White House, depending on the size of the request and political sensitivity of the proposal.

USDA has this authority under at least three statutes — 1) Section 416(b) of the Agricultural Act of 1949; 2) Section 32 of the Agricultural Adjustment Act Amendment of 1935; and 3) Section 5 of the Commodity Credit Corporation (CCC) Charter Act of 1948. The only similar Federal authorities of which I am aware, are for Medicaid demonstration projects. While those are theoretically supposed to be budget neutral, my impression is that is not always the case.

Section 416(b) Food Aid

Section 416(b) authorized the donation of CCC-owned commodities in excess of domestic program requirements to carry out food assistance programs in developing and friendly countries.[113] While at one time CCC took physical ownership of significant amounts of excess commodities, that was not the case around the year 2000. Instead, the lawyers at USDA had made a legal interpretation that low prices meant commodities were in surplus and, therefore, CCC funding could be used to purchase domestic commodities for distribution in the developing world.

While providing food aid to impoverished countries is an important objective, access to this "free money" had caused the program to explode from virtual non-existence in 1997 to $1.2 billion in FY 2001. This rapid growth resulted in poorly targeted funding that ruined markets for locally grown food and allowed other nations to reduce their food aid efforts. Furthermore, even with the USDA legal interpretation, the use of 416(b) was unpredictable because if might have to be shut down quickly if crop prices rose.

In response, my CCC examiner, Daniel Heath, suggested reforming this program as part of the Bush Administration's Management Agenda in 2002. Working with USDA, the State Department, and the National Security Council (NSC), Daniel developed an alternative approach to replace this food aid. OMB leadership approved his solution of an almost 40 percent increase in the requested food aid appropriation, combined with potential use of a commodity reserve for food aid crises. Consequently, the inappropriate and out of control use of Section 416(b) funding was shut down, and the project became the first item on the President's Management Agenda to be completed.

Section 32 Emergency Surplus Removals

Section 32 is funded by a permanent appropriation set at 30 percent of customs receipts with the bulk of the funding earmarked for child nutrition funding. The remainder, which amounts to several hundred million dollars, can be used to help the farm sector through commodity purchases, direct payments, and other efforts. In most years this funding is used for emergency surplus removals, which raise prices by limiting supply for normal market purchases, to provide "bonuses" to domestic food assistance organizations. These removals are limited to commodities such as meats, fruits and vegetables that aren't eligible for the suite of programs available to row crops.[114]

USDA also had the ability to use clause 3 of Section 32 to make farm disaster payments, a practice they used often during my tenure as NRD DAD for disasters of limited scope. For instance, these were used to compensate farmers for fruit tree losses due to hurricanes and livestock losses due to drought. The Agriculture Branch staff reviewed USDA proposals for both emergency surplus removals and particularly the disaster assistance payments, with a skeptical eye as to whether they were really needed or were just taking advantage of available money.

I signed the apportionments for the bulk of the Section 32 requests, although sometimes with limitations or strings attached to our approval. There were even instances where we worked with USDA on disaster assistance, such as in 2002, when we helped develop a workable drought assistance program for ranchers as a means of heading off a multi-billion-dollar ad-hoc disaster bill. Eventually, however, Congress got annoyed with USDA's use of Section 32 for disaster aid instead of bonus purchases. Consequently, starting from FY 2012 through FY 2017, they included appropriation riders that prohibited the use of salary appropriations to develop discretionary disaster assistance proposals under either Section 32 or CCC Section 5[115], effectively shutting down such assistance.

CCC Section 5 Assistance

The biggest farm piggy bank of all, however, is the Commodity Credit Corporation (CCC), which has permanent indefinite borrowing authority of $30 billion from the U.S. Treasury. CCC authority is used to finance most of the traditional Farm bill mandatory programs, including the commodity support programs, conservation programs, disaster assistance and even agricultural research programs. CCC is automatically replenished annually through an appropriation that equals the prior year level of net realized loss (i.e. the amount CCC spent the previous year).

The purpose of CCC is to stabilize, support and protect farm income, and Section 5 gives the Secretary of USDA very broad discretionary powers to accomplish those objectives. Furthermore, the $30 billion in borrowing authority, which allows USDA to take quick action, is sufficiently high that a huge amount of mandatory funding is usually available for "discretionary" use even after financing the Farm bill mandatory programs. Not only is CCC funding much larger than available under Section 32, but it is available for a broader range of crops and purposes including responses to natural disasters, adverse economic conditions, and USDA priorities.[116]

Among the CCC uses we tried to get control of when I first became DAD for Natural Resources, was funding used for eradication of pests and diseases. Unfortunately, the availability of CCC "free money" had allowed States and the farm industry to shift eradication costs to the Federal level and had diminished their incentives to control pests and diseases.

As a firm believer that cost-sharing results in wiser use of funding, I had my Agriculture Branch staff develop cost-sharing guidelines that allowed the Federal Government to pay for immediate efforts to eradicate new pest infections but required State and industry cost sharing for longer-term efforts. This approach to the problem cut annual CCC costs for pest eradication from $375 million to approximately $50 million and instituted a philosophy of shared responsibility with States and industry.

Administrative PAYGO

Early in 2005, Keith Fontenot, Chief of the Health Financing Branch, came to my office looking for support for an Administrative PAYGO proposal he had developed. Up until this point, the concept of pay-as-you-go only applied to legislative action taken by the Congress in making changes to taxes or mandatory spending. Those PAYGO provisions, which had come out of the 1990 Reconciliation bill, were one of the most important drivers for eliminating annual deficits in the late 1990s.

It took Keith all of 30 seconds to get my support for the proposal because it would provide a useful tool in our jousting with USDA over use of its various "discretionary, mandatory" authorities described above. The concept was parallel to Congressional PAYGO in that it required agencies to provide offsets if they took an administrative action that would increase mandatory spending above the baseline.

It was also an easy sell to OMB Director Josh Bolten, a friend of mine from our Princeton days, who issued a memorandum to agency heads on Administrative PAYGO in May 2005.[117] As a practical matter, few agencies other than USDA and the Centers for Medicare and Medicaid (CMS) services had many authorities to increase mandatory spending through administrative actions and even fewer could easily find offsets. For that reason, Director Bolten wanted liberal authority to waive the offset requirement at his discretion.

The Agriculture Branch loved Administrative PAYGO and even set up their own scorecard to track offsets over time. Surprisingly, USDA wasn't as upset about the new policy as I would have expected, in part because they had numerous potential offsets. These typically might involve tightening up eligibility for a particular program that had been drafted too broadly in the first place. For instance, this might allow the Department to go ahead with say a Section 32 purchase to shore up the price of oranges, while giving them a reason to fix an unintended problem in one of their commodity programs. While the Obama Administration never revoked Bolten's memorandum, the Agriculture Branch seemed to be the only ones still trying to enforce it.

CCC Raids for the Trade War and COVID-19

In fact, the Bolten memorandum stayed in effect until replaced by EO 13893 in October 2019. The new Trump EO included the same Administrative PAYGO requirements as the memo, except it was direction coming from the President rather than OMB. Nevertheless, the offset requirements were rendered meaningless by the Trump Administration's desire to provide lavish CCC assistance to farmers related to Trump's trade war with China and the COVID-19 pandemic.

In March and April 2018, the Trump Administration started applying tariffs against manufactured goods in several countries, but particularly the Chinese for alleged unfair trade practices and national security reasons. In response, China imposed retaliatory tariffs on the U.S. farm sector in a move designed to alienate an important Trump constituency. To compensate the farm community for bearing the brunt of China's retaliatory tariffs, the Trump Administration in July 2018 announced the use of $12 billion in CCC discretionary funding to provide direct financial "trade aid" to farmers.[118] Fortunately for the Trump Administration, the rider on CCC discretionary funding that might have prevented these payments was not in included in USDA's FY 2018 appropriation.

As DAD for International Affairs with trade agencies as part of my portfolio, I supported the tariffs on China for their intellectual property theft and unfair trade practices, and thought it was a savvy move to provide compensation. Nevertheless, I was stunned by the size of the payments, given that they were on top of the Agricultural Risk Coverage (ARC) and Price Loss Coverage (PLC) support programs.

While I was not directly involved, I know that the Agriculture Branch fought, and lost, a pitched battle with USDA over the level of compensation and how these payments should interact with other programs. In May 2019, a second round of $16 billion in "trade aid" payments were announced[119]. Needless to say, the Administrative PAYGO offset requirement had been waived or just ignored for these payments.

Unfortunately, the $28 billion in "trade aid" was not the end of the Trump Administration's excessive use of CCC discretionary funding as COVID-19 provided an additional opportunity. Unlike many other businesses, farming is an essential activity that continued unabated during the pandemic since, pandemic or not, people need to eat. How-

ever, the pandemic did produce adverse impacts on some
farmers, particularly those who sold to institutions, such
as restaurants and hotels, that were shut down during the
pandemic. As supply chains don't adjust instantaneously,
producers supplying those markets suffered greatly.

In response to the pandemic, Congress passed the $2.2
trillion Coronavirus Aid, Relief and Economic Security
(CARES) Act on March 27, 2020, which contained $9.5 bil-
lion in direct financial aid to farmers.[120] A month later the
Trump Administration announced a $19 billion Coronavirus
Food Assistance Program (CFAP). To use poker terminology,
the Trump Administration called the Congress's $9.5 billion
in aid and raised the stakes with an additional $9.5 billion
in discretionary CCC assistance. The additional funding was
split between $6.5 billion to top up the CARES direct assis-
tance and $3 billion went to purchase fresh produce, dairy,
and meat. The $3 billion purchase program was at least well
targeted, as it bought from distributors who would normally
sell to restaurants and hotels and distributed the products
to food banks for citizens in need.[121]

The remaining $16 billion in CFAP assistance went to
producers of commodities with a 5 percent or more price
drop, which was assumed to indicate a COVID-19 loss, even
though it could easily have been normal price fluctuations
based on always changing market conditions. Such a hair
trigger for price support is unprecedented in my experience.

Due to complaints from some commodity groups that felt
left out in CFAP-1, a second round of $14 billion in CFAP-2
CCC discretionary assistance, open to a huge range of commodities, was announced in September 2020[122] — the timing
so close to an election was presumably just a coincidence.
Not to be outdone, the Biden Administration reopened the
CFAP-2 sign-up in April 2021.[123] The justification appears to
have been that, if Trump could to it, so can we.

In the 1960's Senator Everett Dirksen was quoted as saying "A billion here, a billion there, and pretty soon you're
talking about real money." Given the $6 trillion in Trump
and Biden COVID-19 assistance and the over $5 trillion in
Biden FY 2022 Budget initiatives, the Dirksen quote needs
to be rescaled to trillions before your talking real money. In

previous eras, the almost $50 billion in CCC discretionary trade aid and COVID assistance provided between 2018 and 2021 would seem extraordinary. In the trillion-dollar era, it apparently seems trivial to policy makers and OMB staff had little ability to control it under those circumstances.

Credit Reform

My colleagues in BRD would think that I am horribly remiss if I were to write a book about OMB and not mention credit programs. The importance of credit programs becomes clear when you consider that, according to the FY 2023 President's Budget, the value of outstanding credit programs is almost $5 trillion, of which $1.9 trillion is in direct loans and $3.1 trillion is loan guarantees. As Figure 7-1 shows, the value of Federal programs has skyrocketed since the 2008 recession[124].

Federal Credit Instruments

Until the unified budget concept was adopted in the FY 1969 Budget, trust funds and credit activities weren't really captured in the budget. Even under the unified budget, the treatment of credit was a poor measure of both the budgetary and economic impact of credit. The treatment of credit from FY 1969 thru FY 1991 was to measure the cash flows of credit programs.[125]

There are two main types of credit programs — direct loans and guaranteed loans. Under a direct loan, the Federal government enters into a contract with a non-Federal borrower to provide up-front funding which the borrower must repay, usually with interest. The budget treatment of this transaction during this period was to show the cash flow for the full amount of the loan in the year it was lent, with principal and interest showing as offsetting collections in the year those were received. Note that when the U.S. is running a deficit, the U.S. is actually borrowing funds on the open market in order to have money to lend to these non-Federal borrowers.

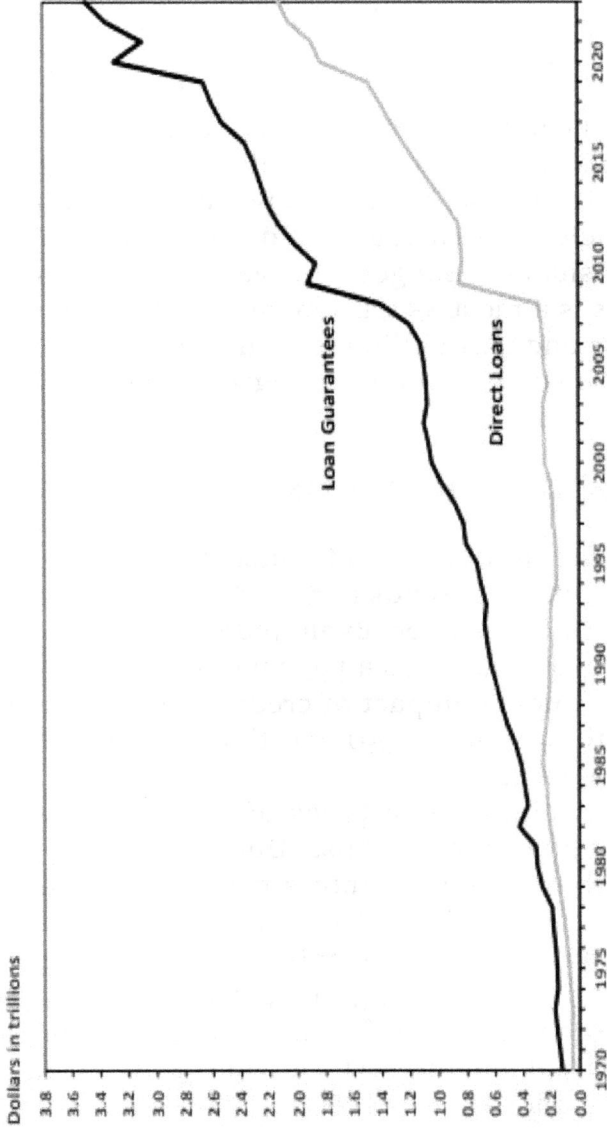

Figure 7-1: Face Value of Federal Credit Outstanding

Under a loan guarantee, a private lender makes the loan to a non-Federal borrower with the Federal government guaranteeing repayment to the lender for all or part of the loan in the event of a default. The budget treatment for a loan guarantee during this period was only to show a cash flow if there was a default and the Federal government, as guarantor, needed to reimburse the lender. Due to the timing of the cash flows under this treatment, loan guarantees tended to look cheaper than direct loans because the cash flows were "out of sight, out of mind".

<u>Enactment of Credit Reform Legislation</u>

During the 1980's, Congress began to debate whether there was a better way to handle credit in the Federal budget. Eventually a consensus evolved that the cost of loans and loan guarantees should reflect the subsidy provided to the borrower and the subsidy amount would be obligated when the loan or guarantee was originated. In essence, this treatment would move credit scoring from a cash to an accrual basis. The real debate hinged on whether to use market prices or Treasury rates in calculating the subsidy.[126]

In the end, a version of a credit reform bill was added on the Senate floor, without any Committee markup, during debate in October 1990 on a massive Omnibus Budget Reconciliation bill. The final Omnibus Reconciliation Act of 1990 was enacted two weeks later with a somewhat different version of credit reform that reflected revisions from OMB's Budget Review Division, an organization that had provided most of the intellectual underpinnings behind the reform.

The Federal Credit Reform Act (FCRA) of 1990 was a short section in Title XIII of the bill and listed four purposes:

1) Measure more accurately the cost of Federal credit programs;
2) Place the cost of credit programs on a budgetary basis equivalent to other Federal spending;
3) Encourage the delivery of benefits in the form most appropriate to the needs of beneficiaries; and
4) Improve the allocation of resources among credit pro-

grams and between credit and other spending programs.[127]

How Credit Reform Works

The key to putting loans on an equivalent budget basis
with each other and non-credit Federal spending was to cal-
culate a subsidy cost for both loans and loan guarantees.
Basically, the subsidy cost is the present value of the cash
flows, both to and from the Government, over the life of
the loan or the loan guarantee including payment defaults.
Under FCRA, the present value is calculated by discounting
(i.e. reducing) future cash flows using the interest rate on
Treasury securities of the same length as the loan or loan
guarantee. For instance, a $100 loan repayment at the end
of year one using a 5 percent discount rate would result in
a discounted cash flow at the time the loan was issued (i.e.
the present value) of roughly $95 (i.e. $100-$5).

Conceptually, the subsidy cost of a direct Federal loan
arises from discounting the stream of future repayments
and netting that amount against the cash disbursed for the
loan. In the case of a loan guarantee, the subsidy cost arises
from putting a value on potential guaranteed loan defaults
that the Federal government is contractually obligated to
cover and discounting those payments back to the present.

Under credit reform, the subsidy cost (aka subsidy BA)
for credit programs must be appropriated, meaning that the
cost of credit programs must be traded off against other discretionary spending within an appropriations subcommittee's 302(b) funding allocation. In most cases, programs
have positive subsidy meaning they have a cost and sometimes a very large cost. As DAD for International Affairs, my
division evaluated some loan guarantees of foreign nation
debt with a 30 percent subsidy level because the country's
credit rating was so poor. This meant that a $1 billion loan
guarantee required $300 million in subsidy BA, an amount
that would be justified only if the country was of major strategic importance, because it was taking funding away from
other foreign policy priorities.

It was also possible to have negative subsidy credit programs that generate a positive return to the Government, excluding administrative costs.[128] For instance, many of the Export/Import Bank loans were negative subsidy. The concept of negative subsidy is hard for many people, including myself, to grasp. As an example, negative subsidy for a loan can occur when the risk of default is low and either origination fees or the interest rate charged to borrowers is sufficiently high to produce discounted cash flows that are higher than the original amount of the loan. In addition to providing subsidy BA, the appropriators also set volume caps for credit programs to avoid agencies from issuing an unlimited level of negative subsidy credit.

The fact that negative subsidy makes money for the Federal Government was used by the Obama Administration in 2010 to pass legislation allowing the Department of Education to make direct Federal loans to students, rather than having the students get guaranteed loans from banks.[129] The use of the Federal government's virtually unlimited and risk free borrowing authority to make money and take business away from private banks is a controversial concept.

That action also reignited the debate about whether to use Treasury, rather than market rates, to discount cash flows under credit reform, with critics of the current approach arguing for a "fair value" approach that adds a risk premium to the current discount rate. Obviously, the "fair value" approach makes credit programs more expensive and would impact education programs particularly hard.

OMB's Role in Credit Reform

One of the downsides of credit reform is that the methodology is complex and difficult to understand. To explain it, OMB issued Circular A-129 concerning the budgetary treatment of credit reform and included a new section in Circular A-11 on how to reflect credit programs in the Budget.[130] FCRA also gave OMB a powerful role in coordinating the estimation of subsidy costs for the Federal Government.

This later role is particularly important in preventing game playing by the agencies, who have an incentive to minimize subsidy costs to maximize the amount of credit they can issue with any given appropriation. The key to preventing game playing is that BRD's "credit crew", an elite team of credit experts, must approve an agency's subsidy model before the agency can issue credit. Even with BRD's best efforts at oversight, GAO found that over a 14-year period, the government had underestimated the cost of credit programs by $42 billion, although that was only 1 percent of the amount of credit issued.[131]

An example of the game playing that OMB tries to prevent is the Development Finance Corporation's (DFC) attempt in 2019 to use credit scoring for purchases of equity in foreign companies. I wasn't wild about the DFC having the ability to purchase equity in the first place. The issue was not new. It had been discussed in the Obama Administration, but no proposal was ever included in the Budgets of that Administration. Although one would think that a Republican Administration would be even more opposed to equity authority, the desire to have a strong DFC to counter China swept away the philosophical concern about the U.S. purchasing private equity.

Under both OMB and CBO scoring rules, the full amount of an equity purchases is scored up-front and any gain from a later sale of equity is recorded later if, and only if, it occurred. The cost of equity purchases would have been significantly lower if the scoring rule were changed to discount the potential gain from the sale of equity and shown as a present value like under credit scoring The key difference, however, is that repayments of interest and principal for a loan are contractually required payments, although occasionally subject to default, whereas there is no such assurance or any commitment of a return on equity. In fact, as equity purchases were only supposed to be made in companies that cannot raise capital in private markets, there is a significant risk of no recoupment from an equity investment.

The attraction of credit scoring for equity is that it would dramatically increase the amount of equity that can be purchased with a given appropriation, as well as dramatically increase the potential loss to the taxpayer. Proponents of this scoring argue that venture capitalists make significant gains taking this type of risk. However, it is also true that the Federal government has always done a terrible job functioning as a venture capitalist.

Another option would have been to identify an acceptable hybrid option that did no harm to Budget accounting procedures and didn't set a bad precedent for other Federal programs. However, there was never an agreement on such an option. This left OMB's leadership in the awkward position of opposing DFC's attempt to change scoring rules since their Chairman, Alan Boehler, was supposedly Jared Kushner's college roommate. Nevertheless, not wanting to set the bad precedent, the Budget never proposed such a scoring change.

CHAPTER EIGHT: Ebola & Zika & Covid, Oh My! --
Fighting Disease Epidemics Internationally

We have already discussed the annual budget development process, which is the typical method for providing
most discretionary budget funding. However, funding is often needed to address crises that come up between budget
cycles (e.g. war and hurricane recovery needs). These funding needs can be addressed in one of two ways: 1) reprogram
existing appropriations originally provided for a different
purpose; or 2) request supplemental appropriations.

This chapter discusses how OMB leverages its control
of the budget process to shape various international health
programs and keep them focused on cost-effective achievement of program goals. Funding for these programs was
provided through a mix of sources, not only those funds requested in the Budget, but through reprogramming of existing funds, and requesting supplemental funds as well. The
chapter will also continue the discussion of the role of the
career OMB DAD.

At the end of April 2010, I moved to a new position at
OMB as DAD for the International Affairs Division (IAD).
After nine years as DAD for Natural Resources, I thought
it was time to move on, particularly as my older, and highest maintenance, daughter had left for college. Although
I had been assuming that I would leave OMB, the DAD for
IAD slot was the first interesting position to come along. I
really didn't think I had much chance, as my involvement
in foreign policy issues was limited to food aid and climate
change. Nevertheless, the PAD for National Security, Steve
Kosiak, was more interested in a good manager than a foreign policy expert and I was selected.

Making the transition was easier than I expected. When
I became DAD for the Natural Resources Division (NRD), I
had to learn how to operate at a higher level within the bureaucracy while at the same time trying to become knowledgeable about the issues faced by the Departments of the

Interior and Agriculture. For this transition, I already knew how to handle the job of a DAD and I just needed to concentrate on learning the substance of my new agencies, including the State Department, the U.S. Agency for International Development (USAID), the Treasury Department's international functions.

I am often asked which of the two DAD jobs was better — IAD or NRD. My answer is always that they have different pluses and minuses that make it impossible to choose. Certainly, the IAD job addresses more important and higher profile issues than NRD. My outside sources of information in the IAD job were the front section of the Washington Post and classified cables, whereas my information sources for natural resources issues were mostly various trade publications.

On the other hand, NRD was a bigger division with three branches, whereas I only had two branches in IAD. Furthermore, I annually had three Director's Reviews each fall in NRD, whereas I only had one in IAD. While my two IAD branches were responsible for very distinct sets of organizations and budget accounts, each staff member was also responsible for any issues that arose in a particular set of assigned countries. Thus, my Iraq examiner was responsible for attending any staff level National Security Council (NSC) or State Department meetings on Iraq but had to coordinate with examiners in both branches because funding for Iraq was included in multiple accounts. This matrix structure drove the need to cram all of our issues into one longer Director's Review session.

Another distinction was that NRD was involved in the full panoply of all of OMB's functions. In contrast, IAD had virtually no mandatory funding and very few regulatory issues. Furthermore, the congressional foreign affairs committees were inept at passing legislation, forcing miscellaneous authorization language to be included in either the appropriations bill or the annual National Defense Authorization Act (NDAA). This meant there was relatively little testimony to review on legislation and the oversight testimony on world hotspots had to be consistent with policies hammered out through the Interagency Policy Committee (IPC) process run by the NSC. Consequently, it was rarely even necessary for me to look at testimony.

While IAD sporadically would get involved in management issues, the bulk of the work revolved around the foreign policy issues coordinated through the IPC process, most of which was classified, and budgeting, most of which was unclassified, to address those issues. Whereas most of the budget work in NRD was in formulating the President's Budget and working to get the President's proposals enacted, in IAD we spent a huge amount of time moving money around after enactment of appropriations in order to address problems as they arose in new hotspots around the world. In addition, working on foreign policy issues necessitated a certain amount of interesting travel. While I only took three trips in 11 years, learning about State Department programs in Rio de Janeiro was much more exciting than visiting a chicken slaughterhouse in the U.S.

Ultimately, however, the question of which DAD role is better comes down to the question of whether it is better to be a small fish in a big pond, or a big fish in a small pond. In IAD, I attended a couple hundred Deputy Committee meetings held by the NSC - so called because Deputy Secretaries were the desired attendees — and got to witness important policy debates including those related to Afghanistan, ISIS, Ukraine, and China.

However, I was a minor player at those meetings, usually attending because the PAD for National Security wasn't available, whose role was to provide budget expertise and function as a liaison to our General Counsel's office on the many sanction EOs. Furthermore, I was a career official in meetings where other agencies were usually represented by political appointees. As interesting and important as those meetings were, the important decisions were either made at NSC Principal's meetings (i.e. cabinet without the President) or National Security Council meetings (i.e. select cabinet members with the President).

Issues on the domestic side were far more numerous than in the national security world and nowhere near as tightly coordinated. Consequently, there were many issues that had to be worked out between OMB and an agency without

White House involvement. For instance, many issues relating to positions on proposed legislation might come up a couple days before a hearing and OMB and the relevant agency would have to resolve what position the Administration would take on the legislation in the agency's testimony.

During the second term of the George W. Bush Administration (which for the remainder of this book I will refer to as Bush 43, as he was the 43rd President, to distinguish him from his father Bush 41), cabinet secretaries were supposed to have office hours weekly at the White House. As a practical matter, USDA was the only Department to actually have these weekly "Kitchen Cabinet" meetings, which were attended by OMB and various White House offices, including Political Affairs, Legislative Affairs, and Council on Environmental Quality. USDA's Deputy Secretary and Chief of Staff almost always attended, and the Secretary came perhaps half the time.

Initially, I only attended when my PAD was unavailable. In 2007, however, there was a lengthy delay in replacing David Anderson when he stepped down as PAD. Consequently, I started attending regularly and decided to keep on attending even after we got a new PAD, because I found the meetings were so useful. I half expected to be kicked out when the new PAD started, but nobody objected to my continued attendance despite being the only career official in the room.

The meetings were largely a discussion on issues brought up by either OMB or USDA, with the White House offices chiming in occasionally. For instance, we might discuss the latest USDA request for "discretionary, mandatory" funding or, after passage of the 2008 Farm Bill, implementation issues such as defining the base for the new ACRE program to administratively limit the potential payments. Unfortunately, OMB staff haven't had this kind of access to the USDA Secretary since the end of the Bush 43 Administration.

Global Health Overview

Working on global health issues was one of the most interesting and rewarding aspects of my IAD experience and one of the few issues without a heavy classified component. There were two types of health issues we addressed, and which posed different budget challenges. The first were continuing health problems, mostly diseases that had become endemic such as AIDS, malaria, and tuberculosis, which were addressed in the normal budget process. Second, there were periodic epidemics or pandemics, such as Ebola, Zika, and Covid-19, which had to be addressed through supplementals and funding transfers. I will discuss both types of health problems below and the associated budget issues we faced.

The State Department's Global Health account during my tenure in IAD was funded at between $8 and $9 billion annually. To put the significance of this funding in perspective, it is roughly equivalent to the size of the total budget for either the Commerce Department or the Environmental Protection Agency.

Assistance can be provided to foreign countries in two forms — multilateral or bilateral. Multilateral means that the U.S. is one of multiple countries contributing funding to an international organization which administers the assistance for the donors. Bilateral means that the U.S. is administering the assistance itself, without going through an international organization. On the ground at the local level, both bilateral and multilateral assistance are usually implemented either through the host government or non-governmental organizations (e.g. Doctors Without Borders).

Relatively few countries provide bilateral assistance because the logistics and administrative expense don't make sense for many small countries such as Belgium or Norway. In fact, the U.S. and the United Kingdom and the only countries with large bilateral assistance programs. The U.S. provides both bilateral and multilateral assistance to a wide range of sectors, including health, education, and economic development.

In the case of global health, there are two primary multilateral funding organizations — the Global Fund to Fight AIDS, Tuberculosis and Malaria, and Gavi, the Vaccine Alliance. Both organizations have new pledging rounds every three or four years. The annual U.S. appropriation for the Global Fund ranges from $1.3 to $1.6 billion per year. However, statutorily the U.S. cannot provide more than one-third of Global Fund contributions, which sometimes results in the U.S. delaying contributions while waiting for sufficient match from other countries.

To put the size of the Global Fund appropriation in perspective, the annual U.S. contribution to the World Bank for helping low-income countries is only $1.1 billion, even though that program finances projects addressing a wide spectrum of problems. This disparity rankles the Treasury Department, which is responsible for most U.S. multilateral contributions other than to health organizations.

While the percentages can vary, roughly one-half of the Global Fund is distributed to combat HIV/AIDS, one-third for malaria, and the remainder for tuberculosis.[132] The U.S. funds Gavi at $250 to $300 million per year, mostly for vaccinations of childhood diseases (e.g. measles, mumps) that are largely controlled in the U.S., but not in many developing countries. More recently Gavi has gotten involved in obtaining vaccines for COVID-19 in the developing world.

As by far the largest global health donor, the U.S. is always under pressure to make large pledges at donor conferences to "leverage" donations from other countries. However, neither the relevant agencies nor the non-governmental organization (NGO) program advocates were ever able to show me any evidence that high U.S. pledges leveraged higher donations by other countries than would have occurred anyway. Furthermore, advocates always viewed the U.S. contribution towards a disease as how much was given for the multilateral effort. One of my pet peeves was how little credit the U.S. got for its huge bilateral programs.

From my perspective, a required match from other donors was the best way to leverage other donations and even that didn't always work. Advocates for a particular cause didn't object to the matching concept, but always wanted the U.S. to provide its full pledge regardless of whether other donors had provided the needed matching funds. Of course, providing unmatched funding totally undermines the concept.

Endemic Disease Programs

State and the United States Agency for International Development (USAID) funded three major bilateral disease control programs out of the Global Health account —HIV/AIDS, malaria and tuberculosis — the same ones addressed by the Global Fund on a multilateral basis. Within the Global Health account total, between $4.2 and $4.7 billion was devoted annually to bilateral HIV/AIDS assistance, although HHS provided an additional roughly $0.5 billion in funding as well. Annual bilateral malaria appropriations were in the $650 to $800 million range and tuberculosis received $250 to $300 million annually.

Polio was another important program, not so much because of the size of the program — $50 million annually — but because polio is so close to eradication. In fact, the Gates Foundation made a couple of pitches to OMB and the NSC about funding a major surge to make polio only the second human disease eradicated after smallpox.

Unfortunately, the barrier to eradication was not lack of money, but the fact that the few remaining areas where the disease was endemic in the wild were in Taliban controlled areas in Afghanistan and Pakistan, and Boko Haram controlled areas in Nigeria. Besides those areas being insecure, the insurgents spread rumors that the vaccines would sterilize the local population. The fact that a fake hepatitis B immunization campaign was used to collect DNA samples to confirm Osama bin Laden's presence in Abbottabad, Pakistan also hurt the credibility of the polio campaign.[133] While eradication of polio is tantalizingly close, a few cases continue to pop up annually in Afghanistan and Pakistan.

HIV/AIDS Programs — the Early Years

The President's Emergency Plan for AIDS Relief (PEPFAR) will go down as one of Bush 43's most enduring successes. It is a program with strong bipartisan support that has endured across Administrations without the need for any rebranding when a new team took office. According to the Office of the Global AIDS Coordinator (OGAC) at the State Department, the U.S has provided almost $100 billion in funding for global HIV/AIDS response since 2003, saving 21 million lives and preventing millions of HIV infections.[134]

The bilateral PEPFAR program has been an unquestioned success story and, as a bureaucrat, I love working on a program with actual outcome measures that can be tracked. However, it also must be acknowledged that it is an expensive program, even with the use of cheap antiretroviral drugs. The reason is that, while the drugs are very good at keeping the disease at bay, the treatments must be continued for the rest of a patient's life or at least until an actual cure becomes available. Stopping treatment will allow the patient to infect others and puts the patient at risk of death.

I got lobbied by many groups advocating for Federal assistance to address a wide range of global health issues. I would often ask about the cost-effectiveness of various health interventions. While rarely wanting to answer that question, if pressed, the groups would usually answer that vaccination programs and family planning were the most cost-effective but would never mention HIV/AIDS programs. Note that family planning does did not include abortion, which the U.S. government does not finance.

In 2011, interim results of a clinical trial showed a 96 percent reduction in HIV transmission in heterosexual couples when antiretroviral therapy (ART) was started immediately after detection of the virus in one of the partners. In essence by suppressing the virus to a very low level, the ART drugs prevent the transmission of the virus to a non-infected partner, even though the virus continues to exist in the infected partner. This HIV control strategy came to be called "Treatment as Prevention" (TasP).[135]

For those of us who grew up believing that an "ounce of prevention equals a pound of cure", this is a counter-intuitive concept to accept. In fact, OGAC had to bring in Tony Fauci to talk about unpublished research to convince OMB and the NSC of the validity of the concept. Basically, in this odd instance, treatment is prevention because it prevents the transmission of the disease, even though the disease still exists in a population of individuals who would eventually need ART anyway to prevent the onset of AIDS. However, it should be mentioned that treatment is not a particularly cheap form of prevention compared to abstinence from unprotected sex or avoiding use of shared needles.

Nevertheless, armed with this research, NSC staff drafted a memo for the President to propose a major new global health commitment for World AIDS Day in December 2011. My comments on the memo concerning costs and programmatic trade-offs forced a reconsideration of the proposed commitment. Unfortunately, an oddity of HIV control is that the ramp-up of participation needs to be managed carefully to prevent an explosion in outyear budgets. The reason is that once an individual begins treatment, the U.S. has a moral obligation to continue treatment for the remainder of that individual's life.

Due to this issue, the original proposed commitment level was unsustainable and might have forced unacceptable trade-offs with more cost-effective global health interventions. However, one of the great successes of the PEPFAR program was declining program costs due to efficiencies and economies of scale as the program ramped up over time. Based on these efficiencies and by devoting a higher percentage of the PEPFAR budget to treatment, my global health examiner, Adam Ross, was able to convince me that we could sustainably increase the number of people on treatment without increasing the PEPFAR budget. Consequently, President Obama was able to announce a new target on World AIDS Day 2011 to help 6 million people on ART treatment by the end of 2013, an increase of 2 million people over the level receiving treatment at that time.[136]

PEPFAR Under Ambassador Birx

One of the remarkable things about the PEPFAR program, was its ability to substantially increase program outputs and outcomes, even though the PEPFAR budget stayed relatively constant over my decade in charge of IAD[137] (See Figure 8-1). Although the program had ramped up successfully during its first ten years, the arrival of Dr. Debbie Birx in April 2014 took the program to new heights.

Figure 8-1: PEPFAR Funding FY 2004 - FY 2022

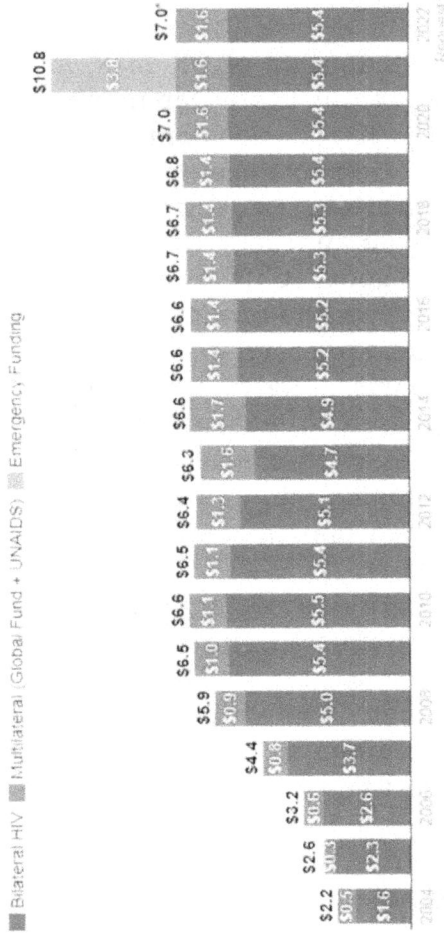

U.S. Funding for the President's Emergency Plan for AIDS Relief (PEPFAR), FY 2004 - FY 2022 Request

(In Billions)

Dr. Birx was a smart, savvy, experienced health care professional who was confirmed as Ambassador-at-Large and U.S. Global AIDS Coordinator with bipartisan support during the Obama Administration. In fact, she was so well respected that she was the only State Department headquarters political appointee kept on by the Trump Administration and was eventually chosen by Vice President Pence in February 2020 to be the White House Coronavirus Response Coordinator.

Under the leadership of Dr. Birx, and in time for World AIDS Day in 2014, the State Department developed the PEP-FAR 3.0 strategy to focus on controlling the epidemic --rather than responding to an emergency — and to deliver an AIDS-free generation. Reflecting Dr. Birx style, PEPFAR 3.0 was a data-driven approach to addressing AIDS that strategically targeted geographic areas and populations to achieve the most impact for the program's investments.[138]

At times, her approach also seemed to involve trying to overwhelm me with lengthy data heavy presentations on the metrics being used to measure progress towards PEPFAR's goals. Nevertheless, her goal-orientation was fully consistent with the Obama Administration's emphasis on evidence and performance management that will be discussed further in Chapter 11.

Dr. Birx' ability to set ambitious goals and hold country program officials accountable for achieving those goals was key to her success. In September 2015, the State Department announced new PEPFAR goals for the end of 2017, including to support 12.9 million people on ART (almost 7 million more than the 2013 goal), and achieve a 40 percent reduction in HIV incidence among adolescent girls and young women (aged 15-24 in 10 sub-Saharan countries). Dr. Birx was also able to convince us starting in FY 2016 to set aside $300 million yearly for a PEPFAR Impact Fund to reward countries that took specific steps to align their national programs to focus on high burden areas that would more effectively achieve epidemic control.

The reduced HIV incidence in girls was to be achieved through a $385 million partnership program ($200 million in PEPFAR funding) called DREAMS (Determined, Resilient,

Empowered, Aids-free, Mentored and Safe). What was different about the DREAMS program was that it was designed to achieve its health goal indirectly by addressing economic and cultural factors that made girls and young women vulnerable to getting infected with AIDS.[139]

While I supported DREAMS, towards the end of the Obama Administration, OGAC wanted to fund two other programs that were even less closely linked to achieving health goals than DREAMS. One was an education pilot program in Malawi and the other was a violence reduction program. The fact that these were being funded by PEPFAR rather than the accounts that fund education and rule of law, told me that PEPFAR had more funding than needed to achieve its goals.

To deal with these proposals, I wanted the office responsible for the primary goal (e.g. improved education or reduced violence) to demonstrate that the projects were actual priorities for them. Consequently, I was able to establish a policy that the office with primary responsibility had to provide at least half the funding to get a contribution from PEPFAR. My recollection is that only one of those two programs could meet that test to move forward.

Malaria and Tuberculosis

The three major endemic infectious diseases are tuberculosis (TB), HIV/AIDS, and malaria as shown in Figure 8-2 on 2019 worldwide deaths by cause[140].

Despite the disparity in the amount the U.S. spends to fight these diseases, it is tuberculosis (1.2 million deaths), not HIV/AIDS (0.86 million deaths) that is the deadliest, with malaria coming in third (.64 million deaths). Part of the reason is that HIV/AIDS requires relatively expensive treatment for life, but the other part of the answer is that malaria and TB are not significant problems in either the U.S. or other developed countries.

When looking at these three endemic infectious diseases and the three epidemic infectious diseases to be discussed later in this chapter, the most international funding goes to COVID-19 and HIV/AIDS because those diseases that have a large impact on and are very visible to U.S. citizens.

Figure 8-2: Worldwide Deaths by Cause

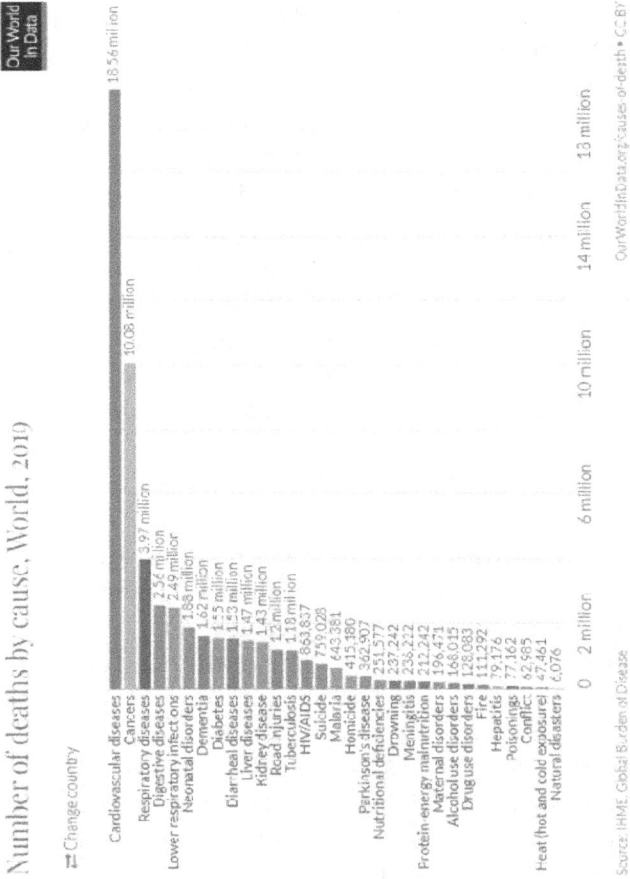

Number of deaths by cause, World, 2019

⇄ Change country

Cause	Deaths
Cardiovascular diseases	18.56 million
Cancers	10.08 million
Respiratory diseases	3.97 million
Digestive diseases	2.56 million
Lower respiratory infections	2.49 million
Neonatal disorders	1.88 million
Dementia	1.62 million
Diabetes	1.55 million
Diarrheal diseases	1.53 million
Liver diseases	1.47 million
Kidney disease	1.43 million
Road injuries	1.2 million
Tuberculosis	1.18 million
HIV/AIDS	863,837
Suicide	759,028
Malaria	643,381
Homicide	415,180
Parkinson's disease	362,907
Nutritional deficiencies	251,577
Drowning	237,242
Meningitis	236,222
Protein-energy malnutrition	212,242
Maternal disorders	196,471
Alcohol use disorders	168,015
Drug use disorders	128,083
Fire	111,292
Hepatitis	79,176
Poisonings	77,162
Conflict	62,985
Heat (hot and cold exposure)	47,461
Natural disasters	6,076

0   2 million   6 million   10 million   14 million   13 million

Source: IHME, Global Burden of Disease

OurWorldInData.org/causes-of-death • CC BY

Our World in Data

Supplemental funding was provided for Ebola and Zika due to the very real threat they posed and the need to keep them from spreading in the U.S. In contrast, TB and malaria have largely been eliminated as a serious problem in the U.S. with only 9,000 cases of TB annually[141] and only 2,000 cases of malaria annually,[142] with few if any deaths. Furthermore, most of those cases are from foreign travelers or those born abroad.

Despite the lower amounts of funding provided for malaria and TB, and the large number of annual deaths, huge strides have been made towards reducing the scourge of these diseases. In the case of malaria, more than 100 countries have eliminated malaria in the last century, including 12 countries since 2000[143]. Furthermore, from 2000 through 2017, malaria incidence declined 36 percent and deaths by 60 percent[144]. In the case of TB, between 2000 and 2019 mortality fell by 45 percent through improved TB diagnosis and treatment[145].

Both diseases are treatable and preventable, but an approved, effective vaccine doesn't currently exist for either. Malaria is transmitted by mosquitoes and is controlled using bed nets, indoor spraying of pesticides, rapid diagnostic tests, and antimalarial treatments. Although malaria is still endemic in many countries, the vast bulk of cases and deaths occur in sub-Saharan Africa.

TB is caused by bacteria that are spread from person to person through the air and largely affects adults in their highest productive years. TB is treated using a set of antibiotics, although newer TB strains are becoming more resistant to the standard antimicrobial drugs. TB is more widely spread around the world than malaria, with 43 percent of cases in southeast Asia, 25 percent in Africa, and 18 percent in the western Pacific region. Although U.S. funding for TB is only one-half to one-third the level of malaria funding, the U.S. still provides 50 percent of international donor funding. Fortunately, 80 percent of TB funding is provided by affected countries.[146]

In addition to HIV/AIDS, Bush 43 deserves a lot of credit for the progress on malaria due to his establishment of the President's Malaria Initiative (PMI) in 2005 to focus resources on 15 high-burden countries. President Obama ramped up the funding for PMI during his first two years as part of his multi-year Global Health Initiative, where it remained relatively flat for the next five years. Malaria funding was supposed to continue to be roughly flat in his final Budget request for FY 2017 as well.

However, the weekend prior to Obama's final State of the Union (SOTU) address in January 2016, a well-connected campaign donor apparently got the President's ear about making a push for malaria eradication. The result was language in the SOTU pledging an initiative to accelerate progress towards achieving the goal of eradicating the scourge of malaria once and for all. While this was a reasonable policy goal, it unfortunately took OMB, the NSC and the State Department by surprise, because there was no such initiative in the Budget. Furthermore, the Budget database was locked, although the print materials were not.

This was the second time in my career that a Budget pledge had been made after the database had been locked. The first time was just before transmittal of the second Clinton Budget when OMB Director Leon Panetta got cold feet about not having any earmarked funding for Boston Harbor wastewater treatment, which was a major contrast to the priority Boston Harbor had been given by the Bush Administration. In that case, the Director just added funding on top of existing totals and an errata page was prepared to be slipped into the already printed budget.

Due to the statutory budget caps in place for the FY 2017 Budget, adding funding on top as Panetta had done was not an option and I was tasked with fixing the problem after getting guidance that the Initiative needed to provide an increase of at least $200 million. The solution that my staff and I developed was to take small reductions in a handful of programs to cobble together a $71 million in increase for malaria within the Global Health appropriation account. The remaining $129 million was to come from unspent emergency supplemental Ebola funds, which required appropriations language to allow Ebola funds to be used for a different infectious disease.

Needless to say, the NGOs involved with malaria were thrilled but, unfortunately, the NGOs that worked on TB control were upset. Inadvertently perhaps, Obama had anointed malaria as the next disease to be targeted for eradication after polio, even though TB was a bigger killer. Bill Gates had already come out with an action plan for achieving malaria eradication by 2040[147], while *The Lancet* medical journal had established a commission which reported in 2019 that eradication was feasible by 2050[148]. What is interesting about those eradication dates is that they conflict with the greatly increased malaria disease estimates being predicted by advocates for global warming control.

While not happy about having to scramble to find funding, at least my global health examiner, Justin Cormier, got an opportunity to make a presentation on malaria at a West Wing Senior Staff meeting (mostly attended by Policy Council Deputies) in the Roosevelt Room. The presentation explained the impact PMI has had in reducing malaria and how OMB had given substance to the President's SOTU commitment for an initiative.

COVID-19 has certainly proven to be more deadly than malaria on a world-wide basis with an average of 3 million deaths for the first two years of the pandemic, levels that scientists think are a vast undercount. In Africa, however, where 90 percent of malaria deaths occur, malaria is viewed as an even greater danger than COVID, leading to frustration about the level of international donor support for malaria compared to the amount spent on COVID.[149] Furthermore, whereas COVID is a disease that disproportionately affects the elderly, three quarters of malaria deaths are in children under the age of 5.

Global Health Budgeting Under Trump

As will be discussed further in Chapter 13 on transitions, my budget guidance in the Trump Administration was to make huge cuts in the State Department/USAID budget. One key skill that OMB budget staff must master is always being prepared to offer the next priority increase or decrease. In fact, during the budget formulation process in some years, we must prepare budget proposals to both increase and decrease the budget in order to give the Director a choice. Most examiners find proposing increases to be relatively easy. The ability to identify thoughtful, well justified reductions that minimize program impact is a trait most often found in the better examiners.

In preparing the Trump budgets, my objective was always to meet the budget guidance while getting the best "bang for the buck" out of the available resources. Ironically, I found that I could accomplish this best by taking large reductions out of humanitarian assistance and global health, two of the programs I thought were among the most important.

In the case of humanitarian assistance, Congress tended to over fund the humanitarian accounts because they were among the few programs on which the majority and minority could agree were priorities to fund. Consequently, there was always at least two billion dollars in carryover (i.e. unused prior year funding) as well as a current year enacted appropriation that was above the President's request, even in the Obama years. This meant that I could cut $3 billion from the enacted level and still often be able to message that the two-year total (i.e. current and budget years) of available funding was sufficient to fund more in each of those years than the highest amount ever obligated in any prior year.

Program advocates hated the humanitarian assistance reductions but couldn't articulate any significant actual negative impact of the cut. Instead, the claim was that OMB made the cuts only because we knew the Congress would restore the funding. While I certainly didn't expect Congress to make the level of reductions that we were proposing, I never made a cut based on the assumption that it would be restored. On the other hand, I knew that the carryover would only bail me out once, if Congress did take the reduction. In that event, very difficult trade-offs would need to be made in other international programs during the following year's budget process to adequately fund humanitarian aid.

The existence of carryover was also part of the strategy for coping with cuts of at least $2 billion annually in the Global Health account, although there wasn't as much carryover available as in humanitarian assistance. Nevertheless, the strategy of protecting the most important objectives remained the same. Those objectives starting in the FY 2019 Budget included:

1) keep all existing patients on HIV/AIDs treatment;
2) remain on track in meeting the U.S. commitment to the Global Fund;
3) continue progress under the President's malaria initiative toward epidemic control; and
4) maintain robust Gavi vaccination funding until the next replenishment round.

In September 2017, the State Department issued the PEPFAR Strategy for Accelerating HIV/AIDS Epidemic Control (2017-2020), which set a goal of achieving control of the HIV epidemic in 10 high-burden countries by the end of 2020. Epidemic control was often defined as attainment of the United Nations AIDS program 90-90-90 goals, which were that 90 percent of individuals with HIV know their status, 90 percent of those individuals are receiving treatment, and 90 percent of individuals on treatment have suppressed viral loads.[150]

Although the strategy was focused on 13 high burden countries, support continued to be provided to a total of 50 countries. For the remaining Trump Budgets, we made sure that the requests for the bilateral program were consistent with this bold but achievable strategy. The fact that the program had continued to get steadily more efficient and better targeted provided the kind of "bang for the buck" needed to achieve those outcome goals despite the constrained budget environment.

One significant change we made starting in the FY 2020 Budget, however, was to propose a higher matching share as part of the pledge for the next replenishment of the Global Fund. While I needed the savings from shifting more of the Global Fund burden to other nations, such a shift was programmatically justified given that the U.S. government was providing 70 percent of the donations for HIV/AIDS international assistance. Furthermore, it was consistent with the

Trump Administration's philosophy on the need for greater burden sharing by other governments on a host of defense and international issues. While program advocates agreed that other nations should pay more for the Global Fund, they had no interest in reducing the U.S. contribution and neither did the appropriators.

Figure 8-3 shows the impressive PEPFAR results through 2021.[151] AIDS advocates will argue that more could have been accomplished if the PEPFAR budget hadn't been held roughly flat for the past decade. The counterargument is that U.S. funding has been so high as a percent of total donations that it discourages funding from other nations who assume that the U.S. will take care of the problem.

In this case, there is no way to know which assumption is correct, although earlier in my career I saw a very clear substitution effect when a surge of Federal wastewater spending in the 1970s led to a significant reduction in State funding. Unfortunately, this substitution effect resulted in only a relatively small overall increase in funding to address the backlog of wastewater needs, despite the huge slug of new Federal funding.

Unforeseen Epidemics and Pandemics

In December 2013, a serious outbreak of Ebola occurred in West Africa, starting in Guinea, and got worse as the year went along when the outbreak spread to neighboring Sierra Leone and Liberia. Ebola is a particularly dreadful, fear-invoking disease that is caused by a virus and, like HIV/AIDS, is transmitted through direct contact with fluids. Symptoms include fever, vomiting, diarrhea, and in some cases internal and external bleeding. There is no treatment for Ebola, although supportive care can increase the chances of survival. Nevertheless, 50 percent of cases have been fatal, with a fatality rate as high as 90 percent in some outbreaks.[152]

In West Africa, this kind of epidemic had to be dealt with by quickly identifying and isolating infected individuals, while contact tracing was done to identify individuals exposed to the virus, to make sure they were isolated and didn't transmit the virus further. A vaccine was later devel-

Figure 8-3: PEPFAR Results 2021

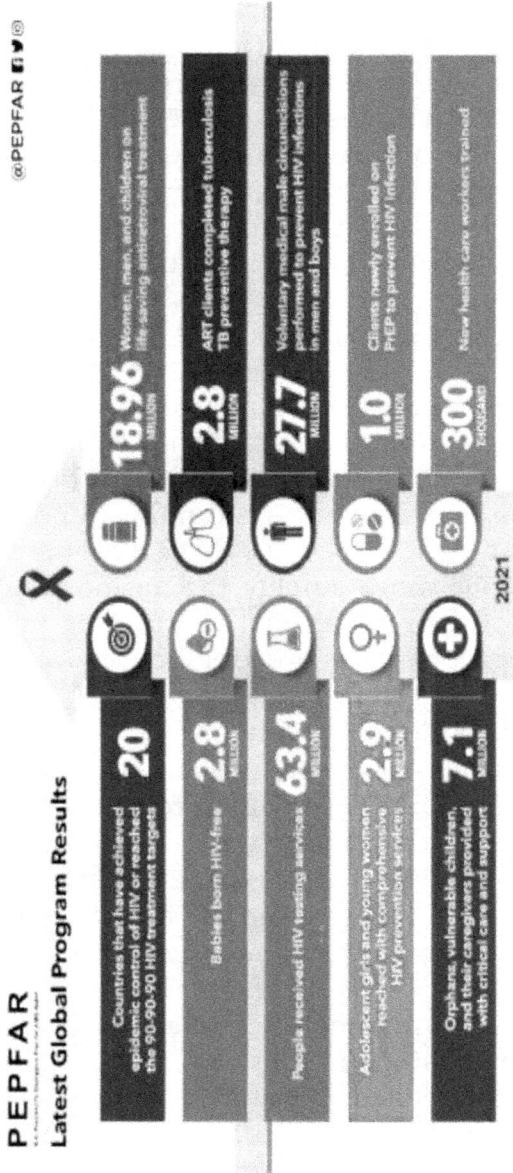

PEPFAR

Latest Global Program Results

@PEPFAR

20 Countries that have achieved epidemic control of HIV or reached the 90-90-90 HIV treatment targets

18.96 MILLION Women, men, and children on life-saving antiretroviral treatment

2.8 MILLION Babies born HIV-free

2.8 MILLION ART clients completed tuberculosis TB preventive therapy

63.4 MILLION People received HIV testing services

27.7 MILLION Voluntary medical male circumcisions performed to prevent HIV infections in men and boys

2.9 MILLION Adolescent girls and young women reached with comprehensive HIV prevention services

1.0 MILLION Clients newly enrolled on PrEP to prevent HIV infection

7.1 MILLION Orphans, vulnerable children, and their caregivers provided with critical care and support

300 THOUSAND New health care workers trained

2021

Source: PEPFAR. Latest Global Results, 2021

oped and used in a subsequent outbreak in the Republic
of the Congo. However, it is not a vaccine being used for
entire populations. Instead, it is used for medical workers
and individuals in contact with an infected person to prevent further spread of the virus.

Although the World Health Organization (WHO) declared
the outbreak a Public Health Emergency of International
Concern (PHEIC) in August 2014, the WHO was unprepared
to respond to the outbreak in a meaningful way. Consequently, the United States government, with the help of the
British and French, had to step in to prevent the outbreak
from spreading beyond the three affected countries.

Options for Funding Emergencies

Ebola presented a classic situation of an unforeseen foreign event that required funding for immediate response.
During budget formulation, the options for funding a new
need are broad in scope, but the funding generally won't be
available for at least a year. In this kind of situation when
funding is needed more quickly the options are: 1) request
a supplemental appropriation (i.e. funding provided after
the normal appropriations process for the fiscal year); or 2)
reprogram existing funding.

State and USAID will always prefer a supplemental to
avoid making trade-offs with existing priorities. However,
Congress may not always be willing to provide a supplemental or may want to include extraneous provisions that the
President may find unacceptable. Furthermore, even supplementals often aren't enacted for a few months after being requested, meaning that funding must be reprogrammed
in the interim.

In IAD, we were fortunate to have several authorities allowing reprogramming of funds and, in some cases, transfer
of funds to other agencies. Not all agencies had similar authorities. In NRD, for instance, USDA had many small accounts, which hindered reprogramming, but they did have
7 percent transfer authority allowing no more than 7 percent to be transferred out of an account and no more than
7 percent could be received by an account. In contrast, DOI

had many small accounts and little ability to move money between them. EPA had no transfer authority but had some reprogramming flexibility because its funding was concentrated in a handful of relatively large accounts.

I used to think about options for reprogramming funds as akin to the statistical concept of "degrees of freedom". While not being used in a statistical sense, I saw it as an analogous because, just as more degrees of freedom led to a more robust and meaningful statistic, the more reprogramming options I had the better solution I could construct to achieve a policy outcome. One thing I learned over time was that you <u>always</u> needed to know what your options were for addressing unforeseen priorities.

In terms of reprogramming, my most important option involved use of Overseas Contingency Operations (OCO) funding, which was also sometimes known as Global War on Terror (GWOT) funding. DOD had been getting OCO funding since near the beginning of the 2003 war with Iraq. The availability of this funding, which was essentially emergency funding provided outside of normal budget constraints, allowed DOD to fund several activities (e.g. economic development and weapons procurement) in several conflict zones that were traditional State Department functions.

When Jack Lew became Deputy Secretary of State for Management and Resources at the beginning of the Obama Administration, he sought to change that by obtaining OCO funding for State. At the State Department he prepared a large OCO Budget request for FY 2012, which he approved as OMB Director when he switched jobs during the FY 2012 budget process. The $8.7 billion in State Department OCO funding for FY 2012 was for "temporary and extraordinary" assistance in a limited number of accounts for the conflict zones of Iraq, Afghanistan, and Pakistan. I was opposed to using OCO for Pakistan, since there was no war going on in Pakistan, but my logic fell on deaf ears.

Once our OCO request got to Congress, the appropriators almost immediately began to play games with OCO, first by increasing the number of accounts with OCO funding and also increasing the number of countries in which it could be used. With the passage of the Budget Control Act of 2011 and the imposition of caps on discretionary spending, the Appropriations Committees realized that they could essentially increase the non-defense discretionary cap by cutting State Department funding under the cap and backfilling the funding with OCO funding that was not subject to the cap. For instance, the FY 2012 OCO level increased to $11.2 billion, even though Congress considerably cut the overall State Department request.

This game playing ultimately led to a State/USAID OCO level of over $20 billion or about 40 percent of the State/US-AID budget. The concept of OCO being for "temporary and extraordinary" assistance was quickly discarded and Congress never put any constraints on where it could be used. I finally drew a line in the sand with the State Department and established a policy that OCO funding could not be used in the Western Hemisphere on the theory that, if you could drive to a country, it wasn't "overseas". Fortunately, I was able to get OMB leadership in both the Obama and Trump Administration to back me up on what one individual jokingly referred to as the "Fairweather" doctrine.

Leaving aside the Congressional game playing, OCO for Iraq, Afghanistan and Pakistan was over funded from the beginning. For instance, $1 billion was budgeted for police training in FY 2012, a level that the State Department never came close to using. Furthermore, for a few years the transfer authority between OCO accounts was very broad and applied to about three-quarters of the total. However, the longer OCO was in existence the more limited the transfer authority became.

In those early years, a huge amount of OCO funding couldn't quickly be used and was available for transfer. Consequently, I had the impression that some people at State viewed Rob Goldberg, the head of the Foreign Assistance Office (aka "F") and my predecessor as IAD DAD, as akin to a god because he could always find money when needed. Rob and I had an explicit understanding not to let others outside our budget offices know how much money was available. If they knew, it would be like ringing the dinner bell and all sorts of supplicants at State, USAID, and the NSC would come running to feed at the trough.

While some of the OCO accounts were useful for responding to health emergencies, such as the Economic Support
Fund (ESF) and International Disaster Assistance (IDA) accounts, OCO couldn't be transferred to the Global Health
(GH) account because GH received no OCO funding. Fortunately, the $1.6 billion IDA account could be used for a broad
range of activities including response to drought, hurricane,
earthquake, and tsunami disasters. Ebola marked the first
time IDA was used for a purely health disaster, although
medical care was often provided in response to disasters
along with food and shelter.

The final ace up my sleeve for funding emergency health
needs was a State Department appropriations general provision (Section 7058) which, in the event the Secretary determined:

> "that an international infectious disease outbreak is
> sustained, severe, and is spreading internationally, or
> that it is in the national interest to respond to a Pub-
> lic Health Emergency of International Concern, funds
> made available under Title III of this Act may be made
> available to combat such infectious diseases or public
> health emergency"

As Title III encompassed around $18 billion annually, sig-
nificant amounts of funding could be made available if the
determination was made. The State Department also had
a set of authorities to reprogram funds for security assistance, but those authorities could not be used to respond to
disease outbreaks.

Ebola Response

After WHO declared the PHEIC in August 2014, the three
West African countries of Guinea, Sierra Leone and Liberia
were isolated from their neighbors by border controls, and
travel bans were imposed by various countries to keep the
disease from spreading beyond those three nations. While
USAID had funding to help address the crisis in the near
term, mainly through IDA, HHS did not. HHS's ability to
reprogram funding was much more limited, primarily a Sec-

retarial transfer authority like USDA's 7 percent transfer authority. However, HHS has a broad portfolio of potential needs and, consequently, guarded that authority jealously, particularly early in a fiscal year. For instance, in 2014 HHS had already used the authority to address the crisis of unaccompanied minors showing up at the Mexican border, one of multiple international crises which IAD had to address in 2014, including the ISIS takeover of parts of Iraq, and the Russian incursion into Ukraine.

Fortunately, as part of the continuing resolution enacted in late September 2014, HHS received $88 million for Ebola response. Congress also gave the go-ahead for DOD to reprogram $750 million in funding from the Overseas Humanitarian Disaster and Civic Aid (OHDACA) account to support U.S. efforts in the region. This was followed in October 2018, by President Obama announcing that the U.S. would launch a "whole-of government" response to the Ebola outbreak coordinated by a USAID Disaster Assistance Response Team (DART).[153]

Most people don't recognize how important DOD is in responding to various disasters around the world. It is literally the only organization in the world with the ships, aircraft, supply chains, and logistical expertise to quickly respond to a disaster virtually anywhere in the world. The OHDACA account is also crucial to making this happen in conjunction with USAID's expertise in disaster response and the inter-agency coordination provided through the DART. Sadly, the U.N. has virtually no ability to provide such a response.

In the end, DOD deployed nearly 3,000 troops to the western Africa region to construct 17 Ebola Treatment Units (ETU) to help bring the epidemic under control. CDC contributed over 1,000 staff and USAID posted 465 personnel to the region on a temporary basis.[154] While this effort began largely with reprogrammed funds, my staff was working with our colleagues in the Health Division (HD), the State Department, USAID, and HHS to prepare a $6.2 billion amended FY 2015 Budget emergency funding request. IAD had three objectives in this effort: 1) adequately fund State and USAID efforts to end the epidemic in West Africa; 2) provide funding to strengthen future developing country response to similar epidemics through what became known as the Global Health Security Agenda; and 3) reimburse funds borrowed from other programs to fund the response prior to congressional action.

As State and USAID's options for reprogramming additional funds were dwindling, in December 2014 Congress enacted the Consolidated and Further Continuing Appropriations Act of 2015, which provided the State/USAID appropriations for the year as well as $5.4 billion in emergency Ebola funds, of which $2.5 billion was for State and USAID.

In part due to DOD's ability to get medical units on the ground quickly, the epidemic was controlled more rapidly than anticipated. The DART was disbanded in January 2016, a little over a year after the emergency funding was provided, and the WHO ended the PHEIC in March 2016. At the time the PHEIC was terminated, State and USAID had obligated only half of the $2.5 billion available, in part due to IAD efforts to keep the Ebola funding focused on critical epidemic control efforts rather than "nice to have" programs. Unfortunately, only a portion of that remaining total could be used for anything other than Ebola response.

Zika Response

An epidemic caused by the Zika virus was first identified in Brazil in May 2015. While Zika causes only a mild illness in most people, in pregnant women it can cause birth defects, particularly a severe brain abnormality known as microcephaly. Like malaria, Zika is transmitted by mosquitoes, although a different species than transmits malaria, but a species prevalent in much of the U.S. In a twist, however, Zika was also linked to sexual contact with an infected individual.[155]

One thing many people don't understand about mosquito borne diseases is that the disease does not naturally occur in mosquitoes. Instead, the mosquito is the vector or carrier that bites an infected person and transmits it through a bite to another person. Thus, the best method of control is to: 1) quickly identify infected individuals and isolate them to keep them from being bitten by a mosquito and spreading the disease; and 2) spray areas near the infected individual to kill any mosquitoes that might already be transmitting the disease. Mosquito borne infections are like forest fires, stamping it out quickly prevents it from spreading, while a slow response allows it to get out of control quickly as unchecked epidemics grow exponentially.

In February 2016, the WHO declared a PHEIC for the Zika outbreak. By that point, infected travelers had already brought the virus to the U.S., with Puerto Rico being particularly hard hit. However, the first locally transmitted cases of Zika in the continental U.S. were not confirmed until July 2016 in the Wynwood neighborhood of Miami.[156] The appearance of Zika in the U.S. led the Obama Administration on February 22, 2016, to make an FY 2016 supplemental budget request of $1.89 billion, all of which was classified as emergency funding outside the budget caps. The bulk of the funding was for HHS, with $335 million requested for USAID and $41 million for State, and most of the State money was intended to support organizations such as the Pan American Health Organization.

OMB staff helped develop the supplemental in conjunction with an effort to look for existing funding that could be reprogrammed to Zika response. On April 6, 2016, OMB and HHS announced that $589 million had been identified for such reprogramming, of which $510 million was from Ebola balances. Two days later, USAID announced that it was transferring $295 million of ESF Ebola funds to other accounts, including $158 million to CDC for its international control efforts. This transfer was possible only because of the transfer authority to other agencies available under the Foreign Assistance Act. HHS used its limited Secretarial authority to reprogram an additional $81 million in August 2016.

With our ability to reprogram funds almost exhausted, Congress finally enacted a bill on September 28, 2016, which included $1.1 billion in supplemental Zika funding. The bill reflected a conference agreement reached in late June 2016, but Senate Democrats blocked cloture on the bill three times over a provision preventing certain assistance through Planned Parenthood health centers and a $750 million rescission of Affordable Care Act (aka Obamacare) funding. The enacted bill largely funded HHS, but provided $175 million for State and USAID, offset by a $117 million rescission of unused Ebola funds that were going to expire at the end of September anyway.[157]

In the end, the bulk of the heavy lifting in preventing Zika from spreading during the worst part of the mosquito season had been accomplished over the summer with the reprogrammed funding, not the supplemental. Within two months of the enactment of the supplemental WHO declared the end of the epidemic.

COVID-19

As virtually all readers have lived through the COVID-19, I won't go into the public aspects of the pandemic. When we first start tracking COVID while it was still in China in December 2019, those us in IAD and the Health Division thought "here we go again", not suspecting how much worse it would turn out to be. While the soon to be released FY 2021 budget request for State included $90 million for the Global Health Security Agenda and $25 million for a new Emergency Reserve Fund within the Global Health account, there was obviously nothing specific for COVID in either the State/USAID or HHS budgets.

As the outbreaks on the Diamond Princess cruise ship and in Italy began to unfold at the end of January 2020, IAD and HD briefed OMB's Deputy Director, Russ Vought, on our respective authorities to reprogram funds, since he hadn't been through the Ebola and Zika epidemics. It was the same story with HHS having fewer options and much more immediate needs than State/USAID.

By the end of February, Ambassador Debbie Birx had been called back from an AIDS conference in South Africa to become the Coordinator for the White House Coronavirus Response Task Force. I was thrilled with her appointment, not only because of her eminent qualifications, but also her political and bureaucratic skills in thriving during the transition from Obama to Trump. Unfortunately, she took on an impossible job.

I was less thrilled that she asked to have one of my examiners, who had been with her on the South Africa trip, to be detailed to her staff. While I like my examiners to be successful and have opportunities, this examiner had not been in IAD for very long. There was also a pattern developing of my examiners being detailed to the White House, having their details extended multiple times, and never coming back to OMB. That turned out to be the case in this situation as well.

Towards the beginning of the pandemic, the Trump Administration was criticized for not being better prepared for a pandemic and for having eliminated an office in the NSC for coordinating biological threats. I felt those criticisms were somewhat off the mark, at least in terms of preparing internationally. First, the Global Health Security Agenda (GHSA) was embraced by the Trump Administration and continued to be funded. Second, there is only so much you can prepare for, without wasting a lot of money, when you don't know the nature of an unknown disease or how it is transmitted (i.e. stockpiling ventilators does no good for an Ebola or Zika type of outbreak). The most important type of preparation is to build up the underlying health systems so they can react and adapt to different situations as they occur. However, that was exactly what GHSA was designed to do in the most poorly prepared countries in Africa and southeast Asia.

Unfortunately, COVID had its least impact in the GHSA countries. In fact, none of the three countries where the pandemic spread first — China, Iran, and Italy — would have ever been eligible for GHSA. Due to it being a highly contagious, air-borne respiratory disease, COVID spread quickly around the world due to airline travel by relatively well to do tourists. In many ways, it was a disease of the developed world, unlike every other disease discussed in this chapter.

The fact that COVID hit the developed world hardest meant that State and USAID didn't play the kind of role they had in the Ebola and Zika epidemics. In fact, many State and USAID programs were shutting down and non-essential staff being recalled home due to the pandemic. Furthermore, medical assistance that USAID wanted to provide, was hampered by critical supply shortages and White House policy direction that USAID could not buy domestically any medical supplies critically needed in the U.S. Oddly, the White House directed us to work with State, USAID, and DOD to pull together a $100 million aid package for Italy which, because it was delivered so late, provided little help when the Italian hospital system was overwhelmed in early 2020.

My staff and I also spent a lot of time helping resolve issues on the ground to keep the government running smoothly. These included helping with the recall of Peace Corps volunteers world-wide, reprogramming money to finance the repatriation of tens of thousands of U.S. citizens abroad and addressing the severe revenue shortfall in State's normally fee funded passport and visa programs, which weren't collecting any fees once travel started to shut down. We also worked on meeting various White House commitments to provide excess ventilators to developing countries in need, once the shortage in the U.S. had been addressed.

One typical activity in which we were not very involved was developing the COVID emergency funding bills. For the two enacted during the Trump Administration — the Cares Act of 2020 and the emergency portion of the Consolidated Appropriations Act of 2021 — OMB, or at least IAD, was very much in a reactive mode to make sure that the funding was appropriately targeted.

The broad outlines of the American Rescue Plan (ARP) of 2021 were developed by the Biden transition team due to the need to act quickly after Biden's inauguration. Furthermore, as will be discussed in Chapter 13, OMB staff were not allowed to work with the incoming team prior to Biden's Inauguration as had been the case in every one of my previous transitions. As the ARP was enacted as mandatory funding in a reconciliation bill, the language had to be crafted differently to be consistent with the Byrd rule in the Senate and not appear to be an appropriations bill. Consequently, IAD's role was to work with the White House, who had the lead on communicating with the Senate, on targeting the funding and making sure that the way the bill was structured would still allow State and USAID to implement the programs as intended.

Out of the $5 trillion provided in those emergency COVID bills, State and USAID received only $17 billion, a tiny amount compared to the domestic spending. The $1.1 billion in the CARES Act in March 2020 was targeted to address some of the operational issues discussed above and provide humanitarian assistance as the world began to shut down. The $5.3 billion in the Consolidated Appropriations Act in December 2020 was largely to pay for COVID vaccines for developing countries as well as bail out the revenue shortfall in the passport and visas programs.

Finally, the $10.8 billion in the ARP, which was enacted in March 2021 shortly before my retirement, was largely split between humanitarian assistance and global health issues, particularly to pay for more vaccines. For better or worse, due to my retirement, I missed having to work on the Delta and Omicron variant surges and the continuing shortfall in vaccines for less developed countries.

CHAPTER NINE: Between Scylla and Charybdis -- *Withholding Funds for the Ukraine*

While much of the last chapter was about finding money for new priorities either through reprogramming or supplementals, this chapter is about the flip side. In this chapter, I will discuss how foreign assistance funds for particular countries are routinely withheld by both the Administration and the Congress, often resulting in the funds being reprogrammed for other uses. I will also talk about the Trump Administration's attempts to rescind State and USAID funding as well as the controversial 2019 withholding of military assistance funds for Ukraine.

Foreign Assistance Primer

First, I need to explain the complicated relationship between the State Department and the United States Agency for International Development (USAID). Theoretically, USAID is an independent agency and not a bureau within the State Department. In fact, USAID is represented separately at meetings within the NSC process and can take positions in those meetings different from those of the State Department representatives. On budget matters, however, the State Department makes all the decisions on a unified State and USAID budget request, with USAID essentially functioning as a bureau within the Department. Furthermore, at U.S. embassies around the world, the Ambassador is a State Department employee and, with some DOD exceptions, all Federal employees in the country, including USAID staff, report to the Ambassador under Chief of Mission status.

The Office of Foreign Assistance, or "F" as it is known within the Department, essentially functions as the State Department budget office for foreign assistance. There is a separate budget office within State for operations. I am not aware of any other Department in the Federal Government that has such a dual budget office structure. To complicate matters further, USAID has its own budget office, although they must work through "F" on many issues.

Part of the reason for this odd budget structure for foreign assistance is that several key budget accounts include funding for both State and USAID. For instance, over a third of the Global Health account discussed in the last chapter is USAID funding, including the TB and malaria programs. However, PEPFAR is a State Department program headed by a Coordinator who provides policy guidance, and who has the rank of Ambassador to facilitate negotiations with foreign governments, even though much of the program is implemented on the ground by USAID.

As of FY 2021, the DAD for IAD was responsible for over $40 billion in foreign assistance, not including emergency supplemental funds. This included around $3 billion for the Treasury Department's international programs as well as several smaller international agencies including the Millennium Challenge Corporation, and the Development Finance Corporation. It did not include DOD foreign assistance funding, mainly for weapons, which was targeted at a few high-profile countries including Afghanistan, Israel, and Ukraine.

Two of the three big components of the funding for which IAD was responsible were discussed in Chapter Eight, including over $9 billion for global health, and close to $10 billion for humanitarian assistance. This chapter will focus on a set of five accounts totaling $15 billion in FY 2021 enacted funding that are largely allocated by country. These accounts are:

> *Economic Support Fund (ESF) — $3.2 billion:* ESF funds projects in countries of strategic importance to the U.S. to help them meet economic, development, and political needs to foster allies with stable governments and prosperous economies. ESF is a State Department controlled account, but the bulk of the funding is implemented by USAID.

> *Assistance for Europe, Eurasia & Central Asia (AEECA) — $0.8 billion:* AEECA has the same function as ESF,

and the same relationship with USAID, except that it is focused exclusively on countries that were formerly part of the Soviet Union.

Development Assistance (DA) — $3.5 billion: DA aids underdeveloped countries which do not have strategic importance to the U.S., to help them reduce extreme poverty and develop democratic societies. In theory, the ESF, AEECA, and DA accounts are mutually exclusive, meaning that no country should get funding from more than one of these accounts. In practice, however, that is not always the case. DA is a USAID account, largely controlled by and fully implemented by USAID.

International Narcotics Control and Law Enforcement (INCLE) — $1.4 billion: INCLE funds programs to combat transnational crimes and illicit trafficking as well as promote rule of law by helping countries strengthen weak or corrupt law enforcement institutions. INCLE is a State Department account that is also implemented by the State Department.

Foreign Military Financing (FMF) — $6.2 billion: FMF funds procurement of U.S. built weapons systems and support for those systems to help friendly and allied countries defend themselves and counter terrorism. Although many countries receive FMF, over two-thirds each year goes to Israel ($3.3 billion) and Egypt ($1.3 billion) in funding specifically earmarked for those countries. FMF is a State Department account implemented by the State Department.

As FMF has some unusual features that are important in understanding the situation with the State Department's military assistance to Ukraine, it will be discussed separately. The other four accounts are all two-year accounts that face several hurdles in getting their funding obligated expeditiously. During the bulk of my tenure, most of these accounts had OCO funding in addition to their normal base appropriations. The one exception is that there has never been any OCO funding in DA, since the account is supposed to help countries without strategic significance.

Very little of the funding in these accounts gets obligated in the first year the funding is available and at least a quarter — sometimes up to a half -- of the funding doesn't get obligated until the last quarter of the second year that the funds are available. There are several reasons for this, mostly due to Congressional requirements or dysfunction. The first problem is that Congress can't meet its deadlines for enacting appropriations. In fact, in recent years appropriations have rarely been enacted much before Christmas and often not until March, almost half the way through the fiscal year. While State and USAID are allocated funding under a Continuing Resolution (CR), such funding is rarely used since there is so much carryover of prior year funding that needs to be obligated first.

Once OMB receives the apportionments after appropriations are enacted, we generally process them quickly for these accounts. An apportionment is a legal document that must be signed by an OMB official before appropriated funds can be obligated by an agency. The original intention of the apportionment was to allocate funding on a quarterly basis to prevent agencies from over-obligating during the year. Given the funds control capabilities of today's computer systems, the apportionment process seemed to me to be something of an anachronism.

Apportionments only apply to a specific year and, as little funding in these accounts gets obligated the first year, the apportionments in that first year have little meaning. A new apportionment is required for the second year of availability and OMB guidance requires those apportionments to be signed prior to the beginning of the new fiscal year in order for the funding to be available in the event of a CR and particularly if there is a shutdown. Generally, these carryover apportionments made all the funding available immediately. To the extent we had disputes with State on funding allocations, those were generally dealt with during later steps in the process.

Congressional Control of Foreign Policy Funding

Much of the funding in these five accounts is "earmarked" for specific purposes or economic sectors and/or for specific countries. This is a different use of the term "earmark" than for domestic agencies, where the term generally is synonymous with a Congressional "pork" project. These sector earmarks were not account specific but were always spread among multiple accounts. For FY 2020, for instance, there were 13 different categories of earmarks spread across the accounts. In fact, a huge portion of each account was earmarked by sector ranging from 33 percent of INCLE to 95 percent of DA.

Sector earmarks can be in bill language, which means they are legally required to be met, or report language, which means there is more flexibility because report language is generally not legally binding. In most years, there was a mix of bill and report earmarks. Due to the appropriators distrust of the Trump Administration, however, all sector earmarks in the FY 2020 bill were in bill language.

This is even though Lindsey Graham, Chairman of the Senate Subcommittee for State and Foreign Operations, was a confidant of President Trump. However, they had a complicated relationship and a major point of disagreement between the two men concerned the value of the "soft power" of State and USAID funding. It was an issue on which they apparently agreed to disagree.

Overlaid on top of these sector earmarks were earmarks for specific countries. Most of these earmarks were specific to a particular account, but not always. Some of the country earmarks were binding requirements in bill language, although the majority were in report language. As indicated above, while report language is generally not binding, the State/USAID appropriations bill includes bill language that codified country allocations included within a table in the conference report for the bill. This bill language essentially made those allocations in report tables legally binding.

The sheer magnitude of these legally binding earmarks posed a huge and complex allocation problem for "F". Although Section 653 (a) of the Foreign Assistance Act requires State to report to Congress on funding allocations by foreign country and category of assistance within 30 days of enactment of appropriations, the process to simultaneously meet all the earmarks always takes much longer. Unfortunately, the tighter the earmarks, the longer the process takes. Even after the staff at "F" identify a viable solution that fits all the constraints, there are three more steps in the process before the 653(a) report can officially be sent to Congress.

First, "F" must circulate the allocations within State and USAID, including to all the embassies worldwide. While the embassies usually appreciate any increases they receive above the President's request, they often complain and appeal the allocation of various earmarks. For instance, an embassy might get more than they need for their country in earmarked biodiversity funding, but less than needed for unearmarked types of economic development funding. Unfortunately, if a specific level of biodiversity funding is earmarked in bill language, State has no option other than to force the embassies to use the funding for that purpose.

Once the State Department finishes the internal review process, the 653(a) allocations are sent to OMB for review. While we consulted with the NSC on specific issues, we avoided sending them the full report for review. Annually, my staff and I would propose a couple of changes before clearing the report. In most cases our changes related to State underfunding various White House priorities in order to fund Secretarial priorities. These issues often had to be elevated to the political level for resolution.

Finally, the allocations are sent informally to State's authorizers and appropriators for review. Although the committees claim they do not clear the allocations — wink, wink — in fact that is what happens. State can't formally submit the 653(a) report to Congress until they complete negotiations with the committees over allocations that didn't turn out as one the Committees had hoped. Unfortunately, the formal allocations are usually not ready to submit to Congress until summer, or more than three quarters of the way through the fiscal year. The bulk of funding in these accounts can't be obligated until the 653(a) report is sent.

Unfortunately, the 653(a) report is not the end of the process, as much of the funding in these accounts is still subject to what is known as congressional notification (CN). Section 7015, an annual general provision in State's appropriations bill, is the most extensive congressional notification provision, although there are numerous other CN provisions scattered throughout both appropriations and authorization bills for State and USAID. These provisions, which apply to a significant portion of foreign assistance funding, require State and USAID to notify both the appropriations and authorization committees of plans for spending funds allocated to a particular country 15 days prior to obligation of funding.

Congressional Withholding of Foreign Policy Funding

It is important to understand that there is a huge philosophical disagreement between the Executive and Legislative Branches over the control of foreign policy. The Executive Branch believes that the Constitution gives the President all the authority to conduct foreign policy, while the Legislative Branch cites its constitutional authority over spending as giving is a measure of control over foreign policy. In fact, according to GAO, between FY 2015 and 2018 the appropriations bills for State and USAID included an annual average of 730 requirements or directives for those agencies to follow[158].

Nobody disagrees with the legality of the "report and wait for a fixed period" type of congressional notification legislative requirement. However, once the 15-day waiting period for a congressional notification expires, State is still often not able to obligate the notified funding due to what are known as congressional "holds". These holds are not included in the 730 average annual congressional directives to State and USAID, because holds have no statutory basis.

Holds work somewhat differently depending on the issue and the committee involved. In some cases, a committee must affirmatively place a hold on a CN, while in other cases a hold is assumed until State is given an affirmative clearance. In essence, each CN requires sign-off, either implicit or explicit, from eight separate organizations, four in the House and four in the Senate. The four in each house are the majority and minority in both the authorizing committees — House Foreign Affairs Committee (HFAC) and Senate Foreign Relations Committee (SFRC) —, and the appropriations subcommittees — House Appropriations Committee Foreign Operations (HACFO) and Senate Appropriations Committee Foreign Operations (SACFO).

The committees do not have to give State a reason for a particular hold. In many cases the hold is to allow time for the committee to negotiate with the department over the types of projects being funded through the CN or the allocation of the funding between countries.   However, in other cases, the hold is a form of "hostage taking" to provide leverage over State on an issue unrelated to the CN and, occasionally, to provide leverage over the Administration on an issue unrelated to State or USAID. It should be noted that, as it only takes one of the eight organizations to hold up the funding, the other seven may be in favor of it moving forward. However, in most cases, the principle of maintaining Congressional leverage over the executive branch, through the hold mechanism, apparently is more important to the committees than any delay in releasing funding to achieve an important policy goal!!!

While State and USAID are not legally required to comply with these holds, only rarely do they defy the committees and "blow" the hold by obligating the funding. The relevant committees view State and USAID's compliance with the holds as a matter of comity between the executive and legislative branches. While in some cases there are legitimate issues needing resolution before the funding is provided to a particular country, State and USAID comply mainly because they fear retribution from the committees either in terms of reduced funding or even more or tighter directives.

A State Department review of CNs that State and USAID submitted to Congress during FY 2019 for funding expiring that year, showed that holds were placed on $2.5 billion (i.e. roughly 50 %) of the $5.0 billion in total funding for those CNs. Holds were placed on 87 CNs, lasting between 1 and 61 days beyond the expiration of the statutory 15 day waiting period. Congress was relatively restrained in FY 2019. In FY 2017, holds of more than 10 days beyond the statutory waiting period were placed on $6.7 billion in funding with 5 holds beyond 100 days, including one hold of 321 days. In FY 2018 holds of more than 10 days were placed on $3.5 billion in funding with five holds of more than 100 days, including one of 201 days.[159]

Administration Withholding of Foreign Policy Funding

For better or worse, U.S. foreign policy is fluid and ever changing as governments change power around the world and uncontrollable events scramble regional or world political dynamics. Whether the changes are the result of peaceful or violent events, in many cases they change the relationship between the U.S. and a particular country, necessitating a review of whether the U.S. should continue to provide funding to that country. Consequently, there are many situations where the U.S. may withhold funding while the U.S. relationship with a country is reevaluated. As we shall see, the State Department's ability to address these situations is much more limited when the funding has been statutorily earmarked for a particular country.

Democratic Administration Withholding

In most cases, money is withheld as leverage to get the government of the affected country to take certain actions, while in other cases the funding may be withheld as punishment for actions already taken. Fortunately, I had retired before the Taliban took over Afghanistan. Prior to the takeover, the U.S. had been appropriating $0.5 billion annually through the State Department, with another couple of billion in previously appropriated but unexpended funds still available, much of which was waiting to be sub-obligated onto actual projects. DOD was providing another $4 to $5 billion annually for the Afghanistan National Security Forces. Obviously, after the Taliban takeover, none of this funding was going to be used for its intended purposes and State was going to be de-obligating as much funding as possible.

To the extent that funding continues to be provided for Afghanistan, it will all be previously unbudgeted humanitarian assistance, none of which will be provided to the Taliban government.

While Afghanistan is a particularly stark example of a funding cutoff, it also happens in response to a range of circumstances. In 2014 during the Obama Administration, for instance, enactment of an anti-homosexuality bill in Uganda created a huge backlash in the European Union (EU) and U.S., even though homosexuality was illegal in other African countries. The World Bank, Sweden, the Netherlands, Norway, Denmark, and the U.S. all suspended or reprogrammed funds that would have gone to Uganda. The $13 million the U.S. reprogrammed was small, particularly given that the U.S. was providing on the order of $700 million to Uganda at the time. However, a huge portion of that funding was global HIV/AIDS and humanitarian funding, which the U.S. rarely if ever withholds as leverage against a country[160].

Civil wars also present a problem for continuing to provide U.S. foreign assistance. The U.S. was responsible for brokering the agreement that led to the partition of Sudan in 2011 into two countries — Sudan and South Sudan. While Sudan was a pariah regime guilty of extensive human rights abuses and arguably ethnic genocide, the U.S. had high hopes for South Sudan and wanted to do everything possible to make the new country a success. In fact, over $200 million in ESF was appropriated for South Sudan in 2013, in addition to assistance through the global health, humanitarian assistance, and peacekeeping operation accounts.[161]

Unfortunately, everything went awry when a power struggle between South Sudan's President and Vice-President, the leaders of the countries two biggest tribes, led to a civil war in December 2013. Much of the available economic funding was withheld for both policy reasons (i.e. the power struggle) and programmatic reasons (i.e. the civil war made implementation impossible). Consequently, a significant amount of expiring funding was reprogrammed to fund initiatives for Obama's 2014 U.S. Africa Leader's Summit.

The Obama Administration also withheld funding for Ukraine. After pro-Russian President Viktor Yanukovych fled Ukraine in February 2014, an interim government was established, and Presidential elections held in May 2014. The Obama Administration moved quickly to help stabilize the new government, amid a weak economy, by providing a $1 billion loan guarantee in May 2014 at a subsidy cost of $195 million. Due to the need to find offsets to finance such guarantees, as well as approve the subsidy model, my staff was heavily involved with every sovereign loan guarantee. Unfortunately, fighting in the Donbas region that broke out in April 2014 and intensified with the undeclared Russian invasion in August, substantially further weakened the Ukraine economy.

Consequently, in January 2015 the U.S. Treasury announced plans for $2 billion in additional loan guarantees in 2015, $1 billion early in the year and an additional $1 billion later in the year.[162] In fact, a second $1 billion loan guarantee was signed in May 2015 to support the economic reform agenda of President Petro Poroshenko. The loan guarantee was part of a package, along with debt restructuring of private credit, that was needed to unlock an $18 billion tranche of an International Monetary Fund (IMF) bailout package.[163]

Unfortunately, due to the war and weakened economy, the $459 million subsidy cost of the May 2015 loan guarantee was over double the cost of the first guarantee. Furthermore, we had to reprogram the funding from other sources, since the Obama Administration decided not to request supplemental funding for Ukraine, despite the fighting raging in the Donbas. This was even though the Administration had already proposed supplementals or budget amendments that year to: 1) counter ISIS; 2) address unaccompanied alien children arriving at the border from Central America; and 3) fight the West African Ebola outbreak.

Only a handful of countries (i.e. Israel, Jordan, Egypt, Tunisia, and Iraq) have ever received U.S. sovereign loan guarantees and Ukraine was the first recipient outside the Middle East. In general, they are only provided to countries of major strategic importance that can't access private credit markets without the U.S. guarantee. While no country has ever defaulted on one of these guarantees, the high subsidy cost relative to the size of the guarantee reflects the significant credit risk. Consequently, the guarantee provides a huge financial advantage to the country, because they get a rate close to the U.S. cost of borrowing, rather than the sky-high rate they would have to pay if the country could get a loan without a guarantee.

Due to the significant credit risk, the U.S. uses the leverage of the loan guarantee to protect the U.S. investment and obtain financial reforms in the recipient country through the use of "conditions precedent". These are conditions that the country must meet before the U.S. will sign the loan guarantee. I don't recall whether firing Prosecutor General Viktor Shokin was an explicit "condition precedent", but the guarantee was not moving forward without his firing. Vice President Biden made this clear to President Poroshenko multiple times.[164]

My staff and I were following the situation in Ukraine closely during this period and, contrary to the claims of Trump supporter Rudy Giuliani, I never saw anything to indicate that the Administration wanted to fire Shokin to protect the Vice President's son. As unseemly as Hunter Biden's activities were, the U.S. wanted Shokin fired because he wasn't pursuing corruption and was undermining existing cases. Furthermore, it was not just the U.S. government that wanted to get rid of Shokin, but the EU and the IMF as well, because combating corruption was so key to reforming the Ukraine economy as well as protecting these institution's investments in Ukraine. Finally in March 2016, Shokin was formally dismissed by the Ukraine Parliament once the IMF threatened to withdraw funding.[165] After this lengthy delay the U.S. signed the third $1 billion loan guarantee on June 3, 2016[166] at a subsidy cost of $275 million.

Trump Administration Withholding

While President Trump's withholding of Ukraine aid got most of the media's attention, Trump withheld funding in multiple other situations. My observation of Trump's foreign policy is that he didn't like throwing good money after bad and he was always looking for leverage to achieve his foreign policy objectives. In some cases, that leverage might involve imposing tariffs on counties like China that abused trade rules and, in other cases, it involved withholding funds.

Trump also didn't care if his approach was unconventional and he seemed to enjoy flaunting the often, inflexible rules of the foreign policy community. For instance, Trump's unconventional approach to North Korea was blasted by the foreign policy community for giving Kim Jong-Un some unwarranted legitimacy by simply meeting with the President. While Trump's approach failed to get North Korea to give up its nuclear weapons, it at least stopped North Korea from conducting further nuclear testing during his Administration.

Trump similarly stunned the foreign policy establishment in August 2018 when he froze most U.S. aid to organizations providing services in the West Bank and Gaza. The exception was law enforcement aid to the Palestinian Authority which the Israeli government wanted continued to help control militants in the West Bank. Even though the U.S. virtually never withholds humanitarian assistance, Trump's freeze also ended the $300 million annual U.S contribution, through the Migration and Refugee Assistance account, to the United Nations Relief and Works Agency (UNRWA).

UNRWA provides social services at 59 Palestinian refugee camps in multiple countries, which are dense urban dwellings very similar to their surroundings.[167] The Trump Administration view was that the U.S. had gotten little benefit from over 60 years of U.S. contributions to UNRWA and that very few of the camp inhabitants were actual refugees who had been dislocated after the establishment of Israel. Despite the conventional wisdom that the funding cut-off would spark unrest in the Palestinian community, the reaction was relatively mute, in part because other countries picked up some of the funding slack. Given the Trump Administration view that the U.S. provides more than its share of foreign assistance, this kind of reaction was viewed as a win.

Trump's use of carrots to further his unconventional approach to foreign policy was on display when he cut a deal with Sudan in October 2020. This deal allowed Sudan to sign the Abraham Accords and normalize relations with Israel, only a month after the United Arab Emirates and Bahrain had become the first countries to sign. This was a stunning reversal for Sudan which had sent troops to fight against Israel in earlier Arab-Israeli wars and was only possible due to the overthrow of the Bashir government in April 2019.[168] The carrots included sanctions relief as well as funding, after my staff had scrambled to find the needed funding trade-offs to make the deal happen.

Despite an NSC led inter-agency policy process that is designed to think through the implications of various foreign policy actions, President Trump tended to make a lot of seat-of-the-pants decisions without policy input from key cabinet agencies. For instance, once the last ISIS stronghold in Syria was defeated in March 2019, Trump wanted to end U.S. assistance to the portion of Syria controlled by the Syrian Democratic Forces, a coalition of Arab and Kurdish fighters opposed to the government of President Bashar al-Assad. It appeared that Trump didn't want any further entanglement in Syria and, since Syrian refugees were streaming to Europe, he thought the EU should be paying a larger share of the significant Syrian humanitarian assistance costs. Most agencies thought that abandoning our Kurdish allies was a mistake and sought carve-outs to the funding freeze with some success.

A somewhat similar dynamic took place when Trump froze security assistance for Pakistan in January 2018, a position not totally consistent with the FY 2019 Budget that we were just finishing up at the time. Most agencies agreed that Pakistan had failed to act against Afghan Taliban militants who used the border region as a safe haven, but felt the U.S. got value out of certain types of assistance. In particular, a small amount of military training funding for high ranked officers was viewed as critical for maintaining high level links to the Pakistani military. That funding was finally restored in the FY 2021 Trump Budget request.

In February 2019, the Departments of State and Homeland Security (DHS) had signed a Joint Statement with the Northern Triangle countries of El Salvador, Honduras, and Guatemala on migration and security to address the causes of illegal immigration. This was largely a continuation of programs to address the root causes of illegal immigration. These programs had been ramped up by the Obama Administration after the Deferred Action for Childhood Arrivals (DACA) program — which allowed temporary work permits for illegal alien children who had spent most of their lives in the U.S. — was established in June 2012. Unfortunately, DACA had inadvertently triggered a wave of unaccompanied alien children (UAC) coming to the U.S.

President Trump almost immediately undercut the efforts of State and DHS when he tweeted in mid-March that he was ending all foreign assistance to those countries for FY 2017 and 2018 — roughly $500 million — because those countries hadn't done enough to deter illegal immigration to the U. S[169]. The recently enacted FY 2019 appropriations and FY 2020 request were also frozen, but not targeted for reprogramming in case the Northern Triangle countries did more to stem the flow of illegal immigration before those funds needed to be obligated.

This unexpected policy reversal put IAD in the position of having to quickly work with "F" to: 1) identify which funds were affected; 2) determine how the freeze was to be applied to funds that had technically been obligated but for which projects had not been started; and 3) identify options for using those funds consistent with any statutory constraints or earmarks. OMB Acting Director Russ Vought was tasked by the President with enforcing the policy and wasn't happy when we raised several issues which had to go back to the President for further clarification.

As in the case with Syria and Pakistan, the President backed off his hardline position in a few instances where a Cabinet official was able to convince him that certain cuts hurt the interests of the U.S. more than the Northern Triangle countries (e.g. counter-narcotics assistance). Nevertheless, the President's strategy of using the funding cuts as leverage did result in Asylum Cooperation Agreements with the Northern Triangle countries that did help roll back the 2019 surge in illegal immigration.

Deferrals and Rescissions

The Impoundment Control Act (ICA) of 1974 was enacted in the wake of President Nixon's refusal to obligate $12 billion in appropriated funding in 1973 to 1974 in an attempt to reign in the deficit.[170] The Act established formal rules for both withholding appropriated funds, referred to as a deferral, and for canceling appropriated funds, referred to as a rescission. In both cases, the President must transmit a special message to the Congress indicating the amount of budget authority being proposed for deferral or rescission and the rationale for the proposal. Once the special message is transmitted, the funds are reflected on the apportionment as either deferred or withheld pending rescission.

The special message for a deferral must also specify the time period for which the budget authority is deferred, but it may not extend beyond the fiscal year in which the message is transmitted. The deferred funding must be reapportioned for obligation if either House of Congress passes a resolution disapproving the proposed deferral. As demonstrated above, foreign policy funding is at times withheld by the Administration as well as at the behest of Congressional committees. I used the wording "at the behest of Congressional committees" because those committees have no legal authority to require withholding the funds beyond the 15-day waiting period. Consequently, it is technically State or USAID that is withholding the funding, although they would not do so in the absence of the hold.

Rescissions work differently than deferrals. Under a rescission, funds included in the special message are automatically withheld from obligation for 45 days of continuous congressional session or until Congress passes and the President signs a bill which rescinds the funding. Rescissions bills are considered by Congress under special floor rules, which make it harder to delay floor consideration and easier to enact the bill. Under these special rules, Congress is free to enact only a portion of the President's proposal but may not include any proposed rescissions that were not included in the President's special message. Funds withheld pending rescission must be released following expiration of the prescribed 45 days of continuous session if a Presidential rescission proposal is not enacted into law.

As will be discussed later in the chapter, there are two major disagreements between OMB and GAO concerning implementation of the ICA. The first issue concerns under what circumstances withholding funds triggers the requirement to transmit a special message because the withholding meets the definition of a deferral under the ICA. The second issue concerns whether the Administration can transmit a rescission proposal where the 45-day withholding period extends beyond the period of availability for the funds. Under such a circumstance, even if Congress does not enact a rescission bill, the funding will have expired and no longer be available for obligation. This situation became known within OMB as a "pocket rescission" due to its similarity to a "pocket veto" of a bill. While there is a partisan element to a pocket rescission, the deferral issue reflects an institutional dispute between the executive and legislative branches.

Developing a Pocket Rescission for State and USAID Funding

As was discussed earlier, President Trump was not a fan of State and USAID "soft power" spending and OMB Deputy Director Russ Vought was even less supportive. Consequently, the potential for a State and USAID "pocket rescission" package of funding that would expire at the end of FY 2018 (i.e. September 30, 2018) was explored. As the funding could not be put on hold until the President signed the rescission proposal, State and USAID were not told such a proposal was being considered until late in the process to avoid accelerated spending that would minimize the amount of funding rescinded.

OMB estimates the amount potentially available for rescission by looking at the spending pattern for the relevant agencies in prior years. While this is the best available method, its accuracy depends on the stability of the spending pattern between years. In this case, however, somebody apparently tipped off USAID, most likely an NSC staffer, and they went on a spending rampage. Whereas 49 percent of FY 2017 DA funding was available at the end of July, only 22 percent was available two weeks later, after $1.5 billion had been hurriedly obligated. Consequently, the unobligated amount available for rescission was smaller than hoped.

Needless to say, Russ Vought, who had been honchoing this effort, was not happy with the final amount. As the amount of savings was too small given the expected backlash, no rescission proposal was sent to Congress. I am sure that he knew that I had not tipped off USAID but, nevertheless, I think he held me responsible for his embarrassment anyway. The outcome of the 2018 rescission proposal also most likely had an impact on some of the events related to a second pocket rescission proposal and Ukraine funds withholding in 2019 that I will discuss next. Unfortunately, these two matters are closely inter-twinned.

Withholding Ukraine Military Assistance Funding

For FY 2019, there were two sources of funding assistance to help Ukraine purchase U.S. made weapons. The first was the State Department's Foreign Military Financing (FMF) account, which had been aiding Ukraine since FY 2014, and the second was DOD's Ukraine Security Assistance Initiative (USAI), which came into existence in FY 2016. As indicated earlier, FMF is supposed to be the source for all such military assistance, but funding is easier to find within DOD's budget than State's. However, the programs were essentially redundant in purpose, as most of the same weapons and services could be purchased through either account.

For FY 2019, $115 million was earmarked specifically for Ukraine within FMF, while $250 million was earmarked for Ukraine through USAI. The State Department FMF funding was part of a broader $445 million in total State/USAID assistance to Ukraine, the largest piece of which was $250 million in economic assistance through AEECA. In turn, the Ukraine assistance was part of a broader $1.4 billion initiative referred to as Countering Russian Malign Influence (CRMI), which had been established in response to Russian annexation of the Crimea and fighting in the Donbas.

On June 19, 2019, my colleagues in the National Security Division got word that the unobligated portion of the $250 million in DOD Ukraine funding had been put on hold. Two days later, State submitted a CN for FY 2019 earmarked FMF allocations which included the $115 million for Ukraine.

There was confusion initially about whether the hold on Ukraine military assistance funding just applied to the DOD funds or the similar State funding. Eventually, it was clarified that the hold extended to the State funding as well. The amount of the State funding subject to the freeze expanded when State allocated an additional $26 million in FMF funding for Ukraine from expiring two-year OCO funding that was not earmarked for any specific country. This brought the total amount of State Department frozen funding to $141 million.

Controversial Issues with Withholding

There are three separate and distinct issues that have been raised concerning the Ukraine funding delay that I will address in turn. These issues are: 1) whether any withholding of funds for Ukraine is justified; 2) the rationale for withholding funds; and 3) whether withholding the funds prevents their obligation.

Can Withholding Funds Be Justified?

Concerning the first issue about whether any withholding of funds can be justified, my answer is a resounding yes! As this chapter has demonstrated, foreign assistance funds are withheld at times for a variety of reasons and have been done so in the recent past by the Obama and Trump Administrations as well as routinely by the Congress. In October 2019, as part of the House impeachment inquiry, deputy chief of mission for Ukraine Bill Taylor testified how terrible it was to delay military assistance during an active conflict. I met Bill when he was at the U.S. Institute of Peace and have great respect for his abilities. However, I think he dramatically overstated the impact of the delay.

First, the delay was relatively short. Due to the bureaucratic DOD procurement process, the $250 million in DOD funding was unlikely to be obligated much before the end of the fiscal year under any circumstances. In the case of the State funding, the earmarked FMF funding routinely did not get obligated until the last week of the fiscal year and the $26 million in extra funding was totally unexpected and must have been viewed by the Ukraine military as a form of "manna from heaven".

Furthermore, while people were still occasionally being killed near the line of contact in the Donbas area of Ukraine, the conflict was basically simmering in the summer of 2018. It was nothing like the heavy fighting in 2014, during a period when President Obama wouldn't provide any lethal assistance to Ukraine. In particular, Obama refused to provide the Javelin anti-tank weapons, despite Vice-President Biden's urging, that have been so effective against Russian tanks during the 2021 war. In fact, it was the Trump Administration that reversed the policy and allowed Ukraine to receive Javelins.

What is the Rationale for Withholding Funds?

This was a big mystery to us, although it is not uncommon for career staff not to receive an explanation for certain decisions by political appointees. In this case, however, IAD was put in the position of having to explain the funding pause to other agencies at an inter-agency meeting without knowing either the rationale or, even more importantly, whether the funds would be unfrozen in time to obligate them before they expired.

From my standpoint, there could be two legitimate reasons for withholding the funding. First, consistent with long standing concerns about corruption in the Ukraine, it would be legitimate to withhold funding until the Ukraine Government had taken certain actions to reign in corruption. Second, consistent with the Trump view that the U.S. pays too great a share for militarily protecting Europe, it would plausibly be justified to hold U.S. funding until other European countries contributed more to the defense of Ukraine.

The problem with both these potential explanations is that they take time to implement and would be unlikely to have an impact before the DOD funding needed to be obligated. For instance, even a very specific action of the Obama Administration to combat corruption, by having Prosecutor General Shokin fired, took on the order of six months.

Furthermore, the Trump Administration did not have a good track record in opposing corruption. The only real successful anti-corruption measure I have ever seen was the establishment of the UN backed International Commission Against Impunity in Guatemala (CICIG), which brought down Guatemala's President in 2015. While his successor got elected on an anti-corruption platform, when CICIG started investigating his family, President Morales banned the key prosecutors from the country and defied an order from Guatemala's Constitutional Court to let them return.[171] If the Trump Administration was serious about corruption, it should have used its leverage to get CICIG's mandate extended, and the prosecutors returned to their jobs.

The official explanation for the Ukraine funding delay, given around the time the funding was released, was that the President wanted data on the size of contributions to Ukraine by the EU countries. Using funding leverage for a data collection, as opposed to obtaining bigger contributions, seems like a flimsy rationale, since OMB would always do its best to compile data in response to a Presidential request.

On the other hand, OMB staff had no reason to think the funding was being withheld until Ukraine dug up dirt on Hunter Biden. In fact, at the time I don't think I knew that Biden even had a son aside from Beau, let alone the family black sheep who was profiting on the Biden name. However, if the Democrat's position is correct, that the funding was withheld to get dirt to harm the Biden candidacy, I would agree with the Bill Taylor view that such behavior is "crazy", not to mention totally outrageous. Unfortunately, other than Gordon Sondland, the only individuals with firsthand knowledge never talked.

Would Withholding Funds Prevent Their Obligation

For OMB staff, this was by far the biggest issue because none of us wanted to be involved in an illegal impoundment. Avoiding an impoundment does not mean that all funding must be obligated before it expires. In fact, agency budget officers are more worried about Anti-Deficiency Act violations for overspending, because those can potentially result in criminal penalties. A budget officer's goal generally is to avoid any overspending and limit the amount of funding lapsing in any year to less than one percent of the account total.

The threat of an impoundment was a much larger problem for my National Security Division counterpart, Mark Sandy, related to the DOD funding than it was for me with the State funding. The reason is related to the amount of flexibility available in each circumstance. Mark faced a very difficult situation as the $250 million in Ukraine DOD funding was one year funding that had to be obligated by September 30th through a cumbersome procurement process and could not be transferred to other projects.

In contrast, I had several options to avoid the problem. First, the $26 million in FY 2018 funding was not earmarked for Ukraine and could be reallocated to other countries. Second, while the $115 million in FY 2019 FMF funding had to be obligated for Ukraine, the FMF account included a mix of regular funding with one-year availability, as well as OCO funding with two-year availability. Ukraine funding had been designated as OCO in the past and that option was available in FY 2019, which would allow an extra year to get the funding obligated and avoid an impoundment.

Finally, FMF is unlike any other account in government in that statutorily the funding is considered obligated upon apportionment. Furthermore, unlike my other foreign assistance accounts, I couldn't apportion the funds all up front knowing that I could address any disagreements with State during the CN process. Instead, statutorily I <u>could not apportion</u> the funds until <u>after</u> the 15-day CN period had expired.

The logic of this oddity is that because funding was obligated upon apportionment and obligation can't take place until after the CN period expires, it follows that apportionment (i.e. obligation) also can't occur until the CN expires. As a practical matter, this often meant that FMF funds were apportioned close to the last day of the fiscal year. In fact, that was the norm for the Ukraine FMF funding. Obligation upon apportionment also meant that, unlike for DOD, the funding didn't need to go through the procurement process and be put on specific contracts to avoid a funding lapse.

The Apportionment Controversy

The situation took an unexpected turn on July 30th when Acting Director Vought re-delegated apportionment authority from Mark and I and gave it to our PAD Mike Duffey. This action was totally within the Acting Director's discretion, but it was the first time that anybody could remember it happening.

I never found out the real reason for the re-delegation, although it most likely relates to concerns about our willingness to sign upcoming apportionments. The DOD apportionments related to Ukraine, while the State apportionments related to another potential pocket rescission. In both cases, the apportionments involved pausing obligations to allow policy processes to play out.

DOD Ukraine Apportionments

Mark signed an apportionment on July 25th with a footnote pausing obligations for USAI until August 5th based on DOD assurance that DOD's procurement work would continue, and the pause would not preclude timely execution of the Ukraine funding. Mike Duffey signed two identical apportionments that extended the pause through August 19th. These apportionments only affected $214 million of the original $250 million appropriation.[172]

Mike signed an additional six apportionments that lasted through September 11th, but these contained a red flag that might have given Mark pause about signing if he still had the authority. The red flag was that the sentence with the DOD assurance that the pause would not prevent timely execution of the funding was deleted. This did not mean that DOD couldn't get it done, but that they weren't willing to give any assurances. My observation has been that even very bureaucratic organizations can get things done quickly when properly motivated in a crunch. This was certainly demonstrated the previous summer when USAID obligated $1.5 billion in two weeks to keep them from being rescinded.

In the end, the USAI funding was released on September 12 and the vast bulk of it was obligated by September 30th, with the remainder obligated early in the following fiscal year after Congress extended the availability of the funding. Nevertheless, in January 2020 decision, GAO concluded that OMB violated the Impoundment Control Act (ICA) by withholding funds for policy reasons without submitting a deferral[173].

Not surprisingly, OMB's General Counsel's Office vehemently disagreed and responded to a draft of the GAO decision in December 2019. As this is the kind of issue that the lawyers for the two organizations could have a multi-hour legal tea party and only reach an agreement to disagree, as a non-lawyer I won't even try to recap the debate. However, the decision appears to turn on whether the funds were withheld for policy reasons, in which case the withholding would be a deferral, or programmatic reasons, in which case it would not be a deferral.

The only deferral I have prepared in my forty-year career was the wastewater treatment grant deferral in my first year that was discussed in Chapter 3. However, that case was a straightforward policy deferral designed to prevent obligations in order to reduce outlays. The situation is much murkier in most cases because policy and programmatic issues are often two sides of the same coin. For instance, withholding a loan guarantee until Ukraine fired its Prosecutor General is policy, but ensuring that taxpayer dollars are well spent by minimizing corruption is programmatic. OMB's position on programmatic delays has resulted in no President issuing a deferral in over twenty years.[174]

Ultimately, if Congress wants to clarify this issue and adopt the stringent GAO interpretation of a deferral, they can amend the ICA. However, I don't expect that to happen, because Congress is often complicit in withholding funds for policy reasons (i.e. State and DOD might have to submit a deferral every time they comply with an informal Congressional hold).

Prelude to Another Pocket Rescission Proposal

I have no idea whether OMB Acting Director Vought knew the real rationale for the Ukraine funding delay, but it is plausible that he didn't because at heart he was a policy nerd and wouldn't necessarily be in the loop on political issues. While Russ was a good soldier who would carry out the President's wishes, he also didn't really care about Ukraine. A more important goal for him was to implement a pocket rescission of international funding and atone for the failed attempt the previous summer.

Unlike for DOD, apportionment action wasn't necessary for the $115 million in State FMF funding because the CN was held up awaiting policy guidance. The controversial State apportionments in August 2019 related to the development of rescission proposals. As the prior year's attempt failed because word of the rescission leaked, OMB political staff was closed mouth, even with IAD staff, about whether there would be another attempt in August 2019.

Nevertheless, earlier events would indicate they were developing a strategy. First, our General Counsel, Mark Paoletta, wanted to get smart on apportionments and had a meeting with me and technical experts from BRD to better understand the general process as well as how apportionments were handled by IAD. Second, Russ and Mark Paoletta met with me and my branch chiefs just before July 4th to better understand the obligation patterns for State and USAID accounts.

It is possible that Paoletta had asked Mike to have us pull together data for that meeting on State/USAID obligations to date for the year and Mike never conveyed the tasking to us. As the PADs are typically overstressed, it was not unusual for assignments not to be conveyed to the career staff in a timely manner, forcing us to scramble to get the work done. In any event, Fouad Saad, my branch chief for Economic Affairs, and I received some criticism for not having provided the requested data that we didn't know had been requested. This left Fouad fuming.

While I found Mark Paolleta could be very personable in a social setting, he was an ideological warrior on the job. At a later time, Paoletta made a statement that he couldn't get data on State and USAID obligations until Mike Duffey arrived as PAD. I held my tongue, but I was furious that I essentially was being publicly accused of insubordination. Not only was that incorrect, but Mike Duffey was clueless about such issues and had little role in getting data from State. Fortunately, I don't think Fouad was at that meeting.

We started preparing a pocket rescission in late July, which basically included the same accounts as the prior year. The formula was simple, propose to rescind all remaining funding in these accounts that was above the level requested in the President's Budget and would expire after September 30th. The rescission proposal included the extra $26 million in FMF that State wanted to allocate to Ukraine. However, it did not include the frozen $250 million in DOD and $115 million in earmarked FMF State funding. I have always wondered whether President Trump would have wanted it included if he knew that option was available.

State Department Apportionment Issues

Mike Duffey signed his first apportionment on August 3rd which made the funding in ten accounts unavailable for obligation until three business days after OMB received an accounting of the remaining unobligated balances in those accounts. It is possible that concern about my willingness to sign this kind of apportionment was behind the apportionment authority re-delegation. However, I would have signed that apportionment because the short obligation delay would not have resulted in a funding lapse. In fact, in my twenty years as a DAD, I had only balked at signing one apportionment and that was in the Obama Administration for a program the Trump Administration declined to fund. As with all apportionments, the Director always has the option to sign the apportionment instead of the DAD if the Director really wants the apportionment to take effect.

The problem in that situation was that the proposal was to use FY 2017 CR funding for the Green Climate Fund (GCF). However, the House appropriations bill explicitly included a ban on GCF funding and the CR included standard language prohibiting expenditure of funding that would preclude Congressional funding options (i.e. no GCF). In that case, however, there was a viable alternative. The alternative was to reprogram up to $500 million in FY 2016 ESF funding for GSF. This was on top of the $500 million we had already reprogrammed for a program which had received no funding in the appropriations bill.

While this alternative was a somewhat smaller amount than the proposal to use FY 2017 CR funding, it was legal. However, it left the State Department with virtually no reprogramming flexibility for the remainder of the year. Not surprisingly, when this funding was announced the political left was ecstatic and the political right was furious. Ironically, in an analogous situation in the Trump Administration, funding was reprogrammed for the border wall from accounts which included no such funding. In that case, however, the roles were reversed with the political left being furious and the political right being ecstatic.

After receiving the requested data, Mike signed a second apportionment on August 9th which made the funding for those accounts available at a daily rate calculated to obligate the remaining funds by September 30th. By knowing how much funding remained as of August 8th and the maximum amount that could be obligated daily, this approach was not only legal but also prevented a repeat of the previous year's "August surprise" of panicked spending. The result was that $4 billion would be available for a late August rescission.

Making the Funds Available

Despite the effort to ensure a significant level of State and USAID funding was available for a pocket rescission, the rescission package was never submitted to Congress. Whether the decision was influenced by the Ukraine controversy or opposition to the rescission by Secretary of State Mike Pompeo is unclear, but it was a major disappointment to Russ. State was informed that no funds would be rescinded, and Mike Duffey signed a new apportionment on August 29th which apportioned the remaining funds on a weekly basis for the month of September.

If the rescission had been sent forward, it would have faced bipartisan opposition in Congress. However, the only way for Congress to make those funds available was to re-appropriate the funding after the rescission and it is not clear the votes would have been available to take that action. Most likely the issue would have wound up in court with opponents of the pocket rescission citing a December 2018 GAO opinion that such an action would violate the ICA.

It is unclear how the courts would rule on this issue since the 2018 GAO opinion reversed the view GAO held in the 1970's when it allowed smaller pocket rescissions in the Ford Administration. Furthermore, the ICA is very explicit in prohibiting deferrals from extending beyond the year of the deferral but is silent on any such prohibitions for rescissions.[175] Even if the court ruled that a pocket rescission violated the ICA, it is unclear if the court had any authority to restore expired funding or whether that would be left to the Congress.

While the President's decision meant that the $26 million in FY 2018 FMF funding for Ukraine wouldn't be rescinded, it still had to go through the CN process. In fact, while we had the flexibility to prevent any State funding from lapsing, we only had until September 14th to submit CN's to either: 1) obligate the funding for Ukraine; or 2) reallocate the funding to other countries and shift the $115 million for Ukraine to OCO with two-year availability. Fortunately, the President released the funding and State sent the CNs to Congress on September 11th, even though we didn't hear the news until the next day. Consequently, all the State Ukraine FMF funding was obligated by September 30th.

Impeachment Inquiry

Our hope was that life would get back to normal after the rescission proposal was rejected and the President allowed the Ukraine funds to move forward. Unfortunately, that hope was dashed when the whistleblower compliant alleging the President had abused his power became public on September 9th and Speaker Pelosi initiated the impeachment inquiry on September 24th.

As the inquiry proceeded, the potential for being deposed started to become real by mid-October, particularly after Mike Duffey refused to appear for his deposition. My FMF examiner was panicked about the possibility that she could be subpoenaed. I told her that it was very unlikely the inquiry would reach down to her level. Part of her concern stemmed from the fact that she was not eligible for professional liability insurance. By this time, OMB had implemented a new benefit to subsidize up to half the cost of the insurance for its executives. I took advantage of this new benefit to upgrade the insurance I had been getting for fifteen years since I first started working on the Cobell case. I didn't realize at the time, but the upgraded insurance paid for representation at Congressional hearings, whereas the base insurance was just for representation in court cases.

To Testify or Not to Testify, That is the Question

Unfortunately, once Mike Duffey and Russ Vought decided not to be deposed, it increased the chances that the House Intelligence Committee would seek statements from Mark Sandy and I, as they didn't want to take the time needed to litigate the refusal of Mike and Russ to comply with their subpoenas. Internally, there was pressure on career staff to follow the Director's lead and not comply with any subpoenas because the President had ordered Executive Branch staff not to comply. I personally did not find that very comforting.

In my mind, this seemed like the dilemma Odysseus faced in returning from Troy and having to try to steer the

narrow passage between the monster Scylla and the whirl-
pool Charybdis. In this case, the decision was between
defying the direction of the President and OMB leadership
(i.e. Scylla) and defying an enforceable Congressional subpoena (i.e. Charybdis). To me it was an unfair choice and, if
my testimony had been requested, I was thinking seriously
about counter-suing the President and Congress in order to
get judicial direction about which order to comply with and
which to ignore.

In fact, in late October Charlie Kupperman, the Deputy
National Security Advisor, followed essentially this strategy. Furthermore, the strategy worked as the Committee withdrew its subpoena for his testimony on November
6th.[176] However, I was later told that, as Charlie was a White
House employee, he had an additional defense available to
him that I didn't and, therefore, a stronger case for defying
a Congressional subpoena.

In early November, my NSD counterpart Mark Sandy received an order to appear for a closed-door deposition as
part of the impeachment inquiry. The short time frame to
comply put Mark under incredible pressure at an already
stressful time of year. Acting Director Vought was very
proud that no current or former OMB employees had agreed
to testify and wanted Mark to maintain the company line.
The budget DADs were unanimous in telling Mark that they
would support him no matter what he decided.

After talking to a lawyer, Mark decided to give the deposition on Saturday November 16th, but his lawyer insisted
that he receive a subpoena first.[177] Mark told me that, on
advice of counsel, he didn't wouldn't answer any questions
about State Department funding, even though that would increase the chances that I would be called for a deposition. I
told him that his position was perfectly appropriate. While
some witnesses at the inquiry reportedly had to raise funds
to pay their lawyer bills, Mark was fortunate in having the
high level of professional liability insurance. As his lawyer
was willing to accept the insurance company rates, I don't
think that Mark ever paid a nickel in legal costs.

As might be expected, given that he didn't have any
bombshell information to reveal, both sides came out of the

five-hour deposition spouting that Mark's testimony provided support for their position on the legality of the President's actions regarding Ukraine[178]. In the absence of a real
bombshell, some in the press tried to manufacture one, once
the transcript of Mark's testimony was released, by imply-
ing in reports that two OMB staff members quit over the
withholding of Ukraine aid.[179] That reporting was, at best,
a misrepresentation of what Mark said and, at worst, incorrect.

One of those staffers was an OGC lawyer, who had had
several disagreements on legal positions with her political
boss, Mark Paoletta. However, I never heard that the withholding of Ukraine aid was the reason she left. Furthermore, as a sharp and highly capable lawyer, it was not surprising she could get a job elsewhere with a promotion.

The other staffer who resigned was my branch chief
Fouad Saad who, as Mark pointed out in his testimony, was
not responsible for the State FMF funding that was being
withheld. Furthermore, when Fouad told me he was leaving, he said that he made the decision before the Ukraine
funding hold. Nevertheless, Fouad had issues with both
Trump Administration policies as well as with some of the
appointees. I was never sure whether his raised voice at
that awful meeting with Russ and Paoletta in early July reflected long-standing tensions with the Administration or
was the trigger for his deciding to leave.

When it came time in August to rate SES staff for the
year, Russ essentially dictated all the ratings even though,
as a third line supervisor for the branch chiefs, the Director
would never normally have such a role. Unfortunately, he
directed me to downgrade Fouad's rating to a "Meets". It is
unclear how much of this was due to his lowering the overall curve of SES ratings and how much was score settling. In
any event, Fouad was a high-performance branch chief who
deserved a better rating even in a world of overall lower
ratings.

I appealed the rating and pointed out that, if it reflected
dissatisfaction with Fouad's behavior at the July meeting,
that meeting occurred a few days <u>after</u> the end of the rating period and couldn't be considered. Alternatively, if the

downgrade was to meet a lower curve, I offered to let him reduce my rating to raise Fouad's. However, what I think convinced Russ to restore Fouad's rating was when I let Russ know that Fouad was leaving, and I didn't want him to have to compete for new jobs with a ratings downgrade.

In the case of Mark Sandy, Russ never took any overt action to retaliate against him for defying the President's order and testifying, but the relationship seemed irreparably damaged. However, the following summer, Russ unilaterally took action to downgrade one of Mark's branch chiefs to a special assistant position on the management side. Although Mark was highly opposed to this action, he didn't have the political capital to reverse it.

Dodging the Bullet

When Mark's attorney returned from his deposition, she told our Counsel's office that House Intelligence Committee staff were reporting that I would be the next witness called for a deposition. While ignoring a subpoena like Russ and Mike Duffey had done was never an option, I still hadn't decided whether to provide the deposition like Mark had, or whether to follow the Kupperman strategy of taking the issue to court. While I wanted to talk through the issue with a lawyer, my concern was that the decision on whether to contact Sandy's lawyer or Kupperman's lawyer might have dictated the advice I would get.

Given the Democrats stated desire to have an impeachment vote in December, before the primaries and election year activities became a distraction, I knew they were running out of time for fact finding. My assumption was that they would need to depose me before Thanksgiving, and I was concerned about being jammed on the deposition and having trouble lining up a lawyer for a deposition a couple of days before Thanksgiving.

On November 25th, the Monday before Thanksgiving, however, House Intelligence Committee Chairman Adam Schiff announced that the Committee would release its report after the Thanksgiving recess. At that point, I figured that I had dodged the bullet, most likely because the

Democrats had run out of time, although possibly in con-junction with their coming to the correct conclusion that I would have little to add to what Mark had told them. As a policy wonk who is often appalled by political outcomes, it is somewhat ironic that a political consideration was what saved me from having to testify.

CHAPTER TEN: Balancing Costs and Benefits -- *Presidential Regulatory Review EOs*

This chapter will discuss OMB's regulatory review function, starting with its history. In particular, the chapter will discuss the regulatory review and paperwork reduction authorities, the roles of OIRA and RMO staff, and what issues, such as risks and costs, are considered during a review.

When I attended my first DAD budget markup in the fall of 1979, my branch chief, Jim Tozzi, wasn't present, much to the annoyance of his boss, Don Crabill, the DAD for NRD at the time. Unfortunately for Don, Jim Tozzi was a power unto himself. At the time he was working directly for OMB Director Jim Lynn on a project to develop a regulatory budget. The regulatory budget would be somewhat analogous to the funding budget in that a cap would be set on regulatory costs that an agency would not be allowed to exceed. The proposal, however, was a bridge, or two, too far and eventually imploded due to technical, legal, and political issues.

Nevertheless, at the end of budget season in January 1980, Tozzi moved to the management side of OMB to become the DAD for the small and weak Regulatory Policy and Reports Management Division (RPRMD). The division's key responsibility was implementing the Federal Reports Act of 1942, which sought to limit information collection burdens imposed by Federal agencies, excluding the Internal Revenue Service (IRS). However, as the IRS currently accounts for 70 percent of the information collection burden imposed by the Federal government, that exemption was huge.

At the time, RPRMD didn't have any formal regulatory review responsibilities. However, Tozzi had been involved in regulatory reviews previously in the Nixon and Ford Administration's as part of the Quality of Life program. While that program was before my tenure, Environment Branch staff had expressed to me how annoyed they were when it was terminated at the beginning of Carter's term, because the branch had played a central role in those reviews.

The Carter Administration replaced the Quality of Life reviews with a limited set of regulatory reviews by the Regulatory Analysis Review Group (RARG), which was an inter-agency group chaired by a Senate confirmed member of the Council of Economic Advisers (CEA). However, much of the staff work, and development of public comments, for those reviews was done by employees at the Council on Wage and Price Stability (CWPS), as the impetus for many of the reviews was to mitigate the impact of rulemakings on inflation, which was soaring in the late 1970's.

Paperwork Reduction Act

While OMB policy officials have never wanted OMB career staff freelancing on the Hill, Jim Tozzi was an exception. He had extensive Congressional interaction in his previous job at the Army Corps of Engineers and saw no reason to stop once he was at OMB. Consequently, Tozzi became a significant lobbyist for OMB in passing the Paperwork Reduction Act (PRA) late in 1980.

Like Superfund, the PRA was passed in the lame duck session of Congress after Reagan's election victory over Carter. Unlike Superfund, the PRA could have been enacted after Reagan took office. However, Tozzi helped persuade business groups not to wait. According to an aide to Senate Committee Chair Lawton Chiles, the fact that Tozzi would probably be running the new program helped overcome their reservations.[180] For his efforts, Tozzi got a framed signed copy of the PRA to hang in his office.

While OIRA review of regulations is very controversial with many groups, paperwork reduction has wide public and bipartisan support because EVERYBODY hates paperwork. The implementation of the PRA and subsequent amendments is certainly OIRA most popular success. The reason is that federally imposed paperwork is a burden for the entire citizenry, because by far the biggest paperwork burden consists of tax forms, with the decennial Census and federally imposed medical paperwork being a far smaller, but still very significant, additional burden.

In contrast, current regulatory review focuses primarily on significant rules imposing costs of more than $100 million in any year, which in most cases means large effects on very large businesses and factories or, occasionally, small effects across many small businesses, households, and individuals. While the large industries affected by these rules are critical to the success of the U.S. economy, they are easy for the press to demonize if industries push back that the marginal cost of a portion of the rule is greater than the marginal benefit. While the public and the press are usually not sympathetic to big business, they are sympathetic to the travails of average citizens drowning in incomprehensible paperwork.

Paperwork or its electronic equivalent, nevertheless, is critical to the functioning of the Federal Government. In fact, even with OIRA review, the public spent roughly 11.5 billion hours in 2018 responding to various Federal information requirements.[181] For agency bureaucrats, more paperwork is often better than less if it provides some marginal utility for enforcement or statistical analysis of the program. The task for OIRA desk officers is to advocate for a positive value of information collected, to avoid or mitigate against duplication, and to use statistically sound sampling as opposed to census-like collections. In essence, to find the happy medium between providing sufficient data collection for agencies to successfully implement their programs, while not needlessly burdening the public.

Under the PRA, agencies must get a "control number" from OMB, which lasts for three years, before imposing an information collection burden on the public. This burden may include recordkeeping, and third-party disclosures, such as food labels or gas-mileage estimates for new vehicles.[182] An information collection can be in paper form, website survey, or electronic submission. In order to get OMB's approval for a control number, the agency must define the objective being met by the collection, estimate the paperwork burden, and justify the use of the information. Usually, the information collection is subject to a 60-day public comment period after publication in the Federal Register.

OIRA staff rarely question the need for an information collection because most are renewals of an earlier approved Information Collection Request (ICR). However, like budget examiners reviewing the budget, they will review the proposed information collection with a skeptical eye as to whether all the collection's data elements are really necessary or if the information is still needed. OIRA is also required to annually publish a report called the Information Collection Budget of the United States, which allows OIRA and the public to see the overall burden that government forms place on the public.

Regulatory Review EO 12291

In addition to enhancing OMB's paperwork review authority, the PRA also established the Office of Information and Regulatory Affairs to be headed by a new Presidentially appointed Senate confirmed Administrator. OIRA's authority was further enhanced by other two actions: 1) President Reagan's February 17, 1981, issuance of E.O. 12291 — Federal Regulation; and 2) the transfer of much of the former CWPS staff to OMB to provide a needed boost in staffing and expertise. The EO was issued with the following goals:

> "reduce the burdens of existing and future regulations, increase agency accountability for regulatory actions, provide for presidential oversight of the regulatory process, minimize duplication and conflict of regulations, and insure well-reasoned regulations".[183]

The Administrative Procedure Act (APA) requires that all agencies publish notices of proposed rulemakings (NPRM) for public comment in the Federal Register and that agencies consider and respond to those comments when the agency publishes the final rulemaking (FRM) in the Federal Register. The APA is a crosscutting statute that applies to rulemaking across the Federal Government unless a statute explicitly exempts a rulemaking from the APA. The APA itself includes an exemption to the requirement for an NPRM in emergency circumstances. In emergency situations, agencies are allowed to issue interim final rules (IFR), which allow the rule to become effective immediately but also opens a simultaneous comment period which can result in an amended FRM, if valid adverse public comments are received.

Essentially EO 12291 piggybacks on the APA process by giving OIRA the responsibility to review all agency rules, excluding independent regulatory agencies, in both proposed and final form before publication in the Federal Register. For all major rules, agencies were required by the EO to provide a Regulatory Impact Analysis (RIA), which is essentially a cost-benefit analysis that was to be quantified whenever possible. Furthermore, for these major rules OIRA was to get 60 days to review the draft RIA and NPRM and 30 days to review the final RIA and FRM. For non-major rules, OIRA had 10 days of review time at both the proposed and final rulemaking stages.

All of a sudden, this put OIRA in the role of having to review over 2,000 rules annually, a backbreaking burden even with the additional staff from CWPS, which had pushed OIRA's total staffing level to around 80.[184] This put OIRA staff in the position of having to devote at least some time to hundreds of minor rules that may have been better spent focusing on the major rules given their staffing constraints. Nevertheless, changing major rules required more political capital than the minor rules so some OIRA staff felt more effective when they tackled the efficiency of minor rulemaking.

As discussed in the Superfund chapter, OIRA was also limited by the fact that they only had the authority to review, not approve agency proposed rulemakings. As EO 12291 was issued under the President's general constitutional authority to manage the Executive Branch, it could not override explicit statutory authority that vested in the heads of departments and agencies the authority, and often mandate, to promulgate various rules. Agencies that understood this relationship between the EO and applicable law were, therefore, in a position to ignore OIRA's comments on the rules in the absence of strong White House pressure to take OIRA's recommended changes.

As OIRA struggled to assert itself in those early days, the issue came to a head in a dispute between EPA and OIRA over a hazardous waste rule. EPA decided to ignore OIRA's comments and send its rule to the Federal Register for publication. Jim Tozzi, however, was a master at wielding power and his motto was "speak softly and carry the biggest stick you can find"[185]. In this case, the stick was the PRA.

Tozzi chose this particular rule for a fight because its implementation was dependent on a major information collection. Consequently, he informed EPA that, while he couldn't stop them from sending the rule to the Federal Register, he wouldn't issue a PRA control number for the information collection needed to implement the rulemaking. Furthermore, he told EPA that he would include language in the Federal Register letting the business community know that they didn't need to comply with the rule due to the lack of an OMB control number.

EPA, of course, was furious but had no choice but to come back to OMB and negotiate over how to address the OIRA comments. Tozzi had made his point and, in the process, sent a message to EPA and other agencies about how OIRA could leverage its approval authority under the PRA to strengthen its hand in EO 12291 reviews.

Regulatory Review EO 12866 and Data Quality Act

OIRA's ability to make changes to rules consistent with the objectives of the regulatory review EOs has ebbed and flowed over time. Generally, OIRA is in a stronger position during Republican Administrations and a weaker position during Democratic Administrations. It is notable that OIRA's regulatory review authority has never been fully codified, although some reporting requirements have been enacted, because there has never been sufficient political support in Congress to accomplish that objective.

Especially in the 1980s, left-leaning activist organizations, particularly environmental groups, wanted to get rid of the EO. However, that hasn't happened for a couple of reasons. First, even Democratic Presidents are leery of the costs and potential economic disruption that unchecked regulatory agencies, particularly EPA, can impose. While agencies tend to have a single mission focus, the White House has multiple objectives, including political ones, and Presidents need some measure of White House control over agencies. Second, the political cost of rescinding the EO was too high to make it worthwhile, particularly since the next Republican President could simply restore it anyway. Consequently, the calculus appears to have been that it was better to manage the regulatory review process than get rid of it.

The Clinton Administration approach to this problem was to revoke EO 12291 and issue a new EO 12866. In most ways, the new EO was very similar to the old one except that it changed some definitions, lengthened OIRA review time and limited OIRA review to "significant" regulatory actions. This included all rules imposing a cost of over $100 million in any year, but also other rules that OIRA deemed to be significant because of their novelty, budget effects, or inconsistency with another agency's mission. This change cut the number of rules subject to OIRA review to between 500 and 700 per year[186]. Given that OIRA's staffing level had drifted downward since its 1981 high, consistent with overall OMB staffing, this meant that OIRA didn't need to waste time on the minor rules. EO 12866 also increased the transparency of OIRA review by requiring agencies to disclose changes made to the rule due to OIRA review.

In addition to the EO changes, Clinton appointed a particularly strong and capable individual, Sally Katzen, as OIRA Administrator to ride herd over both the agencies and OIRA staff. Ms. Katzen had previously served during the Carter Administration as General Counsel to CWPS from 1979 to 1981. Nevertheless, these changes didn't necessarily guarantee smooth sailing with the agencies. Clinton's EPA Administrator, Carol Browner, was the quintessential team player on budget issues, submitting budgets close to her budget ceiling even when the rest of the Cabinet did not. Whether this was a calculated strategy or not, it gave her more leeway to play lone wolf on regulatory issues in disputes with the White House.

The most consequential rules of that era were EPA's proposals to simultaneously tighten the NAAQS standard for ozone and establish a standard for PM 2.5 (i.e. particulate matter particles no larger than 2.5 micrometers), which hadn't been regulated previously. This provoked a major battle within the Clinton Administration over the stringency and timing of the new rules. At least a few key White House staff were very upset with Browner's inflexibility on the levels of the new standards.

Some of the concerns related to the economic impact of the new rules, but some may have also reflected tensions caused by the debate over the proposed rule occurring just prior to the 1996 Presidential election. However, Browner stood her ground and the proposed rules were issued in late November 1996. President Clinton issued an implementation memorandum to ease the transition to PM 2.5 as there were no monitors to detect such small particles, and to determine whether health effects were due solely to size or the composition of the small particles. The Obama Administration faced similar tensions when Obama was up for reelection in 2012 but was able to shift controversial EPA regulations until after the election with less resistance.

E.O. 12866 has remained in place since 1993 and has been implemented in all succeeding Administrations. This is noteworthy since many EOs remain on the books but are ignored when a President from a different party is elected. The most important amendment to EO 12866 occurred during the Presidency of George W. Bush who explicitly clarified that OIRA's review authorities included guidance documents in case anyone had any doubt that "regulatory action," as defined in EO 12866, was broad enough to include them.

Industry viewed these guidance documents as tantamount to rulemakings that should have been subject to OIRA review and that didn't necessarily go through the APA notice and comment process. EPA, HHS, and other agencies have argued that such guidance should not go through OIRA review since the guidance is not enforceable. The controversy over review of guidance has split along partisan lines, with OIRA review being imposed during Republican Administrations (i.e. Bush & Trump) but rescinded in Democratic Administration (i.e. Obama & Biden). Nevertheless, it should be noted that virtually all regulatory actions by the Food and Drug Administration are guidance documents and most significant such actions have been reviewed by OIRA across multiple administrations both Democrat and Republican.

Perhaps the most important, certainly the most controversial, change to OIRA's statutory authority since its creation, was the enactment of the Data Quality Act (DQA) (aka Information Quality Act) in December 2000. It was the brainchild of Jim Tozzi who had left OMB in 1983 to start his own regulatory lobbying firm. Whereas environmental organizations have always wanted more transparency about the OIRA process, industry wanted more transparency about the science used to justify regulations, as the data was often not publicly available nor was the science reproducible.

At Tozzi's behest, the language was slipped into a huge omnibus appropriations bill as a general provision by Representative Jo Emerson and Senator Richard Shelby, which President Clinton signed in late December 2000 shortly before he left office.[187] Most appropriation general provisions apply only to the agencies covered by a specific bill and only for one year. However, Tozzi had drafted the language to be permanent law and had it inserted into the one section of the bill that had government-wide applicability.

The provision consisted of two short sections and required OMB to issue guidelines for "ensuring and maximizing the quality, objectivity, utility and integrity of information (including statistical information) disseminated by the agency"[188]. Basically, the law allowed private parties to petition agencies to withdraw information that did not meet the statutory standard.

The DQA sent the activist community into a froth about it being an anti-science provision that would derail or delay numerous regulations. In reality, the DQA was neither the strong tool that regulated entities hoped, nor the nemesis that environmental and other NGO groups feared. The Act's brevity, which allowed the provision to be slipped into the appropriations bill undetected, also undermined its usefulness. Unlike most regulatory statutes, it included no enforcement language. In particular, it did not include a citizen suit provision that would allow an aggrieved party to take an agency to court for failure to correct a problem with the data.

Types of Rulemakings

The enactment of the Clean Air Act Amendments (CAAA) of 1990 triggered the need for hundreds of new regulations, many of them highly consequential and costly. While my branch stayed heavily involved, it was the OIRA branch responsible for EPA that took the lead in reviewing the new rules. Although many rules follow new legislation such as the CAAA, others are imposed under long-standing statutes. In some cases, these are needed because the statute requires periodic review and updates to the rules (e.g. National Ambient Air Quality Standards), while in other cases a new need may have arisen (e.g. vehicle CO_2 standards to address global warming or implementation of the Obamacare act).

Like on the budget side, the workload of individual OIRA desks officers varies depending on the nature of the workload in the agencies they cover. Some agencies impose large paperwork burdens (e.g. Treasury, Census Bureau, Health and Human Services, and the Securities and Exchange Commission) requiring relevant OIRA staff to spend huge amounts of time on PRA issues. Other agencies promulgate major rules requiring OIRA staff review under EO 12866.

Of the 85 major rules promulgated (i.e. issued in final form) in FY 2016, 31 fell in a specific category referred to as "transfer rules". In general, transfer rules implement Federal budgetary programs authorized by Congress. These would include rules relating to the Medicare program and Pell education grant programs[189]. These rules are often of more interest to the examiners on the budget side than the OIRA desk officers. For instance, my Agriculture Branch examiners would spend a lot of time reviewing these types of rules, particularly after passage of a new farm bill that would change the requirements for various price support programs. Similarly, the Health Division closely scrutinizes Medicare and Medicaid regulatory actions because such review was the best mechanism available to shape enacted mandatory programs.

The remaining major rules are the most important for OIRA review, because those are the rules that impose the biggest burden on the private sector, cities and states. EPA is the most important of the regulatory agencies, and imposes the most costs, but there are key bureaus within multiple departments, such as the Departments of Health and Human Services, Transportation, Energy and Labor, that also have significant regulatory responsibilities.

The packages that OIRA staff receive from agencies on economically significant rules tend to be lengthy and complex. The package will usually include a draft of the Federal Register notice, proposed or final, and the Regulatory Impact Analysis. In addition, to reading the material, OIRA staff often hold marathon, multi-hour interagency meetings to go over the rule language in detail.

At the proposed stage, the draft NPRM will include both the proposed rule as well as text providing the authority for the rule, the rationale for the proposal being chosen over other alternatives, and, ideally, the key evidence supporting the proposal. At the final stage, the draft FRM will include the final rule language, a summary of the comments received during the comment period as well as the agency's rationale for either rejecting comments or making changes in response to comments.

Regulatory Impact Analysis

The development of the RIA is intended to inform the decision-making process. The ideal RIA has a detailed cost-benefit analysis that quantifies all the costs and benefits. Such an ideal is rarely achieved as many benefits, in particular, are difficult to quantify. However, that does not mean they are ignored in the analysis. Lack of quantification just makes decision-making more difficult and subjective. In fact, the conceptual balancing of costs and benefits is the same whether all cost and benefits can be quantified or not.

Benefits that can't be quantified are to be described qualitatively in the RIA and considered in choosing the preferred regulatory option. In the absence of benefit data, the agency can alternatively resort to a cost effectiveness, or break-even analysis to help choose an option. Of course, the purpose of the RIA is to balance societal benefits. However, some agencies resort to including private benefits to dial up or dial down the justification of their regulatory actions. For instance, Corporate Average Fuel Economy (CAFÉ) standards and EPA's CO2 standards were justified by private benefits from consumers' fuel cost savings counted against the rise in vehicle costs.

OMB Circular A-4, issued in 2003 when John Graham was the OIRA Administrator, provides guidance to agencies concerning how to conduct regulatory analysis. While finding the option that generates the largest net benefits is generally the goal of cost-benefit analysis, it should be noted that cost-benefit analysis does not consider distributional effects. As economic efficiency is not always the only public policy objective in rulemaking, distribution effects and other policy goals often must be considered in decision-making to comply with statutory requirements. For instance, EPA prepares an RIA when it considers a revision to ambient air quality standards for transparency purposes. However, as previously noted, the NAAQS standards are health-based standards that must be established without regard to costs.

Ideally, quantified costs and benefits should be monetized wherever possible. However, benefits and costs do not always take place in the same time period. Furthermore, benefits and costs that occur sooner are generally considered more valuable than those that occur later. Thus, benefits and costs distributed over time cannot just be added together. Instead, the stream of benefits and cost over time must be discounted to the present using an appropriate discount rate to produce a net present value of the costs and benefits. According to OMB Circular A-94, the default position for regulatory analysis is to use a real discount rate of 7 percent, which is an estimate of the opportunity cost of capital. However, Circular A-4 also recommends providing an alternative analysis using a 3 percent real discount rate, which is an estimate of the social rate of time preference[190].

Understanding Risks

One of the key objectives in many regulatory statutes is managing risks. In the early rounds of controls under the Clean Air and Clean Water Acts (CWA), the primary health issues of concern revolved around respiratory ailments under the CAA and sanitation related diseases (e.g. diarrhea, dysentery, hepatitis A, typhoid, and polio) under the CWA. As the worst of those problems were addressed through the initial rounds of pollution control under those statutes, considerable emphasis under virtually all environmental laws subsequently was placed on cancer prevention.

As discussed briefly in the Superfund chapter, the health risk posed by a substance is a function of the toxicity of a chemical and the exposure of the chemical to the public. This relationship applies not only to carcinogens but to other health effects (e.g. birth defects) as well. It also applies to ecological effects (e.g. harm to birds and fish), although the science for determining ecological risks lags far behind health risks.

The toxicity of a substance for humans is often extrapolated from animal studies (e.g. rats and mice) where animals are exposed to high doses of a chemical to see what percentage of the exposed animal population develops cancerous tumors or other health effects. Unlike some health effects, cancer is assumed to have a non-threshold linear dose response relationship, which means that doubling the dosage doubles the number of health effects.

As dose response is typically demonstrated at a limited number of high dose levels, this assumption is very useful in extrapolating health effects to the low dose levels that most toxic chemicals pose. High doses are used in experiments for cost reasons, since it reduces the sample size needed to notice statistically significant effects. As there is no known threshold for cancer causing substances, it is also assumed that the linear dose response relationship will hold down to exposure levels of zero.

It may be preferable to determine toxicity through epidemiological studies that measure actual disease occurrence in human populations. However, there are at least three significant limitations to these studies. First, the data sets need to be large enough to pick up the relatively small number of cancer cases that chemical exposure might cause. While the lung cancer risk of smoking tobacco is so high that the association between smoking and lung cancer leaps off the page, that is not the case with most pollutants. Second, unlike controlled animal studies, exposure information may not be available and may vary considerably across the study population. Finally, an epidemiological study can only demonstrate a <u>correlation</u> between exposure to a chemical and a health effect such as cancer. It takes a body of accumulated evidence for scientists to conclude that the chemical actually <u>causes</u> cancer.

Once a dose response curve is developed, EPA or another regulatory agency makes other key assumptions about exposure to the chemical in an occupational or residential setting for purposes of determining risk. For instance, for contaminated groundwater in an aquifer used for drinking, EPA might assume that residents using well water from the aquifer drink two liters per day over a 70-year lifespan. By combining this toxicity and exposure data, EPA might find that traces of arsenic in well water at the assumed exposure levels pose a 1 in 1,000 lifetime risk of getting cancer due to that exposure.

In general, the assumptions used to generate this risk level are very conservative and probably overstate the real risk by an order of magnitude (i.e. a factor of 10) or more. As it is generally impossible to fully eliminate a risk, EPA generally chooses mitigation options that leave a residual lifetime risk of between 1 in 10,000 and 1 in 1,000,000. To put these residual risks in context, the risk to an individual of being struck by lightning is roughly 1 in 1,000,000 in a year and 1 in 15,000 over a lifetime.[191]

While OIRA has some PhD scientists and epidemiologists on staff, it is difficult for them to push back on the risk determination. However, there is more ability to question the risk reduction goal of the regulation (i.e. 1 in 100,000 versus 1 in 1,000,000), because questions of cost and feasibility come into play in those decisions. Unfortunately, the public exposed to a risk generally wants the risk eliminated rather than just reduced to tolerable levels.

Probably due to pressure from citizens living near hazardous waste sites, at one point in the mid-1980s EPA sent us draft Superfund guidance that would have allowed them to clean up sites to a 1 in 100,000,000 residual risk level. This was two orders of magnitude higher than the upper bound risk for any other EPA program and would have set a precedent for setting tighter and more expensive control levels in those programs. As the guidance fell under OMB's approval authority for the NCP, OMB ultimately prevailed, and the guidance level was jettisoned. Given that pump and treat groundwater remediation often takes 20 years or more to achieve a 1 in 1,000,000 risk level, EPA would never have finished any cleanups at the 1 in 100,000,000 level.

While EO 12866 is OMB's main tool for addressing individual regulations, the budget can also be used to address systemic issues. In the late 1970's EPA had recognized that it had a problem in that all its program offices were pursuing regulation of the same toxic chemicals in an uncoordinated fashion. This was resulting in regulation that was not cost-effective, was inconsistent across program offices, and often shifted a problem from one media to another (e.g. a water pollution control concentrates a pollutant in sludge that gets disposed in a landfill). To EPA's credit, they knew that they had a problem and established an internal committee to address it. Unfortunately, the committee failed.

Recognizing that failure, I wrote an issue paper, just prior to the 1980 election, for EPA's FY 1982 Director's Review to establish a path forward. My proposal, which the Director endorsed, was to provide $7 million in FY 1982 funding for EPA's Policy Office to develop a new toxic integration strategy. However, in order to ensure agency buy-in, the proposal also required EPA to reprogram $2 million in FY 1981 funding to get the project established immediately. While EPA reflexively rejects many OMB proposal's, they enthusiastically endorsed this effort. Despite large budget cuts to the FY 1982 Budget once Reagan was elected, I was also able to convince our new leadership of the projects' value and maintain its funding.

The strategy developed by EPA shifted the focus of toxic pollution efforts to an industry-by-industry approach, while recognizing that the existing chemical by chemical and a new geographic hotspot approach were useful in certain situations. Unfortunately, statutory impediments kept the strategy from being fully implemented. Nevertheless, it had an evolutionary impact in pushing EPA toward cost-effective cross-media management of toxic chemical risk and provided some of the intellectual underpinnings for pollutant trading within facilities and EPA's relative risk studies.

Key Issues in Regulatory Analysis

Importance of Marginal Analysis

One of the most important concepts in microeconomics, which applies to regulatory analysis, is the concept of marginal costs and benefits. The public and the press tend to think in terms of total or average costs and benefits. Unfortunately, this can lead to wrong conclusions. For instance, it might be reported that the benefits exceeded the costs for a program which had five distinct components. However, the fact that total benefits exceeded total costs might mask the fact that net benefits (i.e. benefits minus costs) for three components might be positive, while net benefits for the other two were negative. In this case, net benefits to society could be maximized by either dropping the two components with negative net benefits or, possibly, by making changes to those components that would make them reach positive net benefits.

In the case of regulatory analysis, the proper use of marginal costs and benefits comes into play most prominently when OIRA analysts are comparing the difference between various options. For instance, consider a rule for addressing wastewater coming out a pipe from a factory where two types of end-of-pipe technology are available to treat the wastewater, with the second being added to the pipe after the first technology has done its job. Option 1 is to just require the first piece of technology, while Option 2 is to require both.

As Table 10-1 below shows, when looked at from the standpoint of total costs, both options appear to have positive net benefits. However, the marginal costs of adding that second piece of technology exceed the marginal benefits. This means that society is worse off by adding the second piece of technology because net benefits decline from $300 million to $100 million. Thus, unless other statutory factors come into play, Option 1 should be the selected option.

Table 10-1 Maximizing Net Benefits

	Total Costs	Total Costs	Marginal Costs	Marginal Costs
$ in millions	**Option 1**	**Option 2**	**Option 1**	**Option 2**
Benefits	800	1,100	800	300
Costs	500	1,000	500	500
Net Benefits	**300**	**100**	**300**	**-200**

Selection of a Baseline

When estimating the cost and benefit impact of a regulation out into the future, the RIA first must project conditions in the future if the regulation is not imposed. Thus, in the case of a motor vehicle standard, projections would be needed for factors such as vehicle miles traveled and how fast old cars are being replaced by new cars, in order to estimate what vehicle emissions would be in the absence of a regulation. While some of these factors have an impact on projecting costs (i.e. rate of new car replacement), a high baseline can have an even greater impact on benefits.

Furthermore, biases of the estimator, unconscious or not, can slip into baseline projections. For instance, during the acid rain debates of the late 1980s, an industry model projected a declining baseline for future SO_2 emissions and, therefore, fewer benefits from acid rain controls. Their projections were dismissed as the biased work of a vested interest. In contrast, EPA's baseline would show increasing SO2 emissions due to economic growth and therefore greater acid rain control benefits. Unfortunately, every year EPA was wrong as actual emissions would decline, like the industry projections, and EPA would issue a new forecast showing emissions growth starting from the lower actual level. Despite being wrong several years in a row, EPA never adjusted the model to reflect that their assumptions about emissions growth were fundamentally wrong.

The assumptions used to make projections are subject to error on both the high and the low side and the error bounds increase as the projections go further out into the future. Furthermore, baselines typically do not consider estimates of technological change that might have an impact on the baseline in the absence of a rule because most such changes are inherently unknowable. For instance, EPA used the no technological change assumption in developing the baseline for its retrospective cost-benefits estimate of the CAA versus no CAA. In doing so, however, it gave the CAA credit for benefits due to the switch in automobiles from carburetors to fuel injectors which probably would have occurred in the absence of the CAA.

Baselines seem like an arcane and boring aspect of a regulatory debate. However, as shown above, the selection of the baseline can have a significant impact on the regulatory analysis and needs to be scrutinized closely by OIRA in reviewing the RIA.

Appropriate Estimates for Statistical Value of Life

Perhaps the most controversial topic in regulatory analysis is what value to put on a human life, particularly lives saved far in the future. Costs are easier to monetize than health effects such as deaths avoided. At one time, future costs of regulatory programs to protect human health were discounted but the deaths avoided were not, producing a distorted analysis. Unfortunately, the public recoils at the concept of discounting future deaths. However, if the question is reframed as whether an individual would prefer to save one life now or two lives 100 years from now, most people would choose one life now. In making that choice they are implicitly indicating they do discount future lives even if they are revolted by the concept. In fact, a 1992 study found that survey respondents considered six lives saved 25 years from now to be equivalent to 1 life saved today, an implicit discount rate of 7 percent.[192]

A concept known as the Value of a Statistical Life (VSL) was developed to get around the problem of directly discounting human lives. Under this concept, agencies do not place a dollar value on individual lives but estimate how much people are willing to pay for small reductions in their risks of dying from adverse health conditions, such as those caused by pollution. This VSL is then applied to estimates of future lives saved by a regulatory action and can be discounted back to the present. OMB Circular A-4 lets agencies determine the appropriate VSL for use in their rulemakings. In the past, VSL amounts used by agencies varied significantly, but for key agencies they have converged over time to around $9 million in 2015 dollars[193].

The VSL's come from the academic literature that makes estimates using a variety of methods including surveys that ask people what they think lives are worth and studies that impute a value of life from wages of high-risk jobs or revealed preferences from measures taken to reduce risk. Unfortunately, the VSL's from these studies vary widely with the $9 million figure being towards the high end of the range.

The VSL's are effectively an average value and assume that the value of all lives is the same, no matter a person's age. This makes sense if the risk is evenly distributed across the population but doesn't work as well if the risk is concentrated in either children or seniors. While many seniors don't like the idea that their lives are worth less than others, I think that the remaining 60 years of life expectancy of either of my daughters is worth far more than my 20 remaining years. Given how protective parents are of their children, I think most people would agree.

There is also some literature indicating that older people value their lives less than younger people[194]. Consequently, EPA's Science Advisory Board has urged EPA to look at alternative VSL measures that put a value only on an individual's remaining years where the risk primarily affects the elderly. One such measure is the value of statistical life-years (VSLY) which is derived by dividing the estimated VSL by expected life expectancy. While still controversial and only used as an alternative analysis, this approach appropriately values saving the life of a child as greater than saving the life of a senior citizen.

Risk Management Failures

Activists who want to bring attention to an issue have an incentive to decry the existence of trace contaminants to pressure Congress or regulatory agencies to act on an issue. A sympathetic press is often a willing participant in these efforts. Unfortunately, this type of scare tactic ignores the fact that many chemicals (e.g. vitamin A, arsenic, and zinc) are toxic at high levels, but are essential to all life at low levels. Consequently, focusing on toxicity instead of risk can lead to misaligned priorities.

Understanding this problem, EPA Administrator Lee Thomas commissioned a study to look at how environmental risks compared to the problems it was addressing. The 1987 study "Unfinished Business: a Comparative Assessment of Environmental Problems" concluded that the risk rankings developed by EPA staff did not correspond well with either EPA's statutory authorities or its program priorities, but rather aligned more closely with public opinion.[195] Figure 10-1 from a book on problems with the regulatory process by Steven Breyer, before he became a Supreme Court Justice, was based on EPA's work and shows the disconnect between the public and the experts on health risks[196].

A terrific example of misplaced priorities was the effort to remove asbestos from buildings. Asbestos has a complicated history. Its fire-retardant properties made it a godsend and saved countless lives when it was used in World War II to minimize fires on ships during an attack. After the war, however, it became clear that it could cause lung disease, particularly in asbestos miners. The U.S. has been struggling with how to manage asbestos risks ever since.

Figure 10-1 Public Versus Expert Perception of Health Risk

How the Public and EPA Rate Health Risks Associated with Environmental
Problems

Public	EPA Experts
1. Hazardous waste sites	Medium to Low
2. Exposure to worksite chemicals	High
3. Industrial pollution of waterways	Low
4. Nuclear accident radiation	Not ranked
5. Radioactive waste	Not ranked
6. Chemical leaks from underground storage tanks	Medium to Low
7. Pesticides	High
8. Pollution from industrial accidents	Medium to Low
9. Water pollution from farm runoff	Medium
10. Tap water contamination	High
11. Industrial air pollution	High
12. Ozone layer destruction	High
13. Coastal water contamination	Low
14. Sewage-plant water pollution	Medium to Low
15. Vehicle exhaust	High
16. Oil spills	Medium to Low
17. Acid rain	High
18. Water pollution from urban runoff	Medium
19. Damaged wetlands	Low
20. Genetic alteration	Low
21. Non-hazardous waste sites	Medium to Low
22. Greenhouse effect	Low
23. Indoor air pollution	High
24. X-ray radiation	Not ranked
25. Indoor radon	High
26. Microwave oven radiation	Not ranked

Data Source: Frederick Allen, U.S. EPA, based on EPA report "Unfinished Business: A Comparative Assessment of Environmental Problems" (1987) and national public opinion polls by the Roper Organization in December 1987 and January 1988.
Figure Source: BREAKING THE VICIOUS CIRCLE: TOWARD EFFECTIVE RISK REGULATION by Stephen Breyer, Cambridge, Mass.: Harvard University Press, Copyright @ 1993 by the President and Fellows of Harvard College. Used by permission. All rights reserved.

The hazards of asbestos led to a huge effort to remove asbestos from buildings and the U.S. spent $50 billion in the 1980s and 1990s on the effort. The problem was that asbestos in buildings, if left undisturbed, doesn't pose a significant health risk, whereas asbestos removal does pose a risk. However, it took a decade of changing guidance for EPA to finally get right how to handle asbestos in buildings.

In the late 1980s, Congress funded an EPA loan and grant program to remove asbestos in schools. Unfortunately, it took the Administration three years to convince Congress that the effort was a waste of money. In fact, it has been estimated that asbestos removal in U.S. buildings cost $100 million to $500 million for every life saved[197].

Leaving remediation aside, whether to use asbestos presents an interesting risk-risk tradeoff (i.e. lives saved from fire prevention versus lives lost due to asbestos mining). In the case of asbestos, the conundrum can be resolved in most cases by using safe substitutes. The cost availability and safety of substitutes is an issue OIRA grapples with regularly, particularly when considering cancellation of pesticides. In fact, nowhere has the risk-risk trade off issue been more vexing than in the case of the pesticide DDT.

DDT use began in the 1940's to kill mosquitos in a highly successful effort to combat malaria, typhus, and other insect-borne diseases, thereby helping to significantly cut infant mortality rates in many developing countries in the post-war period. However, DDT's significant adverse environmental effects and persistence in the environment slowly became apparent. In part due to public pressure stemming from the 1962 publication of Rachel Carson's "Silent Spring", EPA finally canceled DDT for use in the U.S. in 1972.

In the case of the U.S., cancellation made sense since malaria had already been eliminated and U.S. farmers could afford more expensive pesticides for agricultural uses. However, the cost-benefit calculation relating to DDT was different in many less developed countries which experienced huge numbers of malaria deaths annually. Many of these countries delayed banning DDT and finally did so only under enormous international pressure.

Unfortunately, that sometimes turned out to be a mistake. In South Africa, for instance, DDT was banned in 1996 only to see malaria rates increase tenfold in five years. Consequently, by the early 2000's, malaria was still killing 2.7 million people annually, of which 90 percent were in Africa. Within three years of switching back to DDT in 2000, South Africa's malaria incidence dropped by half.[198] Despite the environmental risks, the World Health Organization (WHO) partially reversed course in September 2006. In a policy that is still in effect today, the WHO declared support for using DDT indoors in much of Africa, because the benefits of malaria risk reduction in affected countries outweighed the environmental risk of its usage.[199]

The Impact of PM 2.5 on Benefit Calculations

In October 1997, EPA completed a statutorily required report on the benefits and costs for the 20-year period between passage of the 1970 Clean Air Act and the 1990 amendments. The central estimate of 20 years benefits was $22 trillion in 1990 dollars, compared to 20-year costs of $523 billion.[200] The benefits estimates reflecting reduced health effects due to actual air emissions levels in 1990 compared to the baseline emissions for 1990 without Clean Air Act controls but with emissions increases due to economic growth.

In order to put in perspective the size of the $22 trillion central benefit estimate for the 1970 to 1990 period — and the upper bound estimate of $49 trillion —, total U.S. Gross National Product (GDP) for the same period in 1990 dollars was $93 trillion.[201] Thus, the central estimate was 24 percent of GDP and the upper bound estimate was a whopping 53 percent of GDP. This suggests that the methods or assumptions used for benefits estimation may be unrealistic. An alternative analysis using a VSYL approach for mortality, cut benefits by $7.5 trillion to a still very high-level total of around $14 trillion.[202]

Within the $22 trillion estimate, $1.4 trillion was due to the 99 percent reduction in lead emissions due to the phaseout of unleaded gasoline. However, $16.6 trillion was due to avoidance of premature mortality, largely from PM-2.5, with 184,000 cases avoided in 1990.[203] One of the interesting things about that figure is that EPA did not have a standard for PM-2.5 until 1997 and didn't even have a standard for PM-10 (i.e. particulate matter particles no larger than 10 micrometers) until 1987. The agency's earlier particulate standard was for total suspended solids. As EPA also didn't have a PM-2.5 monitoring network until after the standard was set in 1997, estimates of PM-2.5 levels were extrapolated from TSP and other pollutants.

Even the existence of PM-2.5 as a health threat wasn't discovered until a series of studies in the early 1990s showed a statistical association between fine particulates and mortality, an association that was not seen for larger PM-10 particles. These studies have been a godsend for EPA in justifying a range of stringent air pollution regulations. Given the high number of deaths attributed to PM-2.5 and the high VSL EPA uses, virtually any regulation that reduces PM-2.5 has positive net benefits.

The effect of PM-2.5 benefits on future benefit cost studies is readily apparent. For instance, in 2011 EPA released a report projecting the benefits and costs of the Clean Air Act Amendments (CAAA) of 1990 through the year 2020. For just the year 2020, the central estimate of benefits in 2006 dollars was $2 trillion (roughly 12 percent of actual 2020 GDP in 2006$),[204] of which $1.7 trillion was attributed to PM, while the annual estimate of costs was $65 billion. The benefits reflect 230,000 early deaths avoided in 2020.[205]

Similarly, OIRA's 2017 Report to Congress on the Benefits and Costs of Federal Regulations, the latest complete report issued by OIRA, demonstrates the dominance of PM-2.5 benefits compared to the benefits of other rules government-wide. The report summarizes the cost and benefits of all significant Federal rules promulgated over a ten-year period, in this case FY 2007 to FY 2016. For that period, EPA rules account for between 71 and 80 percent of the monetized benefits (also 55 to 64 percent of costs), of which 95 percent are air quality rules, which are driven by PM-2.5 benefits.[206]

Issues With PM-2.5 Benefit Valuations

Critics have complained that the data used in the key PM-2.5 studies was not publicly available for other scientists to try to replicate the findings, a key objective in science. Unfortunately, there is a dilemma that compiling the data for these types of studies often requires the scientists who compile the database to commit to patient confidentiality, thereby preventing broad availability of the data. To address this concern, EPA had an independent research organization, the Health Effects Institute, reanalyze the data from the key study and came to similar conclusions as the original studies.

Nevertheless, the inability of other researchers to access the data was a major part of the impetus for passage of the Data Quality Act in 2000. In addition, it directly led to enactment of an FY 1999 appropriations provision, referred to as the Shelby Amendment, which requires that all data produced under a grant award must be made available to the public under the Freedom of Information Act. Making such information available is important, for instance, in attempting to reconcile the conclusions of the earlier PM-2.5 studies with another analysis of PM-2.5 data which indicated that effects on mortality and morbidity became statistically insignificant when education levels were included among the explanatory variables.

Our scientific understanding of PM-2.5 hasn't advanced far since the initial studies in 1990, but far enough for EPA's Clean Air Science Advisory Committee (CASAC) to determine that PM-2.5 is causally related to premature death based on the weight of epidemiological evidence. It has also advanced far enough for EPA to issue new or lower standards in 2006 and 2012.

However, what we don't know is astounding. The chemistry of ambient particulate matter is complex because PM comes not only from direct emissions of particles, but also the conversion of gaseous pollutants, such as sulfur dioxide, into particulate matter in the atmosphere. Yet we don't know what specific types of fine particles are responsible for increased mortality. This makes a difference because we may be attributing huge benefits to rules that regulate the wrong substance and have little or no effect on mortality.

We also don't know how PM-2.5 actually kills people. While some studies show correlations with chronic pulmonary and heart disease, usually there is only a statistically significant correlation with total mortality. This is a huge contrast with other life-saving rules, where the deaths, which the regulations were intended to prevent, were easy to find prior to regulation, such as car crashes, factory accidents, and even lung disease in asbestos miners.

In fact, for PM-2.5 <u>you can't go into any morgue anywhere in the world and find anyone who has ever died from PM-2.5</u>. This seems absurd given EPA's 2011 projection of 230,000 early deaths avoided in 2020 due to the CAAA, some of which reflects deaths avoided due to increased pollution in the absence of the law and some due to actual reductions in emissions[207]. As total U.S. deaths in 2019 (i.e. pre-pandemic) were 2.9 million[208], such a significant change in deaths, even excluding those from the increasing baseline, ought to be easy to spot.

Most likely, PM-2.5 shortens the life of the elderly or other individuals already suffering from chronic health problems and the underlying health issue is listed as the cause of death. To the extent that PM-2.5 shortens the lives of individuals whose health is already poor, it should be a strong argument for using VSLY in benefits estimates rather than VSL. However, estimating the remaining years of life for these individuals would be difficult, particularly when we don't know which individuals, suffering from which illnesses, PM-2.5 affects.

A National Research Council study from 2002 flagged the uncertainty in EPA's PM-2.5 premature death estimates suggested that EPA describe the uncertainty "as completely and realistically as possible"[209]. OIRA's 2017 "Report to Congress on the Benefits and Costs of Regulation" does an excellent job of discussing the uncertainty of six key assumptions underpinning EPA's particulate matter benefit estimates.[210] This chapter has already discussed several of these assumptions, many of which apply to other pollutants as well, including: whether correlation found in studies can be treated as causality; treatment of all types of PM-2.5 particles as the same; baseline estimation issues; and application of VSL in calculating benefits.

One assumption that hasn't been discussed is EPA's taking credit for mortality reduction at levels below the NAAQS. We faced the same conceptual issue in developing cost-effectiveness estimates for various control options when we were developing the Bush Administration's CAAA proposal in 1989. EPA wanted to consider pollutant reductions in areas already in attainment with the NAAQS standards. My PAD, Bob Grady, and I were adamant they shouldn't be included, as NAAQS are established to protect public health, including sensitive sub-populations, with an adequate margin of safety (i.e. there should be no known significant health effects below the primary NAAQS standard). We prevailed in that fight as including benefits at levels below the NAAQS in attainment areas would have distorted the analysis.

Unfortunately, that is not the case with PM-2.5 where CASAC, while noting the uncertainty, agreed to allow EPA to assume benefits below the NAAQS, because they couldn't conclude that effects do not occur. By the same token there is no science to support a conclusion such effects do occur. Thus, EPA can continue to generate huge benefit estimates for PM-2.5 nationwide, even though only 15 areas representing less than 10 percent of the population are currently in non-attainment.[211]

An example where this assumption comes into play is the coal and electric utility air toxic standard under Section 112 of the CAA. The standard was intended to regulate mercury and has a tortured history, in part over the science of whether the small mercury emissions impose health effects. Under Section 112, the standard was based on Maximum Achievable Control Technology (MACT) with benefits for the chosen option ranging from $28 to $77 billion (2001$), with costs of $8.2 billion. Despite the intent of the rule being to regulate mercury, 99 percent of the benefits are particulate matter co-benefits.[212]

The co-benefits stem from the demonstrated MACT technology reducing PM-2.5 in addition to mercury. However, if established as a performance standard, a utility could theoretically achieve the mercury standard without eliminating any PM-2.5, in which case costs far exceed benefits and the MACT standard, which is set taking costs into account, might not be justified. Alternatively, even if co-benefits are allowed, given that PM-2.5 non-attainment is almost entirely in the west and most coal and gas fired utility emissions are in the east, the rule's costs might exceed the benefits if it were not for the fact that EPA assumes benefits below the NAAQS level.

The issues discussed above are just a few of the complex problems that OIRA desk officers confront when they review agency rulemakings. While OIRA does a good job of flagging issues and suggesting alternatives that might be more cost-effective or cost-beneficial, their review authority limits how much they can influence an agency's determinations. Furthermore, OIRA is not in a strong position to question agencies and their science advisers on scientific issues.

Nevertheless, periodically revising OMB Circular A-4 to provide more government-wide guidance on new or evolving crosscutting issues might be useful, if it can be done in a manner that maintains the unbiased nature of the Circular. Furthermore, some of the PM-2.5 issues, such as allowing co-benefits and whether to allow benefits below a standard that already has an adequate margin of safety, seem more like economic or policy issues that properly fall in OIRA's bailiwick. I tried to convince a couple OIRA Administrators that they needed their own advisory board of prominent economists to give them cover in challenging agencies on controversial issues such as those. Wisely or not, I was ignored.

CHAPTER ELEVEN: The Long and Winding Road -- *The Never-ending Quest for Efficient Federal Management*

As mentioned earlier, there has been remarkable stability in the budget process within the Executive Branch over the years no matter which party controlled the Presidency. Unfortunately, the same cannot be said for management efforts. While it is not surprising that new Administrations would have somewhat different management objectives, in most cases a new Administration reinvents the process as well as changing the objectives. This chapter reviews the changes in how administrations address OMB's management responsibilities over time.

There are probably several reasons for the difference in stability between OMB's budget and management processes. First, while the Congressional budget process is clearly broken, the process to produce the President's Budget works exceedingly well. There is no such consensus on an appropriate management improvement process. As will be discussed in more detail later, OMB's leadership in the George W. Bush (Bush '43) Administration thought their program assessment and management scorecard processes should have transcended administrations. However, those processes didn't last a nanosecond in the Obama Administration.

Second, bashing management of the Federal Government is a safe tactic for Presidential candidates on the campaign. Taking stances on controversial policy issues has the advantage of exciting the candidate's base supporters but can turn off voters in the middle. Pledging management improvements doesn't necessarily energize voters, but it is something that everybody can agree is needed. Furthermore, it is a target rich environment of programs and processes needing improvements. However, as a former Federal employee, it is somewhat disheartening that Presidential candidates have been trashing Federal bureaucrats on the campaign trail since at least the Carter Administration (i.e. my whole career).

The fact that Federal management is a target rich environment for improvements should not be taken as indicating that OMB collaboration with the agencies has not produced major successes. For instance, most tax returns are now submitted on-line, benefit payments and the Federal paychecks are distributed electronically, and paperwork collection has been streamlined through improved information collection systems.

What these improvements all have in common is that they are due to the information technology revolution. My recent staff think I joined OMB during the cave man era because — horror of horrors — I had no desk top computer, no email, and no cell phone when I started. I thank God that COVID-19 struck in 2020 rather than 1980, 40 years earlier, because teleworking would not have been an option for coping with the pandemic.

While the Federal Government has successfully adopted the avalanche of new technology in the last few decades to improve Federal management, it is also true that the Federal Government has never been the leader in doing so. Federal implementation has always lagged the private sector and, as these technological improvements are never-ending, the Federal Government is continually a step behind. Furthermore, even with those improvements, the Federal Government hasn't made much progress on intractable problems such as unpaid taxes, which the Internal Revenue Service (IRS) recently estimated could be as high as $1 trillion per year,[213] and improper payments, which were estimated to be $175 billion in 2019[214]

I will draw a distinction between two types of management, although in reality the two are related and it is sometimes difficult to draw a line between the two. The first type of management is the nuts and bolts of government which includes contracts management, financial management, and information technology management. Much of the focus of this chapter will be on the nuts and bolts of management. The other type of management relates to the implementation of programs. Certainly, to implement programs well, the government needs to get the nuts and bolts screwed on correctly.

The success of program implementation, however, is somewhat in the eye of the beholder, depending on the program objective pursued by a particular administration. Control of the U.S./Mexico border provides a particularly stark example of this point. Republican administrations tend to support border walls and other processes to minimize illegal immigration. While Democrats share the desire of Republicans to keep out terrorists and violent criminals, they view success in managing the border as humanely handling refugees seeking asylum from political oppression and economic migrants fleeing poverty.

The fact that the parties can't even agree what to call these individuals (i.e. illegal immigrants or undocumented workers), suggests the difficulty in getting people to agree on whether the border is well managed. Performance management is essentially a process that links the two types of management and will also be discussed in this chapter.

Ongoing Nuts and Bolts Efforts

Despite my earlier assertion about new Administrations throwing out the management initiatives and processes of the previous crew, not everything changes. As briefly discussed in Chapter 1, there are three statutorily established offices in OMB, two of which are headed by appointees confirmed by the Senate. While these three offices are usually heavily involved in a new Administration's initiatives, they also have ongoing statutory responsibilities to carry out as will be discussed below. There is also a fourth important organization, currently called the Performance and Personnel Management Division, which is responsible for some performance responsibilities statutorily assigned to OMB, but the office itself is not statutorily required.

All these offices tend to be small. Consequently, unlike OIRA, they do not have desk officers who have extensive knowledge of a particular agency's programs. Instead, the staff tend to be subject matter experts on issues within their office's domain. In general, they tend to be higher graded and more experienced than RMO staff, to draft and maintain government-wide guidance within their areas of expertise.

However, due to their lack of agency specific expertise, they need to rely on the RMO's to work with the agencies to get their initiatives implemented. Unfortunately, inconsistent integration of Management side (M-side) and RMO efforts is a continuing weakness within OMB.

Office of Federal Procurement Policy (OFPP)

The Office of Federal Procurement Policy Act of 1974 that created OFPP declared it to be the policy of Congress "to promote economy, efficiency, and effectiveness in the procurement of property and services by and for the executive branch of the Federal Government".[215] While an excellent statement of policy it remains an elusive policy goal, despite 16 different public laws that have amended OFPP's original authority.

Through these Federal laws and supplemented by OMB Management Memorandums and procurement policy letters, OFPP strives to get the best value for taxpayers out of the roughly 10 percent of Federal spending that goes to contractors.[216] However, the most important tool for guiding Federal contracting is the Federal Acquisition Regulation or FAR as it generally known. Development and maintenance of the FAR is overseen by the FAR Council which is chaired by the OFPP Administrator.

The core objective of procurement policy is high quality service at low cost. While simple sounding in practice it is almost impossible to achieve because of trade-offs, some of which will be discussed below. The first thing to know about Federal procurement is that it is a very bureaucratic and lengthy process. From the standpoint of obtaining the lowest cost, the ideal contract is competitively bid, with the bids being for a fixed price. The bidding is done through a Request for Proposal (RFP) process that is publicly announced in the Federal Register.

The RFP specifies the requirements for the contract, which can be very complex, particularly for development of information systems or DOD weapons programs. The bids are evaluated by agency procurement and program staff based on criteria set up in advance. Simple contracts (e.g.

supply light bulbs) are awarded to the lowest price bidder whose bid meets technically acceptable criteria. More complex contracts consider quality factors or the prior performance of the contractor in making the award. For instance, the Army may not choose the low bid on a new tank if a higher cost version has superior firepower or battlefield survivability.

In general, the system is designed to be transparent and fair to all parties. Unfortunately, the trade-off is lack of speed as the transparency and fairness objectives make for a slow process. The system is also weighed done by additional crosscutting objectives, unrelated to the specific goal of the contract, that Congress adds to the procurement process, such as participation by small businesses and minority owned firms. While these objectives are well meaning, they contribute to the complexity of the process. As one Air Force General said in testifying before Congress "you've written so many laws that we need to implement that our contracting officers in the trenches can't even follow them all because they actually start to conflict with each other".[217]

Unfortunately, the complexity of the process and the objective of fairness when combined with the complex requirements of major acquisitions, almost ensure that losing bidders will submit bid protest challenges for major contracts. The bid protest process is intended to prevent fraud, which is an important objective on contracts worth billions of dollars. However, my impression is that most bid protests focus on technical issues arising from the complexity of either the process or the procurement rather than the malicious intent of the staff and officials working on the contract. Again, speed takes a backseat to other objectives as this broken process produces many frivolous bid protests.

Contracts can be awarded more quickly if they are awarded as a negotiated sole-source contract. In general, these types of contracts are discouraged because there is no competition, plus they are typically "cost plus" contracts where the contractor has no incentive to hold down costs. During the Iraq War, DOD was heavily criticized for an expensive sole source, cost plus contract awarded to Halliburton for support services on the ground in Iraq. However, the need for speed in that situation, coupled with the fact there are few companies with the global reach necessary to provide those services, made it an appropriate type of contract in that situation.

OFPP staff have implemented many initiatives across multiple administrations trying to find the "sweet spot" between conflicting objectives. Unfortunately, the trade-offs between cost, quality, transparency, fairness, speed and non-program related objectives make finding such a sweet spot nearly impossible.

Office of Federal Financial Management (OFFM)

OFFM was established by the Chief Financial Officers Act of 1990, to be headed by a Senate confirmed Controller (effectively the Chief Financial Officer (CFO) for the Federal Government) who would report directly to the newly created position of OMB Deputy Director for Management (DDM). The Act also established Chief Financial Officer positions in each of the major agencies and created a Chief Financial Officers Council chaired by OMB's DDM.

The Congressional view in creating OFFM was that billions of dollars were being lost each year to waste, fraud, and abuse (WFA) as well as mismanagement of Federal programs. OFFM's role was to improve the efficiency and effectiveness of Federal programs and stem WFA and mismanagement losses through improved central coordination of internal controls and financial accounting.[218]

OFFM strives to achieve this objective by establishing government-wide financial policies for Executive branch agencies. Like other OMB offices, OFFM prepares OMB Circulars for guidance that will have continuing effect and either Bulletins or Management Memoranda for guidance requiring one-time actions or that apply to a specific year. While Federal programs can often be implemented by grants or contracts, OFFM has responsibility for guidance on grants, while OFPP is responsible for guidance on contracts. OFFM is also responsible for payroll and financial management systems, not the Office of E-Gov, which is responsible for most other information technology systems.

In 1994, the Federal Financial Management Act was enacted requiring the heads of executive branch agencies to prepare and submit to OMB audited financial statements, with agency Inspectors General responsible for the audits. OFFM was placed in charge of prescribing the form and content of the statements. Financial statements for individual bureaus are consolidated into a financial statement for a department and the department statements are consolidated into a Federal Government-wide statement. The Department of the Treasury prepares the government-wide statement, which is audited by the General Accountability Office (GAO) headed by the Comptroller General.

The Comptroller General's Statement in the most recent Federal Government Financial Report noted the significant strides made over 25 years in going from six clean opinions (i.e. no significant problems) in the first year to 21 of the required 24 CFO agencies having clean opinions in FY 2021. However, after 25 years of trying, GAO still cannot express an opinion on the Federal financial statements.[219] Unfortunately, getting a clean opinion has become the "white whale" of the Federal Government financial community.

Certainly, the concept of the Federal Government having audited financial statements comparable to those of the private sector sounds logical, but for what purpose? The statements are important in the private sector because people and institutions need them to evaluate whether to buy a company's stock or loan them money. If the opinion of the accounting firm conducting an audit of a private company has any more than three boilerplate paragraphs, that serves as a red flag to investors.

In contrast, the Federal Government doesn't issue stock and its debt instruments (i.e. treasury bonds and notes) are viewed as the safest investments in the world, even without a clean opinion. In fact, I doubt that anybody has ever decided not to purchase a Treasury bond because DOD can't keep track of its inventory in war zones.

As a longtime consumer of Federal financial information, I wanted agencies to have information systems that provided accurate information that was easily accessible. I also expected agencies to address material financial weaknesses whether identified internally, by the Inspector General, or by the GAO. However, I can say unequivocally that I have never found the agency audited financial statements to be useful, nor do I know anybody else who uses them. I don't know whether this is a problem with the statutory requirement or the form and content that OFFM developed, but it seems to me that an extraordinary amount of time and effort are being consumed to produce auditable statements that have no real use.

Office of E-Government and Technology (E-GOV)

The current website for OMB's E-Gov Office notes that information technology (IT) advancements have been at the center of a transformation that revolutionized the efficiency, convenience, and effectiveness in how the private sector serves its customers. It then goes on to say:

> "The Federal Government largely has missed out on that transformation due to poor management of technology investments, with IT projects too often costing hundreds of millions of dollars more than they should, taking years longer than necessary to deploy, and delivering technologies that are obsolete by the time they are completed.[220]"

OUCH!! While that statement doesn't acknowledge the progress that has been made, as I noted earlier, or prior efforts to catch up to the private sector, there is certainly a lot of truth in the statement.

The E-Gov Office wasn't created until enactment of the E-Government Act of 2002, but OMB's information technology efforts predate that statute. OMB Circular A-130 — Managing Information as a Strategic Resource — was first issued in 1985 to implement some requirements of the Paperwork Reduction Act of 1980. The Circular, which effectively serves as a "one-stop" guide for official OMB policy on information technology (IT) management, has been revised several times since, most notably in 1996, after enactment of the Clinger-Cohen Act.

The Clinger-Cohen Act required the Director of OMB to use the budget process for analyzing, tracking, and evaluating the risks and results of major capital investments for information systems, with the process to continue for the life of the system. The criteria for evaluating the projects became known as the "Raines Rules", after Director Frank Raines who issued them. The rules were incorporated in OMB's budget Circular A-11 as an appendix —Principles of Budgeting for Capital Asset Acquisitions — to embed the analysis of these IT capital asset plans in the budget process.

The rationale for having agencies develop and evaluate the plans according to strict criteria was to prevent development of systems that failed, an all too frequent occurrence in that era. Unfortunately, as is often the case in the government, the process quickly became overly bureaucratic. Although RMO examiners are good at making decisions as to whether an information system was needed programmatically, their eyes tend to glaze over at the lengthy capital asset submissions. Consequently, the examiners usually rely on E-Gov staff to advise them on whether a proposal is technically feasible and worthwhile. In addition to being bureaucratic, the process trades off speed and entrepreneurship in order to prevent failures, which is not the same as ensuring success.

Although a ponderously slow process is a problem with all Federal procurement, it is a particular problem given the speed at which IT evolves for both software and hardware. While I am a strong defender of the normal budget process, I must acknowledge that it works poorly for IT investments given that it takes almost two years from the time an agency starts formulating a request until Congress gets around to appropriating the funds.

A $1 billion appropriation to the General Services Administration's (GSA) Technology Modernization Fund (TMF) through the American Rescue Plan Act (ARPA) of 2021 will help address this problem. The TMF is a revolving fund that provides upfront funding to transition antiquated agency legacy systems to modern IT platforms, with the projects chosen by a board chaired by OMB's Chief Information Officer.[221] While the TMF is an important step, it only addresses a portion of the Federal Government's IT budget problem, and the ARPA money is only a one-time infusion of funding.

Despite the stinging indictment of past IT efforts on E-Gov's website, their annual reports on E-Government Implementation paint a much rosier picture. The last published report from August 2017 states that the Office of E-Gov "continues to drive innovation in Government operations, using IT to improve the transparency, efficiency and effectiveness of Federal operations, and increase citizen participation in Government".[222] The report goes on to laud the government's efforts in promoting open-source software and data center consolidation.

In response to several cyber-attacks against the Federal Government, Congress enacted the Federal Information Security Modernization Act of 2014. This made OMB E-Gov responsible for overseeing Federal information security practices and developing related policies and guidelines led by a new Chief Information Security Officer (CISO). While an initial 30-Day Cybersecurity Sprint eliminated many critical vulnerabilities in agency systems, cybersecurity issues have taken an increasing amount of E-Gov's time in recent years. Unfortunately, as Federal systems are a major target for our adversaries and hacking techniques continually evolve, the Federal Government's defenses also must continually evolve to keep up.

The Office of Performance and Personnel Management (OPPM)

Unlike the other management offices, OPPM was not established in statute and its personnel management function is like the role that the RMO's play with respect to their agencies. However, OPPM does have the OMB lead in implementing the Government Performance and Results Act (GPRA) of 1993 and more generally for coordinating an administration's goal setting and performance review process.

GPRA requires agencies to develop five-year strategic plans that contain a mission statement as well as long-term results-oriented goals. In addition, GPRA requires agencies to establish annual performance goals and prepare an annual report on how well the agency did in meeting those goals. The intent of GPRA was to move away from input goals often favored by interest groups, such as how much money did a program get, and output goals, such as how many vaccines were administered, and instead focus on outcome goals, such as how many lives were saved by the vaccines financed by the program. Unfortunately, developing meaningful outcomes goals is easier said than done.

The push to improve performance management over the last thirty years is driven by a desire to make the Federal Government as efficient and effective as the private sector. Unfortunately, businesses have an overriding goal, to maximize profits, which helps drive efficiency and effectiveness, but which doesn't exist in the public sector. This profit goal makes it easier for private companies to set performance goals for its managers that maximize profits. I should note, however, that the major takeaway from my MBA cost accounting course was that, even in the private sector, the incentives for individual managers to maximize their bonuses are never fully aligned with the overall corporation's profit goal.

Nevertheless, having a strategic plan to provide guidance to Department staff on what is most important for the Department to accomplish can be very useful. The goals of individual managers are also supposed to be tied to the Department or agency goals. Unfortunately, this objective also can be very difficult to achieve in a complex organization with a huge number of programs like the State Department. In that situation, the Secretary has to choose between: 1) a limited number of focused goals that don't cover a large share of the Department's programs; 2) a limited set of goals that encompass most of the Department but each is so broad as to be meaningless; or 3) a set of focused goals that encompass most of the Department but that are so numerous than nothing is a priority.

Even small agencies like OMB have trouble coming up with a good strategic plan. During development of OMB's first plan in 1997 there was a huge fight between the career and the political staff over one word in the mission statement. The career staff thought that OMB's mission was "to help the <u>Presidency</u>" because a five-year plan extended beyond a presidential term and the career staff worked for whoever was elected President. The political staff thought the wording should be "to help the <u>President</u>" because they only worked for the incumbent President. It is not hard to guess who won that fight.

Federal agencies also run into the problem that sometimes the most meaningful, appropriate, and measurable goals are also ones over which the agency has only limited control. For OMB Budget staff, arguably the most important goal is to produce a balanced budget. Unfortunately, the President, the Congress, the Federal Reserve Board, economic cycles, and external economic shocks (i.e. war) can easily thwart the incredible work of the OMB staff.

In fact, when I moved from Natural Resources to International Affairs, my predecessor in the Natural Resource job, Ron Cogswell, presented me with a graph showing how the deficit tumbled into surplus at the end of his tenure, but exploded during mine. I think his point was that I should have been fired rather than moved to another job, while I viewed the graph as a spurious correlation over which I had little control.

A final problem is that many goals are not measurable. In the case of the State Department and USAID, there are very good outcome measures showing the success of various global health programs as were discussed in Chapter 8. On the other hand, anecdotally we know that diplomacy is important, but the impact of diplomacy is subtle, and outcomes can't really be measured. The best the Department can do is measure inputs such as the number of demarches (i.e. request for support of a policy) delivered by U.S. Ambassadors to Foreign Ministries.

Despite the importance of performance management and the amount of effort put into developing performance measures, many of the above problems remain intractable. Unfortunately, I am not sure the Federal Government has advanced the ball on performance management very far since the enactment of GPRA.

President's Management Agendas

The sections above describe the statutorily required management efforts that Administrations must implement, although with varying amounts of vigor. However, every Administration comes in with its own Presidential Management Agenda (PMA), although that term was not coined until 2001 in the Bush '43 Administration. Some of the agenda items emphasize the nuts and bolts of government (i.e. financial, procurement, and information management), while some reflect more ideological objectives. Even for objectives that all Administrations have in common (e.g. eliminate fraud, waste, and abuse), the approaches for achieving those objectives are often very different.

The creation of OMB in 1970 during the Nixon Administration was itself an effort to improve Federal management efforts. OMB was established using the President's reorganization authority, an authority that was also used to create EPA, but which expired during the Reagan Administration and hasn't been renewed since. The establishment of OMB involved adding some management responsibilities to the former Bureau of the Budget in order to provide greater focus on improved Federal management. Nevertheless, OMB's management role has always been a lower priority than its budget responsibilities.

Ronald Reagan Agenda (1981-1988)

Not surprisingly, the management initiatives in the Reagan Administration reflected the President's conservative political policy. In particular, the initiatives focused on: 1) reducing Federal costs; and 2) limiting the role of the Federal government. The first two efforts focused on cutting costs in the nuts and bolts of government.

In March 1981, the President established the President's Council on Integrity and Efficiency (PCIE), the first of several inter-agency management councils that still exist today. The PCIE is composed of agency inspector generals and was tasked with providing leadership and support of government-wide efforts to detect and prevent fraud, waste, and abuse. The second effort, launched in 1982, was "Reform 88" which was designed to restructure Federal management and administrative systems.[223]

The signature Reagan management initiative, however, was the Private Sector Survey on Cost Control (PSSCC). This initiative was more commonly known as the Grace Commission after its Chairman, J. Peter Grace, an industrialist who supported Reagan's tax cuts despite being a Democrat. The Grace Commission, which was launched in June 1982, with Reagan using the phrase "drain the swamp" long before it became associated with Donald Trump and presented its report to Congress in January 1984.[224] The Commission was charged with showing the Federal Government how to be more like the private sector and enlisted 161 top executives supported by over 2,000 volunteers who developed 2,478 recommendations.[225]

Although the volunteers were a mix of private sector line and staff managers, their methodology was like that of various Federal consulting firms, but without any marching orders from the agency to focus their inquiries. There was a task force assigned to each major agency and the Commission volunteers would meet with key staff to understand the agency's function, identify problems facing the agency, and propose solutions, which in some cases were radical.

The EPA group came to OMB to meet with the Environment Branch and use us as a sounding board. Towards the end of the meeting, one of their members asked my boss, Dave Gibbons, how many staff members he had. When Dave pointed to his five examiners attending the meeting, Dave was asked how many staff each of his staff had because they couldn't understand how so few people could have such a big impact on EPA's operation. Afterward, we told Dave we either wanted our own staffs or a large raise since the Grace Commission folks seemed to think we were super productive. It didn't dawn on me until later that, since the Grace folks didn't understand OMB's structure, they were probably giving us credit for the government-wide guidance issued by the management side.

The final Grace Commission report offered recommendations to achieve $424 billion in savings over three years, at a time when the overall budget was less than $1 trillion, rising to $1.9 trillion per year by the year 2000, which was 35 percent of the year 2000 projected budget.[226] Needless to say, these savings weren't all due to efficiencies and eliminating fraud, waste, and abuse. Many of the recommendations required statutory change, largely not enacted, to transfer Federal functions to the private sector or states. While many efficiency recommendations were implemented, they did not have a huge impact on the deficit's trajectory.

Many of the Grace Commission recommendations were consistent with two other Reagan Administration initiatives on Federalism and privatization. The Federalism initiative, announced in the 1982 State of the Union message, included a radical proposal for States and localities to assume full responsibility for public assistance programs, including food stamps, while the Federal Government would fully finance the Medicaid program.[227] Needless to say that the states only loved the second half of the deal and the Federalism initiative largely failed.

Interestingly, in the FY 1989 Budget, the Reagan Administration took credit for shifting financing wastewater treatment plants back to state and local governments[228] through a one-time authorization of capitalization funding for new state revolving funds (SRFs). However, it was Congress who offered this Federalism-consistent proposal in response to the Reagan Administration's proposal to simply phase out EPA wastewater treatment construction funding. The legislation authorizing the SRFs ended up being enacted over two Reagan vetoes, the first a pocket veto at the end of a Congressional term, despite Reagan complaints about the excessive level of spending.

The Reagan Administration's privatization efforts were more successful, although even those successes were limited. These included the sale of Conrail, the long-term lease of National and Dulles airports in Washington, and the auction of $5 billion in Federal loan portfolio assets.[229] The Reagan Administration also began an effort, which has spanned multiple Administrations, to sell surplus Federal land and buildings.

George H.W. Bush Agenda (1989-1992)

With some exceptions, the George H.W. Bush (Bush '41) Administration largely continued the Reagan Administration's management efforts. However, its efforts were less ideologically driven and more of a "work the problem" type mentality. Thus, whereas David Stockman tried to eliminate agency evaluation offices as useless overhead, the Bush Administration saw evaluations as an important tool in improving Federal management. They also returned to management by objectives budget concepts that had previously been used in the Nixon Administration.

While the Federal Managers Financial Integrity Act of 1982 (FMFIA), which called for agencies to identify financial risks and weaknesses in their administrative systems, was enacted during the Reagan Administration, it was not central to Reagan's management improvement efforts. However, it became an important piece of the Bush Administration's efforts, in part spurred by the financial risks posed by the savings and loan crisis of the late 1980's.

To the extent that Bush '41 had a signature management improvement effort, it was the use of joint agency-OMB SWAT and review teams to "fix" specific problems in programs on the "High Risk List" that were often identified through the FMFIA process. The SWAT teams were used in situations that could be addressed within three months, whereas the review teams were for longer term actions[230].

A few of my staff got detailed to a review team, led by our PAD Bob Grady, which was looking into how to contain the exploding cost of Superfund and hazardous waste cleanups at DOD and DOE facilities. In the case of Rocky Mountain Arsenal in Colorado, the "fix" was to minimize both cleanup costs and health risks by preventing development of the site and instead turn it into a wildlife refuge.

One of the biggest challenges in reforming government operations is the difficulty in closing any existing Federal installations because of the opposition of the employees and the local Congressional delegation. This was a particular problem for DOD which had numerous military bases, many of which were becoming obsolete as the Cold War ended.

Towards the end of the Reagan Administration, the Secretary of Defense was able to get initial authority to establish an independent Base Closure and Realignment Commission (BRAC) to evaluate and make a recommendation on DOD suggested base closures. These recommended closures were submitted to Congress for an up or down vote on the entire package. The up or down vote meant individual Congressman couldn't strip out their local base closure and would appear to be against huge defense savings if they voted against the bill.

The 1988 base closures were such a success that the Bush Administration was able to secure legislation — the Base Closure and Realignment Act of 1990 — that enabled an additional three much larger rounds of base closures in 1991, 1993, and 1995.[231] A final round of defense BRAC was authorized in 2005. At the time, I was the DAD for Natural Resources and responsible for hundreds of small, inefficient Agriculture and Interior Department district offices. I suggested that a BRAC type commission was needed for domestic facilities but could never get our leadership interested.

Bill Clinton Agenda (1993-2000)

The signature Clinton Administration management initiative was the National Performance Review (NPR) launched shortly after Clinton took office in March 1993, with a challenge to create a government that "works better, costs less, and gets results Americans care about". The effort was inspired by the book "Reinventing Government", whose author, Dave Osborne, served as a consultant on the effort.[232] Instead of having OMB's DDM run the effort, however, Clinton asked Vice President Gore to lead the effort using non-OMB staff[233].

In some ways the effort was like the Grace Commission, with a few key exceptions. First, the task force was composed of roughly 250 career civil servants instead of private sector managers. Second, Gore chose to target overhead costs as he wanted the focus on how government works rather than what government should be doing. Third, he wanted the effort focused on actions that could be accomplished administratively, rather than requiring Congressional action. This contrasted with the Grace Commission which had a large portion of its projected savings coming from policy changes in the Federal Government's role that required legislative action. The 6-month NPR effort produced a report identifying 1,250 specific recommendations that was projected to save $108 billion over 5 years, ostensibly by reducing overhead positions[234].

As Gore also wanted agencies to establish their own reinvention teams, OMB undertook an internal effort known as OMB 2000 to better integrate our budget analysis, management review and policy development roles. The key changes were to eliminate the special studies divisions and move those staff, as well as some of the staff from the management divisions, into the budget branches. The goal was the same as the original creation of OMB, to better integrate the budget and management functions. The budget side was now referred to as Resource Management Offices (RMO) and budget staff positions were reclassified as program examiners rather than budget examiners.[235]

The Environment Branch received four new staff, many of them senior people, which was probably too many. Different branches organized the new management functions differently, with some assigning a specific individual all management tasks, and others, like my branch, distributing the functions among all the staff so that everybody had a management function responsibility.

With so many senior staff, who needed assignments allowing them to work relatively independently, I limited my involvement in many tasks that I might have otherwise been heavily involved in, such as regulatory review. Instead, I focused more on nuts and bolts management issues and not just ones involving NPR recommendations.

Usually when OMB would get involved on a specific issue, the affected program would become very defensive. I was surprised that was not the case with management issues. The management functions in most agencies are considered backwaters. EPA had a highly capable, hard-working staff that was thoroughly devoted to their environmental mission. However, they came to government to work on environmental issues, not management.

Given that EPA leadership was similarly focused, the management functions were the weak sisters of the organization. Amazingly, I found that by simply showing a strong interest in a financial, contracting or IT issue, my involvement gave the affected offices internal leverage. This helped them get action on issues that might otherwise be ignored because they could claim that "OMB was breathing down their necks".

After Clinton took a shellacking in the 1994 mid-term elections in reaction to the failure of his health care plan, he announced Phase II of NPR, which was subsequently renamed the National Partnership for Reinventing Government. The emphasis of this phase was on what government should be doing, including in the regulatory arena, rather than on just efficiency. While NPR continued to have a permanent staff, which lasted through the Administration, OMB had a bigger role in this phase of the reinvention process.

OMB management asked staff for bold ideas to include in the FY 1996 Budget. One of the ideas that my branch championed was to allow States to consolidate thirteen individual EPA grants into one Performance Partnership Grant (PPG). The proposal allowed states to structure more efficient and effective programs by reducing red tape and allowing states the flexibility to target available funding at their biggest environmental problems. EPA was very supportive of our proposal and was able to get the needed legislation enacted. Within two years, twenty states were at least partially using the new grant structure, although stove-piped organizations at the state level limited its acceptance.

One of EPA's NPR proposals, which we supported, was to reduce Superfund funding earmarked for the Agency for Toxic Substances and Disease Registry (ATSDR) in HHS by shifting certain responsibilities to the states. That an agency would surreptitiously go outside normal channels to fight any proposal to reduce its funding is not unusual, although the individuals involved are rarely discovered.

In this case, ATSDR officials organized a lobbying campaign by its grantees against the cut. One of the grantees, however, included the ATSDR request to the grantees as an attachment to their letter to the Director. This was a rare smoking gun providing documentation of an agency going "off the reservation" to thwart an Administration initiative. Given how difficult it is to find such proof, it should have been a great opportunity to send the bureaucracy a message about such inappropriate behavior by firing the individuals involved. Alas, that didn't happen.

In fact, the only time I can remember that happening was the forced resignation of Mike Parker, the Assistant Secretary for the Army Corps of Engineers, an agency for which our PAD at the time, Marcus Peacock, was responsible. In 2002, Parker had the misfortune of being on a panel with Peacock's wife, who went by a different last name, when he went off the reservation and testified before Congress against cuts to his agency that were in the President' Budget. The Bush Administration acted swiftly to punish that no-no!

The other notable Clinton management initiative was the Y2K effort to prevent the meltdown of the nation's computer systems on January 1, 2000, because the systems hadn't been programmed to handle the date change and would confuse the year 1900 with 2000. John Koskinen, arguably OMB's most capable DDM, was pulled off that job to become the Y2K czar in 1998. Under John's leadership, OMB spent a massive amount of time working with agencies and the private sector to prevent a disaster. The Clinton Administration proudly touted how trouble-free computers operated when the new millennium started. Left unsaid, however, was that few countries encountered any major problems despite putting in only a fraction of the effort as the U.S.

George W. Bush Agenda (2001-2008)

The Bush '43 Management Agenda was released in August 2001 and was guided by three principles of governance that programs should be: 1) results-oriented, not process oriented; 2) citizen centered, not bureaucracy centered; and

3) promoting competition rather than stifling innovation. In a shot at the Clinton Administration's efforts, the management section of the FY 2003 Budget stated, "Rather than pursue an endless and disconnected array of initiatives, the Administration has elected to identify the government's most glaring problems — and solve them[236]".

The NPR office in the White House was eliminated and responsibility for management issues shifted back to OMB. Fortunately, for the first time ever, OMB had a Director in Mitch Daniels who was willing to devote a significant portion of his time to management issues. Most Directors, particularly those who came from the Hill, were interested in big picture budget and policy issues, and got involved in M-side issues only when absolutely necessary. Perhaps because Daniels had most recently been a corporate executive, he viewed improving government-wide management as a key part of his portfolio.

Under Daniel's leadership, two process innovations were developed — the Management Scorecard and the Program Assessment Rating Tool (PART). The Management Scorecard used a stoplight system (i.e. red, yellow, and green) to grade agencies on their progress in meeting various government-wide management objectives. All departments and major agencies were graded quarterly on five initiatives, although a few other initiatives, such as improper payments, were added in the second term that applied to a limited set of agencies. The grades were hashed out during internal OMB meetings with the DDM attended by both M-side staff and the RMOs. This consistent, high-level focus on the scorecard was essential to its success.

The five initiatives were the usual suspects (i.e. Human Capital, Commercial Services Management, Financial Performance, E-Government, and Performance Improvement) and lined up with the organizational structure of the M-side. Each of the initiatives included perhaps a half dozen objectives, with the scores for both status (i.e. the ultimate goal) and progress (i.e. movement towards a higher status) based on how the agency had done in meeting those objectives. For instance, green required meeting all the objectives.

Figure 11-1 shows the quarterly status scores for the Bush Management Scorecard posted on Results.Gov for the quarter ending December 2003[237]. At this early point, only Education and EPA received any greens, in this case for financial performance. The dark circles are mostly reds, and the light circles are yellow, while arrows indicate progress since the last scorecard.

With one exception, the objectives themselves were unremarkable and reflected the ongoing work of the OMB management offices (e.g. obtaining a clean audit or upgrading security on IT systems). One problem with the effort was that the objectives were static. Agencies wanting to achieve Green Status complained bitterly about OMB "moving the goal posts" if we tried to change any of the objectives. Unfortunately, the optimal objectives in year one of an administration were often outdated and less meaningful by year eight, due to the evolution of management issues, particularly as IT systems became more sophisticated.

The one innovative objective related to the PART, which was woven through the Performance Improvement initiative. The PART was a methodology for systematically assessing virtually all the over 1,000 Federal programs. While the concept for the PART came from Daniels, he tasked Marcus Peacock, who had written a paper on assessing performance in a previous job, and a few OMB career staff to develop the tool.

The program reviews themselves were designed to make sure that all Federal programs had: 1) specific definitions of success; 2) outcome-oriented performance measures to track success; and 3) concrete improvement plans.[238] The Director's intent was to use the information in the PARTs, and particularly data on the performance measures, in making budget decisions. As a practical matter, that data was not used when it didn't support Administration priorities but was used to justify Administration decisions when the data was supportive.

The burden of assessing these programs fell to the RMO examiners working with agency staff. The participation of agency staff was effectively compelled by the need to complete quality PARTs on their programs in order for their

Figure 11-1: Bush Administration Management Scorecard

EXECUTIVE BRANCH MANAGEMENT SCORECARD
STATUS AS OF DECEMBER 31, 2003

AGENCIES			Human Capital	Competitive Sourcing	Financial Perf.	E-Gov	Budget/ Perf. Integration
AGRICULTURE	HTML	PDF	●		●		●
COMMERCE	HTML	PDF			●		
DEFENSE	HTML	PDF			●	●	
EDUCATION	HTML	PDF			●††		●
ENERGY	HTML	PDF					
EPA	HTML	PDF	●	●	●		
HHS	HTML	PDF	†		●	●	●
HOMELAND	HTML	PDF	●	†	●	●	●
HUD	HTML	PDF	●	●	●	●	●
INTERIOR	HTML	PDF	●		●	●	●
JUSTICE	HTML	PDF	●		●	●	●
LABOR	HTML	PDF		●			
STATE-IAD	HTML	PDF		●	†	●	†
TRANSPORTATION	HTML	PDF			●	†	
TREASURY	HTML	PDF	●	●	●	●	●
VA	HTML	PDF	●	●	●		

agency to move towards Green on the Performance Improvement item of the scorecard.

The PARTs were a back breaking workload for RMO staff, even though the assessments were spaced out over a five-year period. For a new examiner, the PART process was a terrific learning tool by providing a structured deep dive into the operation of one of their assigned programs. For the more senior examiners, a lot of the effort was viewed as "make work". Towards the end, the inertia of the bureaucratic process to complete remaining programs seemed more important than the actual value of assessing the final tranche of lower priority programs.

The value of the PART process was that, for the first time, all agency programs, not just the ones highlighted in the strategic plans, had to undertake critical thinking about what potential outcome measures for their programs would look like. Nevertheless, the difficulties in developing measures, as discussed earlier, remained.

The Bush leadership made the PARTs available to the public on www.ExpectMore.gov and expected the next Administration to find them hugely useful. While some of the performance measures developed in the PART process lived on, the Obama Administration deleted the website, ignored the PARTs, and terminated use of the Management Scorecard.

Barack Obama Agenda (2009-2016)

The Obama Management Agenda seemed like a rerun of past agendas, pursuing efforts such as reducing improper payments, cutting waste in contracting, holding leaders accountable, and eliminating unneeded Federal property. They correctly identified that the Federal hiring process was broken — taking over 150 days on average to make a hire[239] — but made the hiring process even worse by turbo-charging the existing veterans preference. Even the approaches to address hiring problems were simply workarounds because a real overhaul of the system would anger traditional Democratic constituencies.

While the Obama Administration had no signature management initiative, its emphasis on the use of evidence in performance management was new. In meetings with OMB senior staff, Director Peter Orszag would cite a couple examples where evidence obtained by academic research had been highly useful in making specific programs more effective. Consequently, in preparation for making decisions on the FY 2011 Budget, he had the entire budget staff on a wild goose chase to scour the academic literature to find more examples that could support Administration reform proposals.

Unfortunately, that type of academic research was mostly confined to large entitlement and other human resource programs. Nevertheless, evidence can be extremely useful where data exists, and support for evaluations and use of evidence in policy decisions continued to be a key objective throughout both the Obama and Trump Administrations. However, as with PART information in Bush '43, evidence was primarily used only if it supported predetermined Administration initiatives.

At one point, two outside experts, one of whom by chance I had shared an office with at the Department of Labor after college, were brought in to discuss the importance of randomized trials for testing new policy. The reason they supported small, randomized trials was that on the order of 90 percent of policy changes did not result in statistically significant outcome improvements. Consequently, multiple experiments needed to be conducted to find one effective policy change. While I had always viewed new agency policy proposals with a skeptical eye, I was stunned by the failure rate. I remarked at the meeting that, if their statistic was correct, I hadn't been nearly skeptical enough about new programs over my career.

It also struck me that the statistic meant that most new Administration program initiatives were doomed to fail. Many initiatives are promised on the campaign trail to please various constituent groups. The activists for these groups are good at identifying program shortcomings, but their solution is usually to overlay a new program on top of an existing program, rather than reforming or scrapping the existing under-performing program. Unfortunately, at best these "innovative" new solutions are based on anecdotal information and rarely on any hard evidence.

One successful Obama management initiative that should be mentioned is the creation of the United States Digital Service (USDS), which was founded in 2014 after a major hack of the Office of Personnel Management's personnel records. USDS employed an elite team of computer programmers, many of whom were on detail from Silicon Valley firms. They fixed troubled Federal IT systems in the same manner that the broken Obamacare website was fixed in 2013, at a time when it looked like that website might need to be scrapped.

The Administrator of USDS was an OMB employee and its funding came through an OMB controlled appropriations account. However, it had an odd relationship to OMB in part because it was the only part of OMB that had an operational function, as opposed to a guidance and oversight role. Due to this operational role, conceptually it belonged in GSA. However, GSA did not have the cachet to attract top Silicon Valley talent. Consequently, to provide the prestige needed to attract top talent, USDS was listed as an Executive Office of the President agency with its own website that didn't even mention OMB.

If USDS was the Obama Administration's best management innovation, the SAVE (Securing Americans Value and Efficiency) Awards was the worst. The SAVE Award process was essentially a high-profile suggestion box that allowed Federal employees to offer their ideas about how to cut waste, save taxpayer's dollars, and make government efficient and effective. Over the first four years, Federal employees offered 85,000 suggestions of which 80 were incorporated in the President's Budget, and supposedly saved hundreds of millions of dollars.[240]

While the first year generated real employee interest — my staff alone had to review 5,000 nominations — the program was experiencing diminishing returns long before the fifth and final year. I also suspect that the bulk of the savings came from a limited number of suggestions that probably would have happened in the absence of the program.

Agency budget office and RMO staff hated the initiative because it required rating large numbers of suggestions with small dollar savings in a time frame that at least partially overlapped our respective budget season work.

Donald Trump Agenda (2017-2020)

The Trump PMA, released in March 2018, was in many respects a traditional PMA (e.g. modernize IT, enhance customer service, and improve efficiency and effectiveness). It even continued some of the Obama efforts. However, there were two significant efforts that had both a traditional good government component and an ideological component — 1) Getting Government Out of the Way; and 2) Reorganization and Reform.[241]

The nature of bureaucracies is to establish many rules, directives, and organizations, each of which made sense individually at the time, but which over time weigh down the organization, making it slower and less responsive. Getting Government Out of the Way was, therefore, a type of cleanup operation that the government periodically needs. As part of that effort, for example, the State Department eliminated 35 special adviser positions, such as the Special Advisor for Conflict Diamonds, that were overlayed on top of an already complex organizational structure. OMB even practiced what it preached by eliminating roughly 50 OMB directives. While some of these were already ignored by the agencies (e.g. memos on Y2K), others reduced actual implementation burden.

In the regulatory world, OMB issued guidance requiring agencies to eliminate two rules for every new one implemented. In the first year, this mainly involved taking off the books rules that were no longer needed. The Clinton Administration undertook a similar cleanup effort in 1995, which eliminated 16,000 pages of obsolete regulations. Despite primarily eliminating rules that no longer had any impact, Clinton somehow claimed that the initiative saved $28 billion annually.[242] The Trump Administration, on the other hand, was no longer in good government cleanup mode in the last three years. Instead, Trump appointees were targeting rules for elimination, mostly promulgated in the Obama era, that the Administration viewed as regulatory overreach.

The Trump reorganization effort, while only marginally successful, was badly needed as the Federal agency organization structure was badly out of date. From the Nixon era through the first Reagan term, Presidents had reorganization authority that allowed them to propose agency reorganizations subject to Congressional veto. This authority resulted in the creation of OMB and EPA under Nixon and the Departments of Energy and Education under Carter. Congress didn't renew the authority under Reagan because it was viewed as ceding too much authority to the Executive Branch. Both the Bush '43 and Obama Administration's requested such authority, but Congress had no interest in providing it. Instead, after 9/11 when a new Department of Homeland Security was needed, Congress developed the reorganization through its traditional "sausage-making" legislative process. Perhaps due to that process, it was a reorganization that few people thought went well.

In April 2018, OMB issued a Management Memorandum to agency heads requiring them to develop reform plans which would help OMB develop a plan to reorganize the Executive Branch, as we had been tasked by President Trump in EO 13781.[243] My staff in the International Affairs Division had not been happy about the large cuts we had to make to State and USAID for the FY 2018 Budget. However, I convinced them that reorganization was a good government activity for which we were being given a once in a career opportunity, where we would have high level political support for our proposals. Consequently, we threw ourselves into the activity.

State and USAID understood that their organizational structure was out of date and undertook a serious reform effort in the summer of 2017. Although we decided to see what State and USAID developed on their own before trying to shape the reorganization, I had two priority objectives. First, State and USAID had three duplicative and poorly coordinated offices delivering humanitarian assistance, which would be more efficient and effective if consolidated. Second, while State and USAID had needs and challenges for their finance, payroll and other administrative systems that were different from domestic agencies, it was duplicative and inefficient for each to have their own systems.

When the State/USAID reorganization effort fell apart in the fall of 2017, as Secretary of State Tillerson lost interest amidst clashes with the White House, my division started to pursue those objectives on our own. In the case of optimizing humanitarian assistance, we got our proposal included in the Administration's reorganization plan issued in June 2018.[244] Unfortunately, our efforts eventually ran into a brick wall of opposition from State on humanitarian assistance and from USAID on administrative systems integration.

Fortunately, USAID decided to develop its own internal agency-wide reorganization, with our support, which included consolidating their two humanitarian offices into one. While the USAID reorganization did not require Congress to enact legislation, they were required to go through the Congressional Notification process with four different committees. As there were nine separate notifications for different pieces of the reorganization, and both the majority and minority for each of the committees could place an informal "hold" to stop the project, USAID needed to get a ridiculous 72 signoffs for the reorganization to move forward. While USAID had to make some adjustments to their proposal, the committees finally let it go forward in late 2020.

The division's most successful reorganization, however, was the creation of the Development Finance Corporation (DFC). This was an effort spearheaded by my branch chief, Fouad Saad, and his examiner, Erika Ryan. The reorganization was aimed at reducing duplication and better achieving national security and international development outcomes. The reorganization involved consolidating the Overseas Private Investment Corporation and several functions from USAID and other agencies into the DFC, as well as providing the DFC with some new authorities. The proposal was included in the FY 2019 Budget several months in advance of the Administration's release of its reorganization plan.

Fortunately, there was bipartisan support in Congress for a more aggressive use of development finance as a counterweight to China's Belt and Road Initiative. Consequently, the Build Act authorizing the DFC was passed and signed into law in October 2018. My staff then led the inter-agency process to develop the detailed reorganization plan required by the Act. The plan was transmitted to Congress in March 2019 and the DFC became operational on October 1, 2019.[245]

Management Initiative Savings Estimates

Most management initiatives have huge savings estimates attached to them leading the public to conclude that a large portion of our deficit problem can be solved by simply implementing these commonsense management proposals. Unfortunately, these estimates should be taken with a huge grain of salt. First, much of the savings are not budget savings in a normal sense. As with regulatory benefits estimates, they often are measured from an assumed increasing baseline that may not reflect reality. Second, unless funding is being taken out of an agency's budget, there is no downside to using unrealistic assumptions in order to claim enormous savings that the agency will never be called to reconcile. This contrasts with budget cuts where OMB, and particularly the agency, have an incentive to make accurate savings estimates to avoid making unintended cuts that must be absorbed by other programs.

Finally, some savings, particularly those estimated by the Inspector Generals, are for improved use of funding or some other subjective terminology. While Congress and OMB leadership are huge supporters of the IGs, my support of the IGs is much more restrained. As an examiner in the 1980s, I challenged the EPA IG at a budget hearing about data showing they were less effective than other agency IGs. His response was that the data I was using had been provided to the M-side of OMB with the understanding that it would never be used against them. That was when I realized that the IGs acted just like other bureaucrats when it came to their own budgets and that they did not necessarily even hold themselves to the same standard they hold the agencies in conducting their program audits.

In fact, given that Congress acts as their cheerleaders, the IG's basically get no oversight and there is no scrutiny of the savings estimates in their annual reports. Certainly, the agencies don't believe the IG estimates. The only way to get more realistic savings estimates from the IGs, is to make them subject to an independent audit by a private accounting firm, not GAO, that explains to the public what are real budget type savings and what are wishful thinking "might be" savings.

CHAPTER TWELVE: Let's Play Chicken -- *The Story Behind Shutdowns & Debt Ceiling Crises*

Political maneuvering to pressure the other political party to take a distasteful vote or enact unwanted legislation is a standard part of American politics. However, nowhere is this more evident, or the stakes higher, than in the political game of "Let's Play Chicken" that surrounds the potential failure to enact a continuing resolution or extension of the debt ceiling.

While the press sometimes conflates the two situations and occasionally oversimplifies the events by referring to each as "shutting down the Government", the two situations are actually very different. The core difference is that a failure to enact a continuing resolution will result in a lack of authority providing new appropriations, which means that agencies without appropriations can't sign contracts, award grants, or even allow staff to work. On the other hand, expiration of the debt ceiling means that agencies may not be able to issue checks (i.e. make outlays), even though they can continue to sign contracts, award grants, and allow staff to work. This chapter will examine these two situations as well as OMB's role in avoiding or coping with them.

Failure to Enact a Continuing Resolution

As was discussed in Chapter 2, a continuing resolution (CR) is needed when Congress does not enact all appropriations bills by the beginning of the Federal fiscal year, which begins on October 1st. Such resolutions are needed virtually every year, as Congress has enacted all the appropriations bills prior to the beginning of the fiscal year only four times since enactment of the Congressional Budget Act of 1974.[246]

A CR is effectively a mini-appropriations bill, that must be enacted like any other law, in that it requires passage in both the House of Representatives and the Senate and the signature of the President. In that way, it is very different from the budget resolution, which is effectively a fiscal guidance document for Congress that does not require the President's signature and is not legally binding on the Federal Government or the public.

CRs apply only to appropriations bills not already enacted. In recent years, few if any appropriations bills have been enacted by the beginning of the fiscal year, although some do get enacted during the fall. Therefore, CRs usually apply to fewer agencies and programs as the fall progresses. In most years, there are multiple CRs that get enacted before final appropriations are passed, although most are simple date extensions of the original CR.

In recent years, my assumption has always been that final appropriations will not get enacted for most agencies until the end of December, when the lure of the Christmas break (and the ire of congressional spouses) provides the extra incentive for Congress to make the compromises needed to get the bills enacted. This usually occurs in what is referred to as an omnibus appropriations bill, which incorporates multiple appropriations bills into one large bill, rather than enacting them separately as should occur under regular order. Sadly, in some years the appropriations process extends beyond December.

Most CRs are relatively sparse bills with a host of standard provisions (e.g. no new programs can be started, and no staff can be laid off) as well as a limited number of CR "anomalies", which are exceptions to the standard CR language. The guts of the bill, which is what keeps agencies without appropriations operating, is language specifying the amount of budget authority agencies can obligate during the period of the CR. In the past the language often set the amount based on the lower of last year's level, the House passed level for the budget year, and the Senate passed level. In recent years, that language has been simplified to just last year's level as so few bills have passed. This is particularly the case in the Senate, where considering appropriations bill on the floor is so time consuming that the Senator Majority Leader, regardless of party, rarely even bothers to schedule floor time for most of the bills.

While the CR amount is generally based on last year's level, the amount actually made available by the CR is only a prorated amount of last year's level. Thus, if the CR lasts a month, roughly one-twelve of last year's budget authority would be made available. The actual pro rata calculation is the number of days of the CR divided by the number of days in the fiscal year. If the CR gets extended by a week, the calculation updates by adding seven days in the numerator.

<u>OMB's Role in Developing a CR</u>

OMB generally begins its staff work in July to consider what "anomalies" the Administration wants to request be added to the expected CR. In general, the guidance to OMB staff is to only consider "technical anomalies" as opposed to policy anomalies. A "technical anomaly" is a provision needed to allow a program to keep operating normally which, for technical reasons, would not be allowed under the standard CR amounts.

For instance, when the Development Finance Corporation (DFC) was established in 2019, through consolidation of several programs from other agencies, it had no last year's funding level, even though its predecessor programs did have funding. Consequently, the DFC would not have received any funding under the standard CR language and anomaly language had to be written to allow the DFC to commence operations.

In addition to funding, appropriation bills also include various policy directives, funding restrictions, and, in some cases, authorizing language for programs that can't get authorized through the normal process for authorization bills. For these language provisions, the CR includes language that applies the same "terms and conditions" to the CR as were applicable to the prior year appropriations. However, not all the language in an appropriations bill is written in a manner that makes them a "term and condition" under the CR. In those cases, the OMB program examiner must determine whether the language needs to continue under the CR and, if so, work with OMB' Office of General Counsel to craft an appropriate "technical anomaly".

The anomaly process begins when OMB's Budget Review Division issues a Budget Data Request (BDR) to the agencies requesting them to submit needed "technical anomalies". Inevitably, however, agencies often include some "policy anomalies" within their submission. In some cases, these anomalies relate to high priority Administration policies that would be desirable to start at the beginning of the fiscal year and which the Department Secretary feels merits a strong Administration push to include in the CR.

The State Department, however, often sent in a set of "nice to have" policy anomalies that mirrored requested language in the President's Budget. The department budget office knew that these anomalies had no chance of being included in the CR, but it wasn't worth the fight within the department to exclude them. Instead, it was easier to just transmit them to OMB and let the OMB staff be the "bad guys" by turning them down. This "abominable no-man" role is one that OMB staff play in multiple contexts and usefully enhances the perception of the staff's power.

Objective to Obtain a Clean CR

In general, the objective for most CR's is to pass a "clean" bill, which includes appropriate technical anomalies and no policy anomalies. Thus, the bar for the Administration to include an anomaly in its request to Congress (which is usually transmitted informally — i.e. not signed by either the President or the Director) is very high. The standard that OMB staff generally apply to anomaly requests is often referred to as "wheels off the bus", signifying that the absence of an anomaly would result in major damage to a program if not included.

While Congress is usually on-board with the goal of enacting a "clean" CR, the definition of a "clean" is in the eye of the beholder. Consequently, the Appropriations Committees often reject many of the Administration's proposed anomalies, while usually adding many of their own. These additional anomalies often include ones that the Administration would classify as policy anomalies, but which generally are not major policies and have bi-partisan support within the Appropriations Committees.

The reason for pursuing a "clean" CR is that, once any significant policy anomaly gets included, it opens the flood-gates for demands to include a wide-ranging set of policy anomaly proposals (i.e. if you got yours, I want mine). Consequently, the inclusion of any significant controversial policy proposal can bring down the consensus to pass the CR in a timely manner.

I think it is fair to say that CRs work when there is a Congressional consensus to "kick the can down the road" in addressing the issues that either must or could be included in the final appropriations bill. When Congress can't come together on enacting a CR, it results in what is generally referred to as a Federal Government "shutdown".

Shutdown Rules

The term "shutdown" is often used in the press in a misleading manner in that the Federal Government never fully shuts down. In fact, OMB guidance generally refers to the more technically accurate phrase "lapse of appropriations". Several factors account for the distinction between the two terms. The biggest distinction is that a lapse of appropriations is the cause, and the shutdown is the effect of such a lapse. In addition, a lack of a CR or appropriations bill, only applies to discretionary appropriations, which made up only 30 percent of the budget in [247]2019.

Consequently, entitlements and other mandatory spending programs are not prohibited during a shutdown as, with a couple of exceptions, the funding for those programs is provided through authorizing legislation and not through appropriations action. However, there is a major caveat to that last statement in the situation where Federal payments are mandatory, but the administrative costs (e.g. salaries) to process the payments are made using discretionary appropriations. Those programs require a separate determination as to whether they continue.

A shutdown also only occurs in programs whose appropriations bills have not been enacted. Thus, in general fewer programs are affected the later in the fiscal year that a CR or extension is passed as more individual appropriations bills will have been enacted — hence the term lapse of appropriations.

However, some programs will not shut down even if their appropriations bill for the year has not been enacted. These are programs with multi-year funding that still have remaining prior year appropriations that has "carried over" into the new fiscal year. While agencies generally want to obligate older funding first, particularly if it will potentially lapse at the end of the new fiscal year, the incentives for agency budget officers are reversed during a CR. The reason is that unused CR funding does not carry over into a shutdown period and, consequently, is not available for obligation during that period, whereas "carry over" from a full year appropriations bill is available for obligation in the shutdown period. Consequently, any competent budget officer will ensure that the CR funds are used first during a CR when carryover is limited.

Exceptions to Shutdown Rules

The legal rules governing shutdowns are based on two Attorney General opinions from 1980 and 1981 that provide an interpretation of the Anti-Deficiency Act.[248] While the Anti-Deficiency Act prohibits obligation of funding in the absence of an appropriation, the Attorney General opinions provide some important exceptions. The most important of these is the exception for the safety of human life or the protection of property. Thus, in the absence of an appropriations bill or a CR, prison guards would remain at their posts to prevent dangerous criminals from escaping and medical staff at Veterans hospitals would continue to provide life-saving care. Similarly, the military would not be sent home because it would provide an opportunity for our enemies to attack. During the Reagan Administration, military bands were also covered by this exception, although the rationale for excepting military bands still escapes me.

OMB issues guidance to agencies on the development of plans for a "lapse in appropriations", which must be reviewed at least annually for any needed updates. In general, agency heads have a certain amount of leeway in interpreting the Attorney General's memo and OMB guidance, subject to OMB approval of the plans. Among other things, the plans in general terms define which employees will be "excepted" and report for work during the shutdown and which employees will be furloughed. OMB Circular A-11, which is standing guidance covering budget formulation and execution, requires agencies to begin preparations for a shutdown a week in advance of a potential lapse in appropriations.

The interpretation of the exceptions has not been entirely consistent over time, nor has the amount of deference given to the agency head. For instance, before the long shutdown in 1995 during the Clinton Administration, the Administrator of EPA determined that all agency employees would be furloughed, even though the Superfund hazardous waste cleanup program had significant carryover that could be used to operate the program for a lengthy period. The Administrator's rationale was to ensure that all agency employees were treated in an equitable manner. As Chief of the Environment Branch at the time, I had to point out that it would be an illegal impoundment of funds to furlough employees when authority existed to continue paying them.

During the Obama Administration in 2011, the opposite result occurred in a similar situation concerning the State Department while I was serving as the Deputy Associate Director for International Affairs. In 1995, the State Department had little choice but to shut down virtually all its passport and visa operations due to the lapse of appropriations. However, while in 1995 the passport and visa programs were almost entirely funded by appropriations, the situation had changed dramatically by 2011. In fact, by 2011 those programs were 70 percent funded by fees and a large fee balance was available to continue the programs. In this case, however, State was still going to be allowed to shut down the passport and visa programs. Fortunately, a last-minute deal was reached on the CR and a shutdown was never implemented.

Essential Employees

Another exception to the general shutdown rules concerns functions necessary to the discharge of the President's constitutional duties and powers. This is the exception that allows some OMB employees to work during shutdowns but is generally limited to senior executives and a small set or program examiners and analysts. Basically, OMB's role during a lapse in appropriations is to help manage the shutdown, particularly to provide answers to questions agencies have before, during and after the shutdown; provide input on potential deals and legislative language to end the shutdown; and help manage the reopening of the portion of the government that did shut down. OMB's Management side generally takes the lead in issuing guidance and managing the shutdown in close coordination with the Office of General Counsel and the Budget Review Division.

For better or worse, I have worked during every one of the roughly fifteen shutdowns in my 40 plus year career. In each case, I was deemed "excepted" and not subject to furlough. While excepted is the official term for such employees, the more commonly used, if politically incorrect, term is "essential" employee. It is politically incorrect for fear of the morale implications of deeming the remaining employees as non-essential.

Employees who are "excepted" are only allowed to work on excepted activities during the shutdown period. For the military, this limitation may not result in much distinction from their normal duties. For OMB, however, our activities were limited to those related to managing the shutdown that are discussed above. Thus, even though most shutdowns take place during the period when OMB is formulating the next year's budget, I was not allowed to work on the next year's budget. To the extent that I had down time, I was expected to use it for organizing my files.

Even employees not designated as "excepted" are generally required to report for the first four hours the day the shutdown begins. As one of our lawyers in the Office of General Counsel explained to me in the early 1980s, the official purpose of reporting for those four hours was to prepare the employees' files for archiving. The implicit assumption behind this requirement is that the shutdown will be permanent and affected programs will never reopen — an unrealistic assumption. Most likely the real rationale is that shutdowns in the 1980's tended to be very short and having employees report the first day meant that government operations would be minimally affected if a deal on a CR was reached overnight or first thing in the morning.

While this changed recently, historically one of the key distinctions between excepted and non-excepted employees is that excepted employees were legally required to be paid once the shutdown ended, whereas non-excepted employees had no such guarantee. However, even during the month-long shutdown in 2019, excepted employees did not get paid for working during the shutdown until after the Government reopened.

As a practical matter, all Federal employees get paid for the shutdown period regardless of whether they work or not. While there was no guarantee of payment for furloughed workers, they have gotten paid after every shutdown that I have been through. The rationale is that the workers shouldn't be penalized for the failure of Congress to act. However, that logic apparently doesn't apply to contract employees who don't get paid if they don't work.

Paying employees who didn't work is a very real cost of the shutdown which, of course, penalizes the taxpayer for Congress's failure to act. However, the cost is an opportunity cost rather than a financial payment. The reason is that Congress never provides additional funding to agencies to pay such costs as agencies have already budgeted for those staff salaries. Instead, the opportunity cost results from reduced outputs (i.e. fewer tax returns processed) that may result in longer backlogs or foregone activities (i.e. delayed maintenance).

Consequently, if there is going to be a shutdown, one of the dirty little secrets of Washington is that many (perhaps most) employees would prefer to be furloughed than be classified as "excepted", because they get time off with no loss of pay. Nevertheless, Federal employees generally hate shutdowns, due to the disruption of work schedules and the pressure to make up for lost time when the shutdown ends, as well as the uncertainty about the timing of the next paycheck, particularly during a long shutdown.

Causes of Shutdowns

From my observation, there are four potential situations that can result in a shutdown, all of which can be avoided in the short-term by enacting a "clean CR" that kicks the can down the road. In all these situations, it involves one political party or the other using the CR as a "must pass bill" to provide leverage to achieve a policy objective through the threat of an undesirable outcome. In actuality, neither side wants a shutdown, but one side thinks that the other side with be blamed for the shutdown resulting in either a legislative "win" or, alternatively, a political advantage going into the next election.

The four situations (i.e. types of political disputes) that can either threaten or result in a shutdown result from a matrix of two types of legislative actions — stripping provisions from a pending bill and adding provisions to a pending bill — and two types of provisions — funding and language. These four situations will be discussed below in turn.

The most straightforward situation relates to demands to drop or reduce funding in a pending CR or Omnibus appropriations bill. This is the type of situation that resulted in numerous short shutdowns during the Reagan Administration.[249] President Reagan would veto a CR over too much spending, override attempts would fail, and the Democrats in Congress had little choice but to reduce some spending as Reagan demanded. This is the easiest situation for the public to understand and support the action that could trigger the shutdown, because funding is the purpose of the CR, and the public has little ability to judge the importance of specific funding increases over current levels (e.g. water project funding in 1984).

The second situation involves attempts to strip a controversial language provision from the CR. While not resulting in a shutdown, the Democrats addition of the debt ceiling extension to the CR in September 2021 is an example of this situation. While both the CR and debt ceiling extensions are "must pass bills", the Democrats tried to conflate the two bad outcomes as both being needed to avoid shutting down the Government. As discussed earlier, this is not technically correct, and the Democrats also weren't transparent about the different timing for the two outcomes. The Republicans made it clear that they supported a clean CR, which included supplemental funding for recent disasters and Afghanistan refugees. They were also quite willing to endure a shutdown, confident that the public would blame the Democrats, because the debt ceiling extension was extraneous to the bill and not yet needed, as well as the fact that the Democrats controlled all the levers of government (i.e. the House, Senate, and White House). The Democrats folded like a house of cards.

Attempts to add provisions not included in a pending funding bill by threatening to shut down the government are much more fraught with problems. An example of the third situation is the fight over FY 2019 appropriations, that resulted in large parts of the Federal Government shutting down for 35 days when President Trump demanded that $5.7 billion be added to the pending Omnibus appropriations bill for construction of the border wall[250] and refused to sign a CR to keep the Government operating during negotiations. Trump eventually folded because the public didn't support his position and his approval ratings fell. Trump was also influenced by the fact that he had a Plan B -- declare a national emergency and use that declaration to bypass Congress and reprogram existing funding for the wall.

The final situation, involving trying to strong arm extraneous language provisions into a must have funding bill, is probably the most difficult to explain and get public support to justify the shutdown. The best example of this situation was the 16-day shutdown in October 2013. The shutdown occurred because House Republicans wouldn't agree to a CR that didn't include language delaying or defunding the Affordable Care Act (i.e. Obamacare) as it was about to begin implementation using mandatory (i.e. non-appropriated funding).[251] The public put most of the blame on the Republicans and they eventually relented. Senate Democrats made a similar mistake in early 2018 by preventing enactment of a CR unless there was a fix to prevent the Deferred Action for Childhood Arrivals (DACA) from expiring two months later. However, the Democrats retreated quickly in the face of adverse public opinion and the shutdown lasted only three days.[252]

Most shutdowns don't work out well for the party trying to use it as leverage to achieve a policy goal. As OMB Director Jack Lew once opined at an OMB senior staff meeting, the party that prevails in these fights is usually the one that appears most reasonable to the public. As the examples above demonstrate, it is hard to get public support for policy provisions that are extraneous to funding needed to keep the Government operating. Similarly, it is hard to get public support to shut down the Government in order to add a provision not already in the bill. This is especially true for extraneous language provisions but is also true for funding beyond what would be provided until the CR generic funding formula (i.e. usually last year's level). In general, the public greatly prefers its elected officials to negotiate compromises rather than use government operations as a pawn in a political power play.

Debt Ceiling Disputes

The political Kabuki dance that accompanies debt ceiling disputes is even stranger than for shutdowns and the stakes are even higher because they relate to the stability of the world's financial system. The fact that the stakes are so high is the reason that the debt ceiling has never resulted in a financial default, even though creative workarounds are often employed to prevent that from happening.

Implications of Reaching the Debt Ceiling

To better understand the fights over the debt ceiling, it is first necessary to explain what it means and its implications. Basically, the debt ceiling is the total amount of money that the Department of the Treasury can borrow to finance Federal Government operations. Such borrowing is needed because in the vast majority of years, outlays (i.e. checks written) exceed the amount of revenue collected (e.g. taxes and fees). The deficit refers to an annual figure — the amount that outlays exceed revenue in a particular year— while the debt refers to the cumulative amount of the annual deficits (net of any surpluses) accumulated over time.

By itself, some level of debt accumulation is not a bad thing. In fact, Treasury securities (i.e. bonds and notes) issued by the Government are important and desirable financial instruments that individuals, banks, and foreign governments want to hold because they are viewed as the safest financial instruments on the planet. In fact, due to their safety, U.S. dollars, or Federal bonds denominated in dollars, function as a reserve currency for most of the world. These assets are viewed as safe due to the rock-solid assumption that the U.S. will always pay its debts, as the bonds are backed by the "full faith and credit" of the U.S. Government.

The safety of U.S. Treasury securities will only come into question in two circumstances. The first is if the debt ceiling is not raised and the U.S. cannot issue new bonds to pay back the principal and interest on maturing bonds. The second circumstance is if the amount of debt accumulated by the U.S. becomes so high (usually measured by the amount of debt relative to Gross Domestic Product or GDP, which is the amount of the nation's annual production) that there would not be sufficient demand to purchase new Treasury bonds to pay off maturing bonds. Most economists view the debt held by the public (i.e. excludes debt held by Federal Government accounts) to be the better measure of the country's debt liability than the gross Federal debt figure.

Consequently, it is the confidence of the financial community in the safety of Treasury securities that comes into question if the debt ceiling is not raised in a timely manner. Note that the debt ceiling is usually reached roughly three months before a financial default (i.e. failure to pay bond interest or principal) might occur. This delay in triggering a potential default is due to the use of creative workarounds known as "extraordinary measures" (e.g. suspending reinvestment of securities in the Federal Employees Retirement System) that the Treasury Department can undertake to push back the day of reckoning. Despite being called extraordinary measures these workarounds are now used routinely before every debt ceiling extension or suspension.

The big problems start occurring once Treasury exhausts the extraordinary measures. However, the exhaustion of the extraordinary measures does not necessarily mean that the U.S. will default on Treasury securities. The reason is that the Federal Government still can write some checks and make some payments but can make such payments <u>only</u> as fast as new revenue is received.

To the extent that the U.S. is running a large deficit (e.g. collecting three dollars in revenue for every four dollars in outlays needed) the problem is larger than if there is a smaller deficit. In the situation where the debt ceiling has been reached and the extraordinary measures are exhausted, the Treasury Department should have the ability to prioritize what payments to make. Note that any system of prioritized payments is likely to be challenged in court by advocates for programs that have not been prioritized.

Whereas agencies do extensive planning on how to deal with a shutdown, Treasury has resisted doing any planning, or at least has never admitted to any, for setting priorities when all U.S. financial obligations can't be met. The rationale is that the Department believes that the consequences of such a situation are so severe that even contingency planning on payment priorities might make it look like the situation is manageable and undercut the political pressure to either raise or suspend the debt ceiling.

While a suit could take months to play out, aggrieved parties will probably seek an injunction to prevent the prioritized payments from taking place. In deciding whether to grant such an injunction, a judge will have to decide whether he/she wants to compound the financial damage by preventing <u>any</u> payments.

As a practical matter, I would assume that Treasury would give first priority to making interest and principal payments on U.S. financial securities in order to prevent a financial default on the securities. The second priority would probably be to make payments for social security and other entitlement programs. However, as revenue is lumpier (i.e. does not come in evenly across the year) than outlays, there is no guarantee that even all these payments could be made when they are due. Furthermore, while paying off U.S. financial securities somewhat mitigates the financial damage, it poses a huge political problem with the public who won't like that wealthy and foreign (e.g. Chinese) bond holders are being paid while, for instance, food stamps are cut off.

Even if the payment priorities prevented a default on U.S. financial securities, the inability to make payments for salaries or contracts will having lasting damage to the world's perception of the "full faith and credit" of the U.S. Government. This damage will occur even if the lapse in payments for these types of costs is short. The damage will manifest itself in higher interest rates on U.S. securities going forward — worsening our deficit problems -- and may accelerate acceptance of other types of reserve currencies.

The fact that administrations are too scared to even do any contingency planning for a debt ceiling crisis means that OMB has no official role in addressing the crisis. However, should the debt ceiling be reached, and the extraordinary measures exhausted, OMB will undoubtedly be called in to help manage the government under a priority payment system and clean up the mess w hen the debt ceiling crisis is politically resolved.

Reasons for Playing Chicken with the Debt Ceiling

While no politician wants a debt ceiling crisis, very few like having to vote for raising a debt ceiling that might allow hundreds of billions or even trillions in additional deficit spending. This is particularly true for conservatives who campaigned in favor of small government. However, even President's Obama and Biden voted against debt ceiling increases when they were Senators during Republican Administrations only to argue vociferously that it would be irresponsible not to raise the debt ceiling when they became President. Thus, for political reasons, the onus is always on the President's party, but also the leadership of the House and Senate if controlled by the other party, to provide at least a significant share if not most of the politically difficult votes to raise the debt ceiling.

It seems that every time a debt ceiling increase is needed there are calls to eliminate the debt ceiling. The arguments in favor of eliminating the debt ceiling are that no other nation has such a ceiling and that the potential financial system risks posed by debt ceiling brinkmanship are unacceptable. While these are compelling arguments, there has never been a serious attempt to eliminate the debt ceiling. Instead, in recent years the debt ceiling has been suspended for a certain period of time rather than eliminated. However, such a suspension is not a precursor to elimination. In fact, the rationale for suspension is entirely political to shield Congress from having to vote for a specific, and very large, increase in the size of the debt ceiling.

The reason that the debt ceiling has not been eliminated is that each party views the periodic debt ceiling extension as providing useful policy or political leverage, that is much more effective than the threat of a shutdown. Furthermore, the fact that a debt ceiling increase is distasteful provides useful political focus on the Federal Government's spending habits. Unlike the states, the Federal Government is not required to have a balanced budget, in part because such a requirement would come with its own huge set of problems. Nevertheless, the current system, due to the lack of such a requirement, is biased towards producing large deficits. This is reflected in the fact that the Federal debt held by the public to GDP ratio has increased dramatically from 34 percent in FY 2000 to 97 percent in FY 2022,[253] the most recent year for which actual data is available. Table 12-1 shows the dramatic growth in Federal debt in both trillions of dollars and debt to GDP ratios.

Debt Ceiling Crisis Debt Reduction Measures

In the past, debt ceiling deadlines have resulted in some useful budget control measures, although in some cases other factors, such as stock market crashes, have provided

Table 12-1 Growth in Federal Debt 1980-2022

FEDERAL DEBT AT THE END OF YEAR: 1980 - 2022

End of Fiscal Year	In Trillions of Dollars		As Percentages of GDP	
	Gross Federal Debt	Debt Held by the Public	Gross Federal Debt	Debt Held by the Public
1980	0.9	0.7	33	26
1990	3.2	2.4	54	41
2000	5.6	3.4	56	34
2001	5.8	3.3	55	32
2002	6.2	3.5	57	33
2003	6.8	3.9	60	35
2004	7.4	4.3	61	36
2005	7.9	4.6	62	36
2006	8.5	4.8	62	35
2007	9.0	5.0	63	35
2008	10.0	5.8	68	39
2009	11.9	7.5	82	52
2010	13.5	9.0	91	61
2011	14.8	10.1	96	66
2012	16.1	11.3	100	70
2013	16.7	12.0	100	72
2014	17.8	12.8	102	74
2015	18.1	13.1	100	73
2016	19.5	14.2	105	76
2017	20.2	14.7	105	76
2018	21.5	15.7	106	78
2019	22.7	16.8	107	79
2020	26.9	21.0	128	100
2021	28.4	22.3	125	98
2022	30.8	24.3	123	97

needed impetus as well. For instance, the Balanced Budget and Emergency Control Acts of 1985 and 1987 (aka Gramm-Rudman-Hollings I & II) and the Budget Enforcement Act (BEA) of 1990 were largely bipartisan attempts to bring the budget under control while also providing major increases in the debt ceiling.

The BEA's discretionary spending caps and institution of pay-as-you-go (PAYGO) spending rules for mandatory spending and taxes played a major role in producing the budget surpluses in the late 1990's. The need to raise the debt ceiling also helped spur passage of the 1997 Balanced Budget and Tax Relief Act on a bipartisan basis, although that effort benefited by occurring in the wake of the 1995/1996 shutdowns and the re-election of President Clinton at a time when revenues were increasing rapidly.[254]

Perhaps the first serious example of partisan debt ceiling brinkmanship occurred during that 1995/1996 period. In the aftermath of the Republicans gaining control of the House of Representatives in the 1994 midterm elections, House Republicans in October 1995 vowed not to raise the debt ceiling unless their demands were met for a balanced budget in seven years, which included restraints on Medicare and Medicaid growth but also tax cuts which, of course, made eliminating the deficit even harder.

President Clinton was defiant, and the Treasury Department resorted to using the extraordinary measures to prevent a default and take the pressure off the debt ceiling as a lever. While not the first time some of these measures had been used, relatively new authority made that year the most extensive use of such measures. To keep the pressure on the President, House Republicans balked at passing a CR resulting in a five-day shutdown in November 1995 and a 21-day shutdown starting in mid-December extending into January. As opinion polls put most of the blame on Republicans, the second shutdown was ended after an agreement with only modest cuts.[255]

Unfortunately, that agreement did not resolve the debt ceiling issue with Republicans continuing to refuse to raise the ceiling. However, Republican backbone on the issue was put to the test when the Treasury Secretary notified Congress that, without an increase in the debt ceiling, social security payments could not be made in March 1996. Congress provided a workaround for this problem by passing legislation to issue sufficient securities to make the social security payments, but that such borrowing would not count against the debt ceiling.[256] The debt ceiling was eventually raised in late March 1996 after Moody's, the bond rating organization, threatened to downgrade the ratings on U.S. securities. This provided the impetus for a deal that gave minor concessions to Republican goals.

Debt ceiling brinkmanship returned in 2011 during the Obama Administration and again the issue related to reducing the deficit, in part because the debt to GDP ratio was rising. The perception, whether correct or not, was that the Republicans might not be bluffing this time about allowing a default and, with large deficits, the Obama Administration and the Republicans in Congress cut a deal. This deal resulted in enactment of the Budget Control Act (BCA) of 2011, which imposed discretionary spending caps over a ten-year period enforced by automatic spending reductions.[257]

Despite enactment of the BCA, the Standard and Poor's (S&P) rating service downgraded the United States credit rating a few days later, an unprecedented event. However, the U.S. dodged a bullet on interest rates, because the European debt crisis and the potential for a U.S. recession drove down interest rates on U.S. Treasury bonds, the opposite of what should have happened due to a bond downgrade.[258]

Debt Ceiling Crises Unrelated to Debt Reduction

While there is a certain logic to using the need for a debt ceiling extension as leverage to achieve deficit reduction measures, beginning in the Trump Administration debt ceiling showdowns were no longer used for that purpose. Even though the Democrats initially didn't control either House of Congress (the House flipped after the 2018 midterms), the tables were turned and now the Democrats had leverage. The reason they had leverage is that 60 votes were needed to overcome a filibuster in the Senate. In addition, some Republicans won't vote for a debt ceiling extension under any circumstances, thereby increasing the number of votes needing to be supplied by Democrats and increasing their leverage.

What Democrats wanted was not spending reductions but spending increases. Specifically, the Democrats wanted relief from the discretionary spending caps enacted in the BCA of 2011. Thus, bills were enacted in both 2018 and 2019 that suspended the debt ceiling while increasing both the non-defense and defense discretionary spending caps covering the years FY 2018 through FY 2021.[259]

In 2021, despite debt to GDP ratios at levels not seen since the end of World War II, debt brinkmanship was not about trying to get concessions to reduce the debt, but about politics. While politics has always been an element in debt ceiling brinkmanship, the result has been deals enacted on a bipartisan basis. In 2021, Senate Minority Leader McConnell was not even looking for a deal. His position was that if the Democrats were trying to ram through $3.5 trillion in new spending on a party line vote through the reconciliation process, they could also use reconciliation for a party line vote on raising the debt ceiling since they controlled both the Congress and the presidency.

Democrats were outraged about having to take an unprecedented partisan debt ceiling vote to pay for funding already enacted. The later argument is only partially correct as the higher debt level also is needed to cover annual appropriations that have not been enacted. Furthermore, even if the President's proposed $3.5 trillion Build Back Better bill had been fully offset, a debt ceiling increase would still have been needed if the spending was front-loaded and the tax increase offsets were back-loaded, as is usually the case.

The Democrat's position on the bill was just as political as McConnell's because it was based on protecting politically vulnerable members. The party had the clear ability to raise the debt ceiling through reconciliation, but don't want to because reconciliation would require them to raise the ceiling by a very large specific number rather than voting to suspend the debt ceiling as in 2018 and 2019.[260] A suspension would help make the vote easier for the Democrat rank and file by obscuring from the public the enormous size of the needed debt ceiling increase.

The public has every right to be disgusted with debt ceiling brinkmanship due to the huge risk to the financial system if these debt ceiling crises can't be resolved every time. Nevertheless, these crises have resulted in useful deficit reduction legislation. My biggest concern about the current political environment is that few, if any, members of Congress are concerned about deficits. The Republicans are much more interested in increased defense discretionary spending and keeping taxes low, while Democrats want increased non-defense discretionary spending and to create new mandatory spending and benefit programs. While elimination of the debt ceiling is appealing due to the financial risk of these debt ceiling crises, I wouldn't want to eliminate it without creating some other mechanism to force Congress to periodically address deficit spending to bring it back under control.

CHAPTER THIRTEEN: Surviving Chaos -- *OMB's Role in Presidential Transitions*

Working at OMB during a Presidential transition is simultaneously exciting, fun, exhausting, and terrifying. I ought to know as I have worked through seven of them. After the sixth, I told myself that I was too old for this and swore that I wouldn't go through another. Unfortunately, events conspired against me, and I worked through most of a seventh transition — from Trump to Biden -- including two months as OMB's Acting Director.

Understanding OMB's Transition Role

What makes Presidential transitions so exhilarating for OMB staff is that OMB plays a unique but crucial role. OMB's crucial role stems from two factors. First, OMB provides a broad base of institutional memory on Federal Government programs and processes that incoming Administrations need to tap. In fact, OMB has an expert on every Federal Government program. Other portions of the EXOP also have career staff with institutional memory, but in a narrow field (e.g. the Office of the United States Trade Representative (USTR) on trade issues). The institutional memory that OMB provides is particularly important the more that the incoming White House staff is populated by outsiders who have not previously worked in the Executive Branch.

Second, OMB runs most of the key processes that make the Federal Government function smoothly and consistent with the President's agenda. These include the budget, legislative, regulatory, and executive order processes. Incoming administrations need to harness these processes if they want to get the vast Federal bureaucracy to move in a new direction. This means that OMB plays an outsized role in getting the new Administration up and running.

Regulatory Process

More specifically, these processes are central to implementing the President's agenda, including action on campaign promises for immediate implementation as well as setting the tone for the rest of the Administration. On the regulatory front, this usually involves putting all rules on hold that have not taken effect, so that OIRA and incoming Administration officials have time to review them and decide whether they should be allowed to move forward or scrapped. This "regulatory freeze" is usually issued by the White House Chief of Staff on Inauguration Day, with the Director of OMB issuing a Management Memorandum that provides guidance to agencies on how to implement the freeze. As Acting Director of OMB, I issued this Management Memorandum on President Biden's Inauguration Day, a few hours after the regulatory freeze had been imposed.

Executive Order Process

On the executive order front, OMB's role involves helping issue numerous executive orders providing Presidential guidance to agencies on various policy issues, while rescinding some of the EOs issued by the previous President. A classic example of such an EO is what is referred to as the "Mexico City Policy", which prevents non-governmental organizations that receive federal funds from providing abortion related services even using funds raised privately. This is a policy that is usually imposed as an EO on "day one" in Republican administrations and rescinded by EO on "day one" in Democratic administrations.

Unfortunately, there is an increasing tendency of presidents to implement their policies administratively through executive orders when they cannot get them enacted through the legislative process. The upside of this approach is that the policies can be implemented quickly. The downside is that they can be withdrawn just as quickly by the next administration. Furthermore, executive orders cannot override existing law. Instead, they can only provide guidance to agencies to implement policies, to the maximum extent possible, within the constraints of existing law. Consequently, in the future the implementation of more policies is likely to "ping pong" back and forth between administrations in the same manner as the "Mexico City" policy has over the last few.

Legislative Process

The legislative process generally doesn't kick in as quickly. The purpose of the legislative review process, as discussed previously, is to ensure that any legislation submitted to Congress reflects cleared Administration policy and not just the views of one agency. Similarly, agencies submit testimony to OMB for clearance, which OMB' Legislative Review Division circulates to other affected agencies. The purpose of such clearance is to ensure that the new Administration speaks with one voice.

In part due to the dearth of confirmed political appointees and the need for policy processes, including the Budget, to generate legislative proposals, the legislative process lags behind some of the others. Nevertheless, either the White House Chief of Staff or the Director of OMB usually issues a memo to the heads of Executive departments and agencies alerting them to the legislative clearance requirements under long-standing OMB Circulars. For the Biden Administration, as Acting Director, I issued a Management Memorandum for that purpose on March 4, 2021, six weeks after Inauguration Day.

Budget Process

The most important process, however, is the development of the new President's first budget. As discussed earlier, the Budget is a central part of the policy process in any administration. While not every policy has budget implications, most policies do come with a budget cost. The President's annual Budget submission to Congress is the one place where all the President's policies are consolidated and presented in one document. In fact, if a policy has budget implications and is not included in the President's Budget, it will be dismissed by both Congress and interest groups as not an Administration priority.

In transition years, the President's first budget takes on an outsized importance because it must reflect the President's key campaign commitments and rarely includes anything else other than ongoing operations. Political campaign commitments tend to be developed on an ad-hoc basis in response to the needs of key constituencies as well as responding to U.S. or international events as they unfold during the campaign. They are not developed as part of a master plan, they are often not well thought out, and rarely has there been any serious effort to cost them out. In many cases, there is not even a good list of the campaign commitments, which OMB may have to develop on its own as a checklist for consideration during budget formulation.

As will be discussed in detail below, OMB works first with the transition team and then the team for the incoming Director to flesh out these campaign commitments and develop a budget "score". Unfortunately, incoming OMB Directors and other cabinet secretaries often throw out the work of the transition teams and start over, complicating the lives of OMB staff. Regardless of how well the transition team and the new appointees work together, the key task remains the same — the first budget is about delivering on the President's campaign promises and reflecting them for the first time in a consolidated package. As we will see, however, that is often easier said than done.

As I indicated in Chapter 1, the budget process has remained remarkably stable over four decades in non-transition years. In contrast, during Presidential transition years, the budget playbook is literally thrown out the window. In good part, this is because the transition takes place around the time that the Budget in a normal year is about to be released. Instead, each new Director develops a new process to produce a budget in a constrained time frame, with limited administration appointees in place, that implements the new President's campaign commitments.

Simultaneously Working for Two Administrations

Transitions begin in the prior administration and that period between the election and the Inauguration is important for both the incoming and outgoing administrations and a significant challenge for OMB staff. Except for the Trump to Biden transition, the challenge occurs because OMB staff during this period are often simultaneously working for two different administrations. In fact, it is not unusual to be working to implement a particular issue for the outgoing administration while helping the incoming administration figure out how to undo that policy. Consequently, it is useful for OMB budget staff to either have a split personality, or at least be a master at compartmentalizing their work, because we must faithfully do our best to help each administration without telling what we are doing for the other.

As will be discussed is greater detail below, when OMB staff are allowed to start working for the incoming administration is somewhat dependent on the circumstances surrounding the election and the willingness of the outgoing administration to allow OMB staff to help with transition. Under any circumstance, it is always clear that the first call on OMB staff time is to help the outgoing administration and, only if those tasks are completed, could we work for the incoming administration. I used to think of it as working for the outgoing administration was my day job and working for the new crew was my evening and weekend job.

For the outgoing administration, the last couple of months, longer if the President is at the end of his second term, are devoted to finishing as much of the President's agenda as possible. Usually these are activities that can be accomplished administratively, as enacting legislation at the end of a presidency is a daunting task. Much of the activity at the end of an administration involves rulemaking, which puts OIRA staff on the spot.

Ideally, administrations want any rules classified as major (i.e. imposing a cost of $100 million on the economy in any year) published in the Federal Register at least 60 legislative days prior to the end of the Congress. This prevents the rule from being subject to any regulatory freeze that might be imposed by the new administration or to the Congressional Review Act (CRA) of 1996. The CRA allows Congress to overturn a rule by enacting a joint resolution of disapproval (i.e. must be passed by a majority vote in both houses of Congress and signed by the President) under fast-track rules and not subject to a Senate filibuster.

Even if this deadline can't be achieved, by promulgating a rule earlier than later, there still may be advantages in protecting a rule from being withdrawn by the next administration or overturned in court. In fact, so many rules are being promulgated up until the last day of an administration that the outgoing group sometimes is forced to prioritize last day rules because the Federal Register doesn't have the physical capacity to handle the crush.

The result of this regulatory push is an exhausted OIRA staff going into the new Administration. Fortunately for them, OIRA's workload slows down early in the new administration as the pipeline of agency rules coming to OMB for review was flushed at the end of the prior Administration. While they still must review the rulemakings which the incoming administration has frozen for consistency with the new President's priorities and values, they at least are familiar with those rules after having reviewed them in the preceding months. Furthermore, it takes time for a new administration to get its rulemaking process in high gear, particularly given the normal delays in getting agency sub-cabinet appointees, including the OIRA Administrator, confirmed by the Senate.

The end of administration workload for the budget staff is not as heavy as for OIRA in most transitions — Carter to Reagan being a notable exception — because the normal November/December budget formulation activities aren't being undertaken during that period. However, as most Presidents are interested in ensuring a smooth transition for the country's sake, even if the new President is from the other party, OMB staff usually start working on formulating the Budget for the new President well before Inauguration Day. How early this work starts depends on the transition. Below are my recollections of how each transition played out.

Jimmy Carter to Ronald Reagan (January 1981)

Perhaps because this was my first transition, it was one that left a lasting impression even though it occurred four decades ago. At the time of the election, Jimmy Carter wasn't a popular President and had been hurt badly by the Iran hostage crisis, high unemployment, and high inflation. Nevertheless, Reagan's landslide win came as a shock to many people, as Reagan's conservative views were considered extreme at the time, particularly by those who lived inside the Washington beltway. I remember watching the returns come in at the office as my branch was working late to pull together our review book for our Director's Review meeting on the FY 1982 Budget in two days. One of my newer colleagues, Barbara Chow, who would later become a high-level political appointee in the Clinton Administration, was particularly distraught as the returns came in across the country.

Despite delivering our book to the Director that night, we didn't know if it would ever be used. In fact, there was "radio silence" from OMB political officials for the next couple days as they, and others in the White House, were in a state of shock about the outcome. After going through the various stages of grief, the White House and OMB leadership eventually decided on a strategy to impose as much political pain on the incoming Administration as possible. They decided to develop and transmit to Congress a full FY 1982 Budget. This was not uncommon in the past, but not a foregone conclusion either.

While no subsequent outgoing President has submitted a full budget when the Presidency has changed parties, President Ford had done the same thing for the FY 1978 Budget after he lost the election. While that was before my time, I was told that not only did Ford want to transmit the full Budget as his swan song, he conducted the Budget briefing for the press and answered all the questions, a function that would normally be carried out by the OMB Director and the Secretary of the Treasury.

The U.S. Government Publishing Office (GPO) includes digitized versions of the President's Budget back to FY 1996. For historic versions of the Budget, GPO links to the Federal Reserve Archival System for Economic Research (FRASER). What is interesting about those archives is that they contain the FY 1982 Budget for the Carter Administration, but not the more relevant FY 1982 Budget documents for the Reagan Administration. While most Presidential Budgets are labeled dead on arrival by the opposing party in Congress, a budget submitted by a defeated President as he is heading for the door must be even deader than dead.

The Carter Administration's strategy for its FY 1982 Budget after the election was to submit a "scorched earth" budget. Since Reagan had campaigned on a platform of more limited government and reduced spending, the strategy was to take all of the "low hanging fruit" (i.e. the easy budget reductions). The guidance to staff from our leadership was to modify the budget recommendations we had previously developed, when the Carter folks thought they would win the election, by including major reductions and eliminations.

Our branch identified two major EPA programs for elimination — the noise pollution control program, which had already regulated the most annoying sources of noise pollution, and the Section 208 state water quality planning grants, which were never intended to be ongoing grants and were generally viewed as having had little impact in improving water quality. Having both the Carter and Reagan budgets propose these programs for elimination made it easy for the appropriations committees to eliminate them in EPA's enacted FY 1982 appropriations bill. Given how hard it is to eliminate Federal programs — they tend to take on new purposes even if the original mission is complete— I was always amazed that the environmental community never tried to resurrect these programs in future budgets.

The theory behind the Carter Administration's FY 1982 Budget strategy was that, in order to be true to his campaign platform, Reagan would have to make large reductions below the "scorched earth" budget which would be so extreme as to undermine his popular support. While a reasonable strategy it didn't consider one thing — new OMB Director

David Stockman. What the Carter Administration viewed as "scorched earth" David Stockman viewed as tinkering around the margins.

From my perspective, David Stockman was the most capable of the 18 Director's I served under, a group that was uniformly highly intelligent and accomplished. I recognize that my view of Stockman might be influenced by the fact that I was a junior examiner at the time, rather than the senior executive who interacted with most of the rest. Nevertheless, it is quite well accepted that he was the highest profile and most powerful Director OMB had during my tenure.

Stockman came to OMB as a 34-year-old "boy wonder" after serving as a Congressman from Michigan. Prior to being designated as OMB Director, he and Congressman Jack Kemp wrote a lengthy report to the President-elect, which was subsequently leaked to the Washington Post and New York Times, warning of an "economic Dunkirk".[261] In order to avoid economic disaster, they argued that Reagan should postpone action on hot button cultural issues and instead focus on tax and spending cuts in the first 100 days in order to improve the chances of getting those enacted during the Presidential 'honeymoon" period. Once he was designated as OMB Director, he moved quickly to do just that.

The fact that the Carter Administration decided to publish a full FY 1982 Budget meant that there was a delay in allowing OMB budget staff to work for the new administration. We didn't start working for Stockman until the beginning of the new year. It also meant the staff were tired from having to rush out a Budget a few weeks earlier than normal and after a mid-course correction following the election to pivot from increases to reductions. As my Division Director, Don Crabill, liked to describe it, the incoming crew were like Pony Express riders showing up at the station and expecting to jump on fresh horses, only to find a bunch of tired nags.

During most transitions, this would have been a huge problem, but was less so because David Stockman was Director. During normal budget years, the Budget is developed very much in a bottom-up process. In transition years, there is always a much larger top-down component, and this was even more true with Stockman as Director. While each branch (excluding Defense) developed Director's Review materials with suggested deep reductions, in many cases Stockman had his own reductions that went even further. These were reductions that he had identified during his time in Congress and now had the power to pursue.

As I always informed my staff, transitions are inherently chaotic. This is in large part due to the need to develop a process to implement the President' campaign promises in a much shorter period than normal. The political appointee running the process was Executive Associate Director for Budget Glenn Schleede. Glenn was a former OMB career official who had been the Chief of the Environment Branch in 1971 when the branch was first formed after the establishment of EPA in 1970. Despite Glenn's experience, the process and guidance were in a constant state of change. The guidance issued by Glenn, referred to as Schleede-grams, changed so quickly that, to ensure that the correct guidance was being used, you not only needed to know the date of the guidance but the time it was issued.

For Stockman, speed was particularly important as he knew that his proposed reductions would run into fierce opposition in the agencies. His apparent strategy was to blitz the departments with quick decisions while the new cabinet secretaries were largely "home alone" without supporting political staff, whereas Stockman had all his key people onboard. This allowed Stockman to characterize to the White House that any opposition to the cuts was a matter of the secretary being captured by the department's bureaucracy.

While in a typical year each branch had its own Director's Review, in the truncated time frame to produce a transition budget, Stockman had one review for each division. Thus, the entire Natural Resources Division (NRD) was stuffed into the Director's conference room — Room 248 of the Old Executive Office Building — for a meeting in which the Director did most of the talking.

Stockman was not only a brilliant man with an encyclopedic knowledge of Federal programs, but he was also an excellent strategic thinker who thought long and hard about how to sell the cuts we were proposing. In fact, my enduring memory of that Director's Review concerned justifying the cut he wanted to the dairy price support program by comparing the subsidy per cow in that program to the subsidy per kid in the school lunch program. Not only did Stockman tell our Commodity Credit Corporation (CCC) examiner what comparison he wanted, but he also told him exactly how to make the calculation including what data sources to use and how the data would need to be adjusted to make the appropriate comparison.

While the poor CCC examiner furiously scribbled down the Director's guidance, the rest of us just sat there with our jaws wide open. The last thing an examiner wants is for any of his bosses, but particularly the Director, to know more about their assigned programs than the examiner. It was now apparent to NRD staff that, for certain programs at least, Stockman did know more than the examiner.

Our branch came out of the Review relatively unscathed after proposing a 17 percent cut to EPA's Operating Programs. The Operating Programs were the key part of EPA's budget because they funded the regulatory, enforcement, research, and state grant programs for the agency. For an agency used to getting steady increases through its first decade, this kind of reduction was a huge and unprecedented hit. In fact, it was the largest reduction that we felt could be reasonably justified. Nevertheless, we heard later that Stockman was disappointed in the size of the reduction.

Under normal circumstances, the Budget passback is given to a small set of agency officials in our office in the NEOB. For some reason, however, our branch chief, Dave Gibbons, this year agreed to provide the passback at EPA in the Administrator's conference room. The setup was rather intimidating for our very junior staff as the conference room was packed with all the agencies' top career officials. Each examiner in turn had to explain these unprecedented reductions in their programs, give the rationale for the reduction, and answer any questions.

The reaction to the passback was muted. When we finished, Walt Barber, the Acting Administrator and an Environment Branch budget examiner in the early 1970s, indicated that the agency would not appeal the passback. Walt was a realist and joked that, without a confirmed Reagan appointee, nobody in the White House would probably answer a phone call from them.

Having gone into the lion's den and expecting to get ripped to shreds by this group of senior, experienced officials, I was stunned. After exiting, several of the officials actually thanked us for the passback. One of my senior budget officers finally explained to me that nobody held us responsible for the cuts and that they were grateful to us because they were expecting cuts in the range of 25 to 30 percent. In that respect, their expectations were more in line with Stockman's, who was disappointed with our mark.

This was a powerful lesson for me and one that I would observe repeatedly in my career. The lesson being that an agency's reaction to a passback had less to do with the absolute funding level of the passback than the agency's expectations for that funding. In fact, often the most strident budget appeals of passback were of increases that the agency or department thought should be much larger.

Ronald Reagan to George H.W. Bush (January 1989)

Presidential transitions when the incoming President is of the same party as the outgoing President are less momentous and less exciting than if there is a change of the party is in power. This is especially true when the incoming President was the Vice President in the previous administration. To some extent, the incoming administration is an extension of the previous administration, although the new President has to find ways to distinguish himself from the previous President.

In fact, many of the appointees in the new Bush '41 Administration were appointees in the Reagan Administration. Thus, James Baker was Secretary of the Treasury at the end of the Reagan Administration and became Secretary of State for President Bush. Similarly, Dick Darman was a Deputy Secretary of Treasury for Reagan and became the new OMB Director for President Bush. Like Stockman, Darman was a brilliant man, but he was difficult to work for and he didn't have Stockman's unparalleled knowledge of Federal programs. I tended to think that the difference between the two was that Stockman was a legend, whereas Darman was a legend in his own mind.

Despite the Reagan Administration ending, the detailed FY 1990 Budget was developed by the outgoing Reagan appointees, although with an understanding of the campaign priorities of the incoming Bush Administration and guidance from the Vice President's office. Joe Wright had been OMB's Deputy Director for several years but became the OMB Director for the last few months of the Administration when Jim Miller resigned to give Joe the opportunity to be Director. Joe was not well liked by the budget staff when he was Deputy Director, which largely involved running the management side of OMB, but was so thrilled to be Director that he was like a changed man in dealing with budget staff during development of the FY 1990 Budget.

The FY 1990 Budget was my first since being selected as Chief of the Environment Branch and, for a short time, I thought might be my last. We prepared our budget passback that Fall consistent with how we had done it in my previous years in the branch. In this case, however, the EPA Administrator, Lee Thomas, read the entire lengthy document. Rather than submitting the traditional appeal letter, he called Director Wright and complained about the inappropriateness of the directive tone of the document. Director Wright apologized and immediately gave EPA complete flexibility to reallocate resources within totals, a flexibility that OMB rarely grants.

I was told to get a copy of the passback to the acting Deputy Director immediately and prepare to be taken to the woodshed. Fortunately, the acting Deputy Director didn't find anything in the passback to be inappropriate, although there was some poorly worded language deep in a section that wasn't binding anyway. I had known Lee Thomas for a few years, since he became Assistant Administrator for the Superfund program, and I was his examiner. I had always considered Lee to be a savvy bureaucrat and, in this instance, it looked like he snookered the Director in order to win budget flexibility. His over-the-top complaint was the kind of bureaucratic gambit that could be pulled off only once but, at an administration's end, he had nothing to lose.

The Reagan Administration issued a full FY 1990 budget early in January. The incoming Bush Administration issued a companion document called "Building a Better America" about a month later. "Building a Better America" included program initiatives and changes to fulfill Bush campaign pledges. These changes were largely tax cuts and mandatory spending proposals.

The Bush Administration OMB had its own "boy wonder" in the person of Bob Grady, who became the Program Associate Director for Natural Resources, Energy and Science and was my second line supervisor. Bob had graduated with an MBA from Stanford Business School the previous June and immediately joined the Bush campaign team. Bob and I had similar educational backgrounds — he had degrees from Harvard and Stanford Business, while I had degrees from Princeton and Stanford Business. Consequently, it was somewhat humbling that, despite graduating from Stanford nine years after me, he was my boss and had started at OMB in a position three levels above my starting job as a junior examiner.

Only a few people are capable of making that kind of jump from graduate school student to a powerful political appointment, but Bob handled it easily. In addition to being a skilled political operative, Bob also had an extremely rare combination of analytic and communication skills.

At Stanford, my classmates often got characterized as "quant jocks" (i.e. good with numbers but not a great writer) or "qualt jocks" (i.e. good writing skills but struggled with numbers). While I was clearly a "quant jock", Bob excelled at both ends of the quantitative/qualitative spectrum. He was not only a super analyst who picked up difficult concepts quickly, he had first class communication skills and worked as a speech writer on the Bush Campaign. In fact, Bob wrote the first draft of what was essentially Bush's State of the Union message that first year. This was in part due to the proposed budget changes being the key portion of the speech, which Bob knew intimately, but also because Bob had the right skill set to write the speech.

George H.W. Bush to Bill Clinton (January 1993)

Like Carter to Reagan, this was another transition involving a one-term President who was voted out of office. For Bush, it was a stunning turnaround from the stratospheric, but short-lived, popularity he enjoyed after the quick, successful Iraq War to liberate Kuwait two years earlier. However, his popularity was undermined by a weak economy and his failure to keep his "read my lips — no new taxes" pledge when he negotiated the consequential, and ultimately successful, Budget Enforcement Act of 1990.

Unlike Carter, however, the Bush team knew they were going to lose several days in advance based on their own internal polling. Furthermore, they broke the pattern of an outgoing President producing a full budget, although they did produce a baseline document with some Bush priorities to provide a contrast to the forthcoming Clinton Budget. However, this document was produced largely by the political level, meaning that the budget staff could start providing support to the transition team in November, which was much earlier than in the past.

The process for developing the FY 1994 Budget was unlike any of the other transitions I have been through. The new Director was Leon Panetta, who came to OMB from his position as Chairman of the House Budget Committee. Despite this budget background, he viewed budgets more from the 10,000-foot level and didn't have the in-depth program knowledge of many of his predecessors or even his Deputy Alice Rivlin, the former Director of CBO. Panetta also brought with him five veteran staffers from the House Budget Committee. OMB staff began to refer to this tight knit group as "the Family". Whenever I heard that name used, the song "We Are Family" by Sister Sledge would instantly start playing in my brain.

Reflecting the background of Panetta and the Family, the FY 1994 budget process bore more resemblance to development of a Congressional Budget Resolution than formulation of the President's budget in being top down with a focus on programs rather than agencies. As with other transitions, the main goal of this Budget was to reflect the campaign commitments. These commitments related not only to the FY 1994 Budget but also to supplemental funding for FY 1993 considering Clinton's campaigning on the need for economic stimulus to get the country out of recession. The National Bureau of Economic Research would later determine that the short 1990-1991 recession had already ended.

The bulk of the budget proposals were divided into three key buckets — stimulus, investments, and savings. The stimulus and investment proposals largely came from the campaign — Clinton made a lot of commitments — although some White House staff and Cabinet secretaries were able to get others added. The campaign proposed little in the way of spending savings, so those largely reflected suggestions from OMB staff and an annual list of potential cuts produced by CBO.

Which proposals to include in the Budget were debated in lengthy, high-level meetings that often included the President. Unfortunately, as the deliberations continued, the spending buckets tended to get larger while the savings bucket contracted. Towards the end of the policy deliberations, the White House looked at how these proposals fit into the overall fiscal picture, given that the deficit at the time was viewed as very high. As the fiscal outlook couldn't support all the investments, they needed to be scaled back. Rather than going back to the list and eliminating funding for some campaign commitments, the decision was instead made to take a 40 percent "haircut" across all the programs. This was intended to demonstrate good faith in meeting the campaign commitments with more increases expected in future years.

As Chief of the Environment Branch at the time, two additional EPA problems emerged due to the way this budget was developed. First, decisions on stimulus, investment, and savings were made without looking at their impact on agency totals. For EPA, this became a problem because the "optics" of funding for EPA's Operating Program was viewed as a proxy for an Administration's commitment to the environment.

In this instance, there was little in the investment bucket to pump up EPA's Operating Program total. Even worse, the bulk of the savings proposals were in the form of crosscutting reductions in travel and other types of administrative expenses that were distributed government wide. These types of cuts are always popular with politicians because they don't threaten any program specifically, they just create difficulties for the bureaucrats who must keep the government running. Unfortunately, EPA's share of these cuts swamped the investment increases leading to a significant overall cut in the Operating Program. OMB's policy officials were not happy when we reported this to them, but they had no choice but to fix the problem because of the potential political backlash if Clinton and Gore were seen as less committed to pollution control than the Bush Administration.

Second, I was responsible for a program that was in all three buckets — the Clean Water State Revolving Fund (SRF). The Clean Water SRF made capitalization grants to states which in turn made loans to municipalities for construction of sewer pipes and wastewater treatment plants. The loan repayments were the revolving portion of the program, which would provide the funding for future loans once the capitalization grants had ended. While it was a legitimate policy decision to decide whether to increase or cut the size of the program, it should have been self-evident to the policy officials making the decisions that the same program shouldn't be selected for investments and savings at the same time! Nevertheless, when the White House's final decisions were transmitted to OMB staff, the Clean Water SRF was in all three buckets.

This, of course, created a dilemma for me. My first solution was to net the investment against the larger savings level and include the net savings level in the FY 1994 Budget along with requesting supplemental funding for economic stimulus in FY 1993. Unfortunately, this solution was firmly rejected by a member of the Family. The investment proposal needed to stay in the Budget because it was important to Vice President Gore, while the savings proposal had stay because it was one of the few cuts targeting a specific program that hadn't been eliminated during the policy deliberations.

Ultimately, I came up with a Machiavellian solution. The stimulus funding was sufficient to complete the funding authorization for the CWSRF, which at the time of authorization during the Reagan Administration was supposed to be a one-time authorization before Federal funding for municipal wastewater treatment would end. The savings could, therefore, be justified as savings from ending the one-time Clean Water SRF capitalization program. The investment would be for new annual capitalization grants for the same Clean Water SRFs, although as a fig leaf for claiming that this was a different program, the Administration proposed some minor changes to Clean Water SRF project eligibilities.

When the FY 1994 Budget was released, I was expecting the press to tear us apart for the fake savings portrayed in the Budget. Amazingly, nobody called us out on this poorly disguised piece of budget sleight of hand. I was never sure whether it was because the liberal Washington press didn't want to criticize a newly elected Democratic President after 12 years of Republican rule or whether it was because the press was inept on budget reporting. Either way, it forever damaged my respect for the press on domestic policy. Although it was my idea, I named this gambit after my Clean Water SRF examiner. She was none too pleased by the honor. To this day, I view getting away with this budgetary sleight of hand as being my most dubious and embarrassing accomplishment.

Bill Clinton to George W. Bush (January 2001)

This was a transition that OMB staff were prepared to start early but got delayed a month due to the recount of the votes in Florida, which the Supreme Court eventually shut down on December 9th. As the outgoing Clinton Administration wasn't going to issue a Budget, we were in limbo, unable to work for either the Bush or Gore transition teams until the election got resolved.

It was also an unusual transition in that eliminating the deficit was no longer an issue. The country had gone from a period a few years earlier where there were deficits as far as the eye could see, to the current period with budget surpluses as far as the eye could see. One of the issues in the campaign was how to manage and spend these surpluses. Bush's solution was to enact a huge tax cut to give the money back to the people.

The incoming Director was Mitch Daniels, a fellow Princetonian who had graduated just before I arrived. Mitch was a low key, thoughtful man who embraced the full range of the OMB Director' extensive responsibilities. Mitch would eventually leave OMB to use his management skills as Governor of Indiana and President of Purdue University, where he also periodically wrote thoughtful columns for the Washington Post.

My new PAD was Marcus Peacock, a former OIRA desk officer, whom I had interviewed, more than a decade earlier, for a potential budget examiner opening in the Environment Branch. Marcus would later become Deputy Administrator at EPA. Both Mitch and Marcus had excellent decision-making skills, as evidenced by the fact that they selected me to be the DAD for Natural Resources in May that year.

Despite my links to the incoming team, this transition was not particularly memorable for me. I was in my 14th year as Chief of the Environment Branch, I had a capable and experienced staff, and EPA was not central to any campaign commitments. There was the normal transition chaos involved in producing a budget, in part due to the late start as well as the rush to publish an initial FY 2002 budget document — "A Blueprint for New Beginnings" — by the end of February and the normal set of budget documents in early April.

The centerpiece of the Budget was the President's tax cut proposal, coupled with some program reform proposals for education and various entitlement programs. Unlike for most incoming Democratic Party presidents, there wasn't the huge number of campaign commitments for discretionary spending, with the Defense Department accounting for over half of the requested increase in appropriations.

While the projections of budget surpluses were probably illusory in the first place, the 2001 Bush tax cuts and the 2003 establishment of the Medicare Part D prescription drug benefit ensured the elimination of those surpluses. As neither of those expensive bills was offset, they helped push the country back into a period of increasing debt to GDP ratios that continues today.

George W. Bush to Barack Obama (January 2009)

Perhaps due to the messy start for his Administration, President Bush made it known that he wanted a smooth transition to Obama and without any shenanigans like the Clinton folks taking the "W" keys off their White House computer keyboards when they left. Consequently, OMB started to have contact with a well-organized Obama transition team within days of the election and OMB budget staff spent an unprecedented amount of time helping on the transition. Furthermore, the OMB staff had already compiled over the summer a listing of all the Obama and McCain campaign commitments, so we knew what would need to be addressed in the Budget no matter which candidate was elected.

Given the economic turmoil and collapse of the stock market due to the housing bubble having burst, a fast start on transition was very important for the new Administration. The transition team was working simultaneously on both an economic recovery package as well as the traditional activities of standing up a new Administration and preparing the first budget. It appeared that different groups were working on the two tasks, with former OMB staff working on both. T.J. Glauthier, one of my PADs in the Clinton Administration, was working on the climate piece of the recovery package, with significant input from my staff. The OMB transition was co-led by Bo Cutter, the OMB Economic Associate Director for Budget in the Carter Administration, and Barbara Chow, my old officemate as an examiner and a former OMB PAD under Clinton.

The economic recovery package was intended to provide sufficient stimulus to make sure that the recession was "V shaped", which meant that the fast, steep economic decline would be accompanied by a fast, steep economic recovery. To produce that kind of recovery, the economic stimulus needs to be targeted at helping the unemployed and investing in "shovel ready" projects to provide new jobs. Unfortunately, finding "shovel ready" projects is easier said than done, as most kinds of expensive new projects require a lengthy planning period before getting to the big dollar spending portions of the project.

Despite enactment of the $800 billion American Recovery and Reinvestment Act (ARRA) of 2009 within a month of Obama's inauguration, the recession turned out to have a "U shaped" recovery, which meant that the recovery was slow and over an extended period compared to a fast "V shaped" recovery. Many people, particularly progressive Democrats, argue that the slow recovery was due to ARRA being too small, despite its unprecedented size. On the other hand, conservative Republicans argue that the slow recovery was due to the surge of Obama regulations that discouraged business investment.

While there is probably an element of truth in both of those arguments, I also believe that ARRA was poorly targeted on programs and projects that were not "shovel ready". Most of the Obama campaign commitments were formulated by the spring of 2008, at a time when nobody was projecting an economic downturn. As luck would have it, a high percentage of those commitments were determined by the transition team to be the perfect programs to pull the country out of the recession. (What are the odds of that!!!)

While some of the programs were legitimate stimulus candidates, others seem to have been chosen in line with the infamous maxim of Rahm Emanuel (Obama's first Chief of Staff) to "never let a good crisis go to waste". The consequence of trying to stuff so many of the campaign proposals into the stimulus bill is that a large chunk of the funding did not get spent quickly, undermining the goal of a quick economic recovery. This led to an explosion in deficit spending, in part due to stimulus spending and in part due to the lag in economic growth. The ballooning deficit led directly to the enactment of the Budget Control Act of 2011 as discussed in Chapter 12, which constrained discretionary spending for the remainder of the Obama Administration.

OMB staff also worked closely with the OMB transition team, at least until Peter Orszag was designated as Director of OMB. At that point the transition team disappeared, and it seemed that we started over in working on the FY 2010 Budget. While Orszag was a brilliant man, it was the wrong job for him, and he turned out to be one of our worst Directors ever. Given that he was previously Director of CBO, this came as a surprise to OMB staff, although apparently not to CBO staff.

While many OMB Directors gave short shrift to management issues, most understand that they have a huge portfolio that requires their attention to programs across the government. Unfortunately, Orszag gave short shrift to most of his responsibilities. After completing the initial budget decisions, he appeared to focus his time on two of Obama's highest priorities — health care reform and climate change.

It was even hard to keep his attention on issues in front of him. During our Director's Review in the fall of 2009, after the end of daylight savings time, he noticed that the clock at the end of the conference room was an hour too fast. Rather than jotting a note to have it fixed, he got up during the discussion to fix the clock himself. It would have been a blow to staff morale if he had done it while one of my examiners was presenting. Fortunately, one of Orszag's political staff was talking at the time, although she wasn't pleased either.

Orszag's biggest shortcoming, however, was his "failure to communicate". For Peter, the only communication he seemed to value was communication up to him. Communication from him down to staff largely appeared to be a waste of his time, even though such communication is critical to the functioning of the organization. The situation got so bad that the career DADs pleaded with Rob Nabors, the Deputy Director, and a former examiner, to have a weekly staff meeting with us. Although Rob canceled the meeting fairly frequently, the meetings that did occur were extraordinarily valuable. In fact, the DADs eventually noticed that our direct political bosses, the PADs, would come and sit in the back of the meetings. It was only then that we realized that Orszag didn't communicate with them any more than he communicated with us, and they were desperate for the kind of information that the DADs were getting at these meetings.

At least Orszag provided the staff with some comic relief. First, he tried to have a fire in the fireplace of his huge ornate office in the Eisenhower Executive Office Building (EEOB). The fireplace was a relic from the early days of the building, which was constructed back in the late 1880's. Unbeknownst to Orszag, the chimney's flue no longer vented to the outside and instead sent smoke pouring into the fourth floor causing significant smoke damage. After that incident, a plaque was added to all the building's many fireplaces indicating that they no longer worked.

Second, Orszag came into OMB as a nerdy, divorced father of two,[262] who somehow turned out to be a "chick magnet" while at OMB. In the fall of 2009, news came out that he had a "love child" with a former girlfriend, the daughter of a Greek shipping magnet, only to get engaged to a gorgeous ABC correspondent a month later.[263] For an organization that rarely heard anything about the personal lives of our usually boring, low-profile Directors, it was jarring to see Orszag's love life reported in the mainstream press.

Nevertheless, when Orszag was focused, he made good decisions. In part because OMB staff had a good understanding of the Obama campaign commitments, we were able to give the new Director recommendations on meeting those commitments in time for him to make the key FY 2010 Budget decisions prior to the Inauguration. This enabled OMB to publish a blueprint document — "A New Era of Responsibility: Renewing America's Promise" — before the end of February, like the timeline for the prior Bush Administration's blueprint document.

Barack Obama to Donald Trump (January 2017)

Hands down, the Trump Presidency wins the prize for least prepared to take the reins of power. This was perhaps the case because even many of the people on the campaign didn't think they would win. Furthermore, they had a relatively small transition team under former New Jersey Governor Chris Christie. Unfortunately, by the time of the election, Christie was already on the outs with many in the campaign, and possibly the President as well, so his team's work was little used. For OMB, our transition team was largely one individual from the Senate Budget Committee, who would collect material from OMB staff only to have it disappear into a black hole.

Compounding the problem was the fact that Congressman Mick Mulvaney, the designee for OMB Director, was a controversial choice because of his reputation as a "bomb thrower", who took extreme positions and would never compromise. Due to this reputation, there was real concern about whether he could get confirmed. Consequently, Mick became the first transition Director-designate during my tenure who had no visibility to OMB staff and had no apparent role in decision-making prior to his confirmation. In fact, previous Director-designates were making budget decisions before Inauguration Day. Admittedly, I can't say whether Mick was playing a similar role behind the scenes.

Despite his reputation on the Hill, I found Mick to be a gregarious, engaging individual. Although he was clearly very conservative, he was much more of a deal-cutter than I expected. In particular, he demonstrated flexibility when necessary to advance the Trump agenda, which was populist in nature, but not necessarily conservative.

In contrast, Mick's Deputy and later OMB Director, Russ Vought, struck me as an ideologue's ideologue, who was very inflexible about his conservative positions. This inflexibility would later hurt OMB once he became Acting Director because none of the key Congressman or Senators would deal with him. Consequently, OMB was totally sidelined when the budget cap deals of 2018 and 2019 were negotiated by Treasury Secretary Mnuchin.

Despite the inept transition team, a new landing team arrived over the Holidays led by Russ Vought, who would make all the early budget decisions on the FY 2018 Budget. Given campaign commitments to cut non-defense spending, most divisions were expected to meet the stringent guidance given them relative to the FY 2017 CR level (final appropriations had not yet been enacted), as well as to provide options for an additional cut. Top line reviews, so called as there was no Director, to discuss division recommendations to meet guidance levels were held before Inauguration Day.

Even after the top line review, additional cut options had to be developed for the State Department and USAID. As my staff wasn't really trained to think about cuts at this kind of level, and we only had a day to deliver a suggested list, I stayed up late into the night to develop a list for review the following day with my branch chiefs.

After Russ signed off on the list, he arranged a briefing for National Security Council and other White House staff on the FY 2018 Budget levels for international programs. Although Russ opened the meeting, he quickly threw the spotlight on me to explain the reductions. One of my National Security Division (NSD) colleagues years later told me what a remarkable job I had done that afternoon in explaining difficult cuts in a measured tone with rationales that made each cut sound reasonable.

Unfortunately, the White House staff members in attendance were dumbfounded, even though they were a conservative group and expected some cuts. When they started to complain about the sheer size of the reduction, Russ cut them off by saying that the President wanted a cut of this size. Thereafter, they held their tongues.

Budget staff at State were also expecting sizable reductions but were caught off guard by their depth. Consequently, they formulated their appeal to the passback to mitigate the reductions in key areas. By this time, Mick had been confirmed by the Senate. In order to respond to the appeal, he arranged a meeting with Secretary of State Tillerson at the State Department and took me with him. In the cab on the way over, we discussed appeals strategy. I emphasized the tradeoff between dollars and flexibility — in other words the more flexibility he provided the less funding he would need to add back. I like to think that Mick listened to me because we came out of the meeting with a deal consistent with the advice I gave him.

The framework document "America First — A Budget Blueprint to Make American Great Again" was published in mid-March 2017, with the full FY 2018 Budget published in mid-May. Excluding OCO funding, even with the Tillerson/Mulvaney deal State and USAID took a 28 percent reduction relative to the 2017 CR level.

Donald Trump to Joe Biden (January 2021)

Like the Obama Administration, Biden had a huge and well-organized transition team. The OMB team was led by Martha Coven, a former PAD, and current visiting Professor at Princeton. The OMB national security team consisted of two former OMB examiners, one of whom had worked for me and the other had worked in NSD. Our ability to interact with the team was delayed because Emily Murphy, the Administrator of GSA, did not issue the formal "ascertainment" letter until November 23, 2020[264] signifying that a winner had been determined and Federal funds for the transition could be released.

Even after ascertainment, we were only allowed to meet with the transition team to provide "background" information. I use the term "meet" loosely in this context, since this was during the pandemic and all meetings were either conference calls or Zoom meetings. Even worse, we were not allowed to provide any help to the Biden team in formulating the FY 2022 Budget prior to the Inauguration.

As OMB Director Vought explained in a letter to the head of the Biden Transition Team (BTT):

> "What we have not done and will not do is use current OMB staff to write the BTT's legislative policy proposals to dismantle this administration's work," .... "OMB staff are working on this administration's policies and will do so until this administration's final day in office. Redirecting staff and resources to draft your team's budget proposals is not an OMB transition responsibility.[265]"

This position was unprecedented and truly appalling to me. While the date had varied, OMB budget staff had always been turned over to the incoming team to help prepare the upcoming Budget prior to Inauguration Day. We have done so without shortchanging work for the outgoing Administration and without telling either Administration what we were doing for the other. It was particularly hypocritical for Russ Vought to take this position since I and other OMB staff were diligently working prior to Inauguration Day to help him produce the FY 2018 Trump Budget and undo some of the Obama Administration's work.

From my standpoint, George Washington's greatest contribution to this country was his stepping aside after two terms and establishing the precedent of a peaceful transition of power. The events of January 6th and Director Vought's actions trampled all over the U.S. tradition of a smooth transition of power, a concept that eludes so many other nations around the world with disastrous consequences.

One of my predecessors as DAD for IAD, Rodney Bent, served as Controller in Baghdad when Paul Bremer led the Coalition Provisional Authority (CPA) of Iraq after the 2003 invasion. When Rodney came back to Washington to visit, he stated that the CPA was trying to figure out who could be Iraq's George Washington. Apparently, there was nobody who could fill that role. Instead, Nouri al-Maliki became the first full-term post-war Prime Minister of Iraq.[266]

Unfortunately, al-Maliki practiced the same kind of sectarian or tribal politics that hampers so many countries in the Middle East and Africa. In al-Maliki's case, his marginalization of the Sunni directly contributed to the rise of ISIS, which took over large parts of Iraq and Syria in lightning fashion in the summer of 2014. The only silver lining of his tenure is that his failure to contain ISIS resulted in his resignation in 2014, perhaps inadvertently setting a precedent for a peaceful transition of power in Iraq.

Director Vought's intransigence in letting OMB staff work on the Budget prior to Biden's Inauguration was only one of the problems hampering OMB staff. Unlike the previous two transitions, OMB staff hadn't developed a centralized listing or done any significant costing of the Biden campaign commitments because Director Vought would have "freaked out" (not a technical term) if we had. Nevertheless, I had instructed my division to work on such a list, although there were few commitments on international programs.

Finally, OMB did not have a confirmed Director. Neera Tanden struck me as an odd choice for OMB, particularly in December when few people even in the Biden camp thought that the Democrats would control the Senate. While Tanden was not a budget expert, she clearly had a good grasp of big picture policy issues. However, she was a sharp-tongued political operative firmly linked to Hilary Clinton, who had infuriated the Sander's camp with her actions during the 2016 Democratic primary campaign. Thus, it was not surprising when the plug was pulled on Tanden's nomination in early March 2021.

Unfortunately, the delay in being allowed to work for Biden, meant that OMB was not really involved in development of the $1.9 trillion American Rescue Plan, despite providing significant input into the similar Obama economic stimulus package eight years earlier. However, OMB staff did a good job in making up for lost time in formulating the FY 2022 discretionary budget. The intent was to produce a framework budget for discretionary spending, referred to as the "skinny" budget, like the documents produced in previous transitions and in a similar time frame.

Given the lack of a confirmed Director or Deputy Director, the process was led by Aviva Aron-Dine, the Executive Associate Director for Budget. Aviva had previous OMB experience and was a Biden political appointee, but in a position that did not require Senate confirmation. Aviva took her marching orders from various senior White House principals.

As usual, the intent of the framework budget was to demonstrate that the President was fulfilling the campaign promises that related to domestic discretionary spending. While some advocates in the White House thought this would require a 50 percent increase over the FY 2021 enacted level, others (rumored to include Neera Tanden and Deputy Director designate Shalanda Young) argued that it was unrealistic to get such an increase through Congress.

Ultimately, the President' Budget included a 16 percent increase for non-defense discretionary programs over the enacted level. However, a huge chunk of the increase was dedicated to eight programs or initiatives that President Biden had identified as his highest priorities. These initiatives were mostly in the education, housing, and climate spheres.

In contrast to non-defense spending, defense discretionary spending was held flat held to an increase of less than 2 percent above the FY 2021 enacted level. This was a common ploy in Democratic Administrations to hold down defense spending as a negotiating tactic to get more non-defense spending during Congressional negotiations.

Although State and USAID got a huge increase by normal standards, it was way below the Department's expectations. As was true in the past, an agency's reaction to a budget passback is more correlated to expectations than the actual level. While State wanted more, the final President's Budget included a 10 percent increase.

While the target release date was somewhat later than in previous transitions, the development of the skinny budget document on discretionary spending was less chaotic than normal and appeals, other than DOD, were wrapped up quickly. At that point, however, the publication of both the skinny budget and the full budget ran into the chaos surrounding White House development of the American Jobs Plan and the American Family Plan.

These plans were designed to seize the opportunity of Democratic control of the House, Senate, and Presidency to enact funding for a flood of long cherished Democratic Party goals. The plans would provide mandatory funding to finance these initiatives for multiple years (perhaps four to ten years depending on the program), with the funding for each plan provided in a single bill, rather than annually through the appropriations process. The plans were intended to be fully paid for, largely by taxes on the wealthy.

Unfortunately, OMB's involvement in the development of these two multi-trillion plans was limited, mainly relating to scoring once decisions had been made. However, each plan didn't consist of much more than a fact sheet, with the American Jobs Plan fact sheet including paragraphs for over 50 separate initiatives. Political considerations were paramount in developing the plans, which tried to please the full range of Democratic Party constituencies.

The lack of detail was also a political calculation. Typically, when the President's party also controls the Congress, the Administration provides fewer specifics on its initiatives to let its friends on the Hill flesh out the details. Given the slim margins that the Democrats had to work with in Congress, providing flexibility to party leaders in the Congress becomes particularly important in order to develop bills that thread the needle and can actually get enacted. If the opposition party controls the Congress, Presidents provide much more detail on their proposals, in many cases submitting complete draft bills.

The skinny budget was delayed so that the fact sheet on the American Jobs Plan could be released first on March 31st. Even worse for the morale of OMB staff, the skinny budget wasn't even published as a separate document as in past transitions. Instead, key portions of the draft publication were packaged into a letter from the Acting Director to the Chairs of the Appropriation Committees on April 9th, during the Easter Recess and a full month later than the framework discretionary budgets were transmitted in previous transitions.

The full FY 2022 Budget was also delayed as the Budget scoring numbers for both the American Jobs Plan and the American Family Plan had to be incorporated into the Budget. The mantra among senior career OMB staff became "No June Budget", as a May Budget release was incredibly late even for a transition year. The American Family Plan fact sheet wasn't finalized and released until April 28th and considerable staff work was still needed to incorporate those proposals in the Budget.

Even worse, due to the late date, there was a whole set of additional mandatory proposals (i.e. not in the Jobs or Family Plans) developed in response to campaign commitments, that were simply dropped before the full FY 2022 Budget was finally released on May 28, 2021. This was another blow to the morale of OMB staff who were already feeling marginalized by the White House process on the Jobs and Family Plans as well as the failure to even nominate an OMB Director months after Neera Tanden withdrew from consideration.

CHAPTER FOURTEEN: Perks and Quirks -- *The Good, the Bad and the Ugly of Working at OMB*

OMB is not a good fit for many people but, for those who love working on policy and can handle the workload and pressure, it is arguably the best place in Washington, and possibly the world to work. Consequently, OMB is always able to recruit highly qualified staff to fill examiner and analyst positions. Virtually all these staff have graduate degrees and, in addition to being very smart, are highly motivated to work hard at the job.

Due to OMB's seemingly constant budget shortfalls, OMB is only occasionally able to hire analysts at senior levels. Most OMB staff are hired directly out of graduate school, making it difficult for individuals interested in OMB to join mid-career. Even for those coming out of graduate school, there is a huge advantage to having been selected for the Presidential Management Fellowship (PMF) program. OMB branch chiefs like hiring PMF participants because it allows them to avoid the cumbersome civil service posting process, in which the hiring of a super candidate can easily be blocked by a marginally qualified veteran.

Despite the pressure to hire at the graduate school entry level, the career ladder for OMB staff to senior GS-15 positions will, at times, result in a branch having a surplus of senior people. This happened to me as Chief of the Environment Branch during the Clinton Administration after OMB 2000. The task for the branch chief in that situation is keeping people motivated when there are not enough plum assignments to go around. Of course, this is the kind of problem that most managers in government would kill to have. In fact, many Federal managers have the opposite problem, finding themselves struggling to get any level of motivation from staff who are more interested in their paycheck than doing a good job.

Downsides of Working at OMB

OMB staff are known for working long hours when need-ed, particularly during budget season. However, I never found the hours to be backbreaking, and they were much shorter than those worked by friends or classmates at in-vestment banking or top-notch law firms. To me the biggest drawback was not the hours, but the pressure. The fact that I lasted 42 years in the pressure cooker would suggest that I was something of a pressure junkie. Nevertheless, my ob-servation was that it was the pressure of working at OMB that was the most important factor in people deciding to leave the organization.

<u>Coping with Ridiculous Deadlines</u>

The pressure derives in part due to who we are working for — THE PRESIDENT OF THE UNITED STATES — and part-ly due to the always ridiculously short deadlines we work under. Unfortunately, the deadlines for many assignments have gotten worse over time. When I started back in 1979, a lot of assignments revolved around providing budget in-formation by late afternoon to make the press news cycle for the next morning. However, with the advent of 24-hour cable news, the need to respond quickly has intensified be-cause the news cycle is now continuous.

For the many assignments not tied to news cycles, OMB Directors tend to want information quickly anyway in case they need to respond on a moment's notice. This leads to a lot of "hurry up and wait" assignments where we might crash to provide information within 24 hours and later find out it doesn't get used or even looked at for a week or more. Preparing Statements of Administration Policy on pending bills when the timing of floor action is unknown is an all too frequent example of such a "hurry up and wait" assignment.

OMB staff are also known for preparing numerous data collections on the chance that the information might be needed, but which often are never used. Sometimes these are relatively easy exercises to compile and sometimes they involve huge investments of time. The ill-fated "pocket re-scission" proposals of international assistance funds during the summers of 2018 and 2019 are a prime example of a large investment of time that ultimately went unused.

24/7 Availability

An assumed availability on weekends and evenings, especially for members of the SES, is also a drawback. Particularly after I became a branch chief in 1988, the weekend and evening calls from the White House operator became more frequent. These calls usually meant that somebody in the White House needed some information immediately and was pressuring OMB leadership. These calls always created a certain amount of angst, as I was never sure whether I could prepare the needed response in the short time allotted.

My wife, Debby, <u>really</u> hated the calls because they were often disruptive of weekend plans or disturbed the kids when we were trying to get them to sleep at night. By the Obama Administration, most of the White House operator calls had been replaced by emails. In many respects, this was even worse in that there was a presumption that you were continuously monitoring your mobile phone.

I personally refused to take my work cell phone with me during the evening or on weekends when I left the house unless I was expecting an assignment. In fact, I grew to hate the 24/7 culture that cell phones represented that I rarely used my personal cell phone until after I retired. I always assumed that my refusal to take my cell phone with me would at some point come back to hurt me, but I somehow dodged that bullet. As DAD for IAD, I spent a lot of time in secure facilities where cell phones were not allowed. While that obviously didn't apply off-hours, it usefully prevented the PADs for national security from developing the mindset that their DADs were always instantly available. Unfortunately, this was an all too frequent occurrence with some of the PADs for domestic agencies.

Consequences of Being Abominable No-Men

The Abominable No-Men was the name of the OMB soft-ball team for several years and perfectly encapsulates one of the OMB staff's biggest roles — to say NO!! Like it or not, a significant part of any OMB job is to sift through the huge number of well-meaning policy proposals that agencies want to implement and say "No" to a significant portion of them, due to limits on resources or conflicts with broader Administration policies. While the ability to say "No" is ingrained in the culture of the career OMB staff, it is often a difficult concept for many of the PADs to grasp. As they often come from activist groups, they usually want to "green light" everything and feel uncomfortable playing the "bad guy". This is one of the reasons that PADs often don't last very long.

Even for career staff, there is a recognition that working at OMB tends to make you unpopular at the agencies you work on. However, by being professional and providing transparent justifications for rejecting proposals, staff can hope that their agencies will at least respect their work and that it will not hurt their long-term job prospects. Unfortunately, particularly for single staff, OMB's unpopularity can bleed into your personal life.

As examples of the latter, let me cite two instances. When I was young and single back in the mid-1980s during the Reagan Administration, I would often attend parties in the hope of meeting young women. I remember one instance where I struck up a conversation with a pretty blond. As we were exchanging information about our backgrounds she asked where I worked. When I responded that I worked at OMB, her reaction was "Oh, I am not sure I want to get to know you!" Fortunately, I recovered from that handicap and dated her a few times before mutually deciding it wouldn't work.

A year or so later, I was on vacation in Grand Teton National Park attending a day long mountain climbing class. During the lunch break, the instructor asked us to introduce ourselves and say where we were from and where we

worked. When I mentioned that I worked at OMB, I heard
this groan behind me followed by "oh no". It turned out
that the woman with the negative reaction was also from
the D.C. area, but worked at the National Oceanic and Atmospheric Administration, which had suffered budget cuts
under Reagan. After engaging her in further conversation,
she decided that I was not the devil incarnate and we held
the safety rope for each other later in the afternoon when
we practiced rappelling down a cliff. We both survived and
found the experience thrilling.

Those were easy situations to deal with. More difficult, however, was when the Chief Financial Officer (CFO)
at USDA went to OMB's Deputy Director for Management,
Clay Johnson, demanding that my Agriculture Branch Chief,
Adrienne Lucas, and I be fired. The ostensible rationale
was that we were off the reservation and unilaterally
thwarting the agriculture policies of the Bush '43 Administration. He framed the charge as reflecting not just his
opinion, but that of the other USDA Under Secretaries.

Given that Adrienne was a straight arrow, all American
girl next door type, the idea that she was off the reservation in this manner was absurd. Nevertheless, our PAD,
Marcus Peacock, was directed to talk to each of the USDA
Under Secretaries and report back to Clay. What Marcus's
investigation found was that half of the complaints related
to the Management side of OMB and a significant additional portion related to the Food and Nutrition Service, which
was handled by another division. Furthermore, all the
issues provoking complaints in my bailiwick were policy
issues decided by OMB or White House policy officials. In
fact, the other Under Secretaries understood that the complaints related to policy, and it was only the CFO who was
blaming Adrienne and I.

Consequently, we were completely vindicated. What
was disappointing, however, was that Clay neither explained to us why he ordered the investigation, nor apologized to us afterward for putting us through it. Shortly
thereafter, the CFO was confirmed for a similar position at
the Department of Education. It didn't take long, however,
for him to get crosswise with the new Secretary, Margaret

Spellings, and she had him fired. So while Adrienne and I continued to serve OMB for long after the incident, that **j...ass** .. er .. individual got what he deserved.

<u>Words of Wisdom</u>

One of Clay Johnson's quirks was his predilection for quoting famous sayings. During the annual Budget Examiner's Day show one year, the OMB staff did a skit, patterned after a Saturday Night Live sketch, about Clay's quotes titled "Deep Thoughts with Clay Johnson". Director Josh Bolten loved the skit so much that he started calling Clay by the nickname "Deep".

Instead of being embarrassed by the skit and his new nickname, Clay decided to put both the career and political senior staff on a schedule to deliver their own "Words of Wisdom" at the Friday senior staff meetings. While all that was required was quoting a few famous phrases, most people tried to dress them up a bit when it was their turn. I hated having to prepare Words of Wisdom, but when my turn came up, I always wanted to get a few laughs by having a setup and using the famous quote as the punchline.

One of my turns came right at the beginning of Budget season and I used the opportunity to make fun of my agencies' budget requests. Unfortunately, Clay loved my Words of Wisdom too much and, in the spirit of "no good deed goes unpunished", wanted me to repeat the performance the next week at a President's Management Council meeting of department deputy secretaries.

While it is one thing to make such jokes when the audience knows what is coming, it is a completely different situation when the audience has no idea whether you are joking or not. Although I was concerned about how the deputies of my agencies would take the ribbing, my performance went well, and everybody laughed. As my joke about the Interior Department was about the Cobell lawsuit accounting effort, Deputy Secretary Lynn Scarlett sent me a nice note afterward attached to the latest progress report on the accounting effort.

Perks of the Job

As hopefully the excitement, fulfillment, and honor of working at OMB have come through in earlier chapters, I won't cover those aspects of working at OMB in this chapter. Instead, I want to spend time discussing some of the thrilling and unique perks I have experience in working at OMB. It should be noted, however, that the perks have varied over time and may not be offered to staff in the future.

<u>4th of July Fireworks</u>

Every 4th of July the National Park Service holds a massive, fireworks display on the National Mall, with the fireworks launched from the Reflecting Pool in front of the Lincoln Memorial. The weather is usually sweltering and the commute home by either car or Metro takes forever, yet the crowds every year are huge. While there are better vantage points for watching the fireworks, such as the grounds of the Washington Monument, it is hard to beat the experience of watching from the White House lawn.

Early in my career, OMB staff were invited to view the fireworks from the lawn every year. Since the Obama Administration, EXOP agencies invited to the lawn have rotated on a three-year basis to allow more military families to attend. Most years the invitees are just offered the opportunity to attend, but some years have more elaborate festivities with entertainment provided.

In 1982, the Reagan Administration put on a great party with beverages and ice cream provided as well as square dancing on the White House driveway. Security wasn't as tight back then and, after the square dancing, my girlfriend and I climbed the stairway to the gate blocking the second-floor landing of the South Portico. Some friends snapped a picture of us doing our best Ron and Nancy imitation waving to the crowd below, before the Secret Service politely told us we needed to come down. It didn't seem important at the time, but now I deeply regret having never gotten a copy of that photo.

In later years, taking the kids to watch the fireworks from the lawn made for a great family outing. After the fireworks one year, I saw several kids rolling down this one little hill on the edge of the lawn. Much to the chagrin of my wife, the big kid in me decided to roll down the hill with one of my daughters just to say I had done so at the White House. Unfortunately, it made me dizzier than when I used to roll down hillsides as a child.

Due to the hassle of getting home and putting up with the heat, my family began to only go to the fireworks every few years. When I became DAD for International Affairs, I found that my tenth-floor corner office in the NEOB allowed great viewing, in air-conditioned comfort, and we could still hear the fireworks with the window open. Furthermore, if we left as soon as the fireworks ended, we could race to my car in the NEOB garage and beat all the traffic on the way home.

Christmas Perks

The opportunity to take a tour of the White House is exciting for almost all Americans, including those of us who only work a block away. One of the great perks of working at OMB has been the ability to take friends and relatives on the public White House tour. For many years this was done by showing your EXOP badge and being allowed to go to the head of the line any time during the year.

Even more special have been the candlelight tours of the White House for staff to see the decorations at Christmas time. Normally the President doesn't appear at these tours, but in 1982 President Reagan and Nancy decided to come down to the first floor during our tour. My girlfriend was so excited when she got to shake the President's hand that she didn't want to wash it for a week. She was also impressed that the paper towels in the rest rooms were stamped with the Presidential seal.

The candlelight tours, which are available to OMB staff every year, are basically the same as the public White House tours but allow staff to move through the White House at a more leisurely pace. The best parties, however, are the handful of annual parties held for political and sometimes high-level career staff.

For the first time during the George W. Bush years, OMB career staff were allowed to attend. In fact, my division received several invitations each year, which allowed the recipient to bring a spouse or other plus one. This allowed me to make sure that all my NRD staff had the opportunity to attend one of the Christmas parties at some point during the Bush years.

What made these parties so special was the ability to linger and socialize for a couple of hours. Buffet lines were set up in both the East Room and the State Dining rooms and I remember one year having dinner at a table in the East Room while gazing out across the White House lawn at the Washington Monument and Jefferson Memorial. Even more exciting was the receiving line to meet and have your picture taken with President Bush and Laura, which the Marines ran with military precision.

I attended these parties and got my picture taken with the President twice during the Bush years, once with my wife and once with my older daughter, Julia. I took my younger daughter, Diana, to one of these parties during President Obama's first year and she was thrilled at the prospect having her picture taken with Obama. Unfortunately, Obama opted not to have a receiving line and, instead, chose to make brief remarks to the assembled crowd in the front hall. This greatly disappointed my daughter, particularly as the President was even hard to see through the assembled crowd.

President Trump also opted for remarks over a receiving line. Remarkably, he even held a couple of these parties in 2020 during the pandemic and prior to the availability of vaccinations. Although my division got a few invites that year, I ended up returning most of them, since nobody wanted to attend a party that might turn into a COVID super spreader event.

In addition to Christmas tours and parties, OMB staff also get to provide a list of individuals to receive the President's annual Christmas, later Holiday, card. For much of my career, staff could provide addresses for ten recipients, while in recent years the number has declined to four. In general, my relatives have always been happy to show their Presidential Christmas cards to friends and neighbors. Even if they don't want a card, a brother can still get the psychic value of annoying his sister by sending her a Donald Trump Christmas card.

In many years, OMB staff would also receive a larger version, usually 12 by 16 inches, of the cover of the Christmas card. From Reagan through George W. Bush, these were uniformly beautiful painted pictures of the exterior or interior of the White House. Some of my relatives relished them as gifts because they were suitable for framing. Unfortunately, the quality of the artwork on the Christmas cards went downhill after President Bush. In fact, the Trump Christmas cards must rank as among the most boring cards on the planet.

Finally, starting in 2001, EXOP staff started receiving annual "thank you for your hard work" holiday notes from the White House Chief of Staff. I am not sure why we received them, but my confusion didn't prevent me from keeping a file of twenty years of such notes.

OMB Day Care Center

In some ways, the OMB Day Care Center didn't seem like much of a perk since my out-of-pocket costs were the equivalent of sending a child to college. Nevertheless, OMB, EXOP, and two other agencies were instrumental in getting the U.S. Kids Day Care Center up and running in 1991, a few blocks from my office and the White House. OMB's insistence that the center stay open until 7 P.M. was a godsend, since a 6 P.M. pickup time would have been difficult for me and would have been impossible if my children were at a day care center in Arlington. In fact, if not for that 7 P.M. pickup time, I doubt I would be writing this book because I would probably have left my job at OMB in the early to mid-1990's.

The timing of the Center's opening was perfect for me as well, since my oldest daughter was three months old, the minimum age, the day the day care center opened in

September 1991. Furthermore, that summer I had finally been able to get one of the NEOB garage parking passes that were reserved for branch chiefs. The NEOB parking pass also was a godsend for picking up my kids when I received one of the all too frequent calls that one of the kids had come down sick at the Center. In addition, getting into the Center soon after its opening was important because it guaranteed our second daughter a spot in the infant room, rather than having to hope she came off the waiting list that developed quickly in the Center's first couple of years.

As the day care center for the EXOP, the kids got some special opportunities, such as touring the White House one time as part of their morning walk. Even more special was that occasionally the First Lady dropped by. We got some great pictures when Barbara Bush picked up our fussing infant daughter Julia while on a visit in 1992. Years later, Julia's grandmother sent Mrs. Bush a copy of those pictures, at a time when Julia was in college and working on getting her pilot's license. Mrs. Bush sent a nice letter back, with a handwritten note, advising Julia to remain in the pilot's seat and not jump out of airplanes like her 85-year-old husband was prone to do.

Diana also got to meet a First Lady when Hilary Clinton stopped by U.S. Kids when Diana was around three. We also have terrific, framed pictures from that visit. Unfortunately, against my advice, OMB ended its relationship with U.S. Kids a few years ago in favor of alternative means of supporting childcare for staff.

Easter Egg Rolls

One of the longest White House traditions is the annual Easter Egg roll on the South Lawn, which dates from the Presidency of Rutherford B. Hayes in 1878.[267] At the time my kids were young, all OMB staff with kids in a certain age range (my recollection is roughly 3 to 7) could attend the Easter Egg Roll by showing their badges.

Eventually this policy changed during the Obama Administration when the Roll was opened to more of the general public including a broader age range of kids. Under the new policy, OMB staff had to request slots that were doled out subject to a lottery among the staff.

In most years, the kids can participate in not only the Easter Egg Roll, but a small Easter Egg Hunt as well. In addition, there is usually entertainment and story reading by well-known celebrities. The kids also receive a goody bag when they leave the White House grounds, which includes a wooden Easter Egg imprinted with the logo for that year's event. OMB staff also received a free Easter Egg every year from 1993 until the start of the Obama Administration. After that point, staff could still buy the Easter Eggs, first through the National Park Service and now the White House Historical Association. My collection of Easter Eggs spans 31 years, from 1993 through 2023, although not as long as my collection of White House Christmas ornaments, which dates from 1981, the first year the Historical Association started selling them.

My daughters were fortunate to attend the Roll three times each, during their last three years at U.S. Kids. My favorite Roll was the first one in 1994 in part because the weather was great, an infrequent occurrence from my experience. It was also the only year we were treated to pizza and donuts as we exited. Consequently, Julia, my wife, and I had a nice lunch on the lawn just outside the Southwest gate to the White House grounds.

As we were finishing lunch, I noticed the U.S. Kids cart for the little kids, including Diana who was too young to attend the roll, being pushed around the White House near our location. I told Julia and Debby not to look, in hopes that Diana wouldn't see us. A minute later I heard a little girl crying and, when I looked over, I realized that Diana had spotted us and thought we had abandoned her. At that point, we had no choice but to accompany Diana back to U.S. Kids to get her settled down for her afternoon nap.

In addition to the fireworks, Julia came back to the White House lawn two other times. The first was in middle school on Take Your Daughters to Work Day in 2004. One of the cool things arranged for the kids that day was to see a Marine One helicopter landing and greet President Bush upon his return to the White House. Although I have seen numerous Marine One landings over a twenty-year period from my office window, I never saw one up close and in person. Consequently, I was jealous that my daughter got to attend one.

Julia also got a chance to come back to the White House during high school to do some volunteer work. In this case, it was to help the little kids at the Easter Egg Roll, thirteen years after she had been a participant herself. I was very proud that Julia wanted to volunteer for the event. As my kids had been to the White House so many times growing up, I was always concerned that they would take for granted what were very special opportunities. I think that seeing the joy on the faces of the kids and their parents that day helped bring home to Julia the very special nature of the Easter Egg Roll and other White House events she got to attend.

White House Ceremonies

There are three kinds of White House ceremonies to which OMB staff are often invited. These ceremonies are: 1) arrival ceremonies for visiting heads of State; 2) championship ceremonies for professional sports teams or Olympians; and 3) signing ceremonies. The signing ceremonies are the smallest of the three and staff only get invited if they were significantly involved in working on the relevant issue. I have already mentioned attending ceremonies in the Rose Garden, to release President Bush's 1989 Clean Air Act proposal, and in the East Room, to sign the enacted Clean Air Act Amendments of 1990. Among others, I recall attending a ceremony in the OEOB where President Reagan vetoed the 1987 Clean Water Act amendments for a second time.

OMB staff have a better chance of being invited if a ceremony is outdoors on the South Lawn than if the ceremony is inside. While bigger ceremonies are usually viewed as better by White House public relation types, the weather for a particular time of year often dictates whether a ceremony is inside or out. Outdoors ceremonies always have an invited list of dignitaries from outside the Administration who are given seats near the podium. However, invites to EXOP staff are often issued to fill out a large standing room crowd.

A couple of advantages for inviting large numbers of EXOP staff to these ceremonies are: 1) that attendees are uniformly enthusiastic; and 2) more importantly for the Secret Service, all EXOP staff already have been vetted through extensive background investigations to get their jobs. Sometimes staff are allowed to bring guests, for instance I took my wife and parents to see President Jacques Chirac of France in 1996, and sometimes not. The challenge for EXOP staff at these ceremonies is to get close enough for good pictures, while avoiding having your line of sight blocked by the White House press photographers who generally enter after the crowd of onlookers has assembled.

I passed on attending many of the visits by minor heads of state but made every effort to see the major leaders when they came. For instance, I was able to attend the arrival ceremonies for Mikhail Gorbachev, the final leader of the Soviet Union in 1990; Hu Jintao, the Communist Party Secretary of China in 2006; Prime Ministers Berlusconi and Renzi of Italy in 2008 and 2016; and President Macron of France in 2018. The arrival ceremonies for heads of state have much more pomp and circumstance than the sports ceremonies, with music from the Marine band, formal programs, and complementary flags to wave.

On the other hand, the ceremonies for the sports champions give you an often, needed chance to cheer. How can you not cheer your lungs out for the 1980 Winter Olympic team after the "Miracle on Ice" victory of the hockey team over the Soviet Union. In addition to several visit by Olympic teams, I got to see the Washington Redskins after at least one of their Superbowl victories and, most recently, the visit in 2019 by the Washington Nationals to celebrate their World Series victory.

As a Cleveland native and a die-hard fan of their sports teams, I desperately wanted to go to the ceremony for the Cleveland Cavaliers when they won the NBA championship in 2016, breaking the city's 52-year drought of championships. It was the only time I ever reached out to the OMB front office to try to get an invite to any event. Unfortunately, despite my groveling, I didn't get to go since it was a smaller event inside the White House and OMB wasn't allocated any invites. Bummer!!!

Highly Exclusive Perks

While the Obama Administration disappointed OMB staff by cutting back our ability to attend the Easter Egg Roll and the 4th of July Fireworks, they more than made up for it by providing several new perks. I don't remember when OMB career staff were first allowed to sign up to use the White House bowling lanes, but at least I didn't start using it until the Obama Administration. The lanes themselves are in the basement of the EEOB and are not in great condition. Nevertheless, it makes for a great group event and the ability to brag that you bowled at the White House.

Similarly, I don't remember when OMB staff were first invited to sign up for tickets to the President's box at the Kennedy Center for the Performing Arts. Tickets are doled out based on a priority system in which OMB career staff are at the absolute bottom of the pecking order. Consequently, staff only ever got to attend the least popular shows or, occasionally, more popular shows when there was a last-minute cancellation. Given the low odds, I rarely tried for tickets and never got any. On the other hand, one of my staff lucked into some great tickets and sat in the box with a cabinet secretary for the performance.

One perk that was allowed in the Obama Administration, although started late in Bush '43, was the ability to sign up and take friends or relatives on tours of the West Wing after hours or on weekends. By the time that perk had become available I had been to the West Wing well over 50 times, but always had to be escorted to anywhere other than the White House mess or the Situation Room, which were next to the guard desk on the ground floor.

One time in the Bush Administration, I was seated on a couch in the West Wing, waiting for an escort to take me to a Clean Air Act meeting, when Barbara Bush and her dog

Millie walked in. My first impulse was to be a gentleman and stand in the presence of the First Lady. However, my second thought was that quick movements make Secret Service agents very nervous. Ultimately, my concern about being tackled by the Secret Service led me to stay seated and I just nodded and mumbled hello as the First Lady walked by.

For most people, just taking the public White House tour is a thrill. However, touring the West Wing, where so many important decisions are made, is a chance to see the inner sanctum of power that few people get to experience. The tours allowed guests to see the Rose Garden and look into, but not enter, the Roosevelt Room, the Cabinet Room and, most importantly, the Oval Office. For security reasons, pictures are not allowed on the tour, except in the White House press briefing room and once outside the West Wing.

I had taken a West Wing tour once previously during the Reagan Administration when the political Assistant to my PAD took me and my parents around. The Obama Administration, however, was the first time that OMB career staff could lead the self-guided tour (see Figure 14-1). As this was a perk I wasn't sure would be available in the next Administration, I tried to give tours to as many close friends and family members as I could, often followed by dinner or bowling at the White House lanes. Unfortunately, the Trump Administration didn't allow OMB staff to sign up to give these tours — sigh — even before the pandemic totally shut them down.

Other than riding on Air Force One, which I never even got to do or even see, visiting Camp David is perhaps the ultimate White House perk. I was privileged to go twice during the Obama Administration. The only reason such staff retreats were allowed was that Obama, unlike many other Presidents, rarely used Camp David. As the Camp needed to be maintained regardless of how often the President visited, it made sense to open the Camp for retreats by key staff who had been subject to stringent background checks to get their jobs. Furthermore, the retreats helped keep the Camp staff from going stir crazy.

Figure 14-1 West Wing Tour Map

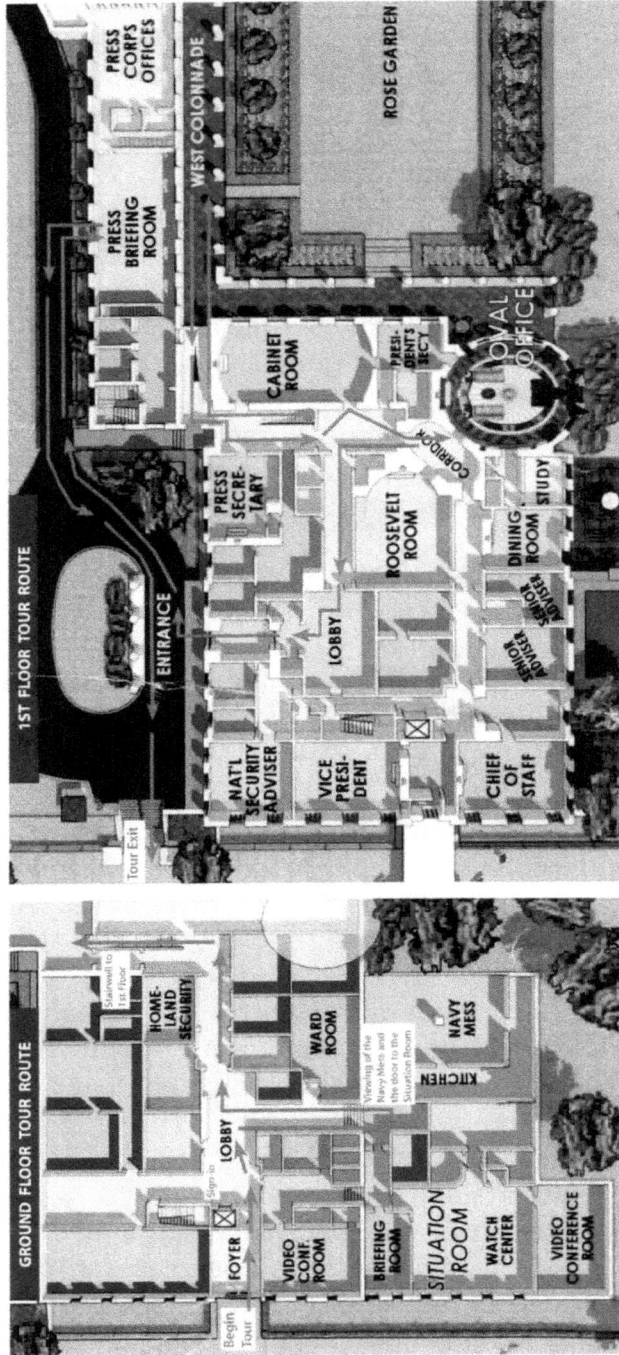

The first time I went to Camp David in August 2014, all of OMB got the chance to attend. However, as only so many guests are allowed to visit each day, OMB's visit had to be split up over several days. In order to justify the visit, the morning was devoted to "work", while the afternoon was play time. The term "work' is used loosely as it mainly involved educating us about the history of Camp David, during a lecture in the Camp Chapel, and a tour of several of the key cabins.

The most notable cabins at Camp David are Aspen, which is where the President stays, and Laurel, which serves as the current conference room for various diplomatic events. There is also a smaller cabin, formerly named Laurel and currently named Holly, where the Camp David Accords were negotiated and signed by Egyptian President Anwar Sadat and Israeli Prime Minister Menachem Begin in September 1978[268].

The second time I visited the Camp in August 2015, was limited to senior career and political staff, and we actually did real work in the morning by discussing and commenting on the draft OMB strategic plan. In both years, play time was somewhat restricted by heavy rain, twice ruining my opportunity to say that I had played tennis on the Camp David courts. Nevertheless, I got to play basketball in the gym and bowl at the lanes at the Camp David Officer's Club. Having bowled at both, I can say categorically that the Camp David lanes are much nicer than the ones in the EEOB.

Although no cameras are allowed at Camp David, there is an official photographer to take your picture. The only catch is that, for security reasons, photos are only allowed in front of the iconic Camp David sign outside the Officer's Club. Each day ended with drinks at the bar in the Officer's Club, which also doubles as the Camp gift shop. While the gift shop items were pretty standard, it is nevertheless very cool to get a jacket or wine decanter embroidered or stamped with the Camp David logo.

Daughter Julia Meets the Easter Bunny at 1995 Easter Egg Roll

First Lady Clinton with Daughter Diana at U.S. Kids in 1996

My Family on the White House South Lawn Waiting for the 4th of July Fireworks to Begin in 2007

White House Arrival Ceremony for Italian Prime Minister Berlusconi in 2008

My Wife and I in a Photo-Op with President Bush and Laura at the White House Christmas Reception in 2001

Jumping for Joy with My Staff at the 2019 White House Christmas Reception

The White House
Bowling Lanes in the
Eisenhower Executive
Office Building

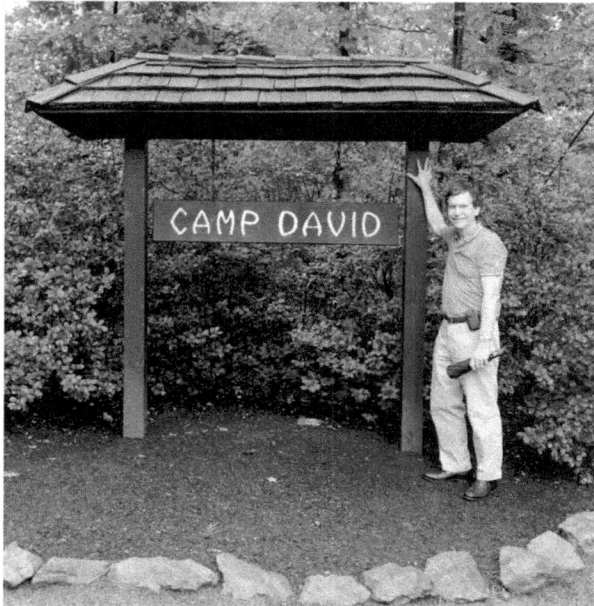

Posing at the Camp
David Sign Outside the
Officers Club on an OMB
Retreat in 2015

View From My 10th Floor Office of the White House Complex and National Mall -- Arguably the best View in Washington

The OMB Director's Conference Room and the Wall of Former Director's Photos

Daughter Julia and Friends Outside the West Wing Entrance Before a Tour in 2016

Fist Bumping with President Biden in the Oval Office on My Final Day in April 2021

CHAPTER FIFTEEN: Fairytale Ending -- *Serving as Acting OMB Director*

I originally intended to retire at the end of calendar year 2019, six months after I reached full retirement age and at the best point in the year to retire from a financial standpoint. However, as discussed in Chapter 9, one of my branch chiefs had left in September and I felt that I needed to replace him before I retired.

It is just as well that I didn't retire on schedule, as the COVID-19 pandemic would have turned me into a shut-in and prevented me from participating in many of the activities that I had planned for retirement. Given my classified responsibilities, I continued to work from the office for most of the pandemic and never felt shut-in. Consequently, I reset my retirement date for the end of calendar year 2020, but didn't tell anybody at OMB, other than the human resource folks who needed to begin processing the paperwork well in advance.

In October 2020, I got a call from Director Vought's Chief of Staff asking if I would serve as Acting Director of OMB in the event of a Biden victory and the failure of Congress to confirm a new OMB Director by Inauguration Day. I hesitated at first and thought about turning down the responsibility and disclosing to the Director's office my intention to retire. On reflection, however, I decided to accept the additional role, in large part because I didn't want the outgoing Administration to replace me if Biden won. My concern was that OMB leadership, or the White House, might try to use my open job to burrow a Trump political appointee into a senior OMB career position.

My thinking was that if Trump won, I could retire at the end of the calendar year anyway. On the other hand, aside from Mick Mulvaney, most OMB Directors have been non-controversial and gotten confirmed around Inauguration Day. Consequently, even if Biden won, I figured the delay in my retirement was short. Unfortunately, as soon as

Biden designated Neera Tanden for OMB Director, I realized that the key assumption in my thinking about an uncontroversial nominee was wrong and that the delay in my retirement would be months, not days.

Taking the Reins...Sort Of

As a career official, serving as Acting Director of OMB is not quite the exulted role that it might appear to be. It is more like being the Queen of England — wave and smile — instead of the British Prime Minister who wields all the substantive power. In a nutshell, my role was to sign official documents on behalf of OMB and to provide a name that could be listed as a defendant in lawsuits against OMB.

Nevertheless, I thoroughly enjoyed my tenure as Acting Director. It provided interesting new responsibilities on top of my day job as DAD for International Affairs. However, as was the case when I took other new jobs, it highlighted how much I had become bored in my current job after 11 years. In many ways, serving as Acting Director was the perfect capstone for my career.

Within a few days of the Inauguration, OMB had perhaps a dozen senior non-Senate confirmed political appointees on-board. If it hadn't been a transition period, a few of them would have been the logical candidates to serve as Acting Director rather than me. However, under the Vacancy Act, a non-Senate confirmed political appointee can't serve as Acting Director until they had been on-board for 90 days.[269] Nevertheless, that does not mean that the new appointees couldn't exert policy control from day one, particularly as many of them were politically connected to the White House.

Consequently, the roles of Acting Director and the two Acting Deputy Directors had to be filled by career staff already in the Senior Executive Service. For that purpose, Russ had selected me to be Acting Director, Matt Vaeth, the DAD for Legislative Reference, as Acting Deputy Director, and Leslie Fields, the DAD for Federal Procurement, as Acting Deputy Director for Management. Figure 15-1 is my recollection of how the key components of the organization chart looked on Inauguration Day.

Figure 15-1: OMB Organization Chart February 2021

February 2021

Acting = A

Office of the Director

Director -- Rob Fairweather (A)

Deputy Director -- Matt Vaeth (A) | Deputy Director for Management -- Lesley Field (A) | Executive Associate Director -- Aviva Aron-Dine
Chief of Staff | Deputy Chief of Staff

OMB-Wide Support Offices

General Counsel
Legislative Affairs
Management and Operations Division
Economic Policy
Legislative Reference Division
Economics, Science, & General Govt Branch
Health, Education, Veterans, & Social Programs Branch
Resources, Defense & International Branch
Budget Review Division
Budget Analysis Branch
Budget Concepts Branch
Budget Review Branch
Budget Systems Branch

Statutory and Management Offices

Senior Advisor (Management)
Office of Federal Financial Management
Office of Federal Procurement Policy
Office of the Federal Chief Information Officer
Office of Information & Regulatory Affairs
Food Health & Labor Branch
Natural Resources & Environment Branch
Transportation & Security Branch
Information Policy Branch
Statistical & Science Policy Branch
Privacy Branch
U.S. Digital Service Administrator
Office of Performance and Personnel Management

Resource Management Offices

Natural Resources	Education, Income Maintenance & Labor	Health	Transportation, Homeland security, Justice & Services	Housing, Treasury & Commerce	National Security
Energy, Science & Water Division; Energy Branch; Science & Space Br.; Water & Power Br.; Natural Resources Div; Agriculture Branch; Environment Br.; Interior Branch	Education, Income Maintenance & Labor Division; Education Branch; Income Maintenance Br.; Labor Branch	Health Division; Health & Human Services Branch; Medicaid Branch; Medicare Branch; Public Health Br.; Health Insurance, Data, & Analysis Br	Transportation, Homeland security, Justice & Services Division; Transportation & Services Branch; Homeland Security Branch; Justice Branch	Housing, Treasury & Commerce Div; Housing Branch; Treasury Branch; Commerce Br.	International Affairs Div; State Branch; Economic Affairs Br; National Security Div; Intelligence Prog Br; Defense Ops, Personnel & Support Br; Defense Investment Br; VA & Defense Health Br

By the day before the Inauguration, however, I was getting nervous because the delegation paperwork hadn't been signed and I wasn't even sure who would sign it. Later in the day, however, I was told that the Chief of Staff's office for the Trump Administration had made an agreement with the Biden Transition Team to allow Biden to make the key agency delegations government wide.

That bit of unconfirmed news, however, left open some ambiguity as to whether I would be Biden's choice for Acting Director. As Matt, Leslie and I were the selections of the Trump team, it was not unreasonable to think that the Biden team might want to make alternative selections. While I was a logical choice as the longest serving career DAD, I was also the senior DAD at the end of the Obama Administration and was not selected. In fact, all the DADs who were selected for the acting positions at that time by Director Donovan were still in OMB and could easily have been viewed as more trusted selections for the posts by the Biden folks.

In the end, Biden made the delegations to the career folks chosen by the Trump Cabinet officials. The President signed my delegation memo in the first wave of such delegations a few hours after he was sworn in as 46th President. Shortly afterwards I got a congratulatory call from Brian Deese — a former OMB Deputy Director under Obama and the new head of the National Economic Council — who offered to provide any assistance I should need in carrying out my duties.

Inauguration Day Actions

It was good that the delegation had come when it did, because my DAD colleagues and I had mapped out several early actions for me to take that day — with the concurrence of the Biden transition team — that were of great importance to the career OMB staff. The first was to direct the White House Office of Administration to put on hold implementation of several personnel actions including the new Schedule F personnel classification category as it related to OMB employees. This action was needed to ensure that no employees were reclassified prior to a Biden Administration policy decision on Schedule F.

Schedule F was a late attempt by the Trump Administration to get more control over the bureaucracy by reclassifying many employees into a new personnel category with fewer civil service protections. It was established by an October 21, 2020, Executive Order and required agencies to identify policy development or advocacy positions for reclassification by January 19, 2021.[270] Director Vought, however, wanted to get it fully implemented at OMB before the end of the Trump Administration. Unfortunately for him, he couldn't get the Office of Personnel Management and the White House Office of Administration to work fast enough to achieve that goal.

Most OMB staff clearly would have fallen under Schedule F, due to our policy development activities. Much of the staff was apoplectic about potentially losing their civil service protections. I was not as concerned, as the lack of such protections had posed few problems for the SES or Schedule A attorneys over multiple decades. That said, Schedule F would have left the door open for potential abuse, even if rarely used. In fact, my directive to freeze personnel actions that first day was also a step towards reversing two recent SES reassignments. To the career staff, these reassignments seemed more in the mode of score settling than legitimate job transfers to benefit the organization.

The advantage of Schedule F for managers would have been to allow more flexibility and speed in hiring. From my perspective, the major disadvantage was that staff brought in under such appointments would have no civil service status when they wanted to leave OMB for another agency. Given how many mid-level vacancy postings do not allow competition outside of the affected agency, this would have been a huge disincentive for people to want to join OMB. In any event, President Biden rescinded Trump's Schedule F Executive Order two days after I had put its implementation for OMB on hold.

Another action I took that first day was to restore the delegation of apportionment authority to the career DAD level. As discussed in Chapter 9, Director Vought had originally taken away the apportionment authority from me and my NSD colleague, Mark Sandy, in the summer of 2019, during the period when the Ukraine funding was being frozen. The authority was taken away from the remaining DADs the following year and given to their PADs.

Most of the time signing apportionments was a ministerial function, although at times an apportionment could be a powerful policy control lever for OMB. For instance, an apportionment could be used to add conditions to funding which agencies legally had to comply with to avoid violating the Anti-Deficiency Act. Such a typical "footnote" to the apportionment might require an agency to report and wait five days before undertaking certain controversial spending while OMB obtained policy clearance. However, there were limits on the usefulness of such footnotes because they had to be crafted to avoid an illegal impoundment of funds.

Director Vought was of the view that giving the PADs apportionment authority would increase their power and result in greater use of apportionment footnotes to reduce spending. However, the PADs struggled to find creative uses for this authority beyond the ones that the DADs had traditionally applied, which in most cases had been cleared with the PAD before DAD signature. Thus, rather than strengthening the PADs, I felt that their new apportionment authority actually weakened them, because the process was a drain on PAD time that could have been used in more productive ways.

Personally, I was not upset at losing my apportionment authority because it was time consuming process of limited value, plus I didn't want my name on any legally dubious Ukraine apportionments. Nevertheless, from a good government standpoint, it makes more sense for the DADs to carry out the function. Furthermore, given the press reporting of Trump Administration overreach in stripping the DADs of the authority in the first place, it was important for staff morale to overturn Director Vought's redelegation of the authority.

While the two actions I took above were of importance to OMB staff, the remaining two actions had government-wide significance. First, I signed a Management Memorandum to the Heads of Executive Departments and Agencies, providing the implementing guidance concerning a White House

Chief of Staff's memo from earlier in the day. That memo imposed a freeze on regulations which had not yet taken effect pending review by the new Administration. This was like the regulatory freeze imposed on day one by several previous administrations, as discussed in Chapter 10.

Second, I issued an OMB Bulletin releasing $27 billion in funding withheld from obligation pursuant to the Trump Administration's January 14, 2021, rescission proposal. The proposal would have rescinded funding provided in the Consolidated Appropriations Act of 2021, which funded most of the Federal government and which the President had signed into law less than three weeks earlier.

The rescission proposal was symptomatic of Director Vought's Don Quixotesque penchant for "tilting at windmills". The proposed rescission, half of which came from my agencies, had zero, none, nil chance of being enacted, but forced me to work during part of my planned Christmas leave to prepare the package. My Inauguration Day action allowed agencies to obligate the funding, but the rescission proposal itself had to be withdrawn by the President, which the President did January 31st in response to the request I sent him.

The Power of the (Auto)Pen

The day after the Inauguration, I went over to the Eisenhower Executive Office Building (EEOB) --formerly the Old Executive Office Building (OEOB) — to look around after the Trump folks had vacated. While there I introduced myself to the two Biden appointees who were working out of the EEOB. Most of the appointees were teleworking due to the pandemic, with a few still living in California.

When I mentioned that I had looked around the Director's office, one of them asked me if I was planning to move in. I politely declined, as I thought it would be rather presumptuous of me to claim the office. The Director's second floor office is enormous and probably larger than any office in the Executive Office complex other than, perhaps, the Oval Office. In earlier times it had been the office of the Secretary of War and had a private bath as well as doors that opened onto a large porch that looked out onto Pennsylvania Avenue and Blair House. Nevertheless, the view from the Director's office didn't hold a candle to the view from my 10th floor NEOB office, which overlooked the White House and had a panoramic view of most of the National Mall.

As the not so pretty "face" of the agency, part of my role was to kick off various internal OMB meetings. These included a weekly meeting of the political staff and the career DADs, as well as an OMB all-hands meeting the first week, where I touted the actions that had been taken to roll back unpopular Trump policies of great interest to staff. I also represented OMB at meetings of principals (i.e. cabinet secretaries, or in this case often career officials acting in such positions), including weekly COVID meetings and an NSC meeting to sign off on an interim foreign affairs strategy.

As this was during the pandemic, none of these meetings were in person, but rather were Zoom calls. This created an odd situation for me as I worked out of my 10th floor office in the NEOB. However, our office is part of the "security suite", a secure area in which no cameras, cell phones, laptops or even Fitbits are allowed. Thus, on Zoom calls I could see the other participants on my computer monitor, but they could not see me because I was participating by a land line phone. For newer staff who hadn't met me, it must have seemed like something out of the Wizard of Oz — who is that man behind the curtain?

Despite not exercising policy clout (i.e. decisions on the FY 2022 Budget), the political staff were largely deferential to me given my role as titular head of the agency and, perhaps, due to my long experience having been through six previous transitions. While I avoided being heavy-handed, if I made comments on a document needing my signature they were always made.

Prior to the Inauguration, I was asked to provide samples of my signature that could be affixed to official documents after I had approved them. As the vast bulk of OMB staff was teleworking, having me physically sign or initial every document was not practical. I provided several samples including one done with a Sharpie marker. As it looked less professional, I was surprised that the Sharpie version became my standard signature. I am guessing that somebody decided that the versions in pen looked like a "girly man" signature that needed to be "pumped up" with the bold Sharpie pen to look more authoritative.

Despite my length of service at OMB, I was nonetheless surprised at the number (roughly 90) and variety of documents that I had to sign, initial, or otherwise approve in my two months as Acting Director. Fortunately, all these documents were well-written and of uniformly high quality, which made me look intelligent, authoritative, and knowledgeable, whether I understood the document I was signing or not.

Over half the documents on which I signed off related to OMB's role in the executive order (EO) process, with the bulk of those being Budgetary Impact Analyses. These mostly boilerplate analyses were statutorily required for every one of the flood of EOs, which started as soon as the President was sworn in and had to be posted on OMB's website. The early Biden EOs had been prepared by the transition team without OMB involvement. However, by the beginning of February, OMB had regained its historic role in processing and resolving comments on proposed EOs. This included having the OMB Director send the President a memo for each EO recommending his signature. I signed nine of these memos.

As a general rule memos to the President are not made public but become part of the President's historic record. Also included in this category were the three enrolled bill memos that I sent the President. OMB prepares an enrolled bill memo for every bill passed by Congress and sent to the President for his signature or veto. The memos include a concise discussion on the substance of the bill, a summary of agency positions on whether to sign the bill and ends with the Director of OMB's recommendation.

The only significant enrolled bill memo that I signed was for the $1.9 TRILLION American Rescue Plan Act of 2021. The odd part about signing that memo was that I really didn't support the bill. I basically agreed with Larry Summers — a Clinton Treasury Secretary and Obama Director of the National Economic Council — who argued in a February 4th Washington Post opinion[271] piece that the bill would be inflationary because, based on CBO data, it was possibly three times as large as needed. It turned out that Summers was correct. In any event, due to pressure to get the bill's stimulus spending allocated quickly, the President signed the bill as soon as it arrived at the White House and never had a chance to read the enrolled bill memo. At least it will be part of the historic record.

The largest category of documents I signed for external consumption were Management Memorandums to the heads of executive departments and agencies. These memorandums provided guidance to agencies aimed at ensuring consistent implementation of management policies and procedures to keep the wheels of government running smoothly. Part of my role in reviewing these documents was to make sure that my name was spelled correctly. Unfortunately, I failed at that basic task as one memo went out with an incorrect middle initial and had to be corrected hours later.

Although I signed eight of these during my tenure, a ninth which provided guidance on implementing the President's EO on mask wearing was signed by the Executive Associate Director for Budget for reasons I never understood. As one of my daughters was opposed to mask mandates, it was probably just as well for peace in the family that I didn't have to sign that one.

The full range of documents requiring the Acting Director's signature included various budget documents both to the White House and the agencies, OMB personnel related documents, letters to Congress and GAO, and a notification to 1,300 tribal leaders inviting them to tribal consultations with OMB on how OMB's functions affect Tribal Nations. I also received a fair amount of incoming correspondence from cabinet secretaries and Congress, some of which was incorrectly addressed to "The Honorable Robert Fairweather". While I found this amusing, I was not entitled to this honorific as I had never been Senate confirmed.

Aside from the enrolled bill memo on the American Rescue Plan, the only document I had second thoughts about signing was an ethics waiver. It came as a surprise one afternoon that a waiver to the President's ethics EO needed to be signed that day for a political appointee at DHS. It turned out that while the EO allowed for such waivers, the Director of OMB was the only official authorized to provide the waiver!!! Lucky me.

It took a while to convince me that the ethical conflict in this case was very minor, although the publication "The Hill" questioned a couple waivers, including this one, in an article two months later. I ended up signing the waiver and, shortly thereafter, delegated the waiver authority to the Designated Agency Ethics Official of each agency. I thought that delegation would take me totally off the hook for future waivers. Unfortunately, I had to sign another waiver for an OMB official.

Heading for the Door

On March 2, 2021, Neera Tanden withdrew her name from consideration as Director of OMB. When it became apparent that a new nominee wouldn't be named and confirmed quickly, a mad scramble began to get Deputy Director designate Shalanda Young confirmed quickly so that she could become Acting Director. (Was the current Acting Director doing that badly?).

Shalanda was confirmed on March 23rd and my tenure — or what some of my colleagues jokingly referred to as my "reign of error" — came to an end. Under normal circumstances Shalanda would have become Acting Director as soon as she was sworn in. However, as the President had been the one to designate me as Acting Director, he had to formally rescind my authority the next day before Shalanda could assume the Director's duties.

Shalanda invited me over the next day to get my advice on how to manage OMB staff. I used the opportunity to tell her that I was retiring at the end of April. She thanked me for my long years of service and said she was glad I didn't want to be taken out of OMB "in a box" as she feared would happen with some of her long serving Hill colleagues.

In normal times, there would have been pressure to have a big farewell ceremony in the Indian Treaty Room of the EEOB, complete with speeches and the reading of a congratulatory letter from the President. Fortunately, the pandemic saved me from that kind of farewell, as my preference was for a series of lunches rather than the big show. Consequently, I was very pleased that my old NRD staff made a special trip into work to take me to lunch one day and my IAD staff had a small party in my office on another day.

Mark Sandy, my NSD counterpart, also arranged for a lunch with the budget DAD group at his house on a Saturday. I had organized the monthly DAD lunches for almost twenty years, but we hadn't met since the start of the pandemic. I am sure that Mark and his wife assumed that we would impose on their hospitality for perhaps an hour and a half, but the lunch didn't break up until over four hours later. Collectively it had been a significant challenge for the DADs to survive the Trump Administration, the pandemic, and a Presidential transition. Consequently, everybody embraced the opportunity to be together, in person and without masks for the first time in fourteen months. Frankly my farewell was just an excuse for us to get together, but it was the perfect type of farewell for me.

On my last day, OMB's front office had arranged for me to have a photo opportunity with President Biden. As I was escorted to the President's office, I asked what the protocol was for a photo-op during a pandemic. I was told that I would be given an N95 mask to wear under my normal mask, that I could wave to the President but not shake his hand, and that I was to stay six feet away from him.

As the President was running late, I was asked to wait in the Cabinet Room. Although I estimate that I had been in the West Wing perhaps 300 times in my career, I had never set foot in either the Cabinet Room or the Oval Office. Thus, it was an honor to be able to stroll around the Cabinet Room and take an up-close look at the paintings and busts that decorated the room.

When I was at Stanford Business School, I took a seminar with George Schultz that culminated in a dinner at his house. While I had dinner, I sat at a table in one of his three cabinet chairs (State, Treasury, and Labor) with his name and cabinet post on the back. At least at the time, the tradition was that the Secretary's senior staff would buy the chair as a gift when the Secretary left. When I asked why the Biden cabinet chairs didn't have the name plates on the back, I was told that they were still resolving a technical problem that Biden had given Cabinet rank to too many people for the normal chairs to fit around the existing table.

When I was finally ushered into the Oval Office, the President broke protocol by coming up close, giving me a fist bump, and putting his hand on my shoulder. We chatted for five minutes about budgeting and my career while the camera clicked before taking a posed photo three feet apart. The President thanked me for my service, and I wished him the best of luck before I was escorted out. As luck would have it, if I had retired two weeks later, my photo-op would have been without masks, when standards were relaxed for a short period prior to the arrival of the COVID delta variant.

My first OMB boss, Jim Tozzi, used to like to say, "don't let the door hit you on the way out". It was his way of telling his staff not to feel too self-important because the clout at OMB comes from the position, not the individual, and OMB can <u>always</u> get highly qualified individuals to replace you. In fact, recruiting for my replacement got a boost when "Politico" gave it a tongue in cheek mention "**LOVE FREEZING AID TO UKRAINE?** Here's a hot job for you".[272] The fact of the matter is that I didn't stay at OMB for forty years because I thought I was essential to the organization, I stayed because I thoroughly enjoyed the job and was always thankful for the opportunities it provided me.

Nevertheless, all good things must come to an end, and I wanted an opportunity to enjoy some retirement years before I ended up "in a box" to use Shalanda's technical terminology. I had been parking in the garage of the NEOB for almost 30 years, since just before my daughter started at the OMB day care center when she was three months old. Consequently, I was deathly afraid that I would break down sobbing when I got into my car to leave that last day. While it is true that I was uncharacteristically emotional as I left, I made it through the garage door without it hitting my car on the way out.

ACKNOWLEDGEMENTS

I would like to thank my wife, Debby, and my two daughters, Julia and Diana, for their forbearance over three decades in putting up with the strains and demands I faced while working at OMB. If it weren't for their cooperation and understanding, I would never have lasted as long at OMB as I did, nor would I have been able to write this book.

I also want to thank the hundreds of OMB employees that I have worked with over the years whose skills, knowledge, integrity, dedication, and hard work made it such an incredible workplace. I have tried to use this book to convey to the public the importance of the work of the OMB staff, and also the high quality of staff analysis and work products.

I want to particularly thank the numerous staff I worked closely with over the years in both the Natural Resources and International Affairs Divisions. I tried to single out many of these staff by name in the examples of OMB's role in the important issues discussed in this book. However, as I focused the book on a limited set of examples, I necessarily failed to include many other staff who were just as worthy of a mention if I had chosen to use other issues as illustrations of OMB's work.

Finally, I want to thank specifically those current and former OMB staff, as well as family and friends, who helped me through encouragement, advice on publication, or review of the draft book. Their support was critical in helping me through the process and making the book as accurate and clearly explained as possible. These individuals include Diana Fairweather, Jan Radkowsky, Kathy Peroff, Dale Snape, Laurie Adams, Kevin Neyland, Adrienne Lucas, and Jaime Read.

LIST OF FIGURES AND TABLES

ABOUT THE AUTHOR

Prior to his retirement, Mr. Fairweather worked in the Federal Government for 44 years, of which 42 were at the Office of Management and Budget (OMB). His service included 33 years as a member of the Senior Executive Service (SES), of which 20 years was at the Deputy Associate Director (DAD) level, the highest level for career employees within OMB. His outstanding work resulted in his being given SES Presidential Rank awards twice in his career. Mr. Fairweather also served as the Acting Director of OMB for the first two months of the Biden Administration in 2021.

At the time of his retirement, Mr. Fairweather was the DAD for International Affairs at OMB. In that position he managed the International Affairs Division (IAD), which was responsible for budget and policy matters relating to the Department of State, the U.S. Agency for International Development, and other international affairs agencies. He served in that position from May 2010 through April 2021.

Prior to assuming that position, Mr. Fairweather was the DAD for the Natural Resources Division (NRD) for 9 years. In that position, he was responsible for budget and policy issues relating to the Departments of Agriculture and the Interior, as well as the Environmental Protection Agency. Mr. Fairweather began his career at OMB as a Budget Examiner in the Environment Branch in NRD until he was promoted to Chief of the Environment Branch, an SES position, in 1988.

Mr. Fairweather has an undergraduate degree in Civil Engineering from Princeton University and a Master of Business Administration (MBA) from Stanford University. He worked at the Department of Labor as an economist for two years between his undergraduate and graduate years.

Originally from Cleveland Ohio, Mr. Fairweather lives in Arlington, VA with his wife Debby and has two adult daughters.

FOOTNOTES

1   "Executive Policymaking: The Role of the OMB in the Presidency", Meena Bose and Andrew Rudalevige Editors, Brookings Institution Press, 2020

2   "The Office of Management and Budget and the Presidency, 1921-1979", Larry Berman, Princeton University Press, 1979

3   "The Evolution of OMB", Philip R. Dame and Bernard H. Martin, self-published, 2009

4   "The Evolution of OMB", Dame and Martin, page 1

5   "Budget of the U.S. Government for Fiscal Year 2022 — Appendix", Office of Management & Budget, May 28, 2022, Page 1169

6   "Budget of the U.S. Government for Fiscal Year 1981 — Appendix", Office of Management & Budget, January 28, 1980, Pages 64-65

7   "Executive Policymaking: The Role of the OMB in the Presidency" Meena Bose and Andrew Rudalevige Editors, Brookings Institution Press, 2020, page 62

8   "Budget of the U.S. Government for Fiscal Year 2022 — Appendix", Office of Management & Budget, May 28, 2022, Pages 1163-1174

9   "Executive Policymaking: The Role of the OMB in the Presidency" Meena Bose and Andrew Rudalevige Editors, Brookings Institution Press, 2020, page 56, updated with 2020 data from United States Government Policy and Supporting Positions (Plum Book), 2020

10 "Executive Orders: An Introduction", Congressional Research Service, March 29,2021, page 3

11 "Budget of the U.S. Government for Fiscal Year 2021", Office of Management & Budget, February 10, 2020, Page 112

12 "Congressional Budget Resolutions: Historical Information", Congressional Research Service, November 16, 2015, pages 2-4

13 "Congressional Budget Resolutions: Historical Information", Congressional Research Service, November 16, 2015, pages 2-4 updated with information from Congress.Gov and Wikipedia

14 "Congressional Budget Resolutions: Historical Information", Congressional Research Service, November 16, 2015, pages 2-4 updated with information from Congress.Gov and Wikipedia

15 House Appropriations Committee Majority News; www.appropriations.house.gov

16 Senate Appropriations Committee Majority News; www.appropriations.senate.gov

17 "If There's a New Rule, Jim Tozzi Has Read It", Peter Behr, Washington Post, July 10, 1981

18 "Jim Tozzi", www.sourcewatch.org, The Center for Media and Democracy

19 "Budget of the U.S. Government for Fiscal Year 1981", Office of Management & Budget, January 28, 1980, Page M3

20 "Revised Budget Projects $16.5 Billion Surplus", CQ Almanac, 1980

21 Controller General memo (B-196787) to the President of the Senate and the Speaker of the House of Representatives, May 30, 1980

22 "A History of the Love Canal Disaster, 1893 to 1998", Colin Dabkowski, The Buffalo News, August 4, 2018

23 "Executive Order 12316 — Responses to Environmental Damage", Ronald Reagan Presidential Library and Museum, August 14, 1981

24 "Superfund: A Half Century of Progress", EPA Alumni Association, April 2020

25 "Rita Lavelle", Wikipedia

26 "EPA Declares Aides's Dismissal Wasn't Political", Phillip Shabecoff, New York Times, February 10, 1983

27 "Rita Lavelle", Wikipedia

28 "Anne Gorsuch Burford", Wikipedia

29 "Are You Tough Enough?", Anne M. Burford, McGraw Hill Book Company, 1986, page 81

30 "Superfund and Toxic Waste", The Washington Post, February 26, 1985

31 "President Asks 5-Year Extension of Toxic Waste Cleanup Program", The New York Times, February 23, 1985

32 "Statement on Proposed Superfund Reauthorization Legislation", Ronald Reagan Presidential Library and Museum, February 22, 1985

33 "President Asks 5-Year Extension of Toxic Waste Cleanup Program", The New York Times, February 23, 1985

34 "Superfund and Toxic Waste", The Washington Post, February 26, 1985

35 "Statement on Signing the Superfund Amendments and Reauthorization Act of 1986",Ronald Reagan Presidential Library and Museum, October 17, 1986

36 "Executive Order 12580 — Superfund Implementation", Ronald Reagan Presidential Library and Museum, January 23, 1987

37 "Budget of the U.S. Government for Fiscal Year 1997 — Appendix", Office of Management & Budget, February 5, 1996, Page 884

38 "Unfinished Business: A Comparative Assessments of Environmental Problems", Frederick Allen, EPA, 1987

39 "Times Beach Missouri", Wikipedia

40 "U.S. Health Aide Says He Erred on Times Beach", The New York Times, May 26, 1991, page 20

41 "Experts Question Staggering Costs of Toxic Cleanups", Peter Passell, The New York Times, September 1, 1991

42 "Superfund: A Half Century of Progress", EPA Alumni Association, April 2020

43 "Cost Estimate: Senate Amendment 2137 to H.R. 3684, the Infrastructure Investment and Jobs Act", Congressional Budget Office, August 9, 2021

44 "Text — H.R. 3684 — Infrastructure Investment and Jobs Act", www.congress.gov

45 "Clean Air Act Options Papers", OMB Environment Branch, May 1989

46 "Natural Acidity of Rainwater", Department of Chemistry, Washington University, www.chemistry.wustl.edu

47 "The Benefits and Costs of the Clean Air Act, 1970-1990", EPA, October 1997

48 "Acid Rain", Wikipedia

49 "Generic Policy Question: Is a Major Sulfur Reduction Program to Control Acid Rain and its Alleged Environmental Effects Warranted and Justified?", Office of Management & Budget, October 1983

50 "The Triumph of Politics — Why the Reagan Revolution Failed", David A. Stockman, Harper and Row Publishers, 1986

51 "Generic Policy Question: Is a Major Sulfur Reduction Program to Control Acid Rain and its Alleged Environmental Effects Warranted and Justified?", Office of Management & Budget, October 1983

52 "Statement on Acid Rain", President Reagan, March 18, 1987, The American Presidency Project (www.presidency.uscb.edu)

53 "Bush Pledges Efforts to Clean Up Air and Water", John Holusha, The New York Times, September 1, 1988, Section B, page 9

54 "Toxic Air Pollution Control Options Paper", OMB Environment Branch, May 12, 1989

55 "Clean Air Act Options Paper: Ozone Nonattainment", OMB Environment Branch, May 22, 1989

56 "Clean Air Act Options Paper: Ozone Nonattainment", OMB Environment Branch, May 22, 1989

57 "Clean Air: How George Did It", Seymour Chwast illustrator, Time Magazine, August 21, 1989, pages 18-19

58 "President Urges Steps to Tighten Law on Clean Air", Philip Shabecoff, The New York Times, Section A, page 1

59 "President Urges Steps to Tighten Law on Clean Air", Philip Shabecoff, The New York Times, Section A, page 1

60 "Bush Sets Clean Air Strategy; President Embraces Tougher Efforts, Says "Stalemate" Must End", Michael Weisskopf and Ann Devroy, The Washington Post, June 13, 1989

61 "President Urges Steps to Tighten Law on Clean Air", Philip Shabecoff, The New York Times, Section A, page 1

62 "President Urges Steps to Tighten Law on Clean Air", Philip Shabecoff, The New York Times, Section A, page 1

63 "Rep. Waxman Vows to Speed Clean-Air Bill to Floor", Michael Weisskopf, The Washington Post, September 14, 1989

64 "Rep. Waxman Vows to Speed Clean-Air Bill to Floor", Michael
    Weisskopf, The Washington Post, September 14, 1989

65 "Charlatan's Web - John Beale", The Daily Show with Jon Stewart,
    December 19, 2013, https://www.cc.com/video/xwoaft/the-daily-
    show-with-jon-stewart-charlatan-s-web-john-beale

66 "John Beale", Wikipedia

67 "Lawmakers Reach an Accord on Reduction of Air Pollution", Keith
    Schneider, The New York Times, October 23, 1990

68 "Farm Demographics", 2012 Census of Agriculture, National Agricul-
    tural Statistics Service, U.S. Department of Agriculture, May 2014

69 "Parity Pricing — An Outdated Farm Policy Tool?", Lloyd Teigen,
    Economic Research Service, USDA, September 1987

70 "Administration Seeks to Shift Farm Policy From Subsidies", Eliza-
    beth Becker, New York Times, September 20, 2001

71 "Farm Security and Rural Investment Act of 2002", Wikipedia

72 "Agriculture Secretary Says Wartime Budget Leaves $171 Billion
    Farm Bill in Doubt", Elizabeth Becker, New York Times, September
    27, 2001

73 "Budget of the U.S. Government for Fiscal Year 2003", Office of
    Management & Budget, February 4, 2002, page 59

74 "Farm Security and Rural Investment Act of 2002", Wikipedia

75 "President Signs Farm Bill — Fact Sheet and Remarks by the Presi-
    dent Upon Signing the Farm Bill", The White House, May 13, 2002

76 "1996 FAIR Act Frames Farm Policy for 7 Years", Agricultural Out-
    look Supplement, Economic Research Service, USDA, April 1996

77 "Agricultural Disaster Assistance", Congressional Research Service
    Report #RS21212, April 23, 2020

78 "Crop Insurance in the United States", Environmental Working
    Group, Farm Subsidy Database

79 "Federal Crop Insurance: Program Overview for the 115th Con-
    gress", Congressional Research Service Report R45193, May 10, 2018

80 "USDA Secretary Unveils 2007 Farm Bill Proposals", Mary Peabody,
    Women's Agricultural Network Blog, January 31, 2007

81 "Agriculture Dept. Urges Big Overhaul in Farm Policy", Alexei Barri-
    onuevo, New York Times, February 1, 2007

82 "The 2008 Farm Bill: A Summary of Major Provision and Legislative
    Action", Congressional Research Service Report RL33934, June 19,
    2008, page CRS-6

83 "The 2008 Farm Bill: A Summary of Major Provision and Legislative
    Action", Congressional Research Service Report RL33934, June 19,
    2008, pages CRS-33 & 36

84 "The 2008 Farm Bill: A Summary of Major Provision and Legislative
    Action", Congressional Research Service Report RL33934, June 19,
    2008, page CRS-5

85 "Farm Bill's Subsidy Costs May Rise — Billions More Could Be Paid Through Little-Noticed Provision", Dan Morgan, The Washington Post, May 21, 2008

86 "The New ACRE Program: Frequently Asked Questions", Bruce Babcock & Chad Hart, Iowa Ag Review, Summer 2008 Vol. 14 No. 3

87 "American Indians Say Documents Show Government Has Cheated Them Out of Billions", Joel Brinkley, New York Times, January 7, 2003

88 "Poor Indians on Rich Land Fight A U.S. Maze", Timothy Egan, New York Times, March 9, 1999

89 "A Victory for Native Americans?", James Warren, The Atlantic, June 7, 2010

90 "Complaint to Compel Performance of Trust Obligations", Filing in the United States District Court for the District of Columbia, June 10, 1996

91 "Indians Win Major Round in Fight Over Trust Accounts ", Timothy Egan, New York Times, February 23, 1999

92 "Cobell v. Norton: Overview and Chronology", John Ahni Schertow, January 23, 2007, https://intercontinentalcry.org

93 "Cobell v. Norton: Overview and Chronology", John Ahni Schertow, January 23, 2007, https://intercontinentalcry.org

94 "Interior Defendant's Motion For Leave To File Supplemental Authority In Support of Interior Defendants' Motion to Strike Plaintiffs Request For Personal Sanctions", filing in the United States District Court for the District of Columbia, April 30, 2003

95 "Statement of James Cason, Associate Deputy Secretary, Department of the Interior, Before the Senate Committee on Indian Affairs on S.1770, the Indian Money Account Claim Satisfaction Act of 2003", October 29, 2003, page 4

96 "American Indians Say Documents Show Government Has Cheated Them Out of Billions", Joel Brinkley, New York Times, January 7, 2003

97 "Statement of James Cason, Associate Deputy Secretary, Department of the Interior, Before the Senate Committee on Indian Affairs on S.1770, the Indian Money Account Claim Satisfaction Act of 2003", October 29, 2003, page 4

98 "American Indians Say Documents Show Government Has Cheated Them Out of Billions", Joel Brinkley, New York Times, January 7, 2003

99 "Statement of James Cason, Associate Deputy Secretary, Department of the Interior, Before the Senate Committee on Indian Affairs on S.1770, the Indian Money Account Claim Satisfaction Act of 2003", October 29, 2003, pages 3 & 7

100 "The Indian Trust Fund Litigation: An Overview of *Cobell v. Salazar*", Todd Garvey, Congressional Research Service, July 13, 2010, page 4

101 "Parties to Cobell lawsuit still far apart", Jerry Reynolds, Indian Country Today, April 18, 2003

102 "The Indian Trust Fund Litigation: An Overview of Cobell v. Salazar", Todd Garvey, Congressional Research Service, July 13, 2010

103 "Cobell v. Norton: Overview and Chronology", John Ahni Schertow, January 23, 2007, https://intercontinentalcry.org

104 "Statement of James Cason, Associate Deputy Secretary and Ross Swimmer, Special Trustee for American Indians on the Cobell Lawsuit", Senate Committee on Indian Affairs hearing on S.1439, the Indian Trust Reform Act of 2005", July 26, 2005, pages 3-6

105 "Appeals Panel Removes Judge Presiding Over Indian Lawsuit", John Files, New York Times, July 12, 2006

106 "Opinion for the Court", United States Court of Appeals for the District of Columbia Circuit, November 15, 2005

107 "Appeals Panel Removes Judge Presiding Over Indian Lawsuit", John Files, New York Times, July 12, 2006

108 "Cobell v. Norton: Overview and Chronology", John Ahni Schertow, January 23, 2007, https://intercontinentalcry.org

109 "The Indian Trust Fund Litigation: An Overview of Cobell v. Salazar", Todd Garvey, Congressional Research Service, July 13, 2010, page 6

110 "The Indian Trust Fund Litigation: An Overview of Cobell v. Salazar", Todd Garvey, Congressional Research Service, July 13, 2010, page 7

111 "The Indian Trust Fund Litigation: An Overview of Cobell v. Salazar", Todd Garvey, Congressional Research Service, July 13, 2010, pages 7 & 8

112 "U.S. Will Settle Indian Lawsuit for $3.4 Billion", Charlie Savage, New Your Times, December 8, 2009

113 "Foreign Food Aid Donation Cluster", United States Department of Agriculture, OMB Circular A-133 Compliance Supplement, June 2016, https://obamawhitehouse.archives.gov

114 "Farm and Food Support Under USDA's Section 32 Program", Jim Monke, Congressional Research Service Report RL 34081, October 17, 2016, pages 3 and 4

115 "Agricultural Disaster Assistance", Congressional Research Service Report RS 21212, Updated April 23, 2020, page 10

116 "The Commodity Credit Corporation (CCC)", Congressional Research Service Report R44606, Updated January 21, 2021

117 "Budget Discipline for Agency Administrative Actions", OMB, Management Memorandum M-05-13, May 23, 2005

118 "Trump wants $12 billion in aid to U.S. farmers suffering from trade war", David Shepardson and Steve Holland, Reuters July 24, 2018

119 "Trump Gives Farmers $16 Billion in Aid Amid Prolonged China Trade War", Ana Swanson, New York Times, May 23, 2019

120 "USDA's Coronavirus Food Assistance Program: Round two (CFAP-2)", Congressional Research Service Report R46645, December 21, 2020

121 "USDA Announces Coronavirus Food Assistance Program", USDA Press Release No. 0220.20, April 17, 2020

122 "USDA's Coronavirus Food Assistance Program: Round two (CFAP-2)", Congressional Research Service Report R46645, December 21, 2020

123 "Coronavirus Food Assistance Program 2 — Fact Sheet", USDA, Farm Service Agency, September 13, 2021

124 "Budget of the U.S. Government for Fiscal Year 2023 — Analytic Perspectives", Office of Management & Budget, March 28, 2023, Pages 261-262

125 "Budgetary Treatment of Federal Credit (Direct Loans and Loan Guarantees): Concepts, History, and Issues for the 112th Congress", James Bickley, Congressional Research Service Report R42632, July 27, 2012

126 "Learning from History: Correcting the Credit Reform Act", Jason Delisle, Economics 21, December 13, 2010

127 "Budget Enforcement Act of 1990 — Section 13201", House Budget Counsel, Budget Counsel Reference website

128 "What background information should I know", OMB Circular A-11, Section 185 — Federal Credit, 2021

129 "Are Student Loans Backed By The Government", Money Mink, August 13, 2019

130 "Budgetary Treatment of Federal Credit (Direct Loans and Loan Guarantees): Concepts, History, and Issues for the 112th Congress", James Bickley, Congressional Research Service Report R42632, July 27, 2012, page 8

131 "Credit Reform: Current Method to Estimate Credit Subsidy Costs is More Appropriate for Budget Estimates Than a Fair Value Approach", General Accountability Office, GAO-16-41, January 29, 2016

132 "Revising the distribution of funding by disease in the new funding model allocation methodology", www.theglobalfund.org/board-decisions/b29-edp11/, October 2013

133 "The CIA's fake vaccination drive has damaged the battle against polio", Heidi Larson, The Guardian, May 27, 2012

134 "The United States President's Emergency Plan for AIDS Relief", www.state.gov/pepfar

135 "HIV Treatment as Prevention", Centers for Disease Control, December 2020, www.cdc.gov/hiv/risk/art

136 "Obama Marks World AIDS Day With Proposal to Expand Treatment", Charlene Porter, U.S. Mission to International Organizations in Geneva, December 2, 2011

137 "The U.S. President's Emergency Plan for AIDS Relief (PEPFAR)", Global Health Policy, Kaiser Family Foundation, October 5, 2021

138 "PEPFAR 3.0 — Controlling the Epidemic: Delivering on the Promise of an AIDS-free Generation", U.S. Department of State, December 1, 2014

139 "DREAMS: Partnership to Reduce HIV/AIDS in Adolescent Girls and Young Women", USAID Archived Content June 2012 to September 2017, exact date unknown but likely September 2015

140 "Causes of Death", Hannah Ritchie and Max Roser, OurWorldinData.org/causes-of-death, December 2019

141 "Tuberculosis — United States, 2017", Morbidity and Mortality Weekly Report, Centers for Disease Control, March 23, 2018

142 "Malaria", Centers for Disease Control, www.cdc.gov/parasite/malaria, February 28, 2022

143 "Malaria Elimination and Eradication", Chapter 12 in Major Infectious Diseases, 3rd edition, The International Bank for Reconstruction and Development, The World Bank, November 3, 2017

144 "Malaria Could be Eradicated by 2050, Global Health Experts Say", Laura Newman, University of California San Francisco, September 8, 2019

145 "Tuberculosis", Bill & Melinda Gates Foundation, www.gatesfoundation.org/our-work/programs/global-health/tuberculosis

146 "Tuberculosis", World Health Organization, October 14, 2021

147 "Malaria Elimination and Eradication", Chapter 12 in Major Infectious Diseases, 3rd edition, The International Bank for Reconstruction and Development, The World Bank, November 3, 2017

148 "Malaria Could be Eradicated by 2050, Global Health Experts Say", Laura Newman, University of California San Francisco, September 8, 2019

149 "In Africa, Malaria is deadlier than covid-19 and still lacks a vaccine", Henry Wilkins and Danielle Pacquette, The Washington Post, June 8, 2021, page A-13

150 "PEPFAR Strategy for Accelerating HIV/AIDS Epidemic Control (2017-2020)", U.S. Department of State, September 19, 2017, page 1

151 "PEPFAR", Fact Sheet, www.hiv.gov, Department of Health and Human Services, December 7, 2021

152 "Ebola virus disease", World Health Organization, February 23, 2021

153 "Status of the Ebola Outbreak in West Africa: Overview and Issues for Congress", Tiaji Salaam-Blyther, Susan Epstein & Bolko Skorupski, Congressional Research Service, Report R44507, May 25, 2016

154 "Status of the Ebola Outbreak in West Africa: Overview and Issues for Congress", Tiaji Salaam-Blyther, Susan Epstein & Bolko Skorupski, Congressional Research Service, Report R44507, May 25, 2016

155 "2015-16 Zika virus epidemic", Wikipedia

156 "Florida Zika Infections Are the First Confirmed Local Transmissions in the U.S., Officials Say", Ada Carr, weather.com, July 29, 2016

157 "Zika Response Funding: Request and Congressional Action", Congressional Research Service, September 30, 2016

158 "State Department Should Take Steps to Improve Timeliness of Required Budgetary Reporting", U.S. General Accountability Office, September 2019

159 OMB Response to November 25, 2019 GAO letter on Withholding Ukraine Security Assistance, from General Counsel Mark Paoletta, December 11, 2019

160 "Briefing: Punitive aid cuts disrupt healthcare in Uganda", The New Humanitarian, April 2, 2014

161 "Congressional Budget Justification — Department of State, Foreign Operations, and Related Programs, Fiscal Year 2015, U.S. Department of State, March 4, 2014

162 "US to Back $2B in Loan Guarantees for Ukraine", Voice of America News, January 13, 2015

163 "US signs $1 bn loan guarantee for Ukraine", Agence France-Presse, May 18, 2015

164 "Reforming Ukraine After the Revolutions", Joshua Yaffa, The New Yorker, September 5, 2016

165 "What Joe Biden Actually Did in Ukraine", Glenn Thrush and Kenneth P. Vogel, The New York Times, September 1, 2021

166 "U.S. Signs Loan Guarantee Agreement for Ukraine", U.S. Embassy in Ukraine, June 3, 2016

167 "UNRWA", Wikipedia

168 "Israel–Sudan normalization agreement", Wikipedia

169 "Trump cuts all direct assistance to Northern Triangle countries Honduras, El Salvador, Guatemala", Conor Finnegan, ABC News, March 30, 2019

170 "Slaying the Dragon of Debt— 1974 Congressional Budget and Impoundment Control Act", The Bancroft Library, University of California at Berkeley

171 "Jimmy Morales, a President Against Democracy in Guatemala", Francisco Goldman, The New York Times, Jan 17, 2019

172 "Letter to Mr Tom Armstrong, General Accountability Office", RE: B-331564, Office of Management and Budget — Withholding of Ukraine Security Assistance, December 11, 2019

173 "Decision: Office of Management and Budget — Withholding of Ukraine Security Assistance", File # B-331564, January 16, 2020

174 "Letter to Mr Tom Armstrong, General Accountability Office", RE: B-331564, Office of Management and Budget — Withholding of Ukraine Security Assistance, December 11, 2019

175 "Impoundment Control Act — Withholding of Funds through Their Date of Expiration", Letter to Honorable Steve Womack and Honorable John Yarmuth, B-330330, December 10, 2018

176 "Judge Won't End Fight Over Impeachment Subpoena Even After House Dems Back Down". Tierney Sneed, Talking Points Memo, November 7, 2019

177 "White House budget official lays out unusual process in freeze of Ukraine aid for impeachment investigators", Manu Raju, Lauren Fox, Phil Mattingly and Veronica Stracqualursi, CNN, November 16, 2019

178 "Mark Sandy House testimony used to down Trump Ukraine bribery claim", Rowan Scarborough, The Washington Times, December 1, 2019

179 "White House Budget Official Said 2 Aides Resigned Amid Ukraine Aid Freeze", Michael D. Shear and Nicholas Fandos, The New York Times, November 26, 2019

180 "If There's a New Rule, Jim Tozzi Has Read It", Peter Behr, The Washington Post, July 10, 1981

181 "Information Collection Budget of the United States Government, 2018", OMB Office of Information and Regulatory Affairs

182 "Information Collection under the Paperwork Reduction Act", April 7, 2010 Memorandum from Cass Sunstein at https://obamawhitehouse.archives.gov/sites/default/files/omb/assets/inforeg/PRAPrimer_04072010.pdf

183 "Executive Order 12291 — Federal Regulation", February 17, 1981, The Reagan Library and Museum

184 "Telephone Directory", Executive Office of the President, September 1981

185 "If There's a New Rule, Jim Tozzi Has Read It", Peter Behr, The Washington Post, July 10, 1981

186 "Federal Rulemaking: The Role of the Office of Information and Regulatory Affairs" Curtis W. Copeland, Congressional Research Service, 2009

187 "Data Quality Law is Nemesis of Regulation", Rick Weiss, The Washington Post, August 16, 2004

188 "Section 515", Consolidated Appropriations Act of 2001, P.L. 106-554

189 "2017 Report to Congress on the Benefits and Costs of Federal Regulations", OMB Office of Information and Regulatory Affairs, page 1

190 "Circular A-4", Office of Management and Budget, September 17, 2003

191 "How Dangerous is Lightning", National Weather Service, National Oceanic and Atmospheric Administration, (www.weather.gov/safety/lightning-odds)

192 "Discounting Human Lives" Maureen L. Cropper and Paul R. Portney, Resources for the Future, Summer 1992

193 "Executive Policymaking: The Role of the OMB in the Presidency" Meena Bose and Andrew Rudalevige Editors, Brookings Institution Press, 2020, page 156

194 "How Much Are Human Lives and Health Worth", Jocelyn Kaiser, Science Magazine, March 21, 2003, p 1836

195 "Unfinished Business: a Comparative Assessment of Environmental Problems", Office of Policy, Planning and Evaluation, EPA, February 1987

196 "Breaking the Vicious Circle", Steven Breyer, Harvard University Press, 1993

197 "When Removing Asbestos Makes No Sense - Risk of Cancer in USA is Barely Measurable", Dennis Cauchon, USA Today, February 11, 1999

198 "Experts Argue for Using Notorious Pesticide to Fight Malaria", Allison Freeman, Greenwire, December 5, 2003

199 "WHO Recommends DDT to Control Malaria", Christiane Rehwagen, BMJ Publishing Group, September 23 ,2006

200 "The Benefits and Costs of the Clean Air Act, 1970 to 1990", EPA, October 1997, page ES-8

201 Derived from "Gross Domestic Product" and "GDP Implicit Price Deflators" data, Fred Economic Data, St. Louis Fed, https://fred.stlouisfed.org/series/GDP# & https://fred.stlouisfed.org/series/GDPDEF/

202 "The Benefits and Costs of the Clean Air Act, 1970 to 1990", EPA, October 1997, page ES-9

203 "The Benefits and Costs of the Clean Air Act, 1970 to 1990", EPA, October 1997, pages ES-5 & ES-7

204 Derived from "Gross Domestic Product" and "GDP Implicit Price Deflators" data, Fred Economic Data, St. Louis Fed, https://fred.stlouisfed.org/series/GDP# & https://fred.stlouisfed.org/series/GDPDEF/

205 "The Benefits and Costs of the Clean Air Act, 1990 to 2020", EPA, April 2011, pages 5-25, 7-5 & 7-8

206 "2017 Report to Congress on the Benefits and Costs of Federal Regulations", OMB Office of Information and Regulatory Affairs, page 10

207 "The Benefits and Costs of the Clean Air Act, 1990 to 2020", EPA, April 2011, page 5-25

208 "Deaths: Final Data for 2019", National Vital Statistics Reports, Centers for Disease Control, July 26, 2021

209 Estimating the Public Health Benefits of Proposed Air Pollution Regulations", National Research Council/National Academy of Sciences, 2002

210 "2017 Report to Congress on the Benefits and Costs of Federal Regulations", OMB Office of Information and Regulatory Affairs, page 12 - 16

211 "PM-2.5 Designated Area/State Information", Green Book, EPA, data as of January 31, 2022,

212 "2017 Report to Congress on the Benefits and Costs of Federal Regulations", OMB Office of Information and Regulatory Affairs, page 10, 11, and 14

213 "IRS Chief Says $1 trillion in taxes goes uncollected every year", David Lawder, Reuters, April 13, 2021

214 "20 Largest U.S. Federal Agencies Admit To $2.3 Trillion In Improper Payments Since 2004", Adam Andrzejewski, Forbes, Dec. 3, 2020

215 "Office of Federal Procurement Policy Act", Section 2 - Declaration of Policy, August 30, 1974

216 "The Office of Federal Procurement Policy", www.whitehouse.gov/omb/management/office-federal-procurement-policy/

217 "Air Force's next hack of the federal procurement system: One-year funding", Jason Miller, Federal News Network, December 8, 2020

218 "Chief Financial Officers Act of 1990", Public Law 101-576, Nov. 15, 1990

219 "FY 21 Financial Report of the United States Government", Department of the Treasury, February 17, 2022, pages 43 & 44

220 "Office of E-Government & Information Technology", www.whitehouse.gov/omb/management/egov/

221 "Budget of the U.S. Government for Fiscal Year 2022 — Appendix", Office of Management & Budget, May 28, 2022, Page 1184

222 "FY 2016 Annual Report to Congress E-Government Act Implementation", OMB, August 2017, page 9

223 "Major Themes and Additional Budget Details: Fiscal Year 1984", OMB, January 31, 1983, page 271

224 "J. Peter Grace", Wikipedia

225 "War on Waste", President's Private Sector Survey on Cost Control, January 12, 1984

226 "War on Waste", President's Private Sector Survey on Cost Control, January 12, 1984

227 "Budget of the U.S. Government for Fiscal Year 1983", Office of Management & Budget, February 8, 1982, page 3-28

228 "Budget of the U.S. Government for Fiscal Year 1989", Office of Management & Budget, February 18, 1988, page 1-4

229 "Budget of the U.S. Government for Fiscal Year 1989", Office of Management & Budget, February 18, 1988, page 1-5 & 1-12

230 "Budget of the U.S. Government for Fiscal Year 1993", Office of Management & Budget, January 29, 1992, Part One —page 308

231 "Base Closure and Realignment (BRAC): Background and Issues for Congress", Congressional Research Service, April 25, 2019

232 "History of the National Partnership for Reinventing Government", https://govinfo.library.unt.edu

233 "Executive Policymaking: The Role of the OMB in the Presidency" Meena Bose and Andrew Rudalevige Editors, Brookings Institution Press, 2020, page 250

234 "History of the National Partnership for Reinventing Government", https://govinfo.library.unt.edu

235 "Making OMB More Effective in Serving the Presidency — Changes in OMB as a Result of the OMB 2000 Review", Office Memorandum 94-16, March 1, 1994

236 "Budget of the U.S. Government for Fiscal Year 2003", Office of Management & Budget, February 4, 2002, page 43

237 "The President's Management Agenda", George W. Bush Library Archives, https://georgewbush-whitehouse.archives.gov/omb/budget/fy2005

238 "Budget of the U.S. Government for Fiscal Year 2009", Office of Management & Budget, February 4, 2008, page 29

239 "Budget of the U.S. Government for Fiscal Year 2011", Office of Management & Budget, February 1, 2010, page 43

240 "Guidance for 2013 SAVE Award Program", OMB Management Memorandum, M-13-18, July 26, 2013

241 "Budget of the U.S. Government for Fiscal Year 2019", Office of Management & Budget, February 12, 2018, pages 7-11

242 "History of the National Partnership for Reinventing Government", https://govinfo.library.unt.edu

243 "Comprehensive Plan for Reforming the Federal Government and Reducing the Federal Civilian Workforce", OMB Management Memorandum, M-17-22, April 12, 2007

244 "Delivering Government Solutions in the 21st Century", OMB, June 2018

245 "United States International Development Finance Corporation Reorganization Plan", OMB, March 9, 2019

246 "Continuing Resolutions: Overview of Components and Practices", Congressional Research Service, November 5, 2020, page 10

247 "Budget of the U.S. Government for Fiscal Year 2021", Office of Management & Budget, February 10, 2020, Page 112

248 "Shutdown of the Federal Government: Causes, Processes, and Effects", Congressional Research Service, December 10, 2018, page 5

249 "Federal Funding Gaps: A Brief Overview", Congressional Research Service, February 4, 2019, page 3

250 "Government shutdowns in the United States", Wikipedia

251 "2013 United States federal government shutdown", Wikipedia

252 "Federal government shutdown, January 2018", Ballotpedia

253 "Budget of the U.S. Government for Fiscal Year 2024", Office of Management & Budget, March 9, 2023, Historical Table 7-1

254 "Slaying the Dragon of Debt", The Bancroft Library, University of California at Berkeley

255 "Slaying the Dragon of Debt— 1995-96 Shutdown", The Bancroft Library, University of California at Berkeley

256 U.S. General Accounting Office, August 30, 1996, Report B-270619, page 5

257 "The Debt Limit: History and Recent Increases", Congressional Research Service, November 2, 2015, page 23

258 Sweet, Ken (August 8, 2011)"Dow plunges after S&P downgrade". *CNNMoney*

259 P.L. 115-123, Bipartisan Budget Act of 2018 and P.L. 116-37, Bipartisan Budget Act of 2019

260 Romm, Tony (sept 21, 2021), "Budget plan ties funding to debt", The Washington Post, page A1

261 "Emergency Economic Program Urged on Reagan by 2 Advisers", Leonard Silk, New York Times, December 11, 1980, page A1

262 "Peter R. Orszag", Wikipedia

263 Mark Liebovich, "If Peter Orszag Is So Smart, What Will He Do Now?", January 8, 2010, New York Times

264 "Emily W. Murphy", Wikipedia

265 "Trump Budget Chief Hampers Biden Transition With Ban on Meetings", Bloomberg.com, December 31, 2020

266 "Nouri al-Maliki", Wikipedia

267 "White House Easter Egg Roll 2022 — April 18, 2022", White House Easter Egg Roll 2022 - Lottery and Event Details (gov1.info)

268 "Inside Camp David — The Private World of the Presidential Retreat", Rear Admiral Michael Giorgione, Little Brown and Company, December 2017

269 "The Vacancy Act: A Legal Overview", Congressional Research Service, May 28, 2021, page 11

270 "Schedule F Appointment", Wikipedia

271 "Opinion: The Biden stimulus is admirably ambitious. But it brings some big risks, too." Washington Post, February 4, 2021

272 "Politico Playbook", April 28, 2021

www.ingramcontent.com/pod-product-compliance
Lightning Source LLC
Chambersburg PA
CBHW062113020426
42335CB00013B/953